ECONOMIC THEORIES, TRUE OR FALSE?

Economic Theories, True or False?

Essays in the History and Methodology of Economics

Mark Blaug
University of London, University of Buckingham
and University of Exeter

Edward Elgar

© Mark Blaug 1990

Published by
Edward Elgar Publishing Limited
Gower House
Croft Road
Aldershot
Hants GU11 3HR
England

Edward Elgar Publishing Company
Old Post Road
Brookfield
Vermont 05036
USA

British Library Cataloguing in Publication Data

Blaug, Mark *1927–*
  Economic theories, true or false?: essays in the history
  and methodology of economics.
  1. Economics. Theories
  I. Title
  330.1

Library of Congress Cataloguing-in-Publication Data

Blaug, Mark,
    Economic theories, true or false? : essays in the history and
  methodology of economics / Mark Blaug.
          p.   cm.
      ISBN 1–85278–376–1
      1. Economics —History. 2. Economics—Methodology. I. Title.
  HB75. B683 1990
  330. 1—dc20   90–3825
                                                               CIP

ISBN 1 85278 376 1

Printed in Great Britain by
Billing & Sons Ltd, Worcester

Contents

Acknowledgements

I wish to thank the following publishers for permission to reprint: North Holland Publishing Company for two lectures, part of a book, *Methodological Appraisal of Marxian Economics,* 1980; JAI Press for 'A Methodological Appraisal of Radical Economics' in *Methodological Controversies in Economics: Historical Essays in Honour of T.W. Hutchison,* ed. A W Coats, 1983, and 'The Economics of Johann von Thünen' in *Research in the History of Economic Thought and Methodology,* vol. 3, ed. W.J. Samuels, 1985; Duke University Press for 'Second Thoughts on the Keynesian Revolution' in *History of Political Economy,* forthcoming 1990; Cambridge University Press for 'John Hicks and the Methodology of Economics' in *The Popperian Legacy in Economics,* ed. N. de Marchi, 1988; Macmillan Press for 'Classical Economics' in *The New Palgrave: A Dictionary of Economics,* ed. J. Eatwell, M. Millgate and P. Newman, 1987, and 'Nicholas Kaldor's New Enquiry into the Nature and Causes of the Wealth of Nations' in *Pioneers of Modern Economics in Britain II,* eds. D.A. Greenaway and J.R. Presley, 1989; Blackwell for 'Comments' in *Economics in Disarray,* eds. P. Wiles and G. Routh, 1984, and 'Marginal Cost Pricing: No Empty Box' in *Public Choice, Public Finance and Public Policy,* eds. D.A. Greenaway and G.K. Shaw, 1985; and the Institute of Economic Affairs for 'Economics Through the Looking Glass', 1988.

Introduction

The methodology of economics or the principles involved in choosing among competing economic theories has been an interest of mine ever since I started studying economics in the 1940s and 1950s. One of my earliest, and perhaps best known, books in economics, *Economic Theory in Retrospect* (1962), concluded with 'A Methodological Postscript' which left little doubt that, so far as I was concerned, the ultimate reason for studying the history of economic thought, the ostensible subject matter of *Economic Theory in Retrospect*, was to answer such fundamental questions as: how much does economics explain?; what are the grounds on which economic theories have been accepted or rejected?; what are the characteristics of endurable economic ideas?; what practical use is economic knowledge?; and, the grandfather of all such queries, how do we ever know whether any economic theory is true or false? Hence the title of this third collection of my papers.[1] Even after studying economics for over 40 years, I still ask myself frequently: 'Why do I believe in some economic theories and not others?'

From the outset, I was convinced that Popper came closer to providing the answer to such questions than any other philosopher of science I had ever read. In the 1970s, I added the writings of Imre Lakatos to those of Sir Karl Popper, interpreted as a modification and extension of Popper, perfectly true to the spirit, and virtually true to the letter, of Popper. To this day I regard myself as a thoroughgoing 'falsificationist' and opposed to the now so fashionable 'post-modernist' tendency towards 'hermeneutics' and 'rhetorical analysis',[2] not to mention the older tendency towards 'relativism' and 'instrumentalism'. But what is the methodology of 'falsificationism'? I think that I can best answer that by reference to the state of modern economics.

In a letter to *Science*, Wassily Leontief surveyed articles published in the *American Economic Review* in the last decade and found that over 50 per cent consisted of mathematical models without any empirical data, while some 15 per cent consisted of non-mathematical theoretical analyses, likewise without any empirical data, leaving 35 per cent of the articles using empirical analysis (see Table 1).

This is one aspect of modern economics: to pursue economic theorizing like a game, making no pretence to refer to this or any other possible world, on the slim chance that something might be learned which will one day throw light on an actual economy. There is another aspect however: to formulate theoretical hypotheses and to show that they are confirmed by empirical evidence, at the

1

Table 1 Articles published in the American Economic Review

		1972–76 (%)	1977–81 (%)
1	Mathematical models without any data	50.1	54.0
2	Theoretical models without mathematical formulation and without data	21.2	11.6
3	Statistical methodology	0.6	0.5
4	Empirical analysis based on data developed by author	0.8	1.4
5	Empirical analysis using statistical inference on published data	21.4	22.7
6	Other types of empirical analysis	5.4	7.9
7	Empirical analysis based on artificial simulations and experiments	0.5	1.9

Source: Science, 217, 4555, 9 June 1982, p. 104.

same time ignoring alternative hypotheses that might equally well have been confirmed by the same data. Putting these two tendencies together, we end up with a discipline that runs few risks of ever being shown to be wrong. In short, economists are very complacent about their subject. Of course, economists frequently disagree – witness the controversy between Keynesians and monetarists – but the participants in these furious debates spend more energy contrasting their respective ideological positions than formulating truly discriminating tests of their competing predictions. In consequence, such controversies persist for decades and even generations.

Specialists in economic methodology take two sharply opposing views of this state of affairs. Some argue that the business of the economic methodologist is to describe the actual practices of economists. Economists, they say, clearly place a high value on empirical research but only to confirm or disconfirm particular applications of economic theory; economists rarely abandon a theory because it has been repeatedly refuted and some economists even go so far as to argue that economic theory is true by the certainty of its fundamental postulates. In short, the methodology of modern economics is 'confirmationism' or 'verificationism' and there are still schools of thought in modern economics, like the modern Austrians, who remain 'radical apriorists'. In books like Ian M.T. Stewart's *Reasoning and Method in Economics* (1979) and Bruce Caldwell's *Beyond Positivism: Economic Methodology in the Twentieth Century* (1982) we get an exposition of economic methodology that is essentially defensive of modern economics, explaining that what economists do is to make the best of a bad job.

In contrast to the descriptive role of economic methodology are books like those of Homa Katouzian, *Ideology and Method in Economics* (1980), Terence Hutchison, *On Revolutions and Progress in Economic Knowledge* (1978) and my own *Methodology of Economics* (1980), which argue that the role of the economic methodologist is to prescribe as well as to describe. Economists may well fall short of the best-practice methods they themselves preach and even the methods they advocate may be deficient. At any rate, these writers are frequently critical of what passes as modern economics, which is not to say that they agree precisely on where economics went wrong or how to put it right.

To illustrate this opposition between a 'defensive' and an 'aggressive' methodology, let me compare Bruce Caldwell's *Beyond Positivism* with my own account in *The Methodology of Economics*. Our two books are in striking agreement on most of the substantive issues in economic methodology: 'methodology' is not just a fancy name for 'methods of investigation' but a study of the relationship between theoretical concepts and asserted conclusions about the real world; in particular, methodology examines the procedures economists adopt for validating theories and the reasons they offer for preferring one theory over another; methodology is both a descriptive discipline ('this *is* what most economists do') and a prescriptive one ('this is what economists *should* do to advance economics'). Finally, methodology does not provide a mechanical algorithm either for constructing or for evaluating theories and, as such, is more like an 'art' than a 'science'. We also agree that economic theories must sooner or later be confronted with empirical evidence as the final arbiter of truth, but that empirical testing is so difficult and ambiguous that one cannot hope to find many examples in economics of theories being decisively knocked down by one or two refutations. It is vain to seek an empirical counterpart for every theoretical concept employed, which is in any case an impossible objective, but we can achieve indirect testing by considering the network of fundamental concepts embedded in a particular theory and deducing their implications for some real-world phenomena. This is not to say, however, that predictions are everything and that it hardly matters whether assumptions are 'realistic' or not. Economic theories are not simply instruments for making accurate predictions about economic events but genuine attempts to uncover the causal forces at work in the economic system – that is, to depict things as they actually are.

Nevertheless, this is where the agreement between us stops. I argue more or less vehemently in favour of 'falsificationism', defined as 'a methodological standpoint that regards theories and hypotheses as scientific if and only if their predictions are, at least in principle, empirically falsifiable'. My reasons for holding this view are partly epistemological (the only way we can know that a theory is true is to commit ourselves to predictions about events and although a confirming instance does not prove truth, a disconfirming instance proves falsity) and partly historical (scientific knowledge has progressed by refutations of existing theories and by the construction of new theories that resist refutations). In addition, I claim that modern economists do in fact subscribe to the methodology of falsificationism: despite some differences of opinions, particularly about the direct testing of fundamental assumptions, mainstream economists refuse to take any economic theory seriously if it does not venture to make definite predictions about economic events, and they ultimately judge economic theories in terms of their success in making accurate predictions. I also allege, however, that economists fail consistently to practise what they preach: their working philosophy of science is accurately characterized as 'innocuous falsificationism'. In that sense, I am critical of what economists actually do as distinct from what they say they do.

Caldwell, on the other hand, doubts that falsificationism is a recommendable methodology: its strictures are so demanding that little of economics would survive if it were rigorously applied. In addition, he can see no evidence that economists practise falsificationism even innocuously. Instead, he advocates 'methodological pluralism', or 'let a hundred flowers bloom'. To me this seems to be tantamount to the abandonment of all standards, indeed the abandonment of methodology itself as a discipline of study. If all methodological views are equally legitimate, it is difficult to see what sort of theorizing is ever excluded. From the standpoint of 'methodological pluralism', it is not even obvious why we should require theories to be logically consistent, or to assert something definite about the real world, which after all carries the implication that they may be shown to be false. Caldwell is much too sophisticated not to recognize the dangers of ultra-permissiveness and the last few pages of his book are expressly devoted to answering possible objections to methodological pluralism. It is simply that I, for one, found his answers unconvincing.

Caldwell is clearly sympathetic to the methodology of falsificationism but he derives many of his dramatic conclusions – 'falsificationism has never been practised to any significant extent in economics'; 'there exist a number of specific and possibly irremovable obstacles to the practice of falsificationism in economics' - from the subtle distinction between the methodology of 'confirmationism' and that of 'falsificationism'. He notes that most modern economists believe 'that theories should be testable; that a useful means of testing is to compare the predictions of a theory with reality; that predictive adequacy is often the most important characteristic a theory can possess; and that the relative ordering of theories should be determined by the strength of confirmation, or corroboration, of those being compared' (p.124). These four principles, he contends quite rightly, define the methodology of 'confirmationism' (or, as I would prefer to call it, 'verificationism') and not 'falsificationism'. Falsificationism is a tougher doctrine. In its simplest form, it can be stated in Caldwell's own words: 'Scientists should not only empirically test their hypothesis, they should construct hypotheses which make bold predictions, and they should try to refute those hypotheses in their tests. Equally important, scientists should tentatively accept only confirmed hypotheses, and reject those which have been disconfirmed. Testing, then, should make a difference' (p.125).

Thus, the distinction between confirmationism and falsificationism rests partly on the degree to which theories are squeezed to yield risky implications, which are liable to refutation, and partly on whether refutations are taken seriously as possible reflections of fundamental error. Confirmationists make sure that their theories run few risks and, when faced with an empirical refutation, they set about repairing the theory or amending its scope; they never abandon it as false. Falsificationists, on the other hand, deliberately run risks and regard repeated failures to predict accurately as a sign that alternative theories must be considered. Obviously, these distinctions are differences of degree, not of kind, and two methodologists may honestly disagree as to whether modern economists are more appropriately characterized as 'confirmationists' or as 'falsificationists'.

Caldwell provides a valuable discussion of the factors that make falsificationism in economics so hard to practise (pp. 236–42) but he fails to point out that exactly the same factors operate in physics, chemistry and biology, albeit to a lesser degree. Indeed, the so-called Duhem-Quine Thesis states that it is logically impossible decisively to refute any theory, since any test of a theory involves at least some auxiliary conditions besides the statements of the theory, so that a refutation can always be blamed on the auxiliary conditions. The way out of this dilemma is to lay down restrictions on what Popper calls 'immunizing stratagems' adopted solely to protect theories against empirical refutations. These restrictions are important features of the methodology of falsificationism, which Caldwell nowhere mentions or discusses.

Let us agree that there are no tests in economics, or for that matter in any other science, that are unambiguously interpretable. But is Caldwell asserting that disconfirming tests are always ignored in economics, or that they always lead to a repair-job designed to make sure that there will be no further disconfirmations? How then does he account for the wholesale abandonment of the Phillips curve in the 1970s, interpreted as a stable relationship between inflation and unemployment, such that one can be traded off against the other? Or how does he explain the repeated appeal to empirical evidence in the Keynesianism-versus-monetarism controversy? No doubt he would reply that the controversy has persisted for almost 20 years despite numerous refutations and counter-refutations. But, surely, what is remarkable is the insistence of all participants in these debates that they must be resolved by truly discriminating tests of the respective predictions of each school of thought, which so far have simply not been forthcoming. If this is not the methodology of falsificationism in action, what is it?

One difficulty is that Caldwell provides no case studies of economic disputes to illustrate his claim that economists typically adhere to confirmationism rather than falsificationism. His only report of empirical work deals with the attempt to construct a direct test of the fundamental rationality assumption of modern economics and although this succeeds in demonstrating the inconclusiveness of such efforts, it has little bearing on the issue of confirmationism versus falsificationism. The book's central conclusion is stated in these words:

> The invocation to *try* to put falsificationism into practice in economics need not be dropped, although it seems there is little chance for its successful application. What must be avoided is the wholesale rejection of research programs that do not meet the falsificationist criteria of acceptability, for that would lead to an elimination, not only of alternative research programs like those proposed by Austrians and Institutionalists, but much of standard economic theory as well. (Caldwell, 1982, p. 242)

But the dreaded prospect of 'wholesale rejection of research programs that do not meet the falsificationist criteria of acceptability' is a red herring: there is no danger of wholesale rejection of anything in modern economics but rather the danger of never finding any common language of communication between an ever proliferating series of competing research programmes. It is not just Austrian and institutionalist economics versus mainstream economics but Marxism, radicalism, post-Keynesianism, behaviouralism, and so on, many of which purport to contain unique principles for validating their own findings and invalidating everyone else's. Can we really say nothing to appraise these competing research programmes except that 'anything goes' in methodology? Are there no minimum standards which we may demand of any species of economics claiming to be scientific?

'Methodological pluralism', I would contend, is a sham – an excuse for never making any final judgements about competing theories. It is a 'defensive methodology' whereas 'falsificationism' is an 'aggressive methodology'. The difference between these two points of view is rather like the difference between type I and type II errors in statistics. Wade Hands (1989), with whom I have crossed swords even more often than with Bruce Caldwell, expressed it very well:

> ... 'falsificationism is a great methodology for avoiding type II error – it makes it impossible ever to accept a bad theory. On the other hand, since nothing seems to be able to pass the falsificationist test, it makes the chances of a type I error (rejecting a good theory) quite high. Blaug's main concern is avoiding type II errors, making certain the ideologies stay out. I am equally concerned with type I errors'.(Hands, 1989)

Apart from one or two exaggerations ('nothing seems to be able to pass the falsificationist test'), this does pinpoint the vital issue that divides even such methodologists as Caldwell, Hands and myself, all of whom would count ourselves as being in the Popperian camp. Which type of error is it more important for economists to avoid? If we work hard to avoid the danger of swallowing 'bad' theories, we run the risk of rejecting some 'good' ones; but, conversely, if we open the door as widely as possible to all theories, we will never reject good theories but we will also accept many bad ones. In the final analysis, such methodological differences rest on one's view of the current state of economics, or of what is right and wrong with modern economics. I take the view, as Hands said, that modern economics is a garden that needs weeding, whereas apparently Caldwell and Hands consider that more fertilizer is required to encourage still more strange and exotic blooms.

Marxian economics

The first two chapters in this volume take up the issue of Marxian economics.[3] Marxian economics, apart from all its other interests, is a wonderful case in point of the problem of theory appraisal. Why should we give credence to Marxian economics or rather, as in my case, why should we *not* give credence to Marxian economics? The first thing we ask of any theory is that it should be logically consistent, because an inconsistent theory is compatible with any set of events and any prior beliefs; in short, it is meaningless. If it is indeed consistent, there follow a number of other desirable, but not absolutely necessary, criteria, such as simplicity, elegance, generality and fecundity (see Tarascio and Caldwell, 1979), none of which lend themselves to a neat definition. Lastly, there is the litmus-paper criterion of falsifiability: what events, should they occur, would falsify the predictions deducible from the theory?

The first chapter on Marxian economics is therefore concerned with an examination of the internal consistency of Marx's schema: are there logical flaws in Marx's purported demonstration that profits are nothing but 'unpaid labour', that these profits are bound to decline in the course of time and that this is the key to capitalism's inevitable demise? One might have thought that this question lends itself to a definite answer but, in fact, the logical consistency of any complex theory is by no means easy to judge. If it were possible to 'axiomatize' the theory – to reduce it to a logical structure akin to that of geometry as set out in Euclid's *Elements* (the stellar example to this day of a fully axiomatized theory) – we could indeed rule unambiguously on its logical consistency. But very few theories, either in the natural or in the social sciences, have been successfully axiomatized and certainly no one has ever come near to doing so in the case of Marx, whose theory or research programme is even more complex and diffuse, ramifying in all directions, than most social theories.

I take the view that there are no serious logical inconsistencies in the Marxian system, or at any rate none that cannot be repaired by post-Marxian refinements. Indeed, the logical coherence of the stupendous 'house that Marx built' is one of the many intellectual attractions of Marxism, both to me personally and of course to Marxists worldwide. Nevertheless, while one cannot easily fault Marx on purely logical grounds, the relevance of the final conclusions of Marx's arguments is highly questionable: his system is shot through with arbitrary assumptions at all stages in the chain of reasoning. This at any rate is the burden of my first paper.

I conclude at the end of this paper that Marx's theory *could* be true but that it is impossible to know whether it *is* true without examining the accuracy of Marx's predictions. Now, Marx was very fond of making economic, political and social predictions of all kinds and he made literally hundreds of them. Alas, most of them were off-the-cuff and not logically implied by his own theories. Our first task, therefore, is to separate the logically deducible from Marx's purely ad hoc predictions and then finally to consider the empirical record of the former. Here we encounter, for the first but not the last time in this volume, the uncomfortable fact that the track record of any theory is never straightforward: it is impossible to say unambiguously what does, or does not, count as a refutation. Nevertheless, in the case of Marxian economics, the gap between what Marx predicted and what actually happened over the span of 100 years since his death is so great that we may say, without any qualification, that the Marxian system has been decisively refuted, not once, not twice, but over and over again. Capitalism never did collapse as a result of its own inner economic contradictions but, even as I write, communism in Eastern Europe seems indeed to be collapsing because of its inner economic contradictions. Irony of ironies: Marx was right about collapse, but he was wrong about the social system to which it would happen! So much then for Marx's predictive record!

So, why are there still Marxists in the world? Quite simply because any theory can be immunized against any number of empirical refutations, however large, if one refuses to abide by some set of metatheoretical strictures; a 'true believer', whether Marxist or of anything else, is one who refuses to tell you *before* scientific reasoning begins whether there are any metatheoretical principles that must be obeyed by a so-called 'scientific' theory. It is on this note that I conclude the treatment of Marx in Chapter 2.

Radical economics

Chapter 3 continues the theme with a survey of radical economics, a largely but not exclusively, American legacy of the students' revolt of 1968. Radical economists are influenced by Marx but they go well beyond Marx in considering the pervasive influence of sexism and racism in labour markets. One of Marx's great, but underdeveloped, ideas is that of 'the labour process', the methods whereby capitalists obtain 'a fair day's work' for the wage they have agreed to pay. In modern language, the employment contract under capitalism is necessarily 'incomplete' in the sense that the quality of work cannot be specified in black and white; it can only be maximized by a subtly coercive process combining the 'carrot' of promotion with the 'stick' of unemployment. Radical economists have exploited this notion to argue that labour markets under capitalism must necessarily divide the workforce by sex and race, thus explaining sexual and racial differences in earnings in terms of 'labour market segmentation'. This is the core of radical economics, but the total radical research programme extends to business cycles, causes of low growth in the industrialized world, imperialism and the poverty of the Third World. It is an extremely ambitious and continuously developing research programme that aims quite simply to supplant the whole of orthodox economics (see Hunt and Sherman, 1986). To appraise so vast a research programme is no easy task, the more so as it is a young and not entirely coherent structure in all its different parts. Nevertheless, the effort to ask, even provisionally, whether radical economics is a promising new departure in economics is extremely instructive: in the process we learn a great deal about the 'art' of theory choice.

I remain unpersuaded about radical economics as a whole but it cannot be denied that it displays considerable strength and power in special fields like labour economics.

The Keynesian revolution

Chapter 4 on the Keynesian revolution takes up a much disputed historical question: how did Keynesian economics succeed so totally and so swiftly? If ever the term 'revolution' was warranted for any intellectual change in economics in the last 200 years, it is the unprecedented victory of Keynesian macroeconomics over the minds of economists in the late 1930s and early 1940s. Of course, there have been numerous attempts to explain the Keynesian revolution, and yet none of these seem to me to remove the air of mystery that continues to surround the entire episode.

According to the methodology of Lakatos, scientists are the sort of people who subscribe to 'progressive' scientific research programmes; and progressive research programmes, for Lakatos, are those that successfully predict 'novel facts'. What then are the 'novel facts' predicted by Keynesian economics and could the immediate corroboration of these facts account for the swift popularity of the Keynesian system? That is the question posed by my essay to which I gave the unhesitating answer: yes. As the years have passed, I am more convinced than ever that Lakatos does provide a splendid apparatus of thought to help us grasp the nature of something like the Keynesian revolution.[4]

John Hicks

The late Sir John Hicks, a Nobel Laureate and one of the most thoughtful commentators on economic theories past and present, never had much use for the philosophy of science of Popper and Lakatos. However, he always deplored economic theory for economic theory's sake – economics as mere intellectual understanding – and insisted that any important and significant economic theory should have definite policy implications. However, a theory which purports to pronounce on matters of economy policy clearly has to commit itself, at least to some extent, to verifiable and indeed verified predictions about the course of economic events; and, of course, the making of such predictions is the hallmark of Popperian and Lakotosian methodology. How then did Hicks reconcile his rejection of Popper and Lakatos with his belief in economics as a policy science?

I argue in this paper that he never reconciled the two and indeed never even recognized the contradictory stance that he had adopted in all his pronouncements about good and bad economics. Since his brand of intellectual schizophrenia is widely shared, it is worth airing.

Von Thünen

We come now to a number of papers in the history of economic thought in which methodological issues loom less large than before; nevertheless, they are not absent because history of thought without methodology is, strictly speaking, impossible. The first chapter in Part II of this volume is a reader's guide and commentary on *The Isolated State* by Johann von Thünen, one of the most fascinating but easily *the* most difficult book in the entire history of economics.

I deplore antiquarian studies in past economic doctrines conducted solely for their own sake – as if such a thing were even possible. However, I must confess being slightly enthralled by von Thünen because I want to figure him out. In fact, von Thunen had a central message which he never succeeded in selling to the economics profession: space is an essential dimension of economic activity and all sound economics is to some extent spatial economics. However, orthodox economics both before and since von Thünen has remained stubbornly spaceless in its fundamental analytical concerns. In that sense, von Thünen's programme was one of the great failures of economics. It is one of the subsidiary objects of this essay to ask why von Thünen failed, but the central purpose of the essay remains to introduce the reader to one of the strangest, but also one of the most original, books in the history of economics, demonstrating once again that, in a subject like economics, highly abstract theories are nevertheless occasionally capable of throwing surprising light on the real world.

Classical economics

When *The New Palgrave* editors asked me to write an essay on 'Classical Economics' I decided that there were already too many books and articles explaining classical economics, and that my efforts were better devoted to reviewing recent interpretations of classical economics, particularly those that clashed with older writings on the nature and significance of classical political economy. In the course of that review, I soon found that all the recent reinterpretations fell more or less neatly into two groups: those for whom classical economics was a primitive version of neoclassical economics, because the whole of eighteenth- and nineteenth-century economics is in fact a seamless web; and those for whom there was a radical break in the history of economics around 1870, with everything before it (such as classical economics) standing in the light and everything after standing in the dark. The former group is perfectly represented by the voluminous writings of Samuel Hollander and the latter by the almost equally voluminous writings of the neo-Ricardians or Anglo-Italian followers of Piero Sraffa. My position is somewhere in between: I do think there was a genuine marginal revolution in economics in the last quarter of the nineteenth century but I do not believe that pre-marginal classical economics was some wonderful style of economic reasoning that has been rehabilitated and finally put on its feet by the labours of the last Piero Sraffa.

It is a case of a plague on both houses. I do my best in this essay to explain why I disagree with Hollander's reading of Adam Smith, David Ricardo and John Stuart Mill. Similarly, I explain what I think is wrong with the so-called 'surplus interpretation' of classical economics that emanates from the school of Sraffa; this is a quarrel that is further pursued in the last chapter of this volume.

Marginal cost pricing

Chapter 8 on 'Marginal Cost Pricing' is ostensibly about a famous proposition in modern welfare economics: when an enterprise is operated publicly for whatever reason, the goal of economic efficiency is only secured if that enterprise is made to price its products in accordance with their marginal costs of production. This proposition, while absolutely orthodox ever since the 1930s, has nevertheless been attacked and criticized by dozens of economists over the last 50 or 60 years. One purpose of my essay was to review this debate, in order to help me make up my own mind about it.

In the course of this review it gradually dawned on me that the entire debate was not really about marginal cost pricing as such, but about one of the deepest questions in the whole of economics: can we ever separate questions of efficiency from questions of equity when recommending economic policies? Take a small example: Economist A recommends a rise in the costs of parking meters (or the price of petrol) in a town so as to reduce urban congestion; it is economically efficient, he argues, to charge more for space when space has become scarcer. No, says Economist B, because to do so would be unfair to poorer motorists who will be unable to pay those higher parking charges. But, says Economist A, if you don't like the prevailing distribution of income, alter it directly, say by progressive income tax, but do not abandon a recommendation to improve economic efficiency just because you disapprove of the prevailing distribution of income. That is all very well says Economist B, but it is politically impossible to raise the levels of income tax and hence it remains true that, given the income distribution we will have to live with, higher parking meter charges are unfair. End of discussion and a perfect stalemate! Moral of the story? If we refuse to divorce efficiency from equity considerations, if only for the sake of argument, there is almost nothing an economist can say about economic policy that will command anything remotely resembling a consensus!

If we are indeed driven to this depressing conclusion by impeccable logic, it ought to be proclaimed from the rooftops because it certainly is not well understood by most economists. However, I think that there are good reasons to deny the conclusion, in which case many of the critics of modern welfare economics, who have never been made aware of the true nature of their criticism, ought to think again.

If this is not the $64000 question in economics, I do not know what is. Anyone studying economics simply has to make up his or her mind at some stage in their study about whether they are indeed willing to separate questions of efficiency from questions of equity. Can we ever talk about the size of the pie without simultaneously having to say how we are going to divide it? If not, I am afraid that much of the economics we learn must be unlearned and forgotten.

Nicholas Kaldor

The late Lord Kaldor was, like von Thünen, one of the 'Great Failures' of economics: his was a truly original, penetrating mind that struggled for over 40 years to develop a truly dynamic theory of capitalist development in the spirit of Keynes – that is, a theory driven by the demand-side rather than the supply-side of markets – yet he failed, not just in the sense of winning over his peers, but in the sense of never spelling out a convincing version of his theory that would have won over those who were inclined to be sympathetic to his ideas. That, at any rate, is my assessment of Kaldor's chequered career but, it must be said, there are those who take a different view (for example, Thirlwall, 1987).

The purpose of Chapter 9 on Kaldor is to introduce the reader to his ideas, to pinpoint where the ideas went wrong, but also to persuade him of the magnificence of Kaldor's 'vision', an entirely new way of formulating the great question with which Adam Smith launched the science of economics 200 years ago – the nature and causes of the wealth of nations.

The New Palgrave

The last chapter of the book consists of a pamphlet-length review of *The New Palgrave: A Dictionary of Economics* that appeared three years ago in four volumes and one million words. Despite its title, it is an encyclopedia of economics and the first that has appeared in the English language in 60 years. On opening its pages, one discovers that modern economics consists either of relatively advanced mathematical economics or of post-Keynesian, neo-Ricardian and quasi-Marxist disquisitions on a large variety of technical concepts, topics and subjects; the number of times Sraffa and Marx are quoted is quite astonishing and out of all proportion to their acknowledged place in the corpus of received economic doctrines. To put it bluntly, the three editors of *The New Palgrave*, John Eatwell, Murray Millgate and Peter Newman, have in fact edited a broadside on behalf of Sraffian economics on the one hand and mathematical general equilibrium theory on the other.

Nevertheless, *The New Palgrave* was widely reviewed and, amazingly enough, it was almost always well reviewed (by those who usually admitted that they had not read it from cover to cover). Is it conceivable that, nevertheless, I am right in my almost wholly negative judgement on *The New Palgrave*, while everyone else is wrong, or at least too generous?

I have set out the evidence in Chapter 10 and I must let the reader judge for him or herself. Naturally, he or she will need to consult *The New Palgrave* to check my allegations but that is permissible provided that they do not actually buy a copy!

Notes

1. See also my 'Kuhn versus Lakatos, or Paradigms versus Research Programmes in the History of Economics' (1976) and 'Economic Methodology in One Easy Lesson' (1980) in Blaug (1986) and 'The Empirical Status of Human Capital Theory: A Slightly Jaundiced Survey' (1976) in Blaug (1987a).
2. For the hermeneutical approach to economics, see O'Sullivan (1987). For rhetorics, see McClosky (1985), a book which I reviewed in largely negative terms (Blaug, 1987b).
3. I have dealt with Marx elsewhere (see Blaug,1985; 1987a).
4. D. Wade Hands (1989) replied to my 'Second Thoughts on the Keynesian Revolution' with his 'Second Thoughts on Second Thoughts', to which I counter-replied, to which he 'counter-counter-replied'. Naturally, I think that I won the argument but I am sure that he thinks the same about his side of the debate; let every reader decide for him or herself!

References

Blaug, M. (1985), *Economic Theory in Retrospect*, (4th edn.), Cambridge: Cambridge University Press.

Blaug, M. (1986), *Economic History and the History of Economics*, Brighton: Wheatsheaf Books; New York: New York University Press.

Blaug, M. (1987a), *The Economics of Education and the Education of an Economist*, Aldershot: Edward Elgar Publishing.

Blaug, M. (1987b), 'Methodology with a Small m', *Critical Review* 1(2), Spring.

Caldwell, B. (1982), *Beyond Positivism: Economic Methodology in the Twentieth Century*, London: Allen & Unwin.

Hands, D. Wade, (1989), 'Reply to Mark Blaug's Reply to D. Wade Hands, "Second Thoughts on Second Thoughts: Reconsidering the Lakotosian Progress of *The General Theory*"', *Review of Political Economy*, forthcoming.

Hunt, E.K. and Sherman, H.J. (1986), *Economics. Introduction to Traditional and Radical Views*, New York: Harper and Row.

Hutchison, T. W. (1978), *On Revolutions and Progress in Economic Knowledge*, Cambridge: Cambridge University Press.

Katouzian, H. (1980), *Ideology and Method in Economics*, London: Phillip Allen.

McCloskey, D.M. (1985), *The Rhetoric of Economics*, Madison, WI: University of Wisconsin Press.

O'Sullivan, P.J. (1987), *Economic Methodology and Freedom to Choose*, London: Allen & Unwin.

Stewart, I.M.T. (1979), *Reasoning and Method in Economics*, London: McGraw-Hill.

Tarascio, V. and Caldwell, B. (1979), 'Theory Choice in Economics; Philosophy and Practice', *Journal of Economic Issues*, 13,December.

Thirlwall, A.P. (1987), *Nicholas Kaldor*, Brighton: Wheatsheaf Books.

PART I

METHODOLOGY

1   A methodological appraisal of Marxian economics I

What I hope to do in this paper is to appraise Marxian economics in the sense of Imre Lakatos, by which is meant, not deciding its truth-value once and for all, but rather assessing its predictive record for the class of events with which it is concerned. This is by no means an easy assignment. Marxian economics is embedded in a wider scientific research programme, comprising sociological, political, and even anthropological theories, all knitted together by an overarching theory of historical change, and as such it must be appraised in the round as a complex of interconnected theories. Moreover, it must be appraised in relation to its own historical momentum in solving the problems that it set for itself, taking due account of rival research programmes of more or less equal scope. However, to do justice to these methodological precepts with reference to Marxism would require an entire committee of social scientists, not a lone economist with some amateur knowledge of politics and sociology. I must apologize, therefore, for my personal limitations but, at the same time, I must insist that the larger Marxian research programme cannot be understood except in terms of its extensive economic content. In view of the many books on Marx that present him as a philosopher of history, a political theorist, and a sociologist, who incidently had a few ideas on economics,[1] we, as economists, need to remind the world that Marx devoted nearly 20 years of his mature output to questions of economic theory and that the economic aspects of Marxism are the only ones which he himself polished to anything like a finished state. Despite his vast output, he never managed to devote sustained attention to his theory of history, his concept of social classes, or his theory of the state, but he did write some 5,000 pages on problems of value and surplus value. If we can make no sense of these, we are not taking Marxism seriously.

One final introductory remark. I shall approach my principal task indirectly. It is pointless to examine the predictive record of a theory until one is satisfied that it is logically consistent, because a logically inconsistent theory is compatible with any and all events. The logical structure of Marxian economics, however, is complex and the possibility that it is actually logically incoherent cannot be dismissed out of hand. I shall devote the first paper, therefore, to the question whether the theory hangs together coherently and only then, in the second paper, shall I take up the track record of Marxian economics. This examination of coherence and consistency will take us so far afield that there is a real danger of losing sight of my primary aim of appraising Marxism as a scientific research programme which commits itself to a whole series of definite predictions about the future course of events. This point must be kept in mind throughout Paper I.

Many of you must be asking yourselves: do we really need yet another examination of Marxian economics? After nearly 90 years of endless commentaries, there is, surely, nothing left to say? In fact, however, recent developments in economic theory have significantly altered our view of Marxian economics. Indeed, it is not going too far to say that the logical structure of Marxian economics was not properly appreciated, and could not have been properly appreciated, by such older commentators as Wicksteed, Böhm-Bawerk and Pareto. Until the advent of linear production models and interindustry analysis, not to mention modern growth theory, the Marxian apparatus was too alien to prevailing modes of economic thought to have been understood for what it is. Even as recently as 1974, William Baumol (1974) felt it necessary to explain to Paul Samuelson what had been Marx's aim in framing his theory as he did, which surely confirms the view that there are inherent difficulties in grasping what Marx is all about. Consider, as further evidence of that difficulty, the three brilliant commentaries on Marx which appeared simultaneously in 1942 – a golden year for Marxian economics: Schumpeter's critical and yet glowing opening chapter on Marx in *Capitalism, Socialism and Democracy*, Joan Robinson's slim but incisive *Essay on Marxian Economics*, and thirdly, Paul Sweezy's major defensive treatise, *The Theory of Capitalist Development*. Sweezy's book rediscovered two remarkable articles by Ladislaus von Bortkiewicz, published in 1906–07, which argued that Marx had utterly failed to solve the so-called 'Transformation Problem', after which von Bortkiewicz showed that it was indeed capable of being solved, at least on certain special assumptions. Schumpeter cites von Bortkiewicz in a footnote but otherwise makes no more than passing reference to the Transformation Problem. Joan Robinson, on the other hand, never so much as mentions the Transformation Problem. It turns out, however, that the Transformation Problem is absolutely critical to the logical validity of the Marxian system: unless the problem has a formal solution, the system simply lacks an adequate foundation. Moreover, although we now know, thanks to Francis Seton, that the Transformation Problem is in general capable of being solved, the meaning of that transformation in terms of substantive economic consequences is precisely what continues to divide Marxists from non-Marxists. It is an amazing commentary on the history of Marxism that it took a bourgeois economist, writing 23 years after the death of Karl Marx and 12 years after the publication of Volume III of *Capital*, to appreciate the seriousness of the logical puzzle that Marx had bequeathed to his followers, and that it then took another 35 years for any Marxist economist to acknowledge von Bortkiewicz's decisive breakthrough in the solution of that problem. In other words, it is no exaggeration to say that every Marxist economist writing between 1883 and 1942 simply did not know what they were talking about – and some still do not know.

The distinctive feature that sets Marxian economics apart from any other kind of economics is the notion that competitive capitalism conforms at one and the same time to two sets of relative prices, one of which is expressed in terms of the total direct and indirect labour embodied in, or required for, the production of commodities ('values' for short), and the other of which is expressed in terms of ordinary long-run equilibrium prices ('prices' for short). In Volume I of *Capital*, Marx postulates that commodities are priced by marking up the payments made to direct labour at an equal 'rate of surplus value', whereas in Volume III he maintains that commodities are priced by marking up the payments made to both direct and indirect labour at an equal rate of profit on total capital invested; as Samuelson (1972, pp. 279–81) has said, it is as if the only costs of production in Volume I are capital depreciation plus wages plus a proportional payroll tax, whereas in Volume III it is recognized that costs of production are actually equal to outlays on all inputs plus a percentage turnover tax on all transactions. It is a simple matter to state the necessary and sufficient conditions that would make it unnecessary to choose between these two systems of price determination: they are, first, the trivial case where the rate of profit is zero, and, second, the case where the ratios of direct to indirect labour, or the degrees of mechanization in different industries, are the same for all commodities, so that we are faced in effect with a one-sector model of the economy. But Marx refused to commit himself to such artificial assumptions, which raises the problem of the precise status of the Volume I world of labour values: competitive prices simply must deviate from labour values because, in the face of differences in what Marx called the 'organic composition of capital', there is no way in which a system of counting only current wages can result in the same set of relative prices as a system where outlays on all inputs are counted. Böhm-Bawerk called this 'the great contradiction' in the Marxian system, arguing that Volume III simply marked a retreat from the pure labour theory of value of Volume I. Marx's followers replied that Marx was perfectly aware of 'the great contradiction' before he sat down to write Volume I, implying apparently that it is perfectly permissible to operate with two different systems of price determination. But Böhm-Bawerk was right: there may not be a great contradiction between the world of values and the world of prices but there is certainly a great dissonance.

What Marx claimed was that the value system can be logically transformed or 'mapped' into the price system in such a way as to produce the same set of absolute prices and the same rate of profit. The algorithm for carrying out this transformation, he argued, would have to satisfy two of what have since been called 'invariance conditions':

1. the total surplus created by direct labour in the value system must be set equal to the total profits that accrue in the price system;
2. 'total value', as he put it, must be set equal to 'total price', meaning apparently that the weighted average of values is to be equated to the weighted average of prices.

The second condition clearly implies that long-run equilibrium prices are only proportional to relative labour costs in the singular case of those commodities produced by an *average* organic composition of capital, that is, the weighted average of the organic compositions of different industries in the economy, the weights corresponding to the proportions of direct labour employed. Marx made a technical mistake in carrying out this transformation of values into prices: he failed to apply the transformation coefficients to the inputs of constant capital. But we now know that this slip can be corrected and we are then left with two propositions that together constitute the substantive results of the Marxian system. We may call them 'the labour theory of profits' and 'the labour theory of prices': the labour theory of profits says that the equal rate of profit that we observe in the real world is governed by a pool of surplus value that is redistributed among individual industries in inverse proportion to their degrees of mechanization, and the labour theory of prices says that relative prices are determined on average by relative labour costs because all the individual deviations of prices from values cancel out in the aggregate. Now these are difficult propositions both to state and to grasp. If this is what Marxian economics amounts to, it is doubtful that it would ever have been capable of inflaming the proletariat to overthrow the capitalist system. To simplify the argument, therefore, Marx builds a make-believe house of values in Volume I, and then surprisingly, he proceeds immediately to live in it: he applied it directly and without any qualifications to such real-world problems as the struggle to secure a shorter working day via factory legislation and the labour-saving effects of improved machinery in the cotton factories. In so doing, he fooled generations of Marxists into believing that the abstract domain of values in Volume I is in some sense as real as the observed world of prices in Volume III. Indeed, I think that it can be shown that he sometimes deceived himself.

Note, first, that neither the labour embodied in commodities nor the surplus values generated by workers are observable entities. That is, of course, neither here nor there: marginal utilities, production functions, and for that matter long-run equilibrium prices are also not observable phenomena, and, anyway, the physical sciences are full of unobservable theoretical entities, such as genes, photons, and gravitational forces. What is much more serious is that values and surplus values are not behavioural variables, that is, variables that are either maximized or minimized by capitalists and workers. Marx himself was perfectly aware of the fact that neither capitalists nor workers care a fig about surplus value *per se* and he noted this fact repeatedly in Volume III of *Capital* (Marx, 1909, pp. 59, 90, 198, 201, 232). What he wanted to say was that, although capitalists seek to maximize the rate of profit and although workers seek to maximize the rate of wages, the *unintended social consequence* of such individual maximizing behaviour is that the total mass of surplus value is maximized in the system as a whole. This is what I think he meant to say, but what he actually said virtually amounted to endowing the capitalist system as a whole with a concerted objective of maximizing the production of surplus value (for example, Marx, 1976, pp. 338, 449). No wonder that some of his disciples slip easily into talking about 'the capitalist's thirst for surplus value', even implying that workers are profoundly concerned about the rate of surplus value (Mandel, 1968, pp. 153, 155; also pp. 135, 137, 139, 152, 156).[2] This is simply bad Marxism but it is bad Marxism encouraged by Marx's own loose use of language. Oscar Wilde once said: 'What is a cynic? A man who knows the price of everything, and the value of nothing.' In Marx, we are saying, capitalists and workers alike are cynics: the maximization of surplus value works rather like an 'invisible hand' to produce a collective result that is no part of the intention of any individual.

But if surplus value is an unobservable, non-behavioural variable, how on earth do we know that it is uniform throughout all industries and occupations? We recall that in the world of Volume I it is only living labour that is marked up and that this mark-up is always a constant fraction, regardless of whether the labour happens to be employed in digging ditches with the aid of crude shovels or in operating steel mills with the aid of blast furnaces. You may well say: why not drop the rather implausible assumption of a single, uniform rate of surplus value throughout the economy, letting it vary, indeed, in direct proportion to the amount of machinery that workers are equipped with? After all, even Marx admits that machines are physically productive, so he could hardly object if we make the rate of surplus value in a particular industry a function of its degree of mechanization. However, Marx could never have accepted the notion of unequal rates of surplus value in different industries, for the simple reason that we would then have to know precisely how it varied among industries in order to calculate the total surplus value that is said to mark an upper boundary on the profits that can be earned.[3] Besides, to allow the variation to depend in any way on the proportions of machines to labour in different industries would seem to be fatal to any theory that attributes surplus value solely to labour.

There is a modern defence of the idea of a single, uniform rate of surplus value throughout the economy. The origin of this defence is in Marx himself but it has become commonplace in Marxist commentaries only fairly recently.[4] The argument goes like this: if labour is homogeneous in quality, there will be one ruling wage rate in the economy; and if workers prefer a shorter to a longer working day, and if they care nothing about the other aspects of a job, they will choose jobs and firms in such a way that the length of the working day is everywhere equalized; finally, according to the labour theory of value, a given quantity of homogeneous labour always produces an equal quantity of value; it thus follows that every worker in the economy must spend the same number of hours reproducing the value of his wage bundle and hence the same number of hours working to produce a surplus value for the capitalist who employs him; thus, as an unintended by-product of competition in the labour market, the rate of surplus value is equalized throughout the economy. Q.E.D.

The argument is impeccable so far as it goes but it is, alas, totally irrelevant to the question that is being asked, which is: how do we discover from prices alone that the underlying, unobservable, non-behavioural rate of surplus value is in fact the same in all industries and occupations? You will have noticed that it required the pure labour-theory-of-value assumption that relative prices are strictly proportional to labour costs to obtain the theorem of a uniform rate of surplus value, which is to say that the proof of the theorem remains trapped in the abstract world of Volume I (see Samuelson, 1972, pp. 293, 299). Putting it another way, the theorem says that the labour theory of profits is true if the pure labour theory of value is true, whereas we already know from Marx himself that the pure labour theory of value cannot be true of each and every commodity.

It is noteworthy that Marx himself only hints at the theorem of the uniform rate of surplus value, not in Volume I, but in Volume III of *Capital* (Marx, 1909, p. 206), going so far on that occasion as to say that the rate of surplus value tends in fact to be equalized in the real world (Sweezy, 1942, pp. 65, 69, 71). In saying this, Marx had actually forgotten that the regime of values and surplus values cannot manifest itself at the level of observable reality; as an empirical fact, rates of surplus value must be unequal between industries once the rate of profit is equalized in the face of differences in the organic compositions of capital.[5] The theorem of the uniform rate of surplus value never arises in the first volume of *Capital* and it is not difficult to see why. In Chapter 10 of Volume I of 'The Working Day' we are told that capital has 'a werewolf-like hunger for surplus labour' (Marx, 1976 p. 353) and that the length of the working day is only equalized between industries as a result of 'a protracted and more or less concealed civil war' between capitalists and workers; in other words, the length of the working day becomes equalized, not as a result of purely economic forces responding to the mobility of labour, but as a result of a political struggle involving the power of the state (Maguire, 1978, pp. 151–5, Elster 1985, pp. 186–94). But if the theorem of the uniform rate of surplus value is to be believed, the length of the working day is equalized by a competitive process taking place in labour markets. Unfortunately, once we take on board the notion of competitive labour markets, the theorem breaks down on the side of uniform wage rates. Adam Smith in a famous chapter of Book I of the *Wealth of Nations* showed that a competitive labour market tends to equalize, not the rate of wages for homogeneous labour, but the 'net advantages' of different jobs. Some jobs require more skill, more endurance, more indifference to routine and more irksome responsibility than others; in addition, jobs also differ in the variance of both earnings and full-time employment opportunities. However, the notion of workers partly affecting their wages by their own occupational choices was deeply abhorrent to Marx, and so it is no wonder that he only refers obliquely in one or two places to Adam Smith's theory (Marx, 1909, pp. 168–9). Even so, either there is competition in labour markets on the supply-side, in which case there is absolutely no reason to believe in the truth of the theorem of the uniform rate of surplus value – given the enormous variety of working conditions and technical methods in different industries, neither the wage rate nor the length of the working day will in fact be equalized everywhere even for strictly homogeneous labour – or else, there is no competition in labour markets, in which case the theorem is deprived of any foundation. Indeed, it is simply amazing that so many modern theorists have endorsed the logic of Marx's argument about the validity of postulating a uniform rate of surplus value. Perhaps, it is only another case of the tendency to lean over backwards to give Marx even better arguments than he himself supplied.

Possibly, something deeper is involved. So persuasive is Marx's device of creating a completely self-contained world of values in Volume I that it is virtually impossible to stop ourselves from thinking of value and surplus as real entities that are almost, if not quite, observable. Take, for example, the famous discussion in Volume I of the division of the working day into a part when workers work for themselves to earn their wages and a part when they work for the capitalist. Millions of readers have found this distinction between paid and unpaid labour hours to be virtually self-evident, whereas, of course, it can neither be observed nor inferred in any economy with a complex division of labour; workers in wage-good industries work all the time to produce their own and other workers' wages, whereas workers in capital-good industries never even produce their own wages, much less anyone else's. And even if wage rates and the length of the working day are everywhere the same, is it plausible to assume that a worker in a highly labour-intensive industry can produce in a given number of hours a product that has the same power to command wage-goods as an identical worker employed for the same number of hours in a highly capital-intensive industry?[76] And yet this is what Marx in Volume I almost manages to make us believe. The fact that values in Volume I are actually expressed as amounts of money – the value of a commodity is the equivalent total labour time embodied in a physical unit of gold (see Steedman, 1977, pp. 208–13) – merely serves to confer additional realism on the Alice-in-Wonderland parable of Volume I.

Take, as a further example, the chapter on absolute surplus value in Volume I. Why else would capitalists fight to the death to prevent a reduction in the working day, Marx seems to be saying, if not because they strive, however unconsciously, to maximize the number of labour hours on which their profits depend? The fact is, however, that they would act in exactly the same way if instead they maximized the rate of profit in a regime of competitive prices. It *may* be that daily output per man would actually be higher if hours were fewer; even if there were a fall in the productivity of labour, the fall in the user costs of machinery operated for fewer hours *might* be more than enough to warrant a reduction in hours; but competitive pressures make it dangerous for any single capitalist to engage in such experiments, and so, unless capitalists can somehow be made to act in concert by, say, a government, the length of the working day will not be spontaneously reduced under perfect competition. It was by this argument that John Stuart Mill, long before Marx, defended the idea of Factory Acts (see Blaug, 1971; Johnson, 1969). For Marx, the 'werewolf-like hunger for surplus labour' provided a much simpler explanation of the resistance of manufacturers to the Ten Hours Bill, at the end of which discussion he has practically persuaded us to believe that surplus value is no abstract fiction but rather a living force that drives the capitalist system.

The temptation to reify the rate of surplus value, to treat a mere abstraction as something concrete and objective, proved irresistible even to Marx, who was usually more careful, and it has certainly proved irresistible to simply hundreds of Marx's followers. How do we know that relative prices are proportional to direct labour costs, at least on average? Oh, we just add up the direct labour hours expended on the production of commodities plus the direct labour hours expended some time ago on the production of their means of production plus the labour hours expended still longer ago on those means of production, *ad infinitum*. To be sure, they will admit, all this indirect labour is carried forward and accumulated at some uniform and constant rate of surplus value, but since this compounding factor is itself directly proportional to direct labour, it makes no difference to the argument (see Wolff, 1979, pp. 141–6). Now, we know, and have known clearly ever since Knut Wicksell, that this sort of adding-up of embodied labour-time only works if the structure of production is perfectly hierarchical, containing no circular loops because, say, coal is used to fuel machinery which is used to mine coal. Marx recognized the fact that a hierarchical production structure is a special case rarely encountered in reality – an amazing insight for someone writing in the 1860s – and yet he could not resist giving his reader the impression that indirect labour is as easily observable as direct labour, and hence that the decomposition of prices into their historic labour costs yields not approximate results, as Ricardo believed, but exact results in conformity with the labour theory of value.[7]

To have believed less would have undermined the solution to the Transformation Problem that Marx supplied, which was simply erroneous. I am not referring to the slight oversight of failing to calculate capital inputs in terms of prices but rather to the fact that the rate of profit, which is equalized in his Volume III system of prices, is not the *money* rate of profit which motivates capitalists but the *value* rate of profit. A uniform rate of surplus value applied to various proportions of constant and variable capital in different industries yields different rates of profit in different industries and what Marx did was simply to average these arithmetically in order to obtain the general rate of profit in the economy. Now, the *money* rate of profit is equal to the weighted money price of the excess of net output over wage costs, divided by the weighted money price of all inputs and, when prices are not proportional to labour costs, there is no reason to expect this ratio to equal the weighted labour value of the same excess of net output over wages divided by the weighted labour value of the same inputs. The two profit rates are not even close approximations of each other, nor is one a definite function of the other.[8] In other words, Marx first determines the general rate of profit in his value system and only then determines the so-called 'prices of production', failing utterly to see that all the variables in one system must be simultaneously transformed into all the variables of the other. Von Bortkiewicz saw the fallacy of Marx's approach but, as I mentioned earlier, his contribution fell on deaf ears until 1942. All through the golden era of Marxism between 1895 and 1920, Marxists simply failed to notice that Marxian economics as expounded by Marx is logically deficient.

Modern reformulations of the Transformation Problem in terms of linear production theory have hindered rather than helped the simple faith of the 'True Believers'. Marx was wrong to think that one can transform values into prices while retaining both the labour theory of profits and the labour theory of prices; one may retain one of the 'invariance conditions' but not both. But if we retain the labour theory of profits, we throw away the so-called 'proof' of the theorem that the rate of surplus value is equal in all sectors and occupations, after which there is little reason to believe the claim that profit is nothing but appropriated surplus value. On the other hand, if instead we retain the labour theory of prices, we in effect abandon the labour theory of profits, which is absolutely fundamental to Marx's picture of capitalism. Unfortunately, no one has ever been able to produce a single good reason for choosing one 'invariance condition' over another.[9] Moreover, we cannot discover from observations which 'invariance condition' to apply because the problem is essentially a logical one of selecting a *numéraire* whose 'value' remains invariant in the process of transformation, and in principle there is an infinite number of such numéraires. To show that the Transformation Problem is purely a formal one, it is only necessary to note that a 'gibberish model' which marked up all raw material outlays by an equal rate of surplus value would create exactly the same logical problem of transforming the values of Volume I into the prices of Volume III (Samuelson, 1977, pp. 284–5). Suppose we could mathematically solve that Transformation Problem? What would it prove? All of which is to say that Marx's labour theory of profits cannot be shown to be wrong; on the other hand, it *can* be shown to be totally arbitrary.

Once we have taken on board the idea of linear production models in the style of Leontief or of Sraffa, we realize the absurdity of Marx's claim that the rate of profit is left undetermined in bourgeois economists because bourgeois economists are unable to place an upper limit on the volume of profits that appears in the numerator of the expression for the profit rate. When the structure of production of an economy is conceived in input-output terms, it is easy to show that the rate of profit is determined as a ratio of purely physical quantities the moment the rate of wage is specified in physical terms. There is absolutely no need to appeal to any special theory about the ultimate source of profits in order to explain how the rate of profit is in fact determined. Having come this far, however, we realize that there is actually no point in operating with a value system, which is half-way between a system of physical quantities and a system of competitive prices.

No, worse than that: we can only calculate values *after* we have derived the set of competitive prices from a physical specification of production processes. Given certain simplifying assumptions, it is indeed possible to stand the Transformation Problem on its head by transforming prices into values: provided there are no 'whirlpool' structures of production and no joint products of the wool-mutton type, it is possible to calculate what Morishima (1973, p. 12) calls 'employment multipliers', that is, sums of the successive increases in employment which would take place in various industries when the production of a given commodity is increased by one more unit. But it is impossible to follow Marx's procedure of transforming values into prices, even in the simple case of strictly recursive patterns of production, without knowledge of the underlying technology of the economy and the real rate of profit that this technology implies. Since indirect labour is accumulated and compounded into the final product at the going rate of profit, the labour values associated with a given technology, far from being data from which the rate of profit is derived, themselves depend critically on the rate of profit. In general, capitalists will choose new techniques so as to maximize the rate of profit relative to the money wage rate and, hence, the pattern of techniques adopted is part and parcel of the very process of determining the maximum achievable rate of profit. And as Ian Steedman (1977, pp. 65, 147–9) has argued, the mere presence of fixed capital always introduces a choice-of-technique problem for capitalists even when there is no technical progress and no substitutability between capital and labour. The use of machines always raises the problem of when to scrap them and the choice of one optimal life rather than another is an essential element in the process of achieving the maximum rate of profit. Hence, labour values, which depend on the economic life of machines, can only be determined after and not before the rate of profit is determined.

We thus have three levels of analysis: an invisible but potentially observable basement of physical *quantities*, another invisible and totally unobservable basement of *values*, and a visible directly observable ground floor of *prices*, the argument being that we can work backwards and forwards from the price system to the quantity system, backwards from the price system to the value system, and forwards from the quantity system to the value system. But what we can never do is to start with the value system as given independently of the other two systems. If the truth be told, this much is actually implied by Marx himself. His 'socially necessary labour time' is nothing else but the vector of minimum labour requirements that are dictated by the prevailing technology of an economy. In other words, he derived his values by implicitly assuming knowledge of the quantity system.

At one time in the history of Marxism, it was common to regard the Transformation Problem as more than a purely logical exercise; the logical transformation of values into prices was said to correspond to an actual historical transformation from a system of 'simple commodity production', in which all producers own their own tools and income per man is equalized by the mobility of labour between occupations, to a system of full-blown capitalism based on the principle of equal profitability on total capital invested. This historical transformation was supposed to have occurred somewhere between ancient and modern times (see Mandel, 1968, pp. 59–65; and Mandel in Marx, 1976, pp. 14–15). Engels believed categorically in the reality of that historical transformation but Marx himself was more cautious, suggesting it more as a piece of 'conjectural history' than as a well attested historical fact (Marx, 1909, pp. 207–9, 212). However, no one has ever discovered a single piece of evidence that would support the notion of the existence of a system of 'simple commodity production' lasting for centuries somewhere in Europe, and in recent times Morishima and Catephores (1978, ch. 7) have finally laid the ghost of that idea.[10]

We are led to conclude at the end of this saga that Samuelson (1977, pp. 251, 295–6) was quite right when he called the value system of Volume I 'a detour' and a 'wasteful redundancy' from Marx's own standpoint of explaining the determination of the rate of profit, the determination of the pattern of prices, and the distribution of income between wages and profits under a system of competitive capitalism. Indeed, stronger language is warranted: as we shall see later, the Volume I world of values is a veritable incubus that has systematically misled Marx and Marxists in interpreting 'the laws of motion' of capitalism. So much is now common ground between Samuelson and Morishima, on the one hand, and certain Marxist followers of Sraffa, on the other. For example, such Sraffian Marxists as Arun Bose (1975, 1980), Ian Steedman (1977) and Geoff Hodgson (1982) entirely abandon the labour theory of value and totally repudiate the Transformation Problem as meaningless and irrelevant (see also Roemer, 1982; Elster, 1985, ch. 3). Even the late Ronald Meek (1973, pp. xxix–xxx, and 1977, pp. 131–3), a prominent Marxist economist of the Old Left, while not going as far as Bose, Steedman and Hodgson, was prepared, after reading Sraffa, to reformulate his basic attitude to Marxian economics. Indeed, in all of these writings we can witness the enormous liberating value of Sraffa's *Production of Commodities By Means of Commodities*. I doubt that Sraffa's system can be used to analyse 'the laws of motion' of present-day capitalism but it can certainly be used to open the eyes of those who want to employ Marxian tools to analyse these laws. It used to be said that the theoretical writings of Chamberlin and Robinson did more to convince orthodox economists that firms can set prices even under competitive conditions than all the years of advertising and price-fixing by retail outlets. In the same way, it took Sraffa's highly abstract model to convince some Marxists that they had been pursuing the will-o'-the wisp of values for over a century. It is true that some of the so-called 'neo-Ricardians' pretend that Sraffa's technique of constructing a composite 'standard commodity' with which to measure prices amounts to the same thing as Marx's solution of the Transformation Problem once it is assumed that wages are expressed and actually paid in the standard commodity (Medio, 1972, pp. 338–42; Eatwell, 1975; Howard and King, 1975, p. 156, 1976, p. 30; and Nuti, 1977, pp. 99–100), but this is simply to mistake a family resemblance between related concepts for an equivalence (Blundell-Wignall, 1976, pp. 285–6; Pasinetti, 1977, p. 133n; Roncaglia, 1978, p. 79). There is no labour theory of prices in Sraffa because the date at which labour is applied, and hence the period of time for which it earns profits, is correctly regarded as part of the problem of determining prices; there is also no labour theory of profits in Sraffa because the determination of the rate of profit in his analysis depends just as much on indirect as on direct labour.

What then do Sraffians mean when they say that they regard themselves as Marxists? How can one call oneself a Marxist when one has overthrown both the labour theory of prices and labour theory of profits? That question has a number of answers that range all the way from the free-wheeling, do-it-yourself Marxism of the New Left to the ostrich-like intransigence of the Old Left fundamentalists. Notice, first of all, that prices and profits in Sraffa are only determined once the real wage rate is given exogenously. Thus, one could argue that a truly Marxist analysis of capitalism involves an explanation of how the real wage is determined by forces that lie outside the Sraffian and for that matter the Walrasian model of perfect competition, namely, an unequal class struggle between capitalists and workers in which capitalists control the means of employment or what Marxists call 'the labour process'. This is a story that can be persuasively told, but even a well-told story is a far cry from a coherent theory and the theory in question – a type of sociological bargaining theory of wages – has never been systematically written down. That much is conceded by some Sraffians (Bose, 1975, pp. 49, 62, 78–9; Steedman, 1977, pp. 59, 206; Harris, 1978, pp. 89, 184–5; see also Meek, 1977, pp. 132–3 and Wright, 1979) for whom Marxism is perhaps no more than the belief that a satisfactory class-bargaining theory of wages is laid up somewhere and is bound soon to be reprieved.

It is remarkable to what extent this point of view is reminiscent of Oscar Lange's position expressed over 40 years ago, long before the rise of linear production theory. Lange (1968, pp. 77–8) derived a *theory* of 'exploitation' under capitalism, not from a theory of value or a theory of the nature of profits, but from:

1. the institutional fact that capitalists deny workers ownership of the capital they work with;
2. the positive judgement that this is not as it must be; and
3. the normative judgement that this is not as it should be.

The additional normative judgement is vital because the fact that workers lack capital is not by itself enough to 'prove' exploitation unless, of course, we are going to play the semantic game of defining 'exploitation' to mean a situation in which workers do not receive the whole product.[11] But there was nothing that Marx himself despised more that purely negative judgements about property relationships. In a sense, therefore, Lange's argument ceases to be definable as Marxism.

Driven to a line of ultimate defence, some mathematically trained Marxists take refuge in Morishima's 'fundamental Marxian theorem', according to which the money rate of profit in the price system is positive if, and only if, the rate of surplus value in the value system is positive (Morishima, 1973, pp. 6, 53; Wolfstetter, 1973, pp. 790, 797, 807–8; Harris, 1978, pp. 85–8). This theory is said to be a correct mathematical statement of what Marx was really driving at, vindicating his claim that a labour theory of profits is capable of rigorous proof. Morishima (1973, pp. 47–51) takes great pains to show that a physical definition of the rate of surplus value as a ratio of unpaid to paid labour time is equivalent to a value definition of that rate as a ratio of surplus value to variable capital, which seems further to support the Fundamental Marxian Theorem as calculable directly from a Leontief input-output table. Clearly, these are strong claims, which, if upheld, do much to restore validity of Marx's basic results.

Unfortunately, Morishima has changed his mind twice over about the import of the Fundamental Marxian Theorem. In his *Marx's Economics* he interprets the labour theory of value as a theory of aggregation, whose purpose is to reduce the multi-sector model of Volume III to the one-sector model of Volume I, and Morishima (1973, pp. 8, 37, 46, 194) therefore characterizes Marxian economics as operating with 'dual accounting systems', one for values and one for prices. Since Marx explicitly states in Volume I that sectors may and do differ from each other in the compositions of their capital, this modernized interpretation of Marx immediately gives us food for thought.[12] Morishima first establishes the Fundamental Marxian Theorem for a one-sector model without fixed capital, without joint production and without choices of technique. He then shows that multi-sector models that admit fixed capital and joint production can produce nonsensical results, such as negative outputs, negative prices and a negative rate of surplus value – this is no more than the other side of the coin of the impossibility of decomposing prices into their historic labour costs when the structure of production contains recursive loops. For this reason, and also because he denies that different types of labour can be reduced to common labour without invoking prices as weights, he abandons the labour theory of value and with it the Fundamental Marxian Theorem in the final chapter of his book (Morishima, 1973, pp. 181, 194).

In *Value, Exploitation and Growth,* however, Morishima and Catephores (1978, pp. 19–20, 90) restore Marxian value analysis by adopting a linear programming approach that relies on linear inequalities rather than equalities, after which the Fundamental Marxian Theorem is restated as generally valid. But the main feature of their linear programming approach is to derive optimal values by allocating labour to productive processes in such a way as to minimize the total labour inputs of the economy (pp. 33–4, 36). Since choices of technique under capitalism are based on profitability and not upon labour minimization, as they candidly admit, the actual allocation of labour in a capitalist economy bears no obvious relationship to the optimal values obtainable by a linear programming solution (pp. 37–8). Nevertheless, they insist that the rate of surplus value defined à la Marx can in general be shown to constitute the floor below which the physical rate of exploitation, defined as a ratio of unpaid to paid labour hours, cannot possibly fall (p. 44). At this point, we may feel that something important has at long last been rescued from the wreckage. Fresh doubts arise, however, when we are told that the new version of the fundamental Marxian theorem implies the equivalence of the following three propositions:

1. that capitalists exploit workers;
2. that the capitalist system is profitable; and
3. that the capitalist system is productive (p. 51).

In other words, after a lot of hard work and the powerful use of modern mathematical theorems for non-negative square matrices, we learn that Marxian 'exploitation' means growth and that the labour theory of profits is just a roundabout way of saying that the capitalist system normally produces a positive net product which is not handed over to workers. If this is the fundamental Marxian theorem, it is difficult to see what all the fuss is about.

These misgivings are not mine alone: they are echoed by a number of Sraffian Marxists (Blundell-Wignall, 1976, pp. 282–3; Steedman, 1977, pp. 57–9; Bowles and Gintis, 1978, p. 314; Hodgson, 1982, p. 216; see also Samuelson, 1977, p. 291; Roemer, 1981, ch. 5; Elster, 1985, pp. 155–61; Roemer, 1985, pp. 36–7), all of whom deny that the fundamental Marxian theorem carries any causal conclusions about the nature of profits. Ian Steedman (1981, p. 17) puts it very well when he says: 'the existence of (narrowly) defined exploitation and the existence of profits are no more than two sides of the same coin: they are simply 'labour' and 'monetary' expressions of the physical surplus. But Marxist writers only too often suggest that by relating profits to (narrowly defined) exploitation they have explained the existence of profit. They have not; they have simply noticed both ways of expressing the existence of the surplus product.'

At this point, let us collect our thoughts. The doctrine that all profits are created by living labour is easy to prove if you assume that the exchange-values of commodities are always proportional to the direct and indirect labour embodied in their production. But this fictional world of Volume I does not obtain in reality where prices deviate systematically from values. Moreover, it is not true that we can mathematically transform the value system into the price system unless we already have knowledge of the quantity system. We can deduce the price system from a prior set of input-output tables and we can then infer a purely notional set of accounts in terms of labour hours, but all this provides absolutely no clues about the source of profits other than that they are due to the entire structure of production and the actual process of setting wages. Thus, the fundamental Marxian theorem should be turned around to read: the existence of a positive rate of profit is a necessary and sufficient condition for the existence of a positive rate of surplus value, in as much as the latter cannot be determined unless the former is already known.

How then is it that Marxists the world over go on blithely asserting that profits are simply unpaid labour and that workers are being 'robbed' under capitalism? They cannot infer 'exploitation' from simple observations because the real world offers no examples of activities that are either entirely hand-operated or entirely automated. They cannot infer 'exploitation' simply from the coercive social power of capitalists because this is exercised to prevent wages from rising sufficiently to eat up the entire product, and some such mechanism is required even in a socialist economy to secure investment for further growth. They can, of course, deny that private appropriation of the net product encourages technical dynamism and they can also deny the equity of a social system in which some people can live without working for wages; in other words, they do not lack both descriptive and normative arguments to advocate 'euthanasia of the rentier' and expropriation of the coupon-clippers. But what they are not entitled to is the scientific claim that profit *is* 'exploitation.

At this stage of the argument, we are usually greeted with a cloud of familiar rhetoric: that Marxian value theory exposes the unequal social relations between men which are masked by the appearance of equality and freedom of contract – which is like saying that it is all right to retain a bad theory provided it leads to the right conclusions; that workers are literally 'forced' to seek employment, whereas capitalists are not forced to find workers – which is a significant difference but not necessarily a difference relevant to the existence of profit; that labour-power is unique among commodities in a capitalist economy because it alone yields a product with value which is greater than its own value – as if this were not just as true of hired machines and hired land; and that, anyway, there is no satisfactory alternative theory of profit in bourgeois economics.

This last claim can hardly be taken seriously because Marxist writers refuse to distinguish profit from interest, disclaiming all questions having to do with portfolio holdings of money. There is indeed no point to the distinction between profit and interest in a static model of perfect competition and in such a model we can only say that the rate of profit or interest is positive in long-run equilibrium because of the joint outcome of the forces of productivity and thrift. We can then concede (with the usual jibes about the painful sacrifices of Baron Rothschild) that private thrift carries little explanatory power because most investment is financed out of undistributed business profits, so that investment and saving are virtually carried out by the same people for the same reasons. In that case, the brake which keeps profits from being ploughed back to the point of capital saturation is the unwillingness of capitalists to go on investing, preferring instead to take out some profits in immediate consumption. If we do not like the Austrian language of 'positive time preference', we may call it 'a Faustian conflict between the passion for accumulation and the desire for enjoyment' (Marx, 1976, p. 741), but, whatever we call it, it comes to the same thing: the incomes of capitalists are simply the rentals for capital services that originate in the lack of a perfectly elastic supply of capital goods. This is *the* bourgeois theory of profit or interest.

Alternatively, we can admit the presence of uncertainty in a dynamic model of price determination, at which point we do need to distinguish between profit and interest. In that case, however, we will have to supplement a theory of interest by the Schumpeterian theory of profit, in which profits are the disequilibrium windfalls of innovators, and by the Knightian theory of profit, in which profits are the unexpected returns of an enterprise that accrue to those without a contractual claim on its income (see Weston, 1970, and Bronfenbrenner, 1971, ch. 15). At any rate, this is the terrain on which the real issues surrounding the justification of profits under capitalism will have to be fought out. In so doing, the old problem about the relationship between economic and political freedom will have to come into the picture. These sorts of questions have been almost entirely evaded by Marxist economists[13] and bourgeois economists, I must say, have only helped them in such evasions by their own unwillingness to analyse what seem to me to be problems of the sociological roots of entrepreneurship.[14] A meaningful debate between Marxist and mainstream economists on this range of issues is long overdue. Recent developments in Marxian economics have cleared the air for such a debate. Writers such as Cohen (1979), Hodgson (1982), Roemer (1985) and Elster (1985) have gone right back to Lange by reinterpreting the Marxist notion of 'exploitation' as a theory about the lack of justice of capitalism as a social system rather than a theory of the nature of profits as a source of income. The dictionary defines exploitation as 'the improper use of another person for one's own gain' and in standard Marx workers are said to be 'exploited' if they work more hours for the boss than the number of hours it takes to produce the equivalent of the wages their boss pays them, implying that they work in part for the boss without pay. Such a definition of exploitation clearly rests on the validity of the labour theory of value because we cannot actually observe the labour content of goods, whether wage goods or final goods. Having rejected the labour theory of value, we must also reject the standard conception of 'exploitation' as the forced extraction of unpaid labour. However, we may nevertheless argue that workers are exploited because the unequal ownership of the means of production limits the options of workers by compelling them to sell their labour services, thereby surrendering to capitalists any influence over what they will produce and how they will produce it.[15] Although this is not a legal compulsion under capitalism, it is nevertheless as coercive as a legal compulsion, at least in the aggregate for the class of workers as a whole. It is in this sense that such writers condemn capitalism as unjust or ethically exploitation.

One may wonder whether such an ethical interpretation of the theory of exploitation deserves to be called Marxist at all, but that only serves to remind us that Marx himself always had a schizophrenic attitude to the moral condemnation of capitalism: he disdained all arguments resting on moral judgements and yet indulged in such judgements on almost every other page. One may also wonder why this kind of exploitation should be said to characterize capitalism when in fact socialism of the Soviet variety likewise compels workers to sell their labour services and, unlike capitalism, makes the refusal to do so a criminal act. But the point remains that only die-hard Marxists continue to believe in the theory of surplus value and its naive explanation of the nature of profits (see, for example, Fine and Harris, 1979; Foley, 1986; Hunt, 1986). By all means let us ask the ethical question whether profits are truly deserved but against the background, not of the labour theory of value and the static theory of perfect competition, but of the functional role of profits in a dynamic world of pervasive uncertainty generated by incessant technical progress. In other words, it is Schumpeter rather than Marx that ought to inspire the discussion about capitalism and justice.[17]

We promised to appraise Marxian economics in the light of its predictions but we have not yet said a word about Marx's predictions. But, in one sense, there is no point in appraising Marxian economics in the light of its predictions. The system is logically inconsistent because we cannot deduce the money rate of profit, the money rate of wages, or indeed any other money prices, from the Marxian value system. It follows that none of Marx's predictions about the changes in money prices follow logically from the structure of his theory and, hence, the appraisal of his predictions can only satisfy a curiosity value. Nevertheless, all this was totally misunderstood throughout the long history of Marxism during which time the principal scientific appeal of Marxian economics rested almost entirely on the alleged accuracy of Marx's predictions about the long-term evolution of the capitalist economy.

Notes

1. The tendency to shrug off Marxian economics as inessential to Marxism reaches a *reductio ad absurdum* in Louis Althusser's *Reading Capital*, which interprets *Capital* as a study of epistemological problems and actually criticizes economists who 'thought that *Capital* was an economic treatise in the immediate sense of their practice' (Althusser, 1970, p. 76). Peter Bell (1977, p. 190) takes this argument one step further: 'The tradition of reading *Capital* as 'economic theory' was made popular by Paul Sweezy.   In general, the building of economic theory, from *Capital*, removed of the critical elements of Marx's method, puts the theory at the disposal of capital. Cleaver (1979, pp. 11–12) commits himself to a similar piece of nonsense. It is evident that Althusser's doctrine affords much relief to those who cannot be bothered to learn Marxian economics.
2. The better Marxist writers never make this mistake. Desai (1974, pp. 51, 91; 1979, p. 68) and Steedman (1977, pp. 30–1) are particularly clear and unambiguous on this question; see also Morishima (1974).
3. It is not clear that this implication is fully appreciated by some Marxist writers (e.g. Desai, 1974, pp. 70–1, 122; 1979, p. 51; Rosdolsky, 1977, pp. 539–41; and Bowles and Gintis, 1977, p. 181), who are perfectly willing to abandon the assumption of a uniform rate of surplus value as unrealistic; see also Morishima (1973), pp. 180–1).
4. See, for example, Wolfson (1971, pp. 19, 21), Morishima (1973, p. 52), Wolfstetter (1973, p. 798), Baumol (1974, p. 55n), Howard and King (1976, p. 26), Blundell-Wignall (1976, p. 280), Nuti (1977, p. 90), Shaikh (1977, p. 123), Harris (1978, p. 84), Junankar (1982, p. 41), Brewer (1984, pp. 136–7), Wolff (1984, p. 123), and Elster (1985, p. 133).
5. Defining v as 'variable capital, c as 'constant capital', and s as 'surplus value', the 'rate of surplus value' is s_1/v_1, s_2/v_2, etc., and the 'organic composition of capital' is v_1/c_1, v_2/c_2, etc. An equal rate of surplus value in all industries implies

$$\frac{s_1}{v_1} = \frac{s_2}{v_2} \text{ or } s_1 v_2 = s_2 v_1 \tag{3.1}$$

An equal rate of profit in all industries implies

$$\frac{s_1}{c_1 + v_1} = \frac{s_2}{c_2 + v_2} \text{ or } s_1 (c_2 + v_2) = s_2 (c_1 + v_1) \tag{3.2}$$

Subtracting (3.1) from (3.2) leaves

$$s_1 c_2 = s_2 c_1 \tag{3.3}$$

Dividing (3.3) by (3.1) yields

$$\frac{c_2}{v_2} = \frac{c_1}{v_1} \tag{3.4}$$

Thus, only (3.4) will allow (3.1) as well as (3.2); if (3.4) does not hold, either (3.1) or (3.2) may obtain but not both.
6. Only if the wage bundle consists of commodities combined in exactly the same proportions as the commodities applied to the production of capital goods, is it possible to say with Marx that 'workers work half the day for themselves and half the day for the capitalist' (Samuelson 1972, p. 292).
7. Some Marxist writers (Mandel, 1968, p. 167) even pretend, not only that all costs of production can always be reduced to historic labour costs in a finite number of steps, but that capitalists routinely make these calculations.
8. This emerges very clearly in Hodgson (1974a, pp. 61–63), Steedman (1977, pp. 29–31, 43–5, 48–9), and Desai (1979, pp. 52–3).

9. In Seton's words (1976, p. 167), 'there does not seem to be an objective basis for choosing any particular postulate in preference to all the others, *and to that extent the transformation problem may be said to fall short of complete determinacy*'.

10. In reply to Morishima and Catephores, Meek (1973, pp. xv–xvi, 180–1, 198–200; 1977, pp. 128–30, 140–5) succeeds in demonstrating that both Marx and Engels were powerfully attracted to the historical transformation thesis but he studiously avoids raising the question of whether the thesis is tenable. Similarly, Hollander (1981) adduces textual evidence to show that Marx sometimes envisaged the transformation of values into prices as an actual temporal process, which I think is true, implying that this was a perfectly legitimate argument, which is certainly not true.

11. Dobb (1973, pp. 145, 151n) is very fond of this semantic game as are Howard and King (1975, pp. 42, 161) and Nuti (1977, pp. 95–6). To show that even able Marxologists have great difficulty in explaining what is meant by 'exploitation' in Marx, consider Sowell's (1976, p. 71) observation: 'Even Marx's "exploitation" does not depend on the labour value definition. Since "surplus value" is simply the difference between wages and the worker's average product, it would remain unchanged under a marginal productivity theory of wages in a perfectly competitive market' (Bronfenbrenner, 1973, p. 61 makes a similar comment). But surplus value is not simply the difference between wages and the worker's average product but rather the difference between these two variables when both are measured in labour hours, having dimensions that are neither current nor constant prices.

12. Samuelson (1977, pp. 239n, 295) objects to the term *'dual* accounting systems' on the grounds that the word 'dual' suggests something like the duality theorem of linear programming. He should also have objected to the term 'accounting systems' since there is absolutely no evidence to suggest that Marx employed the labour theory of value as an accounting device to add up the components of total output.

13. Marxist commentators to this day characterize bourgeois economics as holding an abstinence theory of profits, as if Nassau William Senior died last week, and they rarely so much as mention the names of Joseph Schumpeter and Frank Knight (see, for example, Sweezy, 1942, pp. 83–92; Dobb, 1945, chapter 5; Fine, 1977 and Linder, 1977, II, chapters 21, 22).

14. I have voiced similar complaints elsewhere (Blaug, 1975, pp. 75–8). A book like that of Wiles (1977) shows what can be done to illuminate these questions.

15. This notion of exploitation as the exercise of coercive social power over the production process can be found in *Capital* alongside and subordinate to the more familiar thesis that runs in terms of surplus value reckoned in labour time (Bose, 1980, App. 2). An entire new Marxist literature on the authoritarian nature of the 'labour process' celebrates this approach but without any recognition that it departs radically from orthodox Marxism.

16. As Geras (1985, p. 70) put it 'Marx did think that capitalism was unjust but he did not think he thought so'. See also Buchanan (1982, chapter 3) and Elster (1985, pp. 216–29).

17. Conway's (1987, pp. 106–14) attempt to rebut the Cohen-Roemer-Elster interpretation of exploitation in terms of the traditional abstinence theory of interest misses the point because this theory of exploitation is not about the nature of profits but about the justice of capitalism as a social system.

References

Please note that the references for this chapter are included at the end of Chapter 2.

2 A methodological appraisal of Marxian economics II

The doctrine that scientific theories must be judged in the final analysis by means of *a comparison between their empirical predictions and the facts of experience* was deeply embedded in mainstream British philosophy of science, as taught by William Whewell and John Stuart Mill, with which Marx was acquainted. However, Marx was also a disciple of Hegel and Hegel did not always accept a purely empirical test as the final arbiter of scientific theories. Despite the presence of other elements in Marx's thinking, however, I think it can be shown that Marx did adopt the standard approach to economic problems that united all the English classical economists from Adam Smith to John Stuart Mill: first, it was argued that a purely economic sphere of action could be legitimately isolated from the wider social context in which human action takes place; second, the subject of economics was conceived as an abstract, deductive science that moved by successive approximations from idealized assumptions about individual behaviour and the characteristics of economic institutions to the concrete phenomena of everyday reality; and, third, it was held that the conclusions reached by this chain of reasoning should always be verified by appealing to whatever factual material was available. Our central interest lies in this dominant strand in Marx's work on economic problems. Nevertheless, we ought to spend a moment on those other elements in Marx's thinking that run in a different direction because these account for many of the difficulties which English and American readers experience when they read Marx.

What were Marx's views on his own economic methods? I wish that it were possible to point to his words for an unambiguous answer to that question. It is true that his writings are strewn with methodological remarks – unlike, say, Ricardo, he was hypersensitive to questions of method – but many of these provoke rather than clarify and the only occasion on which he wrote a sustained essay on 'The Method of Political Economy' in the *Grundrisse,* what emerges is both opaque and paradoxical (Marx, 1975, pp. 71-82). Suffice it to say that his method seems to be made up of seven elements, of which the first is the hypothetico-deductive approach of the classical economists, to which we have already alluded. Let us simply list the remaining six:

1. a fundamental distinction, derived from Aristotle via Hegel, between the underlying 'essence' and the ordinary 'appearance' of things, from which

it follows that the fundamental task of science is to pierce the veil of appearances so as to expose those inner essences;

2.   a Hegelian 'vision', to use that favourite term of Schumpeter, according to which all abstract entities, whether natural or social, are conceived as made up of inner contradictory forces, both at the level of 'essence' and at the level of 'appearance', not to mention at the point of interaction between these two levels - this is what is popularly referred to as 'the dialectical method';

3.   another Hegelian idea, overlapping the first two and yet adding extra dimension to the picture, which conceives of all entities as sets of internal relationships, having what is nowadays called a definite 'structure' (thus, when Marx says that 'capital' is a relation and not a thing, he means that the outward semblance of exchange ratios between commodities disguises what is really a social relationship between people, thereby combining the philosophy of relationism with the essence/appearance distinction and the dialectical method);

4.   an eighteenth-century Scottish historical method, which sees social change as initiating in changing 'modes of production', consisting of both technological forces and the property relations between social classes, which changes in the 'base' are then reflected in a 'superstructure' of ideas and institutions, including scientific ideas – this is what Engels called 'the materialist conception of history';

5.   a logico-historical thesis, or what I would prefer to call 'an anti-genetic thesis', again having its roots in Hegel, which argues that the logical status of abstract concepts reverses the actual course of historical development (in other words, the 'essence' of social institutions is grasped, not by examining their origins, but by examining their mature forms at the highest stage of their evolution); and

.6   a theory of truth which dissolves the Humean is/ought distinction by the concept of *praxis* as the ultimate test of a social theory, particularly the *praxis* of the 'proletariat' fulfilling its historical mission by ushering in socialism.

The last of these will give us a great deal of trouble because it threatens to dissolve, not just the Humean distinction between a domain of empirical facts and a domain of ethical values, but also the very notion from which we started, namely, that the predictions of a social theory can be, and must be, put to a detached scientific test.

Taking all seven propositions together, we have more or less the sum of what other commentators have discerned as Marx's method.[1] I shall resist the temptation to comment at length on each of these propositions but we really must pause to consider essentialism, relationism and the dialectical method, that is, the first three on our list. All three may be regarded as powerful heuristic postulates, or algorithms for solving problems, and as such they are unobjectionable. A social theory should not be praised or condemned for resorting to such postulates; it should be judged on its fruits and not on its metaphysical sources of inspiration. Nevertheless, it has been argued by Popper that essentialism has damaging effects on social theories because it encourages an anti-empirical tendency to solve problems by the use of definitions. For Plato and Aristotle, knowledge or 'science' begins with observations of individual cases and proceeds by simple enumeration until one has grasped by intuition that which is universal in them - their 'essence' - which is then enshrined in a definition of the phenomenon in question. This doctrine that it is the aim of science to discover the true nature or essence of things and to describe them by means of definitions had an enormous influence on Western thought right up to the nineteenth century and Popper (1957, pp. 26–34; also 1976, pp. 18–21, 197–8) contrasts this brand of 'methodological essentialism' with the 'methodological nominalism' that came into scientific debates with Newton, according to which the aim of science is to describe *how* things behave in various circumstances with the aid of universal laws, and not to determine *what* they really are.

There can be no doubt that Marx was a thorough-going essentialist. The three volumes of *Capital* are simply peppered with statements of the essence/appearance distinction, endlessly reiterating the view that the task of political economy is to expose the inner 'essence' of things that is always masked by their outward 'appearances' (for example, Marx, 1976, pp. 168, 421, 433, 677, 679, 714; and 1909, pp. 56, 198, 199, 209, 367, 815).[2] It is his adherence to the doctrine of essentialism that accounts for Marx's steadfast belief in the two-tier approach to money prices and money profits: the domain of prices must rest on an underlying domain of values because competitive prices are only epiphenomena, which cannot themselves explain anything. And, of course, he was right. Prices must be explained in terms of an underlying technology, a set of motives ascribed to economic agents, and a rudimentary structure of economic institutions. Is this not the method of orthodox economics? In other words, there is nothing peculiarly Marxian about the essence/appearance distinction. Where we may quarrel with Marx is on the question whether the nature of the 'essence' of prices is only to be found in the domain of values, as if no other 'essence' will suffice. Thus, when Marx dismissed virtually every economist after Ricardo as a 'vulgar' economist, meaning one who skimmed the surface of things and never penetrated to their inner connections, he was simply equating the doctrine of essentialism with his own labour theory of profits.

Adherents of essentialism are inclined to settle substantive questions by reaching for a dictionary – usually a dictionary of their own making. Marx too was very prone to this tendency. Having adopted the labour theory of profits, he was forced to confront the question whether all living labour creates surplus value, regardless of how or by whom it is employed. He asserted that profits are only created by 'production' and not by 'circulation', which is true by definition of 'circulation' as a zero-sum game, and this led him to view that only labour employed in production, or what he called 'productive labour', creates surplus value, 'unproductive labour' being in effect paid out of the profits created by 'productive labour'. He decided, however, that the packing, storing and shipping of goods is part of 'production', whereas all the commercial functions of middlemen and of course the merchandizing functions of retailers are part of 'circulation', in consequence of which a lorry-driver is 'productive' if he is transporting goods from the factory to the warehouse but he is 'unproductive' if he is merely moving goods from a middleman to a retailer. Marx wrote hundreds of pages on these questions, pondering the issue as to whether school teachers and lawyers could ever be considered 'productive' workers, not all of which are free from inconsistencies. But the point I wish to make about his writings on the subject is simply that he always reaches a decision as to what is or is not 'productive labour' by applying the definition that 'productive labour is labour that creates surplus value'. The problem had considerable importance for him because, obviously, the size of the 'productive' labour force governs the total surplus value that is created, which governs the total profits that are available for distribution among capitalists, which in turn determines the rate of profit in the price system. Nevertheless, it never occurred to him to ask whether any empirical observations could ever assist him in deciding which labour is 'productive' and which is 'unproductive'. Thus, he conceded that any reduction in the 'time of circulation' of goods would act to raise the money rate of profit (Marx, 1909, pp. 329–30) but this did not lead him to abandon the view that the merchandizing function is always 'unproductive'. Marxists (for example, Gough, 1972 and Mandel in Marx, 1978, pp. 38–46) have ever since followed Marx's policy of categorizing labour as productive or unproductive by manipulating definitions, never once asking: how do we *know* that we have arrived at the correct definition? In recent years, for example, British Marxists have debated the question as to whether state employees are 'productive workers' (see Fine and Harris, 1976, pp. 154–9), not by looking at what state employees actually do, but by unravelling the taxonomic question whether the state actually produces or whether it merely 'realizes' surplus value.

Marxism has paid a heavy price for its commitment to the methodology of essentialism. Thus, when Marx in the second volume of *Capital* invented the now so familiar Harrod-Domar technique of stating the necessary conditions for smooth economic expansion or balanced growth, he spoiled what could have been a major contribution to economic thought by expressing the necessary conditions entirely in terms of labour values, instead of the money prices that actually govern the inducement to invest. In consequence, he failed to notice that his arithmetic examples of smooth exponential growth involved purely arbitrary rates of capital accumulation. His disciples always found it difficult to square this picture of feasible steady-state growth with Marx's other analyses of the falling rate of profit and the crisis-ridden nature of capitalism. For 40 years, they heatedly debated the meaning of Marx's so-called 'reproduction schema' – a debate known as the 'Breakdown Controversy' - and all this time none of them recognized that the whole debate was beside the point because it was entirely carried out in terms of the value system of Volume I from which nothing can ever be deduced about the motives for capital accumulation. The Breakdown Controversy is an instructive story of the dangers of 'essentialism' with its tendency towards the reification of the concepts of value and surplus value.[3]

The same anti-empirical note is struck in the now ongoing debate about 'the labour reduction problem'. Marx argued that 'socially necessary' labour costs are countable in units of common, abstract labour, skilled labour being counted as so many multiples of common labour. These multiples must be construed as purely technical conversion coefficients and not as wage rates, because it is obviously illegitimate to invoke prices in what purports to be an explanation of how prices are determined. So long as labour is only differentiated in terms of acquired skills, there is no problem: we can assume that such skills are being produced in a separate training industry, in which case labour skills are simply more means of production that are produced and reproduced at the going rate of profit. In other words, the time-consuming production of skilled labour raises no difficulties for the labour theory of value that are not also raised by the time-consuming production of machines. The argument breaks down, however, the moment we concede that labour is also differentiated in terms of 'ability', regardless of whether those ability differences are inborn or whether they are due to family-rearing. Such 'ability' differences simply cannot be interpreted either as given technical coefficients or as the outputs of a notional industry that is governed by the principle of equal profitability. Marx himself invoked what we have called the 'anti-genetic thesis' to justify the principle of calculating labour costs in the common denominator of abstract labour: labour may have been heterogeneous in the past but capitalism tends constantly to erode all differences between types of labour by the introduction of skill-saving processes, so that purely homogeneous, raw labour represents the appropriate abstraction that corresponds to capitalism at its highest stage of development.

Now, undoubtedly, factor substitution acts to overcome shortages of skilled labour by a continuous process of deskilling, but, on the other hand, technical progress frequently acts in the opposite direction by raising the skill requirements of new products and processes. It is a moot question whether the labour force has in fact become more or less differentiated in the process of industrialisation, but certainly the educational explosion of the last 35 years suggests the very opposite of Marx's belief in the increasing homogenisation of labour. This is not a question we can settle here but what is striking is that the facts, whatever they are, are totally ignored in Marxist contributions to the labour reduction problem.

When Böhm-Bawerk and Hilferding discussed these issues at the turn of the century, very little was known about the structure of wages and particularly the personal characteristics of workers in relation to differential rates of pay. But since then we have witnessed the rise of human capital theory, which has generated a vast body of evidence about the determinants of the distribution of earnings in terms of such individual characteristics as age, education, occupation, family origins, and even measured IQ at an early age. And yet when we examine the numerous writings of Marxists in recent years on the labour reduction problem,[4] we do not find a single reference to this new source of data with which to test Marx's conjecture that capitalism tends historically to reduce all types of labour to raw, undifferentiated labour. Moreover, the new data strongly suggests that the rate of return to the training industry, which of course includes the whole of the formal educational system, is not in fact equalized with the rate on profit on business capital (Blaug, 1976, pp. 838–9), implying that the labour reduction problem is not solved by simply disregarding all 'ability' differences between workers. Besides, these 'ability' differences, whether due to nature or to nurture, show up in all the regressions that have poured out of the human capital research programme (Blaug, 1976, pp. 842–3), in which case the classic Marxist solution to the labour reduction problem falls to the ground.

Some radical American economists with Marxist leanings contend that the labour market under capitalism is always segmented into non-competing sexual, racial and ethnic groups, so that there are as many rates of surplus value as there are segments in the labour market, with some workers exploiting others (Bowles and Gintis, 1977, 1978). Whether true or not, here at least is an attempt to reformulate the labour reduction problem in terms of observable phenomena. But more orthodox Marxist economists show no similar inclination to relate their theoretical discussions to recent empirical research, preferring instead to go on mouthing Marx's own cryptic remarks about the inevitable tendency of capitalism to strip concrete labour of all of its differentiating characteristics.[5]

We turn now to the dialectical method, which friend and foe alike regard as the hallmark of Marx's approach to social problems. It is difficult to know how seriously to take Marx's use of Hegelian dialectics but it certainly inspired him powerfully to see conflict where others saw, only harmony and the reconciliation of opposing interests. He actually claimed no more than that he 'coquetted' with Hegel's modes of expression for the purpose of 'setting traps' for his more philistine readers (Marx, 1976, pp. 102–3). At any rate, why should we take much notice of the inner contradictions of capitalism when we learn that even the elliptical motions of planets around the sun are nothing but the resolution of the 'contradiction' between rectilinear motion and the centripetal force of gravity (Marx, 1976, p. 198). Marx's destructive 'contradictions' are so frequently merely 'contradistinctions', or else mutually counteracting forces that may as easily co-exist in stable as in unstable equilibria. Indeed, the classical economist's habit of pronouncing economic 'laws' that may be offset by 'disturbing causes' was tailor-made for Marx's use of the dialectical method: when evidence fails to confirm a fundamental law, he chalks this up as proof that the disturbing causes are at work, thus exemplifying once again the inner 'contradictions' that will eventually disrupt and destroy capitalism.

I must explain that I am in no way decrying the role of tendency-laws in economics.[6] The classical economist's notion of 'disturbing causes' that are said to be capable of contradicting the predictions of economic theories is echoed in the modern economists' appeal to *ceteris paribus* clauses that are invariably attached to general economic propositions or statements of economic 'laws'. There is a widespread impression that *ceteris paribus* clauses abound in the social sciences but rarely occur in the physical sciences. Nothing could be further from the truth, however. A scientific theory that could entirely dispense with *ceteris paribus* clauses would in effect achieve perfect closure, that is, inclusion of all the variables that could make any difference to the phenomena being studied. It is doubtful whether even Newtonian mechanics achieved such perfect closure and completeness. It might be said, therefore, that just about all theoretical propositions in both the natural and the social sciences are in fact statements of tendency laws. Nevertheless, there is a world of difference between most tendency statements in physics and chemistry and virtually all such statements in economics and sociology, the difference residing in the fact that physicists and chemists usually specify the magnitude of the amount of the distortion which results from the *cetera* that are held *pares*. In the social sciences, however, it is common to encounter tendency statements with unspecified *ceteris paribus* clauses – a sort of catch-all for everything that is unknown – or if specified, specified only in qualitative rather than quantitative terms, which may not help very much when we come to test for the existence of the underlying tendency.

I conclude, therefore, that tendency statements in economics may be regarded as promissory notes that are only redeemed when the *ceteris paribus* clause has been spelled out and taken into account, preferably in quantitative terms. Unless they are so redeemed, the argument will fail to produce a refutable prediction even in terms of the direction of the total change being predicted, much more in terms of the magnitude of that change.

Marx's defence of the famous 'law' of the tendency of the rate of profit to decline fails to meet these methodological standards. He said that the law was subject to five 'counteracting causes', and he went on to spell out what these were – we may summarize them under three headings:

1. increases in the productivity of labour in excess of increases in wages;
2. the introduction of capital-saving innovations; and
3. the expansion of foreign trade.

What he gives us, therefore, is one negative rate of change, expressing the basic 'law' of the falling rate of profit, and five offsetting, positive rates of change; clearly, the joint outcome of these six rates of change could go either way. Furthermore, Marx (1909, p. 277) made it clear that four of the five counteracting causes to the falling rate of profit are themselves induced by the fall, which is like saying that we can never observe the operation of the tendency of the rate of profit to decline without simultaneously observing the operation of these counteracting influences.

In the circumstances, there seems little point in even asking whether he would ever have contemplated an empirical refutation of his law of the falling rate of profit. It must be recalled, of course, that he did not invent that law (just as he did not invent the concept of the recurrent business cycle, nor the idea that the size of business firms will increase in the course of economic progress – both of these are found in John Stuart Mill). What he was doing was to provide a wholly new and rather surprising explanation of a standard classical doctrine. It was surprising because, in Ricardian theory, the rate of profit tends to decline because the growth process runs into the barrier of non-augmentable natural resources, and to this barrier there is only one offset, namely, technical progress with a land-saving bias, whose likely occurrence cannot be predicted from terms within Ricardian theory. Marx refused to regard land as a non-reproducible factor in limited supply and he struggled instead to attribute falling profits directly to the process of mechanization. Since he did not distinguish between factor substitution and technical change, he produced a somewhat paradoxical theory in which the rate of profit tends to fall, not because there is too little technical progress, but because there is too much, or, at any rate, too much of the labour-saving type. The air of paradox that hangs over these propositions is aggravated by his inclination to argue that the falling rate of profit is accompanied by constant and even falling wages – all this in a model in which there is no primary, non-reproducible factor other than labour, in which the introduction of new methods is solely motivated by the money rate of profit, and in which there is no irreversible technical change, such that old processes previously discarded cannot be taken up again. This thesis, associating the law of the falling rate of profit with a vaguely expressed law of the impoverishment of the working class, is simply untenable and it is not made any more tenable by linking it with another one of Marx's great ideas, the so-called 'industrial reserve army' of the unemployed whose function it is to keep wages from rising in a boom.

The theory of surplus value, we recall, rests on the notion that the value of labour power is determined, like that of all other commodities, by the amount of total labour embodied in its production, that is, the amount of labour embodied in the wage goods that workers consume. Once values are suitably transformed into prices, Marx relies on the standard mechanism of demand and supply to keep short-run market prices in line with long-run equilibrium prices. But in Marx this mechanism does not apply to labour power because labour power is not produced by households in accordance with rational cost calculations. Hence, Marx had to find some other mechanism to keep market wages from drifting above the value of labour power, and his answer to that problem was the concept of the 'industrial reserve army'. For him, capitalism and full employment are incompatible except for brief moments at the peak of a business cycle. It is obvious that this mechanism of wage rates fluctuating inversely with the level of unemployment, reminiscent of something like the Phillips Curve, is a dynamic theory. Furthermore, it is predicated in turn on an inverse relationship between the wage rate and the profit rate, that is, on a fairly stable investment demand function that is negatively inclined throughout its entire length.

Here, by the way, is another logical flaw in the labour theory of profits, for it now appears that this theory requires specific dynamic assumptions which take us out of the value system of Volume I of *Capital* where the analytical context is strictly that of static equilibrium, or, at least, balanced growth in a steady state.[7]

To return to the law of the falling rate of profit. Marx defined the rate of profit to be a positive function of the rate of surplus value and a negative function of the organic composition of capital, from which it follows immediately that he was really talking about the value rate and not the money rate of profit. He thought that there were no limits to the increase of the organic composition of capital, whereas increases in the rate of surplus value were subject to an upper bound; hence, the value rate of profit had to fall sooner or later. Unfortunately, the rate of surplus value is not only functionally but positively related to the very same process of mechanization that raises the organic composition of capital, and it is now generally agreed that Marx became thoroughly confused by the problem of reckoning in labour-time as the process of capital accumulation proceeds.[8] The conclusion of a falling *value* rate of profit depends essentially on what happens to the labour-time required to produce wage goods as against the labour-time required to produce investment goods and products consumed by capitalists and landlords, and there is nothing in Marx's arguments that suggests an answer to that question. The more serious difficulty is that the money rate of profit need not fall just because the value rate of profit is falling. Since indirect labour is accumulated and embodied into the final product at one rate in the value system and at quite another, lower rate in the price system, any change in the technology of producing capital goods cannot affect the value rate and the money rate of profit in the same way. In general, there is no reason to expect that the trends in these two rates will even have the same sign (Wolff, 1979). Of course, Marx himself was convinced that the two rates would rise and fall together because he had indeed transformed values into prices by setting the first rate equal to the second. If, as we have argued above, this is both arbitrary and mathematically incorrect, we end up by concluding that Marx simply had no coherent theory of the falling *money* rate of profit.

Once again, we see how fundamental is the transformation problem to Marxian economics. Even now we frequently witness attempts to test his law of the falling rate of profit by invoking data on the capital-labour ratio and on the ratio of profits and wages – I have indulged in this pastime myself – which is to pretend that we can cross over effortlessly from the value system to the price system. But the organic composition of capital is not the same thing as the capital-labour ratio measured in constant prices, and the rate of surplus value is not the same thing as the relative shares of profits and wages in national income.

The money rate of profit has shown no persistent trend in advanced capitalist economies for over 100 years and there is no doubt that this fact would have seriously disturbed Marx, particularly as the trendless rate of profit has been accompanied by a persistent upward trend in real wages. Marx made other predictions about the future course of capitalist development - the increasing severity of recurrent unemployment, the increasing amplitude of business cycles, the steady concentration of capital in ever larger business units, the ever widening geographical extension of the capitalist mode of production, the growing polarization of society into two classes, and the continued alienation of both workers and capitalists from production, from society, and from themselves[9] - all of which are either corollaries of the law of the falling rate of profit, or ad hoc prophecies that are simply tacked on to his system.[10] If the law of the falling rate of profit is a dead letter, so are virtually all of his other predictions.

Some Marxists of the Old Left have stoically accepted the empirical refutation of Marx's analysis of competitive capitalism, insisting, however, that all the improvements of living standards under capitalism over the last century are due, not to the operation of spontaneous economic forces, but to trade union pressures and the independent intervention of the state (Meek, 1967, pp. 108-10, 117–28). But many younger Marxists remain recalcitrant, denying that Marx's laws can ever be expected to reveal themselves in the realm of appearances, and proposing indeed to reformulate the law of the declining rate of profit as 'the law of the tendency of the rate of profit to fall *and* of the tendency for counteracting influences to operate' (Fine and Harris, 1976, pp. 162–3; also Hodgson, 1977, pp. 97–8; Fine and Harris, 1977, pp. 113–17, and Fine and Harris, 1979, pp. 61–5), thus flatly rejecting the requirement that tendency laws in economics must be stated so as to be falsifiable at least in principle.

We may grant that admiration for Marx's predictions is subject to long waves that correspond almost perfectly with the long waves of the capitalist system (Bronfenbrenner, 1970). In the 1930s, Marx's predictions of the growth of big business and the hard-core of chronic unemployment struck contemporaries as remarkable forecasts of the long-term evolution of capitalism. In the postwar euphoria of the 1950s and 1960s, however, the virtual disappearance of business cycles and the continued resilience of small and medium-sized business enterprises threw doubt even on these last remaining predictions of the Marxian system. It is not surprising, therefore, that the 1970s have seen a reaffirmation of virtually all of Marx's concrete forecasts of long-term trends under capitalism. But the fact remains that few of the predictions follow logically from the structure of the Marxian theory of capital accumulation, which is simply overdetermined: it is a pot-pourri of elements that can be endlessly permuted and combined to rationalize virtually any set of events (Howard and King, 1975, ch. 6; Harris, 1978, pp. 282–3). Any moment now, we keep being told, the definite, coherent Marxist theory of accumulation for the current phase of monopoly capitalism will emerge from the mêlée of Marxist discussions - and still we wait, 112 years after the publication of Volume I of *Capital*. However, apart from the fairly trite idea that monopoly capitalism destroys the equalization of the rate of profit, raising profits in the monopolized sector at the expense of the competitive sector, nothing of any significance has been added to the original Marxist model.[11] Compared with these meagre accomplishments, even the admittedly unsatisfactory orthodox theory of oligopoly looks impressive.

Marx never wrote an exposition of his methodology, nor did his work receive the sort of criticism in his own lifetime that might have led him to defend and explain his methodology. We cannot, therefore, be sure how he would have reacted to the fact that so few of his predictions have actually materialized: capitalism has survived and it has survived at growth rates that are generally higher than those achieved in the nineteenth century. What is clear is that Marx would have regarded the continued survival of capitalism as posing a serious challenge to Marxist theory. He had, as I have said before, a complex attitude to the question of truth in social theory because he fondly believed that he had found in the concept of the 'proletariat' a philosopher's stone that would somehow unite theory and practice, making effective social action inspired by a theory the ultimate test of the validity of that theory. This is what is meant by the doctrine of *praxis*, according to which Marxism can only be refuted, not by empirical facts on wage rates, profit rates, and the like, but by the failure of the proletariat in advanced capitalist countries to overthrow the system.

The mystical and essential doctrine of *praxis* has posed serious problems to Marx's followers: they have been reluctant simply to ignore the apparent refutations of so many of Marx's predictions because that would be tantamount to obscurantism; at the same time, they have been embarrassed to defend Marxism simply as a rationalizatation of the belief that Western capitalism must sooner or later break down. As for the doctrine of *praxis*, they were no doubt aware that it amounts to turning majority opinion into *the* criterion of scientific validity. And so, whenever Marxists come to state the grounds on which economic and social theories ought to be validated, we hear a great deal about capturing the 'essence' of the problem as it comes to be reflected in the social experience of men, but very little about predictions, and the verification or falsification of predictions.[12]

Above all, Marxists consistently evade the fundamental question that Popper has taught us to pose to all adherents of theories: Marxists, are there any events, which, if they were to occur, would make you abandon Marxism?

I said that Marxists consistently evade that fundamental Popperian question but I have actually discovered two exceptions to that rule. The first is contained in an authoritative and comprehensive reply to Popper's critique of Marx by Maurice Cornforth, a well known British Marxist philosopher of the Old Left; the second is found in the introduction to a new translation of Volume I of *Capital* by Ernest Mandel, a leading figure in the Fourth International originally founded by Trotsky. I must first explain that Popper agrees that no scientific theory can ever be conclusively refuted because adverse results can always be explained away as due to faulty measuring instruments or, more generally, as due to the absence of the appropriate antecedent conditions. What distinguishes science from non-science in Popper is not so much the proposition that scientific theories ought to be falsifiable in principle, but rather that the development of these theories ought to be subject to a set of methodological rules that forbid what he calls 'immunising stratagems': 'immunising stratagems' are those adjustments to a theory whose only purpose is to protect the theory against repeated refutations and mounting anomalies.[13]

Popper argues that Marxism is indeed a scientific theory, or rather a scientific research programme; however, it has been falsified by the course of events and only the constant resort to 'immunizing stratagems' have kept it alive for so long. He gives Marx credit for correctly foreseeing the inherent technical dynamism of the capitalist system and the equally inherent tendency of that dynamism to be constantly associated with periodic business slumps (Popper, 1962, II, pp. 193, 194, 196) – curiously enough, he fails to mention 'concentration and centralization of capital', one of Marx's more remarkable predictions.[14] But he leaves no doubt that Marx's other economic predictions of growing impoverishment, mounting unemployment, and ever more violent business fluctuations have all been glaringly refuted (II, pp. 183, 189, 193). In Popper's view, however, it is only when the failure of Marx's economic predictions are coupled with the failure of his political predictions that we can judge the Marxist system in the round. Many of Marx's political predictions, unlike at least some of his economic ones, simply do not follow logically from his premises (II, pp. 138–9, 140–1, 146). In particular, the tendency of Marx's followers to identify the socialist revolution that Marx foresaw with the Russian Revolution is a typical example of the use of an 'immunizing stratagem'. The Russian Revolution was the product, not of the contradictions of advanced capitalism, but of industrial infancy, agricultural backwardness, and a power vacuum created by the defeat in war (II, pp. 109, 349). To cite the Russian Revolution as confirming Marxist theory is, according to Popper, to turn Marxism into a metaphysical doctrine that culminates in the empty prophecy that, somehow, some day, there will be a revolution somewhere (II, p. 326).

With these observations in mind, let us now take up Cornforth's (1972, pp. 31, 32, 37) reply to the gauntlet thrown down by Popper:

> If uninterrupted economic development were to be combined with capitalist enterprise and capitalist profit, then Marx's theory would be falsified.... Marxists can, it is true, readily account for the socialist revolution starting in Russia. But if it had started, say, in the Far East or in Central Africa, or if it had never started at all, that could not have been accounted for, and really would have falsified Marxism. But it did start, and started where Marxism permitted it to start ... So far it [Marxism] has not been falsified but confirmed ....

What needs to be explained is how Cornforth can find Marxism confirmed while accepting as much of Popper's methodology as he does. The clue lies in that part of Popper's philosophy of science that he does not accept, namely, the ban on 'immunizing stratagems'. Cornforth (pp. 33–4, 40–1) holds it to be a virtue of Marxism that its fundamental propositions are so framed as to accommodate the widest range of possible events, although on Popper's arguments it is precisely this that weakens rather than strengthens the Marxist claim to science: if Marxism is a living science, it should not hesitate to submit itself to really severe tests.

Thus, to give one more example, Cornforth vigorously endorses what Marx called 'the absolute general law of capital accumulation': 'in proportion as capital accumulates, the situation of the worker, be his payment high or low, must grow worse' (Marx, 1976, pp. 798–9)1. 'Like all other laws', Marx added, 'it is modified in its workings by many circumstances', but we search in vain in his writings for any list of what these circumstances are. Undeterred by the idea of an economic tendency law offset by an unspecified number of counter-vailing forces, Cornforth (1972, pp. 193–4) explains the significance of the 'absolute general law' in these words:

> Marx certainly did maintain that all those hopeful people (like Dr Popper himself) who think that improvements in living standards can go on and on under capitalism, so that everything will get better and better and eventually all poverty, unemployment, class differences and war will simply disappear are blind to the operation of the 'absolute general law'.

In short, so long as poverty, unemployment, class stratification and war persist under capitalism, Marx is confirmed, whatever the logical structure of his argument and whatever the time-scale of his predictions. Clearly, this is an open invitation to invent 'immunizing stratagems' without limit, which virtually reduces Marxism to the fortune-telling practices of gypsies.

Similarly, Mandel (Marx, 1976, p. 24) accepts Popper's challenge head-on and yet hedges his bets by selecting predictions that simply do not discriminate between Marxism and many other competing explanations:

> In fact, it would be very easy to 'prove' Marx's analysis to have been wrong, if experience had shown for example, that the more capitalist industry develops, the smaller and smaller the average factory becomes, the less it depends upon new technology, the more its capital is supplied by the workers themselves, the more workers become owners of their factories, the less the part of wages taken by consumer goods becomes .... If, in addition, there had been decades without economic fluctuations and a full-scale disappearance of trade unions and employers' association ... then one could indeed say that *Capital* was so much rubbish and had dismally failed to predict what would happen in the real world a century after its publication.

But, on the contrary, Mandel (Marx, 1976, p. 23) declares:

> It is precisely because of Marx's capacity to discover the long-term laws of motion of the capitalist mode of production in its essence ... that his long-term predictions - the laws of accumulation of capital, stepped-up technological progress, accelerated increase in the productivity and intensity of labour, growing concentration and centralization of capital, transformation of the great majority of economically active people into sellers of labour-power, declining rate of profit, increased rate of surplus value, periodically recurrent recessions, inevitable class struggle between Capital and Labour, increasing revolutionary attempts to overthrow capitalism − have been so strikingly confirmed by history.

However, 50 pages later Mandel admits that 'contrary to what Marx expected', capitalism was overthrown, not in America or Europe, where 'the proletariat was most strongly developed numerically and economically', but in Russia and China 'where the bourgeoisie was weakest' (p. 85). This was, no doubt, one of Marx's slight oversights for which, of course, he must be pardoned!

Cornforth and Mandel notwithstanding, I would argue that what has been refuted in Marxism is not so much the specific economic predictions, although here too there are fewer hits than misses, as the general conception of how capitalism would gradually come apart at the seams. We are now as far away from Marx as Marx was from Adam Smith and if Marx's picture of what was soon to happen to capitalism is looked at in the cold light of a century of development, the gap between prognosis and reality is actually so large as to be ludicrous. In appraising Marxian economics, let us not forget that Marx died almost a century ago and that what his followers have managed to do, or not to do, with his ideas in that time is all that really matters if Marxism is to be judged as a progressive rather than an ossified scientific research programme.

The heart of Marx's vision was, after all, his concept of the proletariat as a new class of impoverished, wage-dependent workers created by the power-driven factories of the Industrial Revolution. The factory system concentrated large numbers of men, women and children under a single roof and harnessed them to the discipline of machine-paced labour, thus unwittingly fostering among them the consciousness of being members of a group with interests different from, and frequently in conflict with, the owner-managers of factories. At the same time, the pressures of competition and the constant necessity to stay ahead of rivals, compelled the factory owners to cut wages, or at least to resist their upward drift, and to lengthen hours of work as much as possible. Thus, capitalism generated increasing misery amidst increasing plenty, which would inevitably weld workers together even if the alienating experience of factory life failed to do so. Moreover, competition tended to destroy itself because larger business units would always outpace and swallow up smaller units. Hence, society would increasingly polarize into two classes: an ever diminishing class of haves and an ever increasing class of have-nots. In these circumstances, the proletariat would grow more conscious of its identity with every passing day. In short, the proletariat was, or would soon become, the subversive class *par excellence* that simply could not fail to seize the rich fruits of this new social system by political means, so as to distribute them to the many rather than to the few.

All this was a remarkable forecast in 1867, which, I do not doubt for one moment, would have fully persuaded me had I been among the first readers of the first volume of *Das Kapital*.

However, this vision of capitalism, doomed by the very key to rapid economic growth that it had discovered – private property in the means of production - already struck many contemporaries as unrealistic before the turn of the century when Eduard Bernstein launched his revisions of Marx. Karl Kautsky's replies to Bernstein, disputing Bernstein's evidence of rising living standards and reinterpreting Marx's law of impoverishment as a statement about relative shares,[15] began the degeneration of the Marxist research programme, which continues to this day. But Bernstein's revisionism was as nothing compared with the blow that the First World War gave to the notion of the proletariat as an alienated, revolutionary class that never could be seduced by appealing to its love of fatherland. Of course, Lenin had a ready explanation for the patriotic response of workers throughout Europe: it was the treason of socialist leaders and the bribery of the 'aristocracy of labour' out of the windfalls of imperialist exploitation that accounted for the events of 1914. But in truth, the workers had voted with their feet against class and in favour of nation, and most socialist leaders (except Bernstein, the revisionist) simply saved their political skin by going along with working class opinion.

The next blow to Marx's vision was the Russian Revolution. Russia was very near to being the most backward country in Europe and its proletariat in 1917 could at most have numbered 10 percent of the total population. Even Lenin could only justify a proletarian revolution under these circumstances by appealing to the imminence of international revolution, followed by fraternal aid from western socialist countries. War communism shattered these hopes and the retreat to NEP simply registered that fact. When Lenin died, the policy of 'socialism in one country' marked the final demise of Marx's vision: a theory of historical change that posited, if it posited anything at all, the primacy of economic over political forces was now to be read backwards to mean the very opposite.

One could continue in this vein. The Great Depression of the 1930s and the rise of Fascism seemed finally to realize the prophecies of Marx, even if in a distorted form, and we may forgive the fellow travellers of that generation who moved to the left as they read what at the time must have appeared as the handwriting on the wall. Wrong again! The capitalist world emerged out of the Second World War to enter, against the predictions of Marxists and orthodox Keynesians alike, a 25-year period of expansion that was as unprecedented as had been the earlier slump of the 1930s. Marxism died out as an intellectual force in the West, but elsewhere it received yet another dramatic transformation. Mao Tse Tung made a revolution, not just without a proletarian majority and a developed capitalist technology, but without any proletariat at all, and with a level of technology that England had surpassed in the seventeenth and Russia in the nineteenth century. Nevertheless, the Chinese strategy of revolution-among-peasants-before-revolution-among-workers was carried forward under the banners of Marxism. Lastly, the boom of the 1960s completed the circle by promoting students, academics, women, blacks, the oppressed people of the Third World, and even criminals in capitalist prisons – anyone but factory workers – as the new revolutionary element that would soon overthrow capitalism. In the name of Bakhunin? No, in the name of Marx, the young Marx, Marx the humanist, who had not yet read and studied Adam Smith and David Ricardo. And, finally, in the 'stagflation' of the 1970s, we are told to go back once again to the old Marx, not so much for his economic as for his sociological insights.

What a wonderful story is the history of Marxism, refuted again and again, and revised again and again – not by its enemies but by its friends. This is a familiar story in the history of economic thought. It happened to Ricardo before Marx and it happened to Keynes in our own lifetime. Perhaps there are still some among you who think that economic theories can be decisively refuted by the historical record and that there is no need for Popperian rules that positively forbid arbitrary revisions of a theory to accommodate growing anomalies and repeated refutations. If so, study the history of Marxism and consider the error of your ways.

Notes

1. For a small sample, see Sweezy (1942, ch. 1), Wolfson (1966, ch 1), Meek (1967, pp. 93–112, 154–7), Ollman (1971, chs. 2,3), Meek (1973, pp. 146–56), Howard and King (1975. ch. 2), Mandel in Marx (1976, pp. 17–25), Meek (1977, pp. 128–30, 134–45), Morishima and Catephores (1978, pp. 201–7), Kolakowski (1978,I, pp. 312–24; III, pp. 264–80, 297–300), and, particularly, Walker (1978, ch. 8).

2.   This has been noticed by many commentators, most of whom take it as *prima facie* evidence
      of Marx's profundity [e.g. Geras (1972), Howard and King (1975, pp. 39–45), Oakley (1976,
      pp. 414–15), Sowell (1976, pp. 65–9), and Rosdolsky (1977, pp. 561–70)].
3.   Elements of the story can be found in Sweezy (1942, ch. 11), Georgescu-Roegen (1960), and
      Desai (1979, pp. 151–71).
4.   See Rowthorn (1974), Roncaglia (1974), and Steedman (1977, ch. 7), who cite many other
      authors.
5.   See, for example, the curiously one-sided historical treatment of Braverman (1974).
6.   The following discussion of tendency-laws raids Blaug (1980, ch. 2).
7.   Sweezy (1942, pp. 84–5n) candidly admits that 'Marxists have generally overlooked the
      logical difficulties involved in applying the law of value to the commodity labor power',
      adding that Oskar Lange was the first to point out the implications of the problem for Marx's
      theoretical structure. This was in 1935, 52 years after Marx's death! Once again, we see
      evidence that all through the Golden Age of Marxism, Marxists simply failed to understand
      the logical structure of Marxian economics.
8.   For a survey of the latest discussions on Marx's law of the falling rate of profit, see Hodgson
      (1974b), Christiansen (1975), and Steedman (1977, ch. 9).
9.   There is no time to explore the multi-faceted meaning of this theory of 'alienation'. But see
      Plamenatz (1975), who traces the pre-Marxian history of this theory and considers its validity
      as a proposition about capitalism as distinct from a proposition about industrialization and
      urbanization.
10.   For a veritable compendium of Marx's predictions, counting 153 in all, of which about half
      are economic predictions occurring in the four volumes of *Capital,* see Gottheil (1966), and
      for a perfect example of the ambiguities of some of Marx's predictions, see Rosdolsky (1977,
      pp. 300–3) on the law of impoverishment of the working class and Cutler, *et al.* (1977,I, chs.
      4, 6) on the law of the falling rate of profit.
11.   See Mandel (1975), which exhibits all the worst features of dogmatic Marxism, adopting both
      Marx's erroneous method of transforming values into prices and the arbitrary investment
      behaviour built into Marx's reproduction schema, while sternly chastizing other Marxists for
      misinterpreting the words of the Master. Thus, when posing the question whether 'permanent
      arms economy' in late capitalism can raise the rate of profit, his answer runs entirely in terms
      of the tendency of defence expenditures to raise rather than to lower the average organic
      composition of capital in the economy as a whole, irrespective of how these expenditures are
      financed. For a brief but trenchant critique of Mandel, see Desai (1979, pp. 204–6), and for a
      more general critique of Marxist analyses of 'permanent arms economy', see Bleaney (1976,
      ch. 12).
12.   See, for example, Sweezy (1942, p. 20), Dobb (1945. pp. 127–8, 131; 1973, pp. 25, 36), Meek
      (1967, pp. 128, 142), Geras (1972, pp. 94–5), Medio (1972, pp. 318–19), Harris (1978, p. 51),
      and Junankar (1982, pp. 150–1).
13.   For an extended discussion of Popper's methodology, see Blaug (1980, ch. 1).
14.   It must be said that Popper's cogent critique of Marx is not always satisfactory with respect
      to Marxian economics. For one thing, Popper (1962, II, pp. 168–70, 181–9, 329) gives much
      more attention to the law of impoverishment and the notion of increasingly severe business
      cycles than to the law of the falling rate of profit, and he never explicates the theoretical
      underpinnings of the latter as the foundation-stone of all of Marx's other 'laws of motion'. For
      another, his examination of Marx's theory of value (II, pp. 170–7, 344) is open to the charge
      of being simplistic, ignoring as it does the transformation problem, while equating 'exploitation'
      in Marx to low wages and long working hours.
15.   The story of Bernstein's revisionism has been frequently told but never better than by
      Kolakowski (1978, II, ch. 4). The whole of Kolakowski's book can be warmly recommended
      as a breath-taking survey, conceived on a vast scale, of the steady degeneration of Marxism
      over a period of almost 100 years.

References

Althusser, L. and E. Balibar (1970), *Reading Capital*, London: New Left Books.

Baumol, W. J. (1974), 'The Transformation of Values: What Marx 'Really' Meant,' *Journal of Economic Literature*, **12**, March, 51–62.

Baumol, W. J. and S. Blinder (1979), *Economics, Principles and Policy*, London: Harcourt Brace Jovanovich.

Bell, P. F. (1977), 'Marxist Theory, Class Struggle, and the Crisis of Capitalism', in J. Schwartz (ed.) *The Subtle Anatomy of Capitalism*, Santa Monica: Goodyear Publishing Company.

Blaug, M. (1971), 'The Classical Economists and the Factory Acts – A Re-examination', in A. W. Coats (ed.), *The Classical Economists and Economic Policy*, London: Methuen & Co.

Blaug, M. (1973), *Ricardian Economics*, Westport: Greenwood Press.

Blaug, M. (1975), *The Cambridge Revolution: Success or Failure?* London: Institute of Economic Affairs.

Blaug, M. (1976), 'The Empirical Status of Human Capital Theory: A Slightly Jaundiced Survey', *Journal of Economic Literature* **14**, (3), 827–55.

Blaug, M. (1978), *Economic Theory in Retrospect*, 3rd ed. Cambridge: Cambridge University Press.

Blaug, M. (1980), *The Methodology of Economics*, Cambridge: Cambridge University Press.

Bleaney, M. F. (1976), *Underconsumption Theories*, London: Lawrence and Wishart.

Blundell-Wignall, A. (1976), 'On Exposing the Transformation Problem', *Australian Economic Papers*, Dec., 277–88.

Bose, A. (1975), *Marxian and post-Marxian Political Economy*, London: Penguin Books.

Bose, A. (1980), *Marx on Exploitation and Inequality. An Essay in Marxian Analytical Economics*, Delhi: Oxford University Press.

Bowles, S. and H. Gintis (1977), 'The Marxian Theory of Value and Heterogeneous Labour: A Critique and Reformulation', *Cambridge Journal of Economics* **1**, (1), 173–92.

Bowles, S. and H. Gintis (1978), 'Professor Morishima on Heterogeneous Labour and Marxian Value Theory', *Cambridge Journal of Economics*, **2**, (1), 311–14.

Braverman, H. (1974), *Labor and Monopoly Capital*, New York: Monthly Review Press.

Brewer, A. (1984), *A Guide to Marx's Capital*, Cambridge: Cambridge University Press.

Bronfenbrenner, M. (1970), 'The Vicissitudes of Marxian Economics', *History of Political Economy*, **2**, (2), 205–24.

Bronfenbrenner, M. (1971), *Income Distribution Theory*, London: Macmillan.

Bronfenbrenner, M. (1973), 'Samuelson, Marx and their Latest Critics', *Journal of Economic Literature*, **2**, 1, 58–64.

Buchanan, A. (1984), *Marx and Justice. The Radical Outrage of Liberalism*, London: Methuen.

Christiansen, J. (1975), 'Marx and the Falling Profit Rate', *American Economic Review*, **66**, (2), 20–6.

Cleaver, H. (1979), *Reading Capital Politically*, Austin: University of Texas Press.

Cohen, G. A. (1979), 'The Labour Theory of Value and the Concept of Exploitation', *Philosophy and Public Affairs*, **8**, (7), reprinted in *The Value Controversy*, I. Steedman (ed.) (1981), London: Verso.

Conway, D. (1987), *Farewell to Marx. An Outline and Appraisal of his Theories*, Harmondsworth: Penguin.

Cornforth, M. (1972), *The Open Philosophy and the Open Society*, 2nd ed., London: Lawrence and Wishart.

Cutler, A. et al. (1977), *Marx's Capital and Capitalism Today*, 2 vols, London: Routledge & Kegan Paul.

Desai, M. (1974), *Marxian Economic Theory*, London: Grey-Mills.

Desai, M. (1979), *Marxian Economics*, 2nd ed., Oxford: Blackwell.

Dobb, M. (1945), *Political Economy and Capitalism*, New York: International Publishers.

Dobb, M. (1973), *Theories of Value and Distribution since Adam Smith*, Cambridge: Cambridge University Press.

Eatwell, J. (1975), 'Sraffa's Standard Commodity and the Rate of Exploitation', *Quarterly Journal of Economics*, **89**, (4), 543–56.

Elster, J. (1985), *Making Sure of Marx*, Cambridge: Cambridge University Press.

Fine, B. (1977), 'The Concept and Origin of Profit' in F. Green and P. Nore (eds), *Economics: An Anti-Text*, London: Macmillan.

Fine, B. and L. Harris (1976), 'Controversial Issues in Marxist Economic Theory', in R. Miliband and J. Saville (eds), *The Socialist Register 1976*, London: The Merlin Press.

Fine, B. and L. Harris (1977), 'Surveying the Foundations', in R. Miliband and J. Saville (eds), *The Socialist Register 1977*, London: The Merlin Press.

Fine, B. and L. Harris (1979), *Rereading Capital*, London: Macmillan.

Foley, D. (1986), *Understanding Capital. Marx's Economic Theory*, Cambridge, MA: Harvard University Press.

Georgescu-Roegen, N. (1960), 'Mathematical Proofs of the Breakdown of Capitalism', *Econometrica* **28**, 225–43.

Geras, N. (1972), 'Essence and Appearance: Aspect of 'Fetishism' in Marx's Capital', *New Left Review*, 1970, in R. Blackburn, (ed), *Ideology in Social Science*, London: Fontana/Collins.

Geras, N. (1985), 'The Controversy about Marx and Justice', *New Left Review*, **150**, March/April, 47–85.

Gottheil, F. M. (1966), *Marx's Economic Predictions*, Evanston: Northwestern University Press.

Gough, I. (1972), 'Marx's Theory of Productive and Unproductive Labour', *New Left Review*, **76**, 47–72.

Harris, D. J. (1978), *Capital, Accumulation and Income Distribution*, London: Routledge & Kegan Paul.

Hodgson, G. (1974a), 'The Theory of the Falling Rate of Profit', *New Left Review*, **84**, 61–3.

Hodgson, G. (1974b), 'Marxian Epistemology and the Transformation Problem', *Economy and Society* **3**, (4), 357–92.

Hodgson, G. (1977), 'Papering Over the Cracks', in R. Miliband and J. Saville (eds), *The Socialist Register 1977*, London: The Merlin Press.

Hodgson, G. (1982), *Capitalism, Value and Exploitation*, Oxford: Martin Robertson.

Hollander, S. (1981), 'Marxian Economics as 'General Equilibrium' Theory', *History of Political Economy* **13**, (1), 121–55.

Howard, M. C. and J. E. King (1975), *The Political Economy of Marx*, Harlow: Longman Group.

Howard, M. C. and J. E. King (1976), 'Introduction' in *The Economics of Marx*, London: Penguin Books.

Hunt, I. (1986), 'A Critique of Rolmer, Hodgson and Cohen on Marxian Exploitation', *Social Theory and Practice*, **12**, (2), Sumner, 121–71.

Johnson, O. (1969), 'The 'Last Hour' of Senior and Marx', *History of Political Economy* **1**, (2), 359–69.

Junankar, P. N. (1982), *Marx's Economics*, Oxford: Phillip Allan.

Kolakowski, L. (1978), *Main Currents of Marxism*, 3 vols, Oxford: Clarendon Press.

Lange, O. (1968), 'Marxian Economics and Modern Economic Theory', in David Horowitz (ed), *Marx and Modern Economies*, London: Macgibbon & Kee.

Linder, M. (1977), *Anti-Samuelson*, 2 vols, New York: Urizen Books.

Maguire, J. M. (1978), *Marx's Theory of Politics*, Cambridge: Cambridge University Press.

Mandel, E. (1968), *Marxist Economic Theory*, London: Merlin Press.

Mandel, E. (1975), *Late Capitalism*, London: New Left Books.

Marx, K. (1909), *Capital III*, edited by Friedrich Engels, Chicago: Charles H. Kerr.

Marx, K. (1963), *Theories of Surplus Value*, edited by S. Ryazanskaya, 3 vols, Moscow: Progress Publishers.

Marx, K. (1975), *Karl Marx: Texts on Method*, edited by Terrill Carver, Oxford: Basil Blackwell.

Marx, K. (1976), *Capital I*, introduced by Ernest Mandel, London: Penguin Books.

Marx, K. (1978), *Capital II*, introduced by Ernest Mandel, London: Penguin Books.

Medio, A. (1972), 'Profits and Surplus Value: Appearance and Reality in Capitalist Production', in E. K. Hunt and J. G. Schwartz, (eds), *A Critique of Economic Theory*, London: Penguin Books.

Meek, R. L. (1967), *Economics and Ideology and Other Essays*, London: Chapman and Hall.

Meek, R. L. (1973), *Studies in the Labour Theory of Value*, 2nd ed., London: Lawrence and Wishart.

Meek, R. L. (1977), *Smith, Marx, and After*, London: Chapman and Hall.

Morishima, M. (1973), *Marx's Economics: A Dual Theory of Value and Growth*, Cambridge: Cambridge University Press.

Morishima, M. (1974), 'The Fundamental Marxian Theorem: A Reply to Samuelson', *Journal of Economic Literature* **12**, (1), 71–4.

Morishima M. and G. C. Catephores (1978), *Value Exploitation and Growth*, London: McGraw-Hill.

Nuti, D. M. (1977), 'The Transformation of Labour Values into Production Prices and the Marxian Theory of Exploitation', in J. Schwartz, (ed), *The Subtle Anatomy of Capitalism*, Santa Monica: Goodyear.

Oakley, A. (1976), 'Two Notes on Marx and the "Transformation Problem"' *Economica*, **43**, (172), 411–18.

Ollman, B. (1971), *Marx's Conception of Man in Capitalist Society*, Cambridge: Cambridge University Press.

Pasinetti, L. (1977), *Lectures on the Theory of Production*, London: Macmillan.

Plamenatz, J. (1975), *Karl Marx's Philosophy of Man*, Oxford: Oxford University Press.

Popper, K. R. (1957), *The Poverty of Historicism*, London: Routledge & Kegan Paul.

Popper, K. R. (1962), *The Open Society and its Enemies*, 2 vols., 4th ed., London, Routledge & Kegan Paul.

Popper, K. R. (1976), *Unended Quest: An Intellectual Autobiography*, London: Fontana/Collins.

Robinson, J. (1942), *Essay on Marxian Economics*, London: Macmillan.

Roemer, J. (1981), *Analytical Foundations of Marxian Economic Theory*, Cambridge, MA: Cambridge University Press.

Roemer, J. (1982), *A General Theory of Exploitation and Class*, Cambridge, MA: Harvard University Press.

Roemer, J. (1985), Should Marxists be Interested in Exploitation? *Philosophy and Public Affairs*, **14**, (1), 30–65.

Roncaglia, A. (1974), 'The Reduction of Complex Labour to Simple Labour', *Bulletin of the Conference of Socialist Economists*, **9**, 1–12.

Roncaglia, A. (1978), *Sraffa and the Theory of Prices*, Chichester: Wiley.

Rosdolsky, R. (1977), *The Making of Marx's 'Capital'*, London: Pluto Press.

Rowthorn, B. (1974), 'Skilled Labour in the Marxian System', *Bulletin of the Conference of Socialist Economists*, **8**, 25–45.

Samuelson, P. A. (1966), 'A Modern Treatment of the Ricardian Economy: 1. The Pricing of Goods and of Labor and Land Services' in J. E. Stiglitz (ed) *The Collected Scientific Papers of Paul A. Samuelson 1*, Cambridge, MA: MIT Press.

Samuelson, P. A. (1972), 'Understanding the Marxian Notion of Exploitation: A Summary of the So-called Transformation Problem between Marxian Values and Competitive Prices', in R. C. Merton (ed) *The Collected Scientific Papers of Paul A. Samuelson 3*, Cambridge, MA: MIT Press.

Samuelson, P. A. (1976), *Economics*, 10th ed., New York: McGraw-Hill.

Samuelson, P. A. (1977), 'Reply on Marxian Matters', *Journal of Economic Literature*, 1973, 'Marx as a Mathematical Economist: Steady-state and Exponential Growth Equilibrium', in G. Horwich and P. A. Samuelson, (eds), *Trade, Stability and Macroeconomic Essays in Honor of Lloyd A. Metzler*, 1974, 'Insight and Detour in the Theory of Exploitation: A Reply to Baumol', *Journal of Economic Literature*, 1974; all in H. Nagatani and K. Crowley, (eds), *The Collected Scientific Papers of Paul A. Samuelson 4*, Cambridge, MA: MIT Press.

Schumpeter, J. A. (1942), *Capitalism, Socialism and Democracy*, Oxford: Oxford University Press.

Schumpeter, J. A. (1954), *A History of Economic Analysis*, Oxford: Oxford University Press.

Seton, F. (1976), 'The "Transformation Problem"', in M. C. Howard and J. E. King, (eds), *The Economics of Marx*, London: Penguin Books.

Shaikh, A. (1977), 'Marx's Theory of Value and the "Transformation Problem"', in J. Schwartz (ed.) *The Subtle Anatomy of Capitalism*, Santa Monica: Goodyear.

Sowell, T. (1976), 'Marx's *Capital* after One Hundred Years', in M. C. Howard and J. E. King (eds), *The Economics of Marx*, London: Penguin Books.

Steedman, I. (1977), *Marx After Sraffa*, London: New Left Books.

Steedman, I. (1981), 'Ricardo, Marx, Sraffa, in The Value Controversy, edited by I. Steedman *et al.*, London: Verso.

Sweezy, P. (1942), *The Theory of Capitalist Development*, New York: Oxford University Press.

Walker, A. (1978), *Marx: His Theory and Its Context*, London: Longman.

Weston, J. F. (1970), 'The Profit Concept and Theory: A Restatement', in I. H. Rima (ed) *Readings in the History of Economic Theory*, New York: Holt, Rinehart & Winston.

Wiles, P. J. D. (1977), *Economic Institutions Compared*, Oxford: Basil Blackwell.

Wolff, E. N. (1979), 'The Rate of Surplus Value, the Organic Composition, and the General Rate of Profit in the U.S. Economy, 1947–67', *American Economic Review*, **69**, (3), 329–41.

Wolff, R. P. (1984), *Understanding Marx. A Reconstruction and Critique of Capital*, Princeton, NJ: Princeton University Press.

Wolfson, M. (1966), *A Reappraisal of Marxian Economics*, New York: Columbia University Press.

Wolfson, M. (1971), *Karl Marx, Columbia Essays on Great Economists 3*, New York: Columbia University Press.

Wolfstetter, E. (1973), 'Surplus Labour, Synchronised Labour Costs and Marx's Labour Theory of Value', *Economic Journal* **83**, 787–809.

Wright, E. O. (1979), 'The Value Controversy and Social Research', *New Left Review*, **116**, 53–82.

3 A methodological appraisal of radical economics

Introduction

Radical economics emerged in the United States in the late 1960s, and it has remained to this day a largely American phenomenon. Its precise origins are difficult to date but as early as 1968, when the Union of Radical Political Economics (URPE) was formed, there were courses in radical economics at a dozen or more American institutions of higher education and these were drawing on a literature which appeared to be growing exponentially with each passing year. In a first attempt to assess this new development, Martin Bronfenbrenner (1970, p. 748) was struck by the speed with which radical economics had swept through the ranks of the faithful in the preceding five years. As a body of ideas, he found radical economics unstructured but still developing and therefore hesitated to deliver anything remotely like a final verdict. On balance, he concluded, that 'the surfacing of radical economics was overdue and ... is here to stay'(Bronfenbrenner, 1970, p. 765).

Bronfenbrenner's preliminary appraisal, or rather interim report, was followed a year later by John Gurley's (1971) attempt to sum up the positive accomplishments of radical economics, which drew a sharp rebuke from Robert Solow (1971) about 'role-playing' and 'cant'. The same year also saw the publication of Assar Lindbeck's *The Political Economy of the New Left* (1971), subtitled 'An Outsider's View', which was less an appraisal than an attempt to persuade radical economists of the error of their ways.[1] More than 10 years have passed since these assessments were written, and a fresh look at radical economics is clearly overdue. Has radical economics fulfilled its promise? Have the intervening years witnessed a continual development of its concepts with new applications to hitherto unexplored areas of economic activity? Has it proved to be fruitful as a scientific research programme (SRP), generating new insights and illuminating new facts, or are there signs of retreat and degeneration?

One thing is clear: there has been no diminution in the rate of output of radical economists. On the contrary, the radical students of the 1960s have become the radical professors of the 1970s, numbering 'at least a tenth of US economists' (Samuelson, 1980, p. 792),[2] and the literature of radical economics has turned

*   I received extremely helpful comments from M. Abramovitz, M. Bronfenbrenner, M. Carnoy, and M. Reich, which is not to say that they bear any responsibility for the views presented in this paper.

57

from a steady trickle to a veritable flood. Bronfenbrenner relied heavily on the pages of the *Review of Radical Political Economics* and on such books as *Monopoly Capital* (1966) by Paul Baran and Paul Sweezy, *Capitalism and Underdevelopment in Latin America* (1967) by André Gunder Frank, *Marxist Economic Theory* (1968) by Ernest Mandel, and *The Age of Imperialism* (1969) by Harry Magdoff. Since then, however, we have seen three collections of radical readings covering all areas of economics (Mermelstein, 1970; Gordon, 1971; Edwards and Weisskopf, 1972), two textbooks expounding and contrasting radical and mainstream economics (Sherman, 1972; Hunt and Sherman, 1978), and an outright radical text for the first undergraduate course in economics (Riddell *et al.*, 1979), not to mention Benjamin Ward's attempt to juxtapose radical, conservative, and liberal economics as equally legitimate modes of economic reasoning in the *Ideal Worlds of Economics* (1979). To the older *Monthly Review, New Left Review, Review of Radical Political Economics,* and *Science and Society,* we must now add such journals as *Cambridge Journal of Economics, Capital and Class* (formerly the *Bulletin of the Conference of Socialist Economists), Economy and Society, Insurgent Sociologist, Kapitalistate, Latin American Perspectives, Politics and Society, Praxis, Radical America,* and *Socialist Review* (formerly *Socialist Revolution),* even though all these also publish many articles on topics outside economics. A recent URPE *Reading List in Radical Political Economics* (1977) lists hundreds of books, pamphlets and articles exemplifying the radical point of view, of which the larger portion dates from the 1970s rather than the 1960s. Clearly, there is no lack of material on which to base a new assessment of radical economics.

It is not easy to define radical economics. It may be defined by its research agenda, by its style or argumentation, and by its central point of view. Perhaps the last of these offers the fewest difficulties: a radical economist is anyone who regards the existing capitalist system as so hopelessly infected with various evils – inequality, alienation, consumerism, militarism, racism, sexism, imperialism, and environmental pollution – that no remedy short of a socialist revolution will cure them; moreover, by a socialist revolution is meant not just collective ownership of the means of production but the establishment of 'industrial democracy' in the sense of workers' control and management of industrial enterprises.[3] It is immediately apparent that radical economists are a different breed from classical Marxists of the Old Left variety. On the other hand, they are barely distinguishable from New Left Marxists.

The relationship between radical economics and Marxism is indeed so ambivalent that it is difficult to pin down precisely. The main intellectual inspiration behind radical economics is undoubtedly Marxism, but only in terms of certain fundamental ideas of Marx – the class struggle between capital and labour, the exploitation of workers, the inherent instability of capitalism, and so on – and not in terms of the technical details of the Marxian apparatus. Thus, the recent upsurge of mathematical Marxian economics, steeped in the writings of J. von Neumann, W. Leontief, and P. Sraffa, has left most radical economists cold. By and large, and with certain exceptions, radical economists prefer to practise a do-it-yourself Marxism, frequently accompanied by profound criticisms of some of Marx's arguments;[4] moreover, much of radical economics is devoted to exploring topics such as sexism, racism, and imperialism, which Marx hardly touched on. Nevertheless, it may be conceded that the spectre of Marxism continues to haunt the literature of radical economics and that it is impossible rigidly to divorce radical and Marxian economics. All that I will insist on is that the two schools of thought are distinguishable partly by their respective research agendas and partly by the litmus-paper test of obeisance to the letter of Marx's writings.

Radical economics may also be characterized by its style of argument. It repudiates the tendency of mainstream, orthodox economics to address all economic problems in terms of the maximizing behaviour of individuals subject only to the constraints of a given technology and given property rights and instead lays emphasis on the strategic use of economic power by definite social groups to alter both the techniques of production and property rights; radical economists do not deny that class power interacts with market behaviour, but markets alone are not viewed as determining economic outcomes – as they are by orthodox theorists. The result is that historical analysis of the development of economic institutions is given as much scope as static theorizing of the general equilibrium variety. Here again, the Marxian dialectical–historical method is said to be the principal point of inspiration, but as Marx's own method is by no means transparently obvious (see Blaug, 1980b, ch. 2), there is ample room for differences in interpretation and hence differences in the styles of reasoning of individual radical economists. Nevertheless, what identifies a piece of analysis as radical economics is the accent on groups rather than individuals as the agents of social change.

How to appraise

My stated aim is to provide a methodological appraisal of radical economics, which to some readers implies that I am going to pronounce once and for all on the validity of radical economics with the aid of some absolute, metatheoretical criteria. But the notion that one can arrive at a categorical judgement of a theory or set of theories (whether in economics or in anything else) is hopelessly naive. No ongoing body of ideas, or what Lakatos calls a 'scientific research programme' (see Blaug, 1980a, pp. 34–40), is either wholly right or wrong, and it can only be judged in terms of the problems it has set for itself or the events which it is seeking to explain. We may ask whether the theories that comprise the SRP are internally coherent; but once that question is answered, there remains the task of deducing their predictive implications and, finally, the even more critical task of examining the empirical record in favour of these theories (and by 'empirical record', I do not mean just statistical regressions). In the final analysis, nothing matters but the empirical track record. In the nature of things, however, that track record is never unambiguous and, moreover, there is a continuous interplay between testing and theorizing, so that the tests of yesterday become irrelevant because the theory has meanwhile been adjusted to accommodate past refutations. Moreover, an SRP cannot be judged in isolation but only in comparison with alternative SRPs directed at the same range of problems. All this is to say that methodological appraisals of SRPs are inherently difficult, frequently inconclusive, and involve subtle judgements of empirical relevance and theoretical fruitfulness. I hope that these all too brief remarks on the philosophy of scientific method will dispel any notion that I am going to lay down the law about radical economics. I was not inclined to be sympathetic to radical economics when I began this appraisal. Having completed it, I still remain sceptical, but I am also more convinced than ever that radical economics must be taken seriously: it poses a definite challenge to conventional economics, and that challenge has not yet been adequately answered.

The methodology of radical economics

Appraisal implies standards and, while my standards are those of virtually all modern economists, namely, falsificationism,[5] it may be worth asking if radical economists likewise believe that theories should ultimately be judged in terms of their falsifiable implications for the phenomena they are designed to explain; if not, we run the danger of judging one body of ideas by the standards set by another. Unfortunately, radical economists have written almost nothing on questions of methodology, and their views must therefore be inferred from various asides.

On certain topics, like sexism and racism in labour markets, radical writers are indeed falsificationists: they rest their case on the evidence and argue that neoclassical theory has been decisively refuted. In general, however, radical economists are more likely to stake their claims on ideological grounds: where orthodox economists see harmony, they see conflict; where orthodox economists see individuals maximizing their opportunities, they see social classes pursuing their common interests; the preferences of individuals which orthodox economists take as data for their analysis are treated as variables by radical economists; and the moral indictment of market forces, which orthodox economists brush aside as irrelevant to value-free science, they view as the capstone to their arguments.

It is of course perfectly true that all theorizing begins with what J. A. Schumpeter has called 'vision' – 'the preanalytic cognitive act that supplies the raw material for the analytic effort'; all SRPs embody what Lakatos calls a 'hard core' or irrefutable, metaphysical commitments (see Blaug, 1980a, pp. 36-7).

Moreover, there is little doubt that the hard core of radical economics is strikingly different from the hard core of orthodox economics. What is questionable, however, is whether choices between competing theoretical systems can be legitimately reduced to choices between hard cores. Obviously, we all have social, political, and intellectual preconceptions which lead us to be attracted to some hard cores and to be repelled by others. Nevertheless, we also judge ideas by their fruits and, however much we may be reluctant to give up a favoured position, we will eventually abandon a preferred hard core if it consistently leads to implications which appear to be refuted by the empirical evidence. To deny this much would be to adopt the methodology of voluntarism or believing-what-one-wants-to-believe.

All this may seem to be too obvious to require stating, but radical economists frequently imply that orthodox economics can be rejected out of hand because its hard core amounts to an acceptance of the status quo, from which it follows that radical economics is inherently superior simply because it begins and ends with the total repudiation of the existing social order.[6] But although these are relevant considerations in choosing between orthodox and radical economics, there remains the question of assessing the theories associated with the two hard cores in the light of evidence which may or may not vindicate the status quo. We must be prepared to admit that, possibly, the status quo is superior to any alternative social state.

The tendency to reduce social sciences to hard cores selected according to taste is further exemplified by the frequency with which radical economists discuss the problem of how to choose between theories in terms of Thomas Kuhn's concept of 'paradigms'. Because radical economists have a different world view than that of orthodox economists, and because economics asks different questions from those posed in mainstream economics, it is implied that criticism of radical economics from outsiders can be more or less ignored (see Hymer, Roosevelt, and Sweezy in Lindbeck, 1977, pp. 120, 140; Gordon, 1971, pp. xiv, l; Applebaum, 1977, pp. 559-65; Franklin and Tabb, 1977; Reich, 1981, pp. 166–8). Now, it is conceivable that radical and orthodox economics constitute wholly incommensurate SRPs – that is, domains of inquiry which at no points overlap in which case it would indeed be impossible to choose between them in terms of empirical evidence. If so, however, the argument cuts both ways: radical economists would be disqualified from criticizing orthodox economists, on the grounds that they lack the empathy to understand orthodox economics, and they would be barred from citing 'facts' purporting to demonstrate the superiority of radical analysis. It is perfectly obvious, however, that radical economists do not accept any such self-denying ordinance. The two SRPs actually overlap on a number of issues – for example, wage determination in labour markets, the economics of labour-managed firms, and the phenomena of business cycles and stagflation – and are commensurable at least in some respects. The notion of competing 'paradigms' is sometimes helpful, but it can also be deeply misleading and, if taken strictly, would reduce the problem of choosing between SRPs to one of religious conversion (see Blaug, 1980a, pp. 29-33).

To hammer the point home, let us briefly consider Benjamin Ward's *Ideal Worlds of Economics*. This extraordinary book presents in turn the liberal (Keynesian), radical (New Left) and conservative (Chicago School) point of view with equal energy and with almost equal conviction in order to demonstrate that all disagreements in economics stem basically from differences in hard cores. It is not logically possible to hold a number of coherent positions, each one of which is entirely inconsistent with the others, and yet this is what Ward tells us is not only possible but in some sense describes the existing situation in economics.

At the close of his persuasive discussion of the radical point of view, Ward (1979, vol. II, p. 98) finally turns to the question of choosing among alternative 'world views'. Such choices, he contends, can be made in terms of three criteria:

1.   '[H]ow well [does] each one [fit] in terms of one's own experience of life and interpretation of history[?]'
2.   'Do the world view's assertions fit the known facts?'
3.   '[Do] the various parts of the world view fit together to make a coherent whole [?]'

He notes that criterion 2 is ambiguous because the facts themselves are frequently dictated by the world view rather than the world view being dictated by the facts, and also because the same facts look different when seen through different lenses. For that reason, he places far greater emphasis on criterion 3, which he calls 'the compatibility test'. He notes with alarm, however, the tendency of some radicals to deprecate all theoretical inquiry and research and to argue that 'what is needed is to abolish capitalism, not to study it'. While agreeing that 'a central function of radical economics is as an instrument of recruitment', Ward (1979, Vol. II, p. 101) insists that 'an equally central function is to provide a correct understanding of how the world works. Without that, there is no good reason to feel that radicals will be able to bring about a genuine revolution.' Precisely! In making sure that one has achieved 'a correct understanding of how the world works', the compatibility or coherence test is only a necessary and not a sufficient condition. Even the criterion of verification – 'Do the world view's assertions fit the known facts?' – is only a weak sufficiency condition for the simple reason that an almost indefinite number of different assertions will fit the known facts in the same way that an almost indefinite number of different mathematical functions will fit a set of known points. The much tougher criterion for deciding whether 'a correct understanding' has been achieved is to ask whether that understanding has generated surprising predictions – novel facts – which were borne out by the subsequent course of events.

Verificationism is the methodology of the complacent because it is unlikely ever to generate disappointments and is therefore perfectly guaranteed to preserve established intellectual positions. We know that our understanding of the world is correct, not when our assertions agree with known facts, but if we are unable to find any facts that contradict our assertions. Throughout his book, Ward consistently evades the fundamental question that Karl Popper has taught us to pose to the adherents of all world views: Are there any events, which, if they materialized, would make you abandon that world view? If there are no such events, it is pointless to look at the facts. But if there are such events, there is hardly anything more illuminating of 'correct understanding' than to spell them out. In other words, the predictive record of a theory or set of interconnected theories, paradigms, world views, SRPs, or call them what you will, is the ultimate acid test of correct understanding, and every attempt to dilute the impact of that criterion ends up in voluntarism and dogmatism.

Some negative features
Before examining particular radical theories, I want to dwell a moment on some general features of the radical literature that I find disturbing.

The first of these is the tendency to ascribe certain widely acknowledged social ills to capitalism without any examination of socialism to check whether it is free of these ills. Worse than that, 'capitalism' in most radical writings actually seems to mean the United States of America and no other capitalist regimes elsewhere are ever examined to see whether the peculiar historical circumstances of the United States make any difference to the operation of capitalism.[7] Moreover, the experiences of Soviet Russia, China, Cuba, and sometimes even Yugoslavia are frequently dismissed on the grounds that these are not true examples of 'socialism'. This amounts to throwing away all historical and comparative evidence that might serve to vindicate or refute the belief that the phenomena of inequality, alienation, racism, sexism, consumerism, imperialism, and environmental destruction can never be eradicated under capitalism. Since it is frankly admitted (for example, by Edwards, Reich and Weisskopf, 1978, p. xii) that racism, sexism, and militarism predate the rise of capitalism and are not unique to capitalist societies today,[8] the argument is that socialism is a necessary but not sufficient condition for the elimination of these evils. However, in the absence of any analysis of actual socialist countries, this contention comes dangerously close to yet another version of 'Utopian' socialism.

John Stuart Mill complained over 100 years ago of the inappropriateness of comparing ideal socialism as-it-might-be with actual capitalism as-it-is. But he was writing before there was a single example of a socialist society. Radical economists likewise compare their ideal democratic, decentralized, and participatory socialism with actual capitalism as-it-is, but they confine their concept of capitalism to American capitalism and refuse to draw any lessons both from actual socialism as-it-is or actual capitalism as-it-is outside the United States. It seems a curious approach if one is concerned to show that capitalism as such will soon collapse and that it will be succeeded not by barbarism or state socialism but by 'true' socialism. Besides, those who prefer capitalism to socialism do not usually do so because capitalism, judged by itself, is paradise. Capitalism, to paraphrase Winston Churchill, is a rotten economic system – and even worse are all the other alternatives! The tendency of radical economists not to compare and contrast the two systems, therefore, ignores the questions which worry the unconverted.[9] However, there are hopeful signs in some recent radical literature (for example, Albert and Hahnel, 1981; Roemer, 1982) of recognition that modern socialist countries constitute true anomalies in the standard case for socialism in the sense that neither the writings of Karl Marx and Friedrich Engels nor those of any other socialist writers prepare us to expect what we witness today in the USSR, China, and Cuba.

A second feature of radical economics, which is a corollary of the first, is the failure to address the economics and politics of socialism. Lindbeck's (1977, pp. 32-3) critique of the New Left comments on the fact that radical economists reject both competition and coercion as mechanisms of resource allocation and yet fail to demonstrate that there is a third way of making these decisions. But there might well be a third way, namely, what Lindblom (1977, chs. 4 and 19) calls the 'persuasion and preceptoral system', which employs moral pressure to obtain cooperative consent The Chinese and Cuban experience (see Albert and Hahnel, 1981, chs. 3 and 4; MacEwan, 1981, ch. 14), however, suggests that this third way may be inherently unstable. Be that as it may, there is also the question of the relationship between economic freedom and political freedom under both capitalism and socialism. The radical economist's vision of socialism is, as we have said, that of a network of producers' cooperatives with an apparently minimal state apparatus. But who would resolve conflicts between different producers' cooperatives, and why should we believe that no such conflicts would ever arise? These issues are almost never raised in the radical literature.[10] The fact that orthodox economists are just as prone to avoid questions of political mechanisms for resolving economic conflicts in their analysis of capitalism and socialism is, surely, not an adequate defence of the similar disinclination among radical economists?

Another striking and pervasive feature of radical economics is a crude kind of functionalism or what might be labelled 'the conspiracy theory of capitalist behaviour'. According to this theory, if one can find a situation which serves the interests of every individual capitalist taken in turn and which is functional to the survival of the capitalist system as a whole, one may ascribe the situation to the collusive behaviour of the capitalist class, despite the fact that one cannot specify the mechanism of collusion and despite the fact that, for other theoretical purposes, capitalists are pictured as ruthlessly competing against each other in a planless and destructive manner. It is true that this so-called conspiracy theory is rarely stated in so many words and that analytically inclined radical economists have learned from Marx that it is illegitimate to combine class collusion and atomistic competition in the same analytical framework. Nevertheless, the conspiracy theory turns up repeatedly in radical writings (see Elster, 1979, pp. 29-35; Barrett, 1980, pp. 93-6; Roemer, 1981, pp. 8-9), possibly because the missing link in the argument is not recognized but perhaps more so because it is a potent method of 'consciousness raising'. The trouble with the conspiracy theory is, of course, that it proves too much: if capitalists can act in concert to pay women and blacks less so as 'to divide and rule', how is it that wages ever rise or that the length of the working day ever falls? Of course, there are market structures, such as oligopoly, which positively encourage and sometimes even institutionalize collusion in the form of cartels. But collusion cannot be made a general principle of economic organization under capitalism – or, if it is, the whole of radical and Marxian economics will have to be rewritten.

The area which was at one time most deeply affected by this conspiracy theory is the radical-cum-Marxist theory of the state, which has only recently assimilated the view that the state under capitalism has its own 'laws of motion' quite distinct from that of the private sector (Miliband, 1977, pp. 73-4; Jessop, 1977; Clark and Dear, 1981). Nevertheless, many radical/Marxist writers on the state nowadays avoid functionalist arguments only to fall into reductionist ones in which all the actions of governments in capitalist societies are explained with reference to the economic imperatives of sustained capital accumulation (see Gough, 1979, pp. 155–7). Reductionism or economism frequently appears elsewhere in the radical literature, for example, on questions of international relations between nation-states, and in general radical writers give little credence to any explanation of social phenomena which does not invoke economic motives. Some orthodox economists are unhappy about the intellectual imperialism implied by the new Chicago School economics of the family. But this Chicago brand of economism is nothing next to the radical penchant for turning economics not just into the queen of the social sciences but into the *only* social science.

Selected topics in radical economics

So much for preliminaries. Let us now turn to the radical treatment of certain leading topics. The first is the famous question of alienation, 'that most bedraggled cliché of contemporary culture' (Harrington, 1976, p. 150). In common parlance, 'alienation' denotes the drudgery and meaninglessness of factory labour under capitalism, which worried even Adam Smith over 200 years ago. But most radical economists give the term a wider meaning – if only to avoid the implication that there is alienation in the Soviet Union (Hunt and Sherman, 1978, pp. 591–2). In so doing they follow Marx, for whom alienation always meant much more than job dissatisfaction: it denoted the worker's estrangement not just from the products of his own labour but from labour itself as a creative human activity, from other workers (the opposite of 'class consciousness'), and from society as a network of relations between people. Moreover, capitalists are no less alienated than workers because, for Marx, alienation infects all members of a capitalist society, being the product of three separate forces: the phenomenon of scarcity, the phenomenon of factories, and the phenomenon of the commercialization of virtually all aspects of life. In the final analysis, it is the lack of conscious, central direction of economic life under capitalism and hence man's failure to control the economic aspects of his environment – the 'invisible hand' so extolled by bourgeois economists – that constitutes the bedrock of alienation for Marx.

Numerous commentators have disinterred these ideas in the writings of the younger Marx (Bronfenbrenner, 1975; Torrance, 1977). They constitute a profound moral condemnation of a private enterprise economy, but there are probably good intellectual reasons why the older Marx dropped this entire line of argument (without ceasing to believe in it) and instead turned his attention to the positive analysis of 'the laws of motion' of capitalism. For one thing, central planning under socialism would overcome one source of alienation but, like capitalism, it too would suffer from scarcity and from the necessity to carry out production in large industrial plants. Socialism would, therefore, set the stage for the elimination of alienation, but only the final state of communism could promise to eradicate all vestiges of alienation.

This conjecture about the turning point in Marx's intellectual development may be correct or incorrect. However, there is no doubt that the concept of alienation, which at first glance seems redolent with far-reaching implications about the social and psychological consequences of industrial civilization, is difficult to pin down precisely because it cuts too deep and too wide. Could any industrialized, urbanized society ever free itself from its effects? It is easy to see that the radical economist's vision of socialism as one of labour-managed enterprises is precisely designed to answer that question in the affirmative. But would workers' control, assuming it is feasible, succeed in eliminating alienation? There would still be a demand for goods which cannot be produced except by repetitious and therefore monotonous work. There would still be pressures to produce at least cost, which would undermine efforts at job enrichment and job rotation and might threaten the job security of some workers. Unless we conceive of an economy of almost unlimited abundance, it is difficult to see how one would avoid some aspects of what is called 'alienation'

The fact that one cannot run is no reason not to try walking, and the above remarks are not to be read as a condemnation of all efforts at industrial democracy. Its purpose is to suggest some of the thorny questions raised by the concept of alienation. Radical economists deserve credit for putting the question of alienation on the economic agenda but, after 10 or 15 years of radical theorizing, they have left the theory of alienation almost as confused as they found it. A harsh but incisive discussion of *Karl Marx' Philosophy of Man* (1976) by John Plamenatz contains more fruitful analysis of the problem of alienation under capitalism and socialism than all the works of radical economics put together.

There remains the unanswered question as to whether workers' participation in management and investment decisions, and particularly a measure of workers' control over management and investment decisions, is compatible with capitalism. Radical economists are convinced that capitalism and worker self-management will not mix (see Hunius *et al.*, 1973; Hyman, 1974; Bowles and Gintis, 1978; Carnoy and Shearer, 1980, chs. 9 and 10), but the same thing was once said about capitalism and the progressive income tax. It is perfectly true, of course, that if we imagine not power-sharing but total control over the productive process by workers we have denied capitalists the exercise of their property rights over the means of production and thus have in fact destroyed capitalism. But why carry the argument to this extreme? If the hierarchical organization of production confers any economic benefits, if it is, in short, technically efficient, and if there are other advantages in a system in which those who make the fundamental decisions in a firm risk their own capital rather than the entire income of the enterprise, workers' control will never become total and absolute (Lindblom, 1977, pp. 104–5). Here then is the heart of the matter: is private property in the means of production, meaning centralized control over the productive process in the hands of those who ultimately bear the burden of entrepreneurial decisions, conducive to efficiency and growth?

Radical economists are in no doubt about the answer to that question. The origin of the division of labour in the eighteenth-century factory, and thus of the hierarchical organization of production, lies not in the superior efficiency of occupational specialization but in the desire of capitalists to 'divide and rule' the labour force and thus to secure what Marx called 'the despotism of the workplace' (Marglin, 1975, 1976).[11] It is the exercise of coercive social power over the production process which is, according to radical economists, the essence of the capitalist system. Labour is the only human input in the productive process, and the hire of labour at time, rather than piece, rates implies a conscious willingness to work at a minimum level of intensity which cannot be fully spelled out in a contractual agreement. The famous slogan 'a fair day's work for a fair day's pay' highlights this double dimension of the employment contract for production systems in which output cannot be unambiguously traced to individual workers. In short, labour under capitalism is not purely and simply a commodity because its hiring contract is typically 'incomplete' in the sense of specifying the duration of work and the rate of pay but not the intensity and quality of the effort to be expended. Constant monitoring to prevent shirking and the threat of dismissal are the only instruments available to capitalists to secure the cooperation of workers in the productive process, but these are only effective if workers can be prevented from acting in concert. Racial, sexual, and ethnic stratification of the labour force is thus seen to be essential not only to the interests of the capitalist class as a whole but to the profits of each and every individual capitalist. Therefore, the problem is not to explain why there is discrimination against women, blacks, browns, and the like under capitalism but how anyone could imagine that sexism and racism could ever be eliminated in a capitalist society (Gintis, 1971; Gortz, 1976; Gintis and Bowles, 1981, pp. 14–17; Reich and Devine, 1981).[12]

In standard neoclassical economics, labour and capital are treated as perfectly symmetrical inputs which are somehow combined in a 'black box' called the firm. As Ronald Coase argued years ago, firms are nonmarket institutions in which authoritarian allocation replaces the price system, but even he said very little about principles which govern this internal allocation system. More recently, under the twin labels of 'the economic theory of agency' and 'implicit contract theory', neoclassical economists have also taken up the problem of the necessarily incomplete labour contract in the light of the information costs of hiring workers and the transaction costs of assigning them to different tasks (see Alchian and Demsetz, 1972; Williamson, 1975, ch. 4). Indeed, the story of the industrial revolution has been rewritten accordingly, if only to answer Marglin's arguments (North, 1981, chs. 12 and 13). Likewise, the concept of the incomplete labour contract has even entered modern macroeconomics as one explanation of stagflation and the tendency of labour markets to adjust quantities rather than prices (Azariadis, 1975; Okun, 1981, pp. 62-77; Thurow, 1981, pp. 56-9; Hudson, 1982, pp. 30-40, 79-82); in Okun's memorable phrase, employers must rely on an 'invisible handshake' to take the place of 'the invisible hand' that fails to operate in labour markets.

Here is a striking example of overlap between radical and orthodox economics with both 'paradigms' proposing identical explanations of underemployment equilibrium (compare, for example, Calva, 1976; Bowles, 1981). However, orthodox economists pay little attention to, and sometimes even deny, the likelihood of a fundamental conflict of interest between workers and capitalists in maintaining the employment relationship, whereas radical economists of course emphasize the 'contested terrain' of industrial relations (Edwards, 1979). There is little doubt that if workers controlled production, they would choose more job enrichment and more frequent job rotation, that is, a lower division of labour, than capitalists now do; in general, there is no reason to believe that the workers' goal of maximizing the pecuniary and non-pecuniary rewards of labour always gives the same results as the capitalists' goal of maximizing profit. Moreover, workers prefer collective rather than individual labour contracts, and in this sense too the interests of workers and capitalists are bound to clash (here, by the way, is the basis of the radical theory of trade unions).

The neoclassical solution to this problem of avoiding the conflict of interests between labour and capital is the device of paying workers less than their spot marginal product when they are young and more than their spot marginal product when they are old, thus inducing them to cooperate in the maximization of the joint welfare of all members of the firm (Lazear, 1981). Nevertheless, in the words of Okun (1981, p. 86), 'the basic problem of the need of trust [in the employment relation] and the inherent reasons for distrust is not soluble. Radical economists would echo Okun's comment, arguing that the inherent conflict of interests in capitalist firms will only disappear if labour hires its own capital in self-managed enterprises. However, producers' cooperatives or labour-managed firms (LMFs) will face new conflicts not present in capitalist firms as they are now constituted: there is the classic 'free rider' problem whereby individual workers shirk and benefit at the expense of other workers; there is the problem of which workers to lay off in the face of shrinking demand for the firm's products; and there is the problem of how to hire new workers when demand expands without diluting the income claims of the original worker-owners. In general, LMFs confront trade-offs which can become potent sources of conflict depending on whether the disadvantages of mutual supervision relying solely on trust are in fact outweighed by the sense of commitment generated by participation and self-management.

Recent decades have witnessed a small but growing non-radical literature on the pure theory of syndicalism, starting with the work of Benjamin Ward, Evsey Domar, and Jaroslav Vanek in the 1960s, based on the assumption that LMFs maximize net value added per worker rather than profits per unit of capital (see Vanek, 1975; Wiles, 1977, chs. 4 and 6; Steinherr, 1978). Apart from the change in maximand, however, the analysis of LMFs has followed the conventional neoclassical analysis of capitalist firms. It has been shown that, for a given technology, both types of firms will achieve the same general equilibrium solutions with the same Pareto-optimal properties; indeed, under certain restrictive conditions, the performance of LMFs is actually superior to the performance of profit-maximizing capitalist firms. Characteristically, however, this literature has failed to address all the interesting dynamic questions about the internal organization of LMFs, their incentive structures, and their capacity to expand and innovate. If LMFs are statistically as efficient or even more efficient than capitalist firms, why are LMFs so rare in mixed economies?[13] However, many of the arguments against LMFs as a 'third' sector in a mixed capitalist economy fall to the ground if LMFs are the 'first' and only sector in the economy (Chiplin and Coyne, 1980). At any rate, the LMF literature fails decisively to answer the central question as to whether hierarchy and job fragmentation as principles of industrial organization under capitalism are so widely observed because they are superior in output terms or because they furnish capital owners with an effective method of controlling their work force.

Radical economists believe that the latter is nearer the truth than the former, and for that reason they find it impossible to conceive of capitalism without what is called 'segmented labour markets' to secure discipline on the factory floor. The theory of segmented labour markets (SLM) is perhaps the most important contribution which radical economists have made to economics because it bears directly on explanations of sexism and racism as inherent or accidental features of capitalism. The theory of SLM is not itself radical in origin and was first broached by American labour economists of the Institutionalist School in the 1920s and 1930s, culminating in the famous distinction by Doeringer and Piore in 1971 between 'internal' and 'external' labour markets (see Cain, 1976, pp. 1224–8).

In the institutionalist version of SLM, there is a contrast between two *sectors* of the economy – the so-called *primary* labour markets of large corporations (with trade unions, job security, and steady career prospects) and the *secondary* labour markets of small business (with no unions, dead-end jobs, and high turnover rates); moreover, this increasing dichotomization of labour markets is traced to certain structural changes in the twentieth-century American economy. In radical theories of SLM, however, segmentation, apart from involving three rather than two stratas, is not so much a matter of contrasting sectors of economic activities but rather of contrasting categories of workers within each and every firm in every sector: the spread of big business, unionism, and the expansion of public employment creates the superficial appearance of a dual economy, but segmentation runs to some degree through all capitalist enterprises.[14] Despite such differences in emphases, both versions of SLM attempt to account for certain directly observable features of capitalism which appear to challenge the conclusions of neoclassical labour economics: the fact of significant earnings differences between males and females and between blacks and whites even when age, schooling, and years of work experience are held constant; the failure of education and training programmes to erode these differences; and the persistence of chronic poverty among certain social groups even during periods of boom and high employment. The emphasis in all these SLM theories is on the demand for labour, whereas the emphasis in orthodox labour economics, and particularly in human capital theory, is on the supply side in the labour market. But radical economists also attempt to explain the changing nature of the supply of labour: women, blacks, and other ethnic minorities are condemned to casual employment at low pay with few opportunities for on-the-job training; their work habits are then formed by these dead-end prospects, so that employers' expectations that women and blacks are less stable and less promising workers are more often than not borne out by experience. All this is to say that behaviour in the labour market cannot be understood except as a historical process in which tastes and preferences are being continuously moulded by past choices and opportunities.

SLM theories seem to imply two predictions. First, if we select some index of job quality, made up of starting wages, turnover rates, bouts of unemployment, increments of pay with the same employer, and so forth, it will prove to be bimodally or multimodally distributed across different but well defined categories of workers. Second, and more important, there will be little upward mobility over time between these demographic groups. In a highly critical survey of the SLM literature, Cain (1976, p. 1231) complains that radical economists have provided few indications of how to measure job quality except in terms of wages, and even fewer of how to assign workers to different segments, not to mention confusion as to whether the segments are sectors, firms, or occupations. However segmentation is defined, he denies that there is much evidence in the American economy for anything like a stable pattern of labour stratification over time. He sums up:

> SLM theories are sketchy, vague, and diverse if not internally conflicting. Description, narratives and taxonomies crowd out model development. On the positive side the theories evolve from detailed data that are often richer in historical, institutional and qualitative aspects than is customary among econometrically-oriented orthodox theories. (Cain,1976, p. 1221)

Cain's review of SLM studies is actually less than comprehensive. Martin Carnoy (1980) provides a more thorough review of four American and five Third World studies, including a new American test in which the segments are job clusters, not industries or sectors of economic activity. But although Carnoy is as sympathetic as Cain is hostile to SLM theories, even he finds that occupational mobility in the United States is systematically related to age and schooling, which runs contrary to the implications of SLM theory (Carnoy, 1980, pp. 75–7; also Rosenberg, 1979). Furthermore, some Third World studies provide categorical refutations of both of the principal predictive implications of SLM theory (Carnoy, 1980, pp. 105–6).

We are left with an indecisive verdict about the significance of the concept of SLM. Since the question of SLM is intimately related to the causes of sexual and racial inequalities under capitalism, we turn now to theories of discrimination in labour markets. In a system of competitive markets, we ought never to observe earnings differences between identical workers for the simple reason that such differences create profit opportunities which induce behaviour that will act to eliminate them. At one time, it might have been argued that sexual and racial earnings differentials are entirely due to the fact that male and female workers and white and black workers are not identical in their relevant personal characteristics, but recent work on earnings functions has made it impossible to trace all sexual and racial earnings differences to the nature of the supply of labour; it is now generally agreed that age, schooling, work experience, and occupation, even when supplemented by residence, home background, and ability variables, can only account for one-half or at most two-thirds of male-female and white-black earnings differentials. In short, there *is* discrimination on the side of demand in labour markets.

To explain why there has always been discrimination in capitalist labour markets and why it shows no signs of disappearing, we can either invoke specific imperfections in competitive behaviour, including collusion among employers aided and abetted by governments, or we can take the more difficult line of arguing that the lower pay of some workers merely raises the pay of others without having the slightest effect on profits, in consequence of which the competitive mechanism fails to reduce earnings differentials. Most neoclassical theories of discrimination have opted for the second alternative, but there are also one or two versions of the first.

Neoclassical theories of discrimination begin with Gary Becker's *Economics of Discrimination* (1975), and indeed before that date the very question of discriminatory hiring patterns in capitalist labour markets had never been raised in classical, neoclassical, or Marxist economics. Becker's book was at first ignored by his colleagues, but the growth of anti-discrimination policies in the 1960s soon produced a number of other orthodox explanations of demand-determined discrimination in labour markets. Michael Reich's recent book on *Racial Inequality* (1981), a major radical contribution to the literature, provides a thorough review of neoclassical theories of discrimination from Becker's taste for discrimination theory, to L. C. Thurow's cartel theory, to B. Bergmann's occupational crowding model, to K. J. Arrow's screening-signalling theory.[15] With the exception of Thurow's cartel theory, all of these theories imply that capitalists lose and white workers gain from discrimination and, hence, that racial and sexual differentials will disappear as time passes, the more so if market structures are competitive. The efforts of the Equal Employment Opportunity Commission since 1964 encouraged many to believe that racial income differentials would soon begin to dwindle, and, indeed, by the early 1970s a number of American economists claimed that they had virtually disappeared among young whites and blacks (see Reich, 1981, pp. 19n, 59-61). Actually, these findings are susceptible of a number of different interpretations and, moreover, there continue to be marked disparities in unemployment rates between whites and blacks. Besides, sexual, as distinct from racial, earnings differentials have only fallen slightly in recent years (see Deckard, 1979, chs. 5 and 6), so that the problem of explaining the persistence of discrimination under capitalism remains.

If we consult the chapter on the economics of discrimination in Samuelson's *Economics,* we learn that discrimination always lowers the total product, meaning that employers forfeit profits by refusing to hire women or blacks on the same terms as men and whites. Can we therefore expect private enterprise spontaneously to close the gap in pay between men and women and between whites and blacks? 'Few believe this,' Samuelson (1980, p. 792; also pp. 798-9) concludes, and he therefore recommends anti-discrimination controls as well as training and retraining programmes. We are not told, however, why 'few believe this', since orthodox theory suggests that all of us should indeed believe it.

Radical economics is not faced with this anomaly because it claims that, for example, racial discrimination benefits capitalists (and certain highly paid white workers) by weakening the bargaining power of all workers over wages. Since most capitalists are white, this suggests the prediction that racial inequality as measured by the ratio of black to white income has a disequalizing effect on the distribution of income among whites. Reich (1981, pp. 132–45) submits this prediction to an empirical test across metropolitan areas in the United States in 1960 and 1970 and finds it strongly confirmed for both years. Unfortunately, he has been unable to obtain independent data on capitalist income by metropolitan areas and therefore ends up by demonstrating that rich whites rather than capitalists as such gain from discrimination (Reich, 1981, pp. 118, 158). In another econometric test, he shows that racial inequality lowers the degree of unionization, lowers the earnings of white workers, and raises the rate of profit across industries (Reich, 1981, pp. 300–2), but again the theory refers to capitalist behaviour in individual firms and not to industries. Reich (1981, p. 309) frankly admits that none of his statistical investigations 'directly reveal the extent to which the processes that currently produce racial inequality are located within firms or outside the work-place, in schooling, housing, and other community settings', and he agrees that they are probably located in both the workplace and the community. He argues, however, that his econometric evidence can be unambiguously interpreted whatever is the actual mechanism that produces racial inequality. This may be doubted, in this case as in all others – econometrics would be a simple subject if it were true.

Reich (1981, ch. 6) also presents historical evidence that racism hurts both white and black workers and that discrimination against a large racial minority of blacks may serve to explain why America has never developed a politically conscious labour movement committed to some form of socialism. The use of historical in addition to econometric data illustrates one of the features of radical economics that sets it apart from neoclassical economics. On the other hand, there are also striking similarities between radical and neoclassical economics, as, for example, in the very standards employed to validate theoretical arguments. Thus, Reich (1981, pp. 11, 81, 109, 218, 306) is concerned to establish the logical coherence of alternative theories of discrimination, but he also emphasizes the 'empirical plausibility' of both assumptions and predictions as the ultimate test of all theories. Radical and orthodox economics may be different 'paradigms', but on the subject of racial inequality their respective domains of application clearly overlap: both confront the question of whether racial inequality can persist in a competitive economy in the absence of collusion among employers, and both answer it by asking another question – 'Who benefits [from racial discrimination]?'

Orthodox economics has yet to show convincingly why racial and sexual inequality is compatible with profit-maximizing behaviour. It is possible to deny that there is such a thing as 'pure' discrimination (paying identical workers differently) while admitting that there is 'statistical' discrimination in the sense that employers resort to stereotypes (such as sex and colour) to identify the potential productivity of job applicants rather than engaging in expensive hiring search procedures. Since statistical discrimination involves no discrimination on average but only discrimination against atypical members of a group, it does not fail to maximize the total product and does not depend on the notion of employers being willing to suffer a loss in order to indulge their distaste for hiring women or blacks. But however plausible is the concept of statistical discrimination at the point of recruitment of new workers, it is much less convincing in the context of the payment of workers with several years of experience in a firm (see Blaug, 1976, pp. 846–7). Moreover, if the stereotypes which employers make use of to facilitate hiring are sticky in the face of changing facts, or if they lag consistently behind the facts because labour markets are chronically slack, the very distinction between pure and statistical discrimination threatens to break down. At any rate, no one has yet succeeded in measuring statistical as distinct from pure discrimination, and to that extent neoclassical theories of discrimination remain incapable of accounting for the persistence of racial and sexual earnings differentials under capitalism.

Furthermore, all neoclassical theories of discrimination treat sex discrimination as being on a par with racial discrimination, although it is extremely doubtful that economic theories of racial discrimination are applicable without major modification to the case of women: for one thing, gains to men at the expense of losses to women are shared by families, implying that families are in some sense discriminating against themselves, a problem which has no counterpart in discrimination against blacks; for another, sexual earnings differences are much greater for married women than for single women, undoubtedly because family commitments in a sexist society condemn married women to search for jobs in proximity to their homes; finally, sexism is not explained by discrimination in housing, schooling, and the franchise, all of which are key elements in racism. Radical economics has not yet provided an authoritative analysis of sexual inequality on a par with Reich's work on racial inequality, but it has furnished many of the elements of such an analysis. Radical writers have sensed the intimate connection that exists between the occupational and the sexual division of labour, between centralized authority and hierarchy in the business firm and patriarchal authority and hierarchy in the family, and between low-paid female labour in the marketplace and unpaid female labour in the family (see Humphries,

1980; Sokoloff, 1980; Hartmann, 1981; Vogel, 1981).[16] Some of this radical-feminist literature is no doubt excessively preoccupied with the purely formal effort to incorporate women's unpaid housework into the value schema of Marx's Capital (does housework create surplus value?; are housewives 'productive'?; and so on), and it is certainly richer in broad-brush historical generalization than in explanations of such bread-and-butter problems as changes in female labour force participation rates. Nevertheless, it has carved out an area of investigation into the underlying causes of male–female differences in pay and employment prospects that appears more promising than the standard neoclassical analysis of the economics of women's pay and work (for example, see Lloyd *et al.*, 1979).

We turn next to the associated theme of education in radical economics. When Bronfenbrenner published his review of radical economics in 1971, there was little to report on radical views of education. However, a now famous essay by Louis Althusser (1971) on the 'reproduction' of the 'social relations of production' via the educational system soon sparked off a whole series of articles and books (Carnoy, 1972, 1974; Carnoy and Levin, 1976), culminating in Bowles and Gintis's *Schooling in Capitalist America* (1976), which almost immediately became a minor classic.[17] The basic thesis of Bowles and Gintis is that educational reform under capitalism cannot succeed without far-reaching social and economic reform because the educational system necessarily reflects the inherent inequalities of the capitalist economy. Capitalist factories are hierarchically organized, and so are capitalist schools; capitalist factories require obedience and subservience to a central authority, and so do capitalist schools; capitalist factories alienate workers from the products of their labour, and capitalist schools alienate students from the products of their learning; workers are motivated, not by the intrinsic value of work, but by the promise of pay, and students are likewise motivated by the external reward of examination grades; and competition rather than cooperation governs the relations among workers as it governs the relations among students. This is what has been aptly called 'the correspondence principle' (Carnoy and Levin, 1976, pp. 26–9), according to which educational systems lack any coherent rationale of their own, shining only by reflected light emanating from the labour market. As Bowles and Gintis express it in Althusserian jargon: 'the social relations of schools reproduce the social division of labour under capitalism'. It follows that the educational reforms which they favour – 'open enrollment, free tuition, no tracking, curriculum and evaluation procedures appropriate to all students' needs, significantly increased finances, and a critique of ideologies which celebrate the status quo' (Bowles and Gintis, 1976, p. 250) – are impossible to achieve without abolition of private property in the means of production and the establishment of 'socialism with a human face'.

Clearly, the correspondence principle tends to deny the school system any administrative and intellectual autonomy. Strictly speaking, it asserts that educational reform under capitalism is pointless whereas under socialism it is unnecessary.

The centrepiece of the Bowles–Gintis book is the demonstration that the economic value of schooling in a capitalist economy has been grossly misunderstood by economists of 'the technocratic school', meaning, presumably, advocates of human capital theory (Bowles and Gintis, 1975). The widely attested association between an individual's lifetime earnings and the length of schooling he or she has received, which is the fountainhead of human capital theory, is not due to cognitive skills which schooling imparts and which employers prize as indispensable to the productive process. It is due rather, say Bowles and Gintis, to certain personality traits conducive alike to high grades in the classroom and to effective work performance on the job. Up to the level of high school education, these are largely traits of punctuality, persistence, concentration, and obedience. In higher education, on the other hand, they are the values of independence and self-reliance within a definite framework of organizational rules and procedures. In this way, elementary and secondary education prepare the hewers of wood and the drawers of water, while college education trains the junior managers and executives.[18]

This emphasis on affective behaviour rather than mental attainments, argue Bowles and Gintis, is not, as some liberals fondly believe, the unintended consequence of schooling carried out for other purposes. So long as industry is organized along capitalist lines, what is required at the bottom of the job pyramid is the ability to take orders, while at the top of the pyramid what is required is the ability to give orders. Teachers are perfectly aware of this spectrum of vocational demands and hence reward students in classrooms accordingly. Employers, on the other hand, have learnt from past experience that there is a general concordance between the attributes required at various levels of the occupational pyramid and educational attainments. In that sense, educational credentials act as surrogates for qualities which employers regard as important, predicting a certain level of performance without however making any direct contribution to it. This 'screening hypothesis', involving what we earlier called 'statistical discrimination', neatly accounts for the facts that earnings and education are positively associated; it even explains why so many educational qualifications appear to be unrelated to the type of work that students eventually take up; and it certainly explains why repeated efforts to create open classrooms, untracked high schools, and curricula without assessment and grading have always failed.

Unfortunately, this argument is neither radical nor Marxist nor original. Ever since Emile Durkheim, sociologists have appreciated the fact that 'socialization', that is, the inculcation of definite values and attitudes, is one of the principal functions of an educational system in any country. Bowles and Gintis (1976, p. 240) complain that 'the school system has played an important role in preserving the capitalist order'; but, surely, this is an obvious and even trivial proposition.

Would a school system in a socialist society not play a similar role in preserving the socialist order? The viability of any economic system depends on people respecting 'the rules of the game', and clearly schools play a major part in legitimizing these rules, as even neoclassical economists will readily admit (North, 1981, pp. 45–7).

Moreover, it is not true to say that orthodox economists have firmly committed themselves to the notion that the economic value of education is due entirely to the effects of cognitive learning in schools, although undoubtedly their writings lent themselves to that interpretation. What they must be accused of is that of viewing schooling as a 'black box': without pretending or even caring to know what goes on in classrooms, they have insisted that passing through schools increases the earning power of people even if both family origins and inborn or acquired mental abilities are held constant.

Bowles and Gintis, however, deny that the pure effects of schooling outweigh the effects of family background factors – or at any rate they seem to deny it. Actually, their own statistical work predicting personal incomes from childhood IQ, socioeconomic background, age, and years of schooling attributes a slightly greater effect to education than to family origins, at least for the age groups 35–44 and 55–64 (Bowles and Gintis, 1976, p. 292). It is well known that home background does exert an independent effect on earnings. It is also well known that the quantity as distinct from the quality of schooling exerts too small an effect on earnings to allow policymakers radically to alter the distribution of earnings solely by reductions in schooling differences among individuals. Bowles and Gintis devote a great deal of energy to a rebuttal of the IQ hereditarians – but, as far as orthodox economists are concerned, this is preaching to the converted: virtually all statistical attempts to explain earnings give little weight to IQ. What is at issue is the magnitude of the separate effects of IQ, home environment, years of schooling, and years of work experience, and on all these questions the dust has not yet settled even among orthodox economists (see Blaug, 1976, pp. 842–5).

Statistically speaking, only a hair's breadth divides the work of human capital theorists from that of Bowles and Gintis. What Bowles and Gintis bring to the argument is a very different interpretation of the findings, which still leaves open the basic question as to whether schooling merely enforces the personality traits acquired at home or whether it actually produces these traits in certain children. Even if we were to conclude that the latter is more the case than the former, there is the further unanswered question as to whether the authoritarianism of the educational system is not just as much the product of the internal pressures on schools as social institutions than the result of the hierarchical organization of capitalist industry. Without the 'correspondence principle', most of the arguments and many of the recommendations of Bowles and Gintis are deprived of a firm foundation (O'Keeffe, 1978, 1979).

Since the publication of their book, Bowles and Gintis (1980) have had second thoughts. They now admit the possible lack of fit between education and the economic system and concede that, for example, the expansion of higher education since 1945 initially took the form of a vast multiplication of traditional liberal arts courses, quite incompatible with the 'requirements' of capitalism. Their latest argument leaves room for independent educational reform to influence the economic system, with student power running, so to speak, ahead of worker power. Much of the original bite of their book, therefore, is gone, and we are left with the much weaker thesis that the educational system under capitalism only promotes the social integration of individuals as workers and citizens at the cost of repressing their personal development, accentuating rather than mitigating the inequalities that inevitably arise in an economic system motivated by profits.

Perhaps I have now said enough to convey the flavour of radical theorizing about education, which brings me to two other topics in the radical research programme: macroeconomics and imperialism. I shall deal only briefly with both of these.

Radical macroeconomics has not yet settled down to a definite and distinct line of thought. Much of it combines Kaldor–Pasinetti–Robinson growth theory with Kaleckian concepts of full-cost pricing and neo-Marxian notions of conflict-bargaining over wages (Sherman, 1976; Gordon, 1981; Naples, 1981; Rosenberg and Weisskopf, 1981) and is virtually undistinguishable from post-Keynesian economics. Yet another strand combines Marxist theories of crises (falling rate of profit, disproportionalities, underconsumption, and so on) with M. Kalecki's fecund notion of a 'political business cycle' (Boddy and Crotty, 1975; Crotty and Rapping, 1975; URPE, 1975; Edwards *et al.*, 1978, ch. 12; Weisskopf, 1979). A recent paper by Bowles (1981), mentioned earlier, links the non-wage costs of policing the labour force to the famous question of what it is that keeps the economy at underemployment equilibrium. The 'incomplete' labour contract is already the centrepiece of the radical analysis of wage determination, wage differentials, and the economic value of schooling. It now bids fair to become the linchpin of radical macroeconomics. Finally, Cherry (1980, ch. 15–21) attempts for the first time to compare Keynesian, monetarist, post-Keynesian, and Marxist–radical macromodels at the level of an intermediate macrotheory text. He, at least, does not take refuge in the facile thesis that they are incommensurable 'paradigms'.

Last, there is the subject of imperialism. All radical writings on imperialism derive not from the now largely obsolete Leninist theory of imperialism but from postwar 'theories of dependency' or 'the development of underdevelopment', emanating from Latin America and deeply influenced by its special circumstances. It was actually Paul Baran's *Political Economy of Growth* (1957) that was the first to hitch Marxism to problems of the sociology of development, but then the torch has passed to André Gunder Frank, Arghiri Emmanuel, Samir Amin, and many others (see Rhodes, 1970; Owen and Sutcliffe, 1972; Wilber, 1973). Indeed, writings on dependency seem to have exploded around 1970 and by now defy summary at any length short of a massive treatise. Fortunately, the reader can be referred to a comprehensive survey by Brewer (1980; also Palma, 1978), which is at once profoundly sympathetic and profoundly critical of the internal logic and empirical relevance of radical dependency theories.

For our purposes, a few general observations on this literature will suffice. The common core that unites the diverse writings of members of the Dependency School are:

1. an emphasis on the external influences that hinder the process of growth in less developed countries; and
2. the idea that dependency either prevents industrialization altogether or limits it to a special, distorted kind.

The emergence of the so-called newly industrializing countries like Singapore, South Korea, and Brazil, the increased bargaining power of the Organization of Petroleum Exporting Countries (OPEC), and the decline in American industrial power relative to that of Europe and Japan has somewhat discredited the Dependency School even in Latin America itself.[19] Nevertheless, the core of the argument remains, denying that trade and the international division of labour will necessarily close the gap between rich and poor countries and focusing sharply on the role of military power, technology, and vital raw materials in the struggle between strong and weak nation-states. The Dependency School's approach is historical rather than analytical; rigour is frequently sacrificed for the sake of relevance; and even its friends despair at the frequent resort to purely ideological assertions (Seers, 1981, p. 16). For the sake of completeness, a distinction must be drawn between the Dependency School and the new Marxist theories of 'unequal exchange': these achieve a rigour of their own but are so deeply embedded in the entire Marxist framework as to disqualify them as genuine examples of radical economics. More to the point is Block (1977), who analyses US international monetary policy, a subject hitherto monopolized by orthodox economists.

Enough said. Radical theories of imperialism have raised interesting questions about the global capitalist system which have long been ignored in orthodox international trade theory, but in my view radical analysis in this area is too narrow and blinkered to throw much light either on 'the causes of the wealth of nations' or on the foreign policies of major powers.

Conclusion

We have covered a wide canvass and yet we have totally ignored some aspects of the radical research programme, i.e., those dealing with urban economics, health economics, the economics of crime, and the economics of poverty, while moving at breakneck speed through such topics as the theory of the state, feminism, macroeconomics, and imperialism. Nevertheless, we have covered enough to provide the basis for some kind of tentative assessment of radical economics as a whole.

Some would argue that there is no systematic body of ideas called 'radical economics': so-called radical economics is simply an attitude, and a radical economist is anyone left of John Kenneth Galbraith with a graduate degree in economics. Granting that radical economics shades into institutional economics at one end and Marxian economics at the other, I would still insist that it occupies a distinguishable territory of its own. Orthodox economists are apt to dismiss radical economics so conceived as strong in rhetoric but weak in testable hypotheses. But this is an uncharitable characterization. To be sure, there is a strong component of ideology, and even deliberate ideology, in much of the radical literature: it is designed to jolt the reader and it usually succeeds in doing so. There is another side to radical analysis, however, which commits itself to definite empirical implications about economic outcomes and which is content to rest its case against orthodox economics on the strength of the supporting evidence. Starting from a 'hard core' of the irrepressible conflict of interests between capital and labour, radical economists have now succeeded in laying down a definite microfoundation for predicting the operations of labour markets, thus casting new light on such phenomena as sexual and racial earnings differences, the returns to private investments in education, the narrowing of skill differentials over time, the historical switch from the 'family wage' to the two-pay-cheques family, and the wages–profits squeeze. Moreover, the incompletely specified labour contract, which lies at the heart of these radical contributions to labour economics, has also captured the interests of some orthodox economists. Their emphasis is of course different, focusing as it does on the possibility of cooperative solutions for the implicit contract between employers and employees. The point is, however, that 'the new institutional labour economics' clearly competes with radical economics on common grounds, holding out the prospect of genuine choice among theories, not in terms of 'hard cores', but in terms of explanatory power and predictive success.

In other respects, however, there is no effective competition between radical and orthodox 'paradigms'. Radical economists have mounted a powerful indictment of life under capitalism, even if it is only an indictment of life under American capitalism. Furthermore, they have developed a coherent scenario of socialism as a system of democratic, decentralized, and participatory control by workers over all production decisions. Those who would dismiss this picture of socialism as Utopian can draw no support from orthodox economics, which virtually excludes consideration of the institutional organization of an economy (see Furubotn and Pejovich, 1972, pp. 1154–7).

Perfect competition, general equilibrium, static efficiency, and the like have almost nothing to do with the unprecedented economic growth, technical dynamism, and rise in living standards that capitalism has produced in the last two centuries. Even the function of entrepreneurship under capitalism – the fundamental decision whether to invest and how to invest in a world of uncertain economic changes – is relegated to the peripheries of the subject in standard economic theory (see Kirzner, 1973, 1979). Similarly, the great question of the relationship between the structure of ownership and the freedom of individuals, between economic freedom and political freedom, is addressed by some mainstream economists – stridently by Friedman (1962, ch. 1) and Hayek (1979, ch. 15) and dispassionately by Lindblom (1977) and Wiles (1977) – but the economics profession as a whole regards it as falling outside the proper scope of economics. Similarly, orthodox economics is largely silent about questions of alienation, consumerism, militarism, and imperialism, and still treats racism and sexism as peripheral issues. Maybe orthodox economics is rigorous and 'scientific', but it does sometimes have all the appearance of a subject in which issues of no great consequence are carefully examined while those of momentous consequence are consigned to the outer darkness.

I do not say 'a plague on both your houses', for this is advice which can only be followed by abandoning social and economic inquiry. We have to take a stand somewhere and must ultimately choose to work in one or another intellectual tradition. Radical economics has, I think, great failings, and I personally end as I began – an unconverted neoclassical economist. Nevertheless, a study of radical economics leaves one ultimately almost as unhappy with orthodox economics as with radical economics. Moreover, the quality of radical economics, is improving steadily over time, and another appraisal in 1985 or 1990 may well come to more positive conclusions than I have been able to reach.

Notes

1. The second edition of Lindbeck's (1977) study reprints comments by G.L. Bach, S. Hymer, F. Roosevelt, and P.M. Sweezy, as well as book reviews by R.L. Heilbroner, B. McFarlane, and J. Tobin, giving a rounded picture of the discussion generated by the book.
2. The increasing institutionalization of radical economics in the United States is reflected in the existence of several economics departments with large numbers of radical economists on their staff (e.g., the University of Massachusetts), in the number of prestigious universities that now offer graduate fields in 'political economy' (e.g., Berkeley, Harvard, Michigan, and Stanford) and in the programmes of URPE at the annual American Economic Association meetings.
3. This follows the definition of radical economics adopted by Bronfenbrenner (1970, p. 478). Groenewegen (1979), in a survey of radical economics in Australia, adopts a much wider definition, including post-Keynesians, neo-Ricardians, Marxists, institutionalists, and even muckrakers, that is, all critics of conventional economics who want to reconstruct a new economics. Likewise, Vaizey (1972) includes even Alfred Marshall and J.M. Keynes in the list of 'radical economists', thus emptying the label of all specific content.

4.   A textbook like Hunt and Sherman (1978, ch. 16) expounds and defends Marxian economics along strictly orthodox lines, but this is an atypical example. The more usual position is to repudiate the labour theory of value and to reinterpret the Marxian concept of exploitation in terms of the authoritarian nature of the employment relation under capitalism (see, e.g., Steedman, 1977; Harris, 1978; Bose, 1980; Gintis and Bowles, 1981; Roemer, 1981, 1982, and, particularly, Steedman *et al.*, 1981; for a more comprehensive example of the freewheeling attitude of radicals to Marxism, see Albert and Hahnel, 1978).

5.   I cannot take time to justify this remark (but see Blaug, 1980a, pp. 10–13, 127–8). It was Terence W. Hutchison's *Significance and Basic Postulates of Economic Theory* (1938) which first introduced Popper's criterion of falsifiability into modern economics, and he has continued throughout his long career to insist on the relevance of Popper's methodological prescriptions for economics (Blaug, 1980a, pp. 94–9).

6.   Franklin and Resnik (1973, pp. 73–4) provide a typical radical methodological pronouncement along these lines:

From a radical perspective, in which analysis is closely linked to advocacy of fundamental changes in the social order, an abstract model or category is not simply an aesthetic device. It is purposely designed to assist in the changes advocated, or in describing the nature of the barriers that must be broken down if the advocated changes are to occur.

Similarly, Edwards *et al.* (1978, p. xii) remark:

Explanation is not enough. The purpose of social and economic analysis should be to help eradicate the current sources of oppression rather than merely to describe them, or – still worse – to obscure them. We want to place our analysis squarely on the side of the growing movement for radical social change. For, as a result of our studies and our association with the radical movement, it has become clear to us that to achieve a better society the capitalist system must be challenged.

Likewise, certain radical writers (e.g., Wright, 1979, pp. 10–14) feel it necessary to defend an emphasis on the empirical testing of ideas, sensing no doubt that many of their readers are more accustomed to *a priori* styles of argument.

7.   As Robert Heilbroner (1974, pp. 63–4) observes:

It is a common tendency ... for radical analysts to assume that the word 'capitalism' is synonymous with the words 'United States' ... Serious problems arise from the choice of the United States, not as the richest or most powerful, but as the *typical* capitalist nation. The first is the assumption that certain contemporary attributes of the United States (racism, militarism, imperialism, social neglect) are endemic to all capitalist nations – an assumption that opens the question of why so many of these features are not to be found in like degree in all capitalist nations (for instance, England or Sweden or The Netherlands) as well as why so many are also discoverable in non-capitalist nations such as the Soviet Union.
(See also Heilbroner, 1976, pp. 30–1)

8.   Radical feminists have been particularly insistent on the point that one cannot deduce from the fact that capitalism has accommodated itself to sexism, and may well have helped to perpetuate it, the proposition that the elimination of capitalism will serve to eliminate sexism (e.g., Hartmann, 1981, pp. 17, 19, 110, 139).

9.   Thus, a recent issue of the *Review of Radical Political Economics* on the Soviet Union, **13** (1), 1981, shows far more concern with fitting the Soviet case into the Marxian stadial theory of history that with substantial analysis of what has or is taking place in the USSR.

10. See, e.g., Hunt and Sherman (1978, chs. 36–9): they describe some features of existing socialist systems but hardly begin to explore the political economy of socialism. However, the book by Sherman (1972, chs. 13–24) comes closer than any radical text I know of to confronting these vital questions. See also Espinosa and Zimbalist's (1978) radical quantitative analysis of experiments with industrial democracy in Allende's Chile.

11. Marglin's first paper (1976), originally published in the *Review of Radical Political Economics* in 1974, is one of the classics of radical economics, which had a decisive influence on the radical analysis of labour problems. It was followed in the same issue by Stone (1975), arguing that work tasks in the US steel industry were deliberately fragmented in the 1890s to divide a workforce which was becoming a threat to management.

12. Some Marxist economists now also emphasize this facet of capitalism (see note 5, above). According to this interpretation, workers are exploited under capitalism not because labour is supposed to be the only source of value and profits but because capitalists alone decide what and how workers produce, indeed imposing by their investment decisions a particular time pattern of consumption on workers.

13. Meade (1975) has provided one answer in terms of the need to spread risks; O'Mahoney (1979) has provided another in terms of the essentially individualistic role of entrepreneurs in starting up new firms.

14. At one time, radical economists argued that SLM arose during the transition from competitive to monopoly capitalism in the 1890s (Edwards *et al.*, 1975, p. 234), but that view has been largely abandoned: SLM are now seen to date back to the very earliest days of capitalism, and the passage of time has merely intensified the scope of labour stratification. This offers a totally different picture of the evolution of capitalism than is found in classical Marxism, which always regarded capitalism as bringing about the increasing homogeneity of labour and the continuous erosion of all differences in skills and earnings (Braverman, 1974; Rubery, 1981). Radical SLM theory argues that there are forces under capitalism which, on the contrary, bring about the increasing heterogeneity of labour (Gintis and Bowles, 1981; Gordon *et al.*, 1982).

15. Most of the key papers are found in three books of readings: Pascal (1972), Furstenberg *et al.* (1974), and Lloyd (1975).

16. See also three special issues of the *Review of Radical Political Economics* entirely devoted to the political economy of women: **4** (2), 1972; **8** (1), 1976; **9** (3), 1977; and **12** (2), 1980.

17. Radical analysis of education is not to be confused with the radical deschoolers, such as Ivan Illich or Paul Goodman, whose arguments are not linked to the differences between capitalism and socialism (see Gintis, 1972).

18. The argument was first broached in Gintis (1971), which ranks with Marglin (1976) as one of the classics of the radical literature; see also Edwards (1976) and Blackburn and Mann (1979, pp. 102–11).

19. See the special issue on imperialism, *Review of Radical Political Economics*, **11** (4), 1979, and compare it with a previous special issue on imperialism, **4**(1), 1972.

References

Albert, Michael, and Hahnel, Robin (1978), *Unorthodox Marxism. An Essay on Capitalism, Socialism and Revolution*, Boston: South End Press, 1978.

Albert, Michael (1981), *Socialism Today and Tomorrow*, Boston: South End Press.

Alchian, Armen A. and Demsetz, Harold (1972), 'Production, Information Costs, and Economic Organization', *American Economic Review*, **62** (5), pp. 777–95.

Althusser, Louis (1971), 'Ideology and Ideological State Apparatuses', *Lenin and Philosophy and Other Essays*, New York: Monthly Review Press, pp. 127–89.

Applebaum, Eileen (1977), 'Radical Economics' in S. Weintraub, (ed.), *Modern Economic Thought*, Oxford: Basil Blackwell, pp. 559–74.

Azariadis, Costas (1975), 'Implicit Contracts and Underemployment Equilibria', *Journal of Political Economy*, **83** (6), pp. 1183–202.

Barrett, Michèle (1980), *Women's Oppression Today: Problems in Marxist and Feminist Analysis*, London: Verso Editions.

Becker, Gary (1975), *Economics of Discrimination*, Chicago: University of Chicago Press.

Blackburn, Robert M. and Mann, Michael (1979), *The Working Class in the Labour Market*, London: Macmillan.

Blaug, Mark (1976), 'The Empirical Status of Human Capital Theory: A Slightly Jaundiced Survey', *Journal of Economic Literature*, **14** (3), pp. 827–55.

Blaug, Mark (1980a), *The Methodology of Economics*. London: Cambridge University Press.

Blaug, Mark (1980b), *A Methodological Appraisal of Marxian Economics*, Amsterdam: North-Holland Publishing (Chapters 1 and 2 above).

Block, Fred L. (1977), *The Origins of International Economic Disorder*, Berkeley: University of California Press.

Boddy, Raford and Crotty, James R. (1975), 'Class Conflict and Macro-Policy: The Political Business Cycle', *Review of Radical Political Economics*, 7(1), pp. 1–19.

Bose, Arun (1980), *Marx on Exploitation and Inequality: An Essay in Marxian Analytical Economics*, Delhi: Oxford University Press.

Bowles, Samuel (1981), 'Competitive Wage Determination and Involuntary Unemployment: A Conflict Model', Amherst: Department of Economics, University of Massachusetts (processed).

Bowles, Samuel and Gintis, Herbert (1975), 'The Problem with Human Capital Theory: A Marxian Critique', *American Economic Review*, **65** (2), pp. 74–82.

Bowles, Samuel (1976), *Schooling in Capitalist America: Educational Reform and the Contradictions of Economic Life*, New York: Basic Books.

Bowles, Samuel (1978), 'Class Power and Alienated Labor', *Monthly Review*, 1975; reprinted in *The Capitalist System: A Radical Analysis of American Society*, (2d. edn), eds. Edwards, Richard C., Reich, Michael, Weisskopf, Thomas E. Englewood Cliffs, New Jersey: Prentice-Hall, pp. 274–82.

Bowles, Samuel (1980), 'Education as a Site of Contradictions in the Reproduction of the Capital–Labor Relationship: Second Thoughts on the "Correspondence Principle". Amherst: Department of Economics, University of Massachusetts (processed).

Braverman, Harry (1974), *Labor and Monopoly Capital: The Degradation of Work in the Twentieth Century*, New York: Monthly Review Press.

Brewer, Anthony (1980), *Marxist Theories of Imperialism: A Critical Survey*, London: Routledge and Kegan Paul.

Bronfenbrenner, Martin (1970), 'Radical Economics in America, 1970', *Journal of Economic Literature*, **8** (3), pp. 747–66.

Bronfenbrenner, Martin (1975), 'A Harder Look at Alienation', *Capitalism and Freedom: Problems and Prospects*, ed. R.T. Selden. Charlottesville, Virginia: University Press of Virginia, pp. 197–218.

Cain, Glen C. (1976), 'The Challenge of Segmented Labor Market Theories to Orthodox Theory: A Survey', *Journal of Economic Literature*, **14** (4), pp. 1215–57.

Calva, Guillermo (1976), 'Quasi-Walrasian Theories of Unemployment', *American Economic Review*, **69** (2), pp. 102–7.

Carnoy, Martin (ed) (1972), *Schooling in a Corporate Society: The Political Economy of Education in America*, New York: David McKay.

Carnoy, Martin (1974), *Education as Cultural Imperialism.* New York: David McKay.

Carnoy, Martin (1980), 'Segmented Labour Markets', *Education, Work and Employment-II*, Paris: UNESCO-International Institute of Educational Planning.

Carnoy, Martin and Levin, Henry M. (1976), *The Limits of Educational Reform.* New York: Longmans.

Carnoy, Martin and Shearer, Derek (1980), *Economic Democracy: The Challenge of the 1980s*, White Plains, NY: M.E. Sharpe.

Cherry, Robert D. (1980), *Macroeconomics*, Reading, Mass.: Addison-Wesley Publishing.

Chiplin, Brian, and Coyne, John, (1980), 'Some Economic Issues of a Workers' Co-operative Economy' in A. Clayre (ed.), *The Political Economy of Co-Operation and Participation: A Third Sector*, London: Oxford University Press, pp. 119–40, 1980.

Clark, Gordon L., and Dear, Max (1981), 'The State in Capitalism and the Capitalist State' in M. Dear, A.J. Scott (eds), *Urbanization and Urban Planning*, New York: Methuen Press.

Crotty, James R., and Rapping, Leonard A. (1975), 'The 1975 Report of the President's Council of Economic Advisers: A Radical Critique', *American Economic Review*, **6** (5), pp. 791–811.

Deckard, Barbara S. (1979), *The Women's Movement: Political, Socioeconomic, and Psychological Issues*, (2nd edn.), New York: Harper and Row.

Edwards, Richard C. (1976), 'Individual Traits and Organizational Incentives: What Makes a "Good Worker"?', *Journal of Human Resources*, **11** (1), pp. 51–68.

Edwards, Richard C. (1979), *Contested Terrain: The Transformation of the Workplace in the Twentieth Century*. New York: Basic Books.

Edwards, Richard C., Reich, Michael and Gordon, David M. (1975), *Labor Market Segmentation.* Lexington, Mass.: D.C. Heath.

Edwards, Richard C., Reich, Michael, and Weisskopf, Thomas E. (eds.) (1972), *The Capitalist System: A Radical Analysis of American Society,* Englewood Cliffs, N.J.: Prentice-Hall (2nd edn.).

Elster, John (1979), *Ulysses and the Sirens: Studies in Rationality and Irrationality.* London: Cambridge University Press.

Espinosa, Juan G. and Zimbalist, Andrew S. (1978), *Economic Democracy: Workers' Participation in Chilean Industry 1970–1973*, New York: Academic Press.

Franklin, Raymond J. and Resnik, Solomon (1973), *The Political Economy of Racism*, New York: Holt, Rinehart & Winston.

Franklin, Raymond J. and Tabb, William K. (1977), 'The Challenge of Radical Political Economics', *Journal of Economic Issues*, **8**, pp. 127–50.

Friedman, Milton (1962), *Capitalism and Freedom*, Chicago: University of Chicago Press.

Furstenberg, George M. *et al.* (1974) *Patterns of Racial Discrimination*, Lexington, Mass.: D.C. Heath.

Furubotn, Erik G., and Pejovich, Svetozar (1972), 'Property Rights and Economic Theory: A Survey of Recent Literature', *Journal of Economic Literature*, **10** (4), pp. 1137–62.

Gintis, Herbert (1971), 'Education, Technology and the Characteristics of Worker Productivity', *American Economic Review*, **6** (2), pp. 266–79.

Gintis, Herbert (1972), 'Towards a Political Economy of Education: A Radical Critique of Ivan Illich's *Deschooling Society*', *Harvard Educational Review*, 42 (1), pp. 70–96.

Gintis, Herbert and Bowles, Samuel (1981), 'Structure and Practice in the Labor Theory of Value', *Review of Radical Political Economics*, **12** (4), pp. 1–26.

Gordon, David M. (1971), *Problems in Political Economy: An Urban Perspective*, Lexington, Mass.: D.C. Heath and Co.

Gordon, David M. (1972), *Theories of Poverty and Underemployment: Orthodox Radical, and Dual Labor Market Perspectives*, Lexington, Mass.: D.C. Heath and Co.

Gordon, David M. (1981), 'Capital–Labor Conflict and the Productivity Slowdown', *American Economic Review*, **71** (2), pp. 30–5.

Gordon, David M., Edwards, Richard C. and Reich, Michael (1982), *Segmented Work, Divided Workers: The Historical Transformation of Labor in the United States*, London: Cambridge University Press.

Gortz, André (1976), *The Division of Labour: The Labour Process and Class-Struggle in Modern Capitalism*, Hassocks, Sussex: Harvester Press.

Gough, Ian (1973), *The Political Economy of the Welfare State*, London: Macmillan.

Groenewegen, Peter D. (1979), 'Radical Economics in Australia: Surveys of the 1970s' in F.H. Gruen (ed.), *Surveys of Australian Economics, Vol. 2*, Sydney: Allen and Unwin, pp. 171–223.

Gurley, John G. (1971), 'The State of Political Economics', *American Economic Review*, **61** (2), pp. 53–62.

Harrington, Michael (1976), *The Twilight of Capitalism*, New York: Simon and Shuster.

Harris, Donald J. (1978), *Capitalism and Income Distribution*, London: Routledge and Kegan Paul.

Hartmann, Heidi (1981), 'The Unhappy Marriage of Marxism and Feminism: Towards a More Progressive Union', *Capital and Class*, 1979, reprinted in L. Sargent (ed.), *The Unhappy Marriage of Marxism and Feminism*, London: Pluto Press, pp. 1–41.

Hayek, Friedrich A. (1979), *Law, Legislation and Liberty*, vol. 3: *The Political Order of a Free People*. London: Routledge and Kegan Paul.

Heilbroner, Robert L. (1974), *An Inquiry into the Human Prospect*, New York: W.W. Norton.

Heilbroner, Robert L. (1976), *Business Civilization in Decline*, New York: W.W. Norton.

Hudson, John (1982), *Inflation*, London: Allen and Unwin.

Humphries, Jane (1980), 'Class Struggle and the Persistence of the Working-Class Family', *Cambridge Journal of Economics*, 1977, reprinted in A. Amsden, (ed.) *The Economics of Women and Work*, London: Penguin Books, pp. 140–65.

Hunius, Gerry, Garson, David G. and Case, John (1973), *Worker's Control. A Reader on Labor and Social Change*, New York: Vintage Books.

Hunt, Edward K. and Sherman, Howard J. (1978), *Economics: An Introduction to Traditional and Radical Views*. New York: Harper and Row.

Hyman, Richard (1974), 'Workers' Control and Revolutionary Thought' in R. Miliband and J. Saville (eds), *The Socialist Register 1974*, London: Merlin Press, pp. 241–78.

Jessop, Brian (1977), 'Recent Theories of the State', *Cambridge Journal of Economics*, **1**(4), pp. 353–73.

Kirzner, Israel M. (1973), *Competition and Entrepreneurship*, Chicago: University of Chicago Press.

Kirzner, Israel M. (1979), *Perception, Opportunity and Profit*, Chicago: University of Chicago Press.

Lazear, Edward P. (1981), 'Agency, Earnings Profiles, Productivity and Hours Restrictions', *American Economic Review*, **71** (4), pp. 606–20.

Lindbeck, Assar (1977), *The Political Economy of the New Left: An Outsider's View*. New York: Harper and Row, 1971 (2d. edn.).

Lindblom, Charles E. (1977), *Politics and Markets: The World's Political-Economic Systems*, New York: Basic Books.

Lloyd, Cynthia B. (1975), *Sex Discrimination and the Division of Labor*. New York: Columbia University Press.

Lloyd, Cynthia B., Andrews, Emily, and Gilroy, Curtis (eds) (1979), *Women in the Labor Market*. New York: Columbia University Press.

MacEwan, Arthur (1981), *Revolution and Economic Development in Cuba*, London: Macmillan Press.

Marglin, Steve (1975), 'What Do Bosses Do? Part II', *Review of Radical Political Economics*, **7** (3), pp. 43–54.

Marglin, Steve (1976), 'What Do Bosses Do? The Origins and Functions of Hierarchy in Capitalist Production', *Review of Radical Political Economics*, 1974, reprinted in A. Gortz. (ed.), *The Division of Labour*, Hassocks, Sussex: Harvester Press, pp. 13–54.

Meade, James E. (1975), 'The Theory of Labour-Managed Firms and of Profit Sharing', *Economic Journal*, 1972, reprinted in J. Vanek (ed.) *Self-Management*, London: Penguin Books.

Mermelstein, David (ed.) (1973), *Economics: Mainstream Readings and Radical Critique*, 1970, New York: Random House (2nd rev. edn.).

Miliband, Ralph, (1977), *Marxism and Politics*, Oxford: Oxford University Press.

Naples, Michele I. (1981), 'Industrial Conflict and Implications for Productivity Growth', *American Economic Review*, **71** (2), pp. 36–41.

North, Douglas C. (1981), *Structure and Change in Economic History*, New York: W.W. Norton.

O'Keeffe, Dennis J. (1981), 'Profit and Control: the Bowles and Gintis Thesis', *Curriculum Studies*, **10** (3), pp. 251–61.

O'Keeffe, Dennis J. (1979), 'Capitalism and Correspondence: A Critique of Marxist Analyses of Education', *Higher Education Review*, **12** (1), pp. 40–54.

Okun, Arthur M. (1981), *Prices and Quantities: A Macroeconomic Analysis*, Washington, DC: The Brookings Institution.

O'Mahoney, David (1979), 'Labour Management and the Market Economy', *Irish Journal of Business and Administrative Research*, **1** (1), pp. 16–41.

Owen, Roger, and Sutcliffe, Bob (eds) (1972), *Studies in the Theory of Imperialism*, London: Longman Group.

Palma, Gabriel (1978), 'Dependency: A Formal Theory of Underdevelopment, or a Methodology for the Analysis of Concrete Situations of Underdevelopment?', *World Development*, **6**, pp. 881–924.

Pascal, Anthony (ed.) (1972), *Racial Discrimination in Economic Life*, Lexington, Mass.: D.C. Heath.

Reich, Michael (1981), *Racial Inequality: A Political-Economic Analysis*, Princeton, NJ: Princeton University Press.

Reich, Michael(1981) and Devine, James (1981), 'The Microeconomics of Conflict and Hierarchy in Capitalist Production', *Review of Radical Political Economics*, **12** (4), pp. 27–45.

Rhodes, Robert (ed.) (1970), *Imperialism and Underdevelopment*, New York: Monthly Review Press.

Riddell, Tom, Samos, Steve and Shackleford, Jean (1979), *Economics: A Tool for Understanding Society*, Reading, Mass.: Addison-Wesley Publishing.

Roemer, John (1981), *Analytical Foundations of Marxian Economic Theory*, London: Cambridge University Press.

Roemer, John (1982), *A General Theory of Exploitation and Class*, Cambridge, Mass.: Harvard University Press.

Rosenberg, Sam (1979), 'A Survey of Empirical Work on Labor Market Segmentation', Davis: Department of Economics, University of California, Davis (processed).

Rosenberg, Sam and Weisskopf, Thomas E. (1981), 'A Conflict Approach to Inflation in the Postwar U.S. Economy', *American Economic Review*, **71** (2), pp. 42–7.

Rubery, Jill (1981), 'Structured Labour Markets, Worker Organisation and Low Pay', *Cambridge Journal of Economics*, 1978, reprinted in A. Amsden (ed.), *The Economics of Women and Work*, London: Penguin Books, pp. 242–70.

Samuelson, Paul A. (1980), *Economics*, (11th edn.) New York: McGraw-Hill.

Seers, Dudley (ed.) (1981), *Dependency Theory: A Critical Reassessment*, London: Frances Pinter.

Sherman, Howard J. (1972), *Radical Political Economy: Capitalism and Socialism from a Marxist–Humanist Perspective*, New York: Basic Books.

Sherman, Howard, J. (1976), *Stagflation: A Radical Theory of Unemployment and Inflation*, New York: Harper and Row.

Sokoloff, Natalie J. (1980), *Between Money and Love: The Dialectics of Women's Home and Market Work*, New York: Praeger.

Solow, Robert M. (1971), 'Discussion of 'The State of Political Economics' by John G. Gurley', *American Economic Review*, **61** (2), pp. 63–8.

Steedman, Ian (1977), *Marx after Sraffa*, London: New Left Books.

Steedman, Ian *et al.* (1981), *The Value Controversy*, London: Verso Editions and New Left Books.

Steinherr, Alfred, (1978), 'The Labor-Managed Economy: A Survey of the Economics Literature', *Annals of the Public and Co-operative Economy*, **7** (1), pp. 129–48.

Stone, Katherine (1975), 'The Origins of the Job Structures in the Steel Industry', *Review of Radical Political Economics*, 1974, reprinted in R.C. Edwards, M. Reich, D.M. Gordon, (eds), *Labor Market Segmentation*, Lexington, Mass.: D.C. Heath, pp. 113–73.

Thurow, Lester C. (1981), *The Zero-Sum Society: Distribution and the Possibilities for Economic Change*, London: Penguin Books.

Torrance, John (1977), *Estrangement, Alienation and Exploitation: A Sociological Approach to Historical Materialism*, London: Macmillan.

URPE (1975), *Radical Perspectives on the Economic Crisis of Monopoly Capitalism*, New York: Union of Radical Political Economics.

URPE (1977), *Reading List in Radical Political Economics*, New York: Union of Radical Political Economics.

Vaizey, John (1972), 'Radical Economist', *New Statesman*, 2 May, pp. 645.

Vanek, Jaroslav (ed.) (1975), *Self-Management: Economic Liberation of Man*, Penguin Modern Economics Readings, London: Penguin Books.

Vogel, Lisel (1981), 'Marxism and Feminism: Unhappy Marriage, Trial Separation or Something Else?' in L. Sargent (ed.) *Women and Revolution: The Unhappy Marriage of Marxism and Feminism*, London: Pluto Press, pp. 195–217.

Ward, Benjamin (1979), *The Ideal Worlds of Economics: Liberal, Radical and Conservative Economics World Views* (3 vols). New York: Basic Books.

Weisskopf, Thomas E. (1979), 'Marxian Crisis Theory and the Rate of Profit in the Postwar US Economy', *Cambridge Journal of Economics*, **3** (4), pp. 159–82.

Wilber, Charles (ed.) (1973), *The Political Economy of Development and Underdevelopment*, New York: Random House.

Wiles, Peter J.D. (1977), *Economic Institutions Compared*. Oxford: Basil Blackwell.

Williamson, Oliver A. (1975), *Markets and Hierarchies: Analysis and Antitrust Implications. A Study in the Economies of Internal Organization*, New York: The Free Press.

Wright, Oliver, (1979), *Class Structure and Income Determination*, New York: Academic Press.

4 Second thoughts on the Keynesian revolution*

The Keynesian revolution is one of the most remarkable episodes in the entire history of economic thought: certainly never before, and perhaps never since, has the economics profession been won over so rapidly and so massively to a new economic theory. Those who lived through it felt themselves impelled to repudiate virtually the whole of received economic doctrine, and many took up the Keynesian system with an ardour that is more commonly associated with religious conversions. Moreover, it was the younger generation who proved most susceptible to the Keynesian contagion and criticism of Keynes came almost solely from the older members of the profession. In short, the Keynesian revolution comes close to conforming to a 'scientific revolution' in the sense of Thomas Kuhn, involving a perception of theoretical crisis, the emergence of a new paradigm and a pronounced generation gap in the response of scientists to the clash of competing paradigms. This is how the story has often been told (e.g. Winch, 1969, pp. 175–7; Stanfield, 1974; Leijonhufvud, 1976, p. 83; Mehta, 1974, 1979). Unfortunately, these Kuhnian narratives provide few clues to account for the paradigm switch of the Keynesian revolution other than the accumulation of unspecified 'anomalies' in pre-Keynesian economies. I have argued in the past (Blaug, 1976, pp. 160–5) that the methodology of Imre Lakatos provides a better framework for characterizing the nature of the Keynesian revolution and, in particular, for explaining why the conversion to Keynesian economics was so swift and so widespread. This view has now been challenged by Douglas Hands (1985) and his criticisms provide me with the text for today's 'sermon'. I do not accept Hands's argument, but it certainly makes one think again about the Keynesian revolution, not to mention Lakatos' philosophy of science.

Did Keynes predict novel facts?

According to Lakatos, a scientific research programme wins professional approval when it is theoretically and, better still, empirically 'progressive'. Lakatos calls a research programme *'theoretically* progressive' when it has 'excess empirical content' over its rivals – that is, it predicts some 'novel, hitherto unexplained fact'; the programme is *'empirically* progressive' if this excess

* I want to thank Donald Moggridge, Don Patinkin, Robert Skidelsky and G. Keith Shaw for helpful comments on an earlier draft of this essay, which appeared in Italian in *Rasseggna Economica,* 4, Luglio-Agosto, 1978.

empirical content is also corroborated (Lakatos quoted in Blaug, 1980, p. 36). The concept of 'novel facts' is not unproblematic: it does not include facts which are known before a research programme is launched, particularly if these facts are deliberately used in the construction of the programme. Research programmes that merely rationalize known facts deserve litle applause; no doubt, such ingenuity has merit but it involves no 'progress' in knowledge in the sense of establishing the truth-value of a new research programme (Hands, 1985, pp. 5–8).

The Keynesian revolution was one of the great success stories in the history of economics. Yet, asks Hands, what were the novel facts predicted by Keynesian economics? It was not mass unemployment since there was nothing new about asserting the occurrence of unemployment in the 1930s and, besides, Keynes's *General Theory* was written precisely to explain that unemployment.[1] It was not the consumption function, the liquidity preference function and the marginal-efficiency-of-capital investment function because these concepts, and the facts associated with them, were all used explicitly in the construction of Keynesian theory. In short, the Keynesian system explained known facts and did not predict genuinely novel facts. Hence, Hands concludes, the Keynesian programme was not 'progressive' in the strict sense of Lakatos and, by that same standard, the overwhelming professional acceptance of Keynesian economics in the 1930s was simply 'irrational'. It thus follows that we must abandon Lakatos' strictly empirical criterion for theoretical progress, as well as Lakatos' 'internalist' explanation of professional success, at least in a subject like economics.

This is the nub of Hands's case.[2] He takes the story of the Keynesian revolution for granted and uses it to throw doubt on Lakatos' rules of methodological appraisal. We will instead take Lakatos' philosophy of science for granted and use it to throw fresh light on the Keynesian revolution.

What was the anomaly that Keynes explained?
Let us begin, however, by giving Hands's argument a run for its money. We will discard Lakatos' standard of scientific progress and assert that Keynes attracted followers and disciples in large numbers simply because he provided a more ingenious explanation of mass unemployment than did his orthodox contemporaries. I choose my words carefully. It is frequently said that pre-Keynesian or so-called 'classical economics' could not explain the unemployment of the 1930s (see, for example, Skidelsky, 1975, p. 90; Patinkin, 1982, p. 19; Tobin, 1987, pp. 265, 396). But this is careless language because there was never any problem about 'explaining' unemployment with the aid of pre-Keynesian theory by drawing on the general notion of 'frictions' or market imperfections. In particular, unemployment could be explained in orthodox terms by real wages being held above market-clearing levels, by protective tariffs, by an overvalued currency (at least in the case of British unemployment before 1931), by rigid prices due to

monopolies and cartels, by misguided monetary policies, and so forth (see Samuelson, 1985, p. 286). [3]

It is true, however, that, in the United States from 1929 down to the trough of the depression in 1933, both money and real wages had fallen sharply at the same time as American unemployment had worsened. The British data were more ambiguous – relative constancy of money wages and gently rising real wages – but nevertheless it was the worldwide persistence of unemployment in the 1930s that gradually sapped confidence in the orthodox explanations (Patinkin, 1976, pp. 17, 121; 1982, pp. 18–19). Thus, it is possible to argue that Keynesian economics gave a more convincing explanation of protracted mass unemployment than did orthodox theory and that is why it so quickly won over a large part of the professional academic community. In other words, although Keynesian economics predicted no genuinely 'novel facts' it provided a better explanation of the known facts, or at least provided an explanatory schema that made the known facts more probable. [4]

After all, one could argue that even Newton's famous theory of gravitation, the most successful scientific research programme of all time, only rationalized certain well known facts about the elliptical paths of planets, the phases of the moon, the occurrence of tides, the trajectory of bullets fired out of cannons – and, of course, the rates at which apples fall from trees! Newton predicted no novel facts; he merely 'saved appearances' by fitting facts familiar to his contemporaries by means of an exact mathematical generalization – namely, the inverse square law. His achievement was to incorporate many old facts drawn from different areas within one and the same theoretical framework; he furnished what William Whewell called a 'consilience of inductions' that so often has the power of throwing fresh light on old problems. In the decades following the publication of Newton's *Principia* in 1687, improved telescopic observations revealed minor deviations of planetary motion from absolutely elliptical orbits and these proved to be calculable *ex post facto* with the aid of Newtonian physics. However, it was only when Edmund Halley's prediction of the return of 'Halley's comet' was confirmed in 1758 that Newtonian theory finally produced a clinching novel prediction that had not been used in the very construction of the Newtonian system. Newton's triumph was completed 23 years later when William Herschel used the inverse square law to discover Uranus, a trick that was repeated in the middle of the nineteenth century for Neptune and in the twentieth century for Pluto.

None of this counts in any way against a Lakatosian description of the Newtonian revolution, because it took as much as 40 to 50 years to achieve something like universal acceptance of the Newtonian system throughout European scientific circles (Kuhn, 1957, p. 259; Cohen, 1980, pp. 141ff, 1985, pp. 167–79). However, the same argument fails in the case of the Keynesian revolution because it took at most 12 years and, on some criteria, only five or six years to win the approval of the vast majority of economists throughout the world. It is always arbitrary to date the completion of an intellectual revolution but one obvious and simple measure is the number of years it takes for a new research programme to be incorporated into elementary textbooks. The first textbook of elementary economics to expound the Keynesian system was *The Elements of Economics* (1947) by Lorie Tarshis. It failed to catch on, probably because it stuck too closely to Keynes's own exposition in *The General Theory*. The same year saw the publication of *The Keynesian Revolution* (1947) by Lawrence Klein and *The New Economics: Keynes Influence on Theory and Policy* (1947), an influential collection of papers about Keynesian economics edited by Seymour Harris. But it was the appearance of Paul Samuelson's *Economics: An Introductory Analysis* (1948), 12 years after the publication of *The General Theory*, that marked the final triumph of Keynesianism. Samuelson had invented the 45-degree cross diagram in 1939 in which Keynesian schedules of consumption-plus-investment intersect with a 45-degree line to determine the 'underemployment equilibrium' level of income (Ambrosi, 1981; Patinkin, 1982, p. 9n); he used it now to teach Keynesian economics to literally millions of students through what was to become the most successful economics textbook of all times. It took many more years for Keynes to conquer professional opinion in West Germany, Italy and France but in the United States and Britain the battle was definitely won by 1948.[5]

Some would argue that the apotheosis of Keynes came even earlier in 1944 when the UK White Paper on *Employment Policy*, William Beveridge's *Full Employment in a Free Society* and *The Economics of Full Employment. Six Studies in Applied Economics* by the Oxford Institute of Statistics followed one another in quick succession within the space of nine months. One might even claim that the battle was won even earlier, in 1941 or 1942, since the 1941 British budget was conceived entirely along Keynesian lines and Roosevelt's economic advisors in the White House were by then deeply committed to the Keynesian framework (Stein, 1969, pp. 165–8; Jones, 1972). At any rate, such opposition to Keynes as existed among academic economists, civil servants and government advisors virtually disappeared during the Second World War, which indeed proved to be something like a laboratory experiment in the effectiveness of Keynesian ideas of demand management. Thus, it is the amazing rapidity of the Keynesian ascendancy that poses the problem for any convincing account of the Keynesian revolution. Moreover, while thinkers like Michael Kalecki, Bertil Ohlin and Gunnar Myrdal had been working along similar lines as Keynes, none of them in fact anticipated the central message of Keynesian economics (Patinkin, 1982, chs. 2, 3). In other words, the Keynesian revolution is *not* another example of a multiple discovery in economics; and that only deepens the puzzle of why Keynes gained so many adherents in so short a time.

The ingredients of Keynes's success

Still staying outside the Lakatosian framework, let us briefly review the standard explanation for Keynes's rapid success. At one time in the early bloom of the Keynesian revolution it was common to attribute Keynes's triumph quite simply to his superior policy proposals: orthodox economists offered no remedies for the depression except a balanced budget and an all-round deflation to force down real wages; only Keynes advocated a deliberately unbalanced budget and compensatory spending on public works. [6] More recent historical research (Schlesinger, 1956; Stein, 1969; Winch, 1969; Davis, 1971; Howson and Winch, 1977; Hutchison, 1978, chs. 5, 6; Corry, 1978; Collard, 1981; Peden, 1983, 1984, 1988; Blaug, 1985, pp. 671–6; Garside, 1987) has thoroughly undermined this mythical picture of Keynes as a 'voice crying in the wilderness'. Much of the mythology that still surrounds popular accounts of the Keynesian revolution relies on disguising the radical difference in the state of pre-Keynesian economics in the United States and Britain. There were American contractionists like Schumpeter and James Angell and moderate expansionists like Alvin Hansen and Wesley Clair Mitchell who favoured monetary over fiscal measures, but the majority of American economists strongly supported a public works programme financed by open-market sales of government bonds and went out of their way to attack the concept of an annually balanced budget as an old-fashioned dogma (Stoneman, 1979). Indeed, the erosion of the shibboleth of balanced budgets and the adoption of the doctrine of 'spending America out of depression' – what Herbert Stein has called 'the fiscal revolution in America' – had been virtually completed in Washington circles by 1936 without the benefit of Keynes's *General Theory* (Stein, 1969, pp. 131–3; Winch, 1969, ch. 11). Moreover, the American experience with wage deflation discouraged any belief in the efficacy of wage-cutting as a cure for unemployment even among the conservative critics of the New Deal. In short, American economists inside and outside the universities generally favoured policies both before and after 1936 which we would now think of as Keynesian – and the same is true of West Germany and the Scandinavian countries (Garvey, 1975; Patinkin, 1982, ch. 2; Andvig, 1983, chs. 11, 12; Hudson, 1985).

Almost as much might be said of Britain except that the depressed conditions of the 1920s, in contrast to the great American boom of that decade, and the return to the gold standard at the prewar parity between 1925 and 1931 produced somewhat greater diversity of policy recommendations among British than among American economists. Besides, the case for wage-cutting as a cure for unemployment was always better for Britain than for the United States, first because real wages had declined much less in the 1930s in Britain than in the USA (Capie, 1987) and, second, because Britain was more of an open economy than the USA – a point that Keynes (1936, p. 263) himself made. In addition, the gap between official thinking in Whitehall and the academic community of economists was much greater in Britain than in the United States. The 'Treasury view' that public spending must crowd out private investment and thus leave aggregate demand no greater than before had no standing among British academic economists, as Keynes always admitted, but was indeed firmly held by Treasury officials all through the 1930s (Howson and Winch, 1977, ch. 5; Davis, 1971, pp. 217–18; Middleton, 1985, ch. 8, particularly pp. 171–2, 1987). In consequence, Britain alone among the major Western industrial nations eschewed any hint of public works and deficit finance to promote domestic recovery in the 1930s and instead relied on cheap money, high tariffs, devaluation and a number of supply-side policies. There had long been wide support among British economists for loan-financed public works but the overvalued pound in the late 1920s produced a small school of 'structuralists', such as Arthur Pigou, Edwin Cannan and Henry Clay, who attributed unemployment to real wages being too high, especially in the declining staple industries. Although they were not short of explanations for the failure of real wages to decline – the recent rise of union membership, the real wage floor associated with the introduction of unemployment insurance and the regional immobility of labour – they regarded it as impractical to advocate wage cuts; their policy recommendations therefore took the form of arguing for the 'rationalization' of declining industries and subsidies to promote greater mobility of labour (Casson, 1983, chs. 2, 3, 8). These structuralist arguments largely faded away after Britain left the gold standard in 1931, only to be replaced by the Austrian monetary overinvestment theories of the business cycle advocated by Hayek and Robbins.

According to Austrian theory, slumps are the necessary consequence of the 'forced saving' resulting from undue credit expansion in the previous boom and should be allowed to run their course in order to give way to the healthy boom that will inevitably follow. The protracted nature of the interwar slump in Britain was explained by the collapse of the gold standard and the proliferation of wage and price-fixing arrangements that had undermined the natural recuperative powers of the economy. This view, perfectly represented by Lionel Robbins's *The Great Depression* (1934), concluded that wage-cutting, however desirable, was inexpedient and, besides, it was the inflexibility of all prices and not just wages that exacerbated the depression. Little followed from all this in the way of practical action but the conditions for recovery, Robbins seemed to suggest, were a return to free trade, a stable currency based on the gold standard and institutional reform attacking the myriad ways in which governments promoted monopolies and cartels. The Hayek–Robbins viewpoint fell on deaf ears and attracted so little attention that Keynes, in *The General Theory*, did not even bother to mention either Hayek's *Prices and Production* (1931) or Robbins's *The Great Depression*,[7] choosing instead to direct all his ammunition against Pigou's highly abstract and profoundly obscure *Theory of Unemployment* (1933) (Collard, 1981, pp. 122–32). Of course, there was no single canonical text that characterized the whole of British economic thinking on anti-depression policies[8] and so Keynes invented a straw man of 'classical economics' to dramatize the battle with orthodoxy and to convey a heady flavour of iconoclasm (Hutchison,1978, ch. 5; Corry, 1978). In summary, it is fair to say that there was a pre-Keynesian orthodoxy on policy matters in Britain – free trade, the gold standard, balanced budgets, debt redemption, and structural reforms – but it was a creed of bankers, businessmen, civil servants and politicians, not of academic economists. The economists were largely in agreement on everything except free trade and, in any case, were at pains to sink their differences in favour of such proposals as easy money and loan-financed public works (Howson and Winch, 1977, pp. 161–3).

The very first sentence of the preface to *The General Theory* announces that it is a book addressed to Keynes's fellow economists and therefore that 'its main purpose is to deal with difficult questions of theory and only in the second place with the applications of this theory to practice'. Thus, Keynes attacked 'classical' economists not because they disagreed with him about action to remedy the slump but because he thought that they were wedded to ideas which were inconsistent with the policies they were advocating. What he sought was capitulation on the theoretical front and, as he said in the famous letter to George Bernard Shaw, he was certain that he would achieve it 'not, I suppose, at once but in the course of the next 10 years', a prediction that proved to be perfectly accurate. The principal theoretical features of Keynesian economics have been described so frequently that we need merely list them to remind us: a shift from micro– to macroeconomics; from the long period to the short period; from real to monetary analysis; and from the variation of prices to the variation of quantities as the central objects of analysis. Both consumption and saving are taken to be stable functions of income, but investment is treated at least partly as autonomous, inherently volatile, and subject to pervasive uncertainty; saving and investment are said to be carried out by different people for different reasons and are only brought into equilibrium by changes of income itself; the rate of interest is explained purely in monetary terms as a function of the stock demand for money interacting with an exogenously determined supply of money; real wages are treated as determined by the volume of employment rather than vice versa; and so forth. At the base of the entire schema is the 'Great Heresy' that an equilibrium level of income and output need not correspond to a situation of full employment and, indeed, that the economy is very likely to get stuck in a low-level equilibrium trap, there being no spontaneous, self-adjusting mechanism that will necessarily drive the economy to employ the entire labour force and to utilize the capital stock to full capacity. There is no doubt about the fact that it was this heresy, combined with Keynes's demonstration of the 'paradox of thrift', that gave Keynesian economics its subversive, left-wing colouration and which earned it so much obloquy from conservatives, particularly in the United States (see, for example, Hazlitt, 1960; Hutt, 1963; and Collins, 1981). In places in *The*

General Theory Keynes (1936, p. 373) went so far as to suggest that the poor have higher marginal propensities to consume than the rich, implying that output, and hence employment, could be raised by redistributing income. In addition, he suggested that capitalism when left to its own devices was doomed to secular stagnation, not just in the distant, but possibly in the near, future (Keynes, 1936, pp. 217–21, 324, 347–8). No wonder *The General Theory* proved irresistible to young economists, radicalized by years of depression.[9]

Even all this, however, does not suffice to explain the fundamental appeal of *The General Theory*. One of Keynes's critical analytical decisions in moving away from his *Treatise on Money* (1930) towards *The General Theory* (1936) was to abandon the type of sequence or period analysis that characterized monetary economics and much of the business cycle literature of the 1920s and, instead, to adopt static equilibrium analysis in which all the relevant variables of the model refer to a single period of time. It was this decision to handle essentially dynamic problems with a static apparatus that led him to define income, saving and investment in such a way as to make saving identically equal to investment, which related investment and income via the consumption function and which in turn defined the instantaneous multiplier as the reciprocal of the marginal propensity to save. It is true that the use of the equilibrium method confused many of his earlier readers who were accustomed to price theory employing comparative statics and monetary theory employing period analysis, but it was precisely this heterodox use of static equilibrium analysis applied to a monetary economy that was out of equilibrium that gave Keynes's theory its rigour and simplicity (Kohn, 1986).

In addition, Keynes worked hard to define all his variables in operational terms, relating them whenever possible to actual or potentially available data, and in so doing rode on the back of the statistical revolution that was already well on the way when *The General Theory* was published. Colin Clark's *The National Income 1924–1931* (1932) and Simon Kuznets's *National Income 1929–32* (1934) testify to a tradition of national income accounting that pre-dates the publication of *The General Theory*. Nevertheless, Keynes's treatment of income as the chief determinant of consumption and the importance assigned in his theory to final outlays of consumption and investment, not to mention the one-period definitions of saving and investment, gave an enormous stimulus to the statistical measurement of income and outlays. Official estimates of national income appeared first in the United States in 1935, the year before *The General Theory*. By 1939, official and unofficial estimates were available for 33 countries and it is no accident that the first official estimates in the United Kingdom were prepared in 1940 by James Meade and Richard Stone, two of Keynes's disciples, stimulated by Keynes's own casual use of national income estimates to analyse the prospective inflationary gap in *How To Pay for the War* (1940) (Patinkin, 1982, pp. 230–60). By the end of the Second World War, official national income accounts appeared in almost all industrialized countries and were invariably presented in the Y = C+I+G rubric of Keynesian economics.

There was a pre-Keynesian macroeconomics, made up partly of the quantity theory of money and partly of various theories of the business cycle. The quantity theory of money was directed at explaining dramatic changes in the level of prices and provided a general framework for analysing the relationships between the supply of money, the demand for money, the flow of expenditures and the level of real output; however, its power was purely descriptive and it had no definite, unambiguous policy implications. The business cycle literature, on the other hand, was unrelated both in form and substance to orthodox price theory and represented a veritable morass of contending explanations of the periodicity of business fluctuations in terms of real and monetary factors; it was not only contentious, it was complex and it was cast almost entirely in non-operational terms, such as the degree of 'roundaboutness' of the economy, the level of hoarding and dishoarding, forced saving, overindebtedness, underconsumption, and the like.[10]

Keynes achieved a drastic simplification of macroeconomics or, more cynically expressed, he achieved the optimum level of difficulty for intellectual success: not so simple as to be immediately accessible without personal effort and yet not so complex as virtually to defy comprehension (Johnson, 1978, pp. 188–9).[11] But an essential additional ingredient in the success of *The General Theory* was its open-endedness and sheer fecundity. Keynes was no Walrasian; yet his system lent itself readily to a general equilibrium formulation. The famous Hicks–Hansen IS–LM version of Keynes, according to which the equilibrium level of national income and the rate of interest are determined simultaneously in the market for goods and the market for bonds, captures only part of *The General Theory* but is nevertheless a perfectly legitimate realization of some of Keynes' own thinking.[12] Similarly, Keynes was fond of the method of overkill or arriving at the same conclusion from several different angles. Thus, Chapter 17 of *The General Theory* on 'The Essential Properties of Interest and Money' seeks to produce the central Keynesian conclusion that 'underemployment equilibrium' is possible without the aid of any of the building blocks developed in the previous 16 chapters. Likewise, Chapter 19 on the 'Changes in Money-Wages' resorts to as many as seven different arguments intended to demonstrate the impracticability and undesirability of depressing money wages as a cure for unemployment.[13] *The General Theory* is littered with digressions, puzzles requiring solution and a wealth of theoretical hints awaiting further development. And this efflorescence of ideas – a sense of the cup running over – was one of the elements in its appeal. It was a poorly constructed book that frequently reads more like a set of random notes than like a systematic treatise, but even this quality of undue haste only enhanced its intellectual effectiveness.

Keynes's novel predictions

We have now accounted for the Keynesian revolution. Or have we? According to Lakatos, 'rational' economists in the 1930s would have switched allegiance from orthodox to Keynesian economics if and only if Keynesian economics was perceived to be a progressive scientific research programme – that is, one that predicted novel facts. But it is not self-evident that Keynesian economics predicted *any* novel facts. We recall that this is the burden of Hands' criticism of Lakatos and we must now meet this criticism head-on.

The principal novel prediction of Keynesian economics is that the value of the instantaneous multiplier is greater than unity and that the more than proportionate impact of an increase in investment on income applies just as much to public as to private investment, and indeed just as much to consumption as to investment spending; in other words, fiscal policy is capable, at least in principle, of raising real income up to the full employment ceiling within a single time period. The notion that a government can spend its way out of depression pre-dated Keynes's *General Theory* and derived from the quantity theory of money, at least in its short-run version. As early as the eighteenth century, David Hume had argued the doctrine of the benefits of creeping inflation: a steady continual increase in the supply of money is partly transmitted to real output and is therefore not simply inflationary. The monetary writing of Knut Wicksell and Marshall's pupils, including the young Keynes himself, had long familiarized economists with the short-run, disequilibrium interpretation of the quantity theory of money; in fact, this was the standard pre-Keynesian framework for demonstrating the efficacy of a loan-financed public works programme. The trouble was that the argument was loose and imprecise and hence was vulnerable to objections based either on the 'Treasury View' or on the sheer administrative costs of mounting such schemes at short notice.

Keynes learned from Richard Kahn how to calculate, however crudely, a precise value for the income multiplier and, in so doing, he placed the case for demand management on an entirely new footing by making it seem incontrovertible. It required only the notion of consumption as a stable function of income and *The General Theory*'s definition of saving and investment as two sides of the same coin and it followed, as a matter of logic, that any increase in real income and employment could be achieved by a sufficiently large autonomous increase in either consumption, investment or government expenditure. This was a novel prediction not in the sense that it was unknown before Keynes's *General Theory* but that it was an unsuspected implication of the concept of the consumption function combined with the peculiar Keynesian definitions of saving and investment; and not just any consumption function but one in which the marginal propensity to consume lies between zero and one, is smaller than the average propensity to consume and declines as income rises.[14] These three characteristics of the Keynesian consumption function were simply asserted by Keynes in *The*

General Theory but all three mini-predictions were in fact confirmed in 1942 by the first set of comprehensive national product data for the United States (Ackley, 1961, p. 225).

The same thing is not true of the greater-than-unity value of the expenditure multiplier, which was Keynes's principal prediction. Keynes himself estimated the British multiplier to be 1.5, but many of his disciples produced estimates in 1938, 1939 and 1941 of between 2.0 and 3.0 and, in one case, of even more than 3.0 (Middleton,1985, pp. 176–8). Because of various leakages into taxes and imports as well as savings, and the slow rate at which the secondary and tertiary effects show up, the true figure is perhaps only just in excess of unity (Klein, 1966, pp. 41, 216). In consequence, some revisionist historians have recently expressed doubts about Keynes's remedies in the circumstances of the 1930s, arguing that the structural rigidities of the prewar British economy and the low value of the impact multiplier would have required so large a fiscal stimulus designed to produce full employment as virtually to imply physical planning on a wartime scale (Middleton, 1985, pp. 176–80, 182–3; Hatton, 1987; Booth, 1987; O'Brien, 1987; Glynn, 1987).[15] But we are not arguing that the Keynesian research programme was '*empirically* progressive' either before or after the Second World War, but only that it was '*theoretically* progressive' – namely, that it predicted facts that were genuinely novel.

It may be convincingly argued that the Keynesian system was never put to the test before the war, that budgetary deficits in the 1930s were never large enough to produce the Keynesian results, in short that 'Hitler's was the only New Deal that actually succeeded in eliminating unemployment' (Skidelsky, 1977, p. 36; Bleaney, 1985, ch. 2), but that in no way affects the point I am making: *The General Theory* gained adherents because Keynes made a novel prediction that seemed highly likely to be true. The virtual disappearance of unemployment during the Second World War provided, rightly or wrongly, what was perceived to be a dramatic corroboration of the central Keynesian prediction. In the same way, the full employment and overfull employment conditions of the 1950s and 1960s were everywhere attributed to the deliberate pursuit by governments of Keynesian policies, although it was in fact private investment that filled the postwar gap in effective demand (Bleaney, 1985, ch. 4). In other words, the evidence for Keynes's central prediction is not compelling even now but that is simply to say that what it is rational to accept at one time in history is not necessarily rational 20, 30 or 40 years later.

One may well ask how it is that I *know* that it was this central prediction about the expenditure multiplier that was decisive in converting the profession to Keynesianism? Alas, despite the well known studies of Klein, Harrod, Winch, Howson and Winch, and Patinkin,[16] we still lack a blow-by-blow account of the Keynesian revolution to which to refer the sceptic. However, a reading of the six great expositions of the 'new' economics by Abba Lerner, Roy Harrod, James

Meade, John Hicks, Oscar Lange and Joan Robinson that appeared within 18 months of the publication of *The General Theory* leaves no doubt that the practical upshot of Keynes's theoretical argument for each of them is that full employment is achievable via fiscal deficits.[17] The dozen or so reviews that appeared in the same years, 1936 and 1937, some of which were distinctly hostile to Keynes's ideas, would supply further supporting evidence (see Wood, 1983).

If this much is accepted, it follows that it may be a mistake to insist, as I myself have done in the past, that the Keynesian revolution was a *theoretical* revolution and not a normative revolution in the policy prescriptions of economists. Despite the opening lines of the preface to *The General Theory*, Schumpeter (1936, p. 92) was quite right when he said in a review of *The General Theory* that 'everywhere he [Keynes] really pleads for a definite policy, and on every page the ghost of that policy looks over the shoulder of the analyst, frames his assumptions, guides his pen'. This in no way denies the Patinkin thesis that the distinguishing analytical characteristic of Keynesian economics is that idea that it is the change in output or income itself that equilibrates aggregate demand and aggregate supply or, alternatively expressed, that autonomous investment, whether private or public, necessarily finances itself via changes in the level of income (Patinkin, 1982, pp. 9–11). But it is easy to see that this fundamental proposition leads immediately to the implication that fiscal policy must be capable of generating a full employment level of income.

There are many other novel facts predicted by *The General Theory*, some of which were influential in attracting additional adherents to Keynesianism, such as that there are significant differences in the marginal propensities to consume of households defined by their income levels, that the interest-elasticity of investment is very low, that on the contrary the interest-elasticity of the demand for money is very high, and, finally, that the community's average propensity to consume tends to decline as national income rises, indicating that the threat of secular stagnation in mature economies will get worse as they grow richer. It turned out eventually that aggregate consumption and saving is relatively insensitive to changes in the distribution of income (Ackley, 1961, pp. 240–6) but in the 1930s young American Keynesians like George Hildebrand, Lorie Tarshis and Paul Sweezy placed as much emphasis on income redistribution as on deficit spending as a way out of the depression (Gilbert, 1938). Similarly, Keynes himself never ceased to believe that investment was sufficiently responsive to reductions in the rate of interest to make monetary policy a potent instrument for raising employment additional to fiscal policy. But a number of empirical studies by young British Keynesians soon showed that the interest-elasticity of investment was not much greater than zero (Klein, 1966, pp. 65–6) and this encouraged the belief that Keynesianism was tantamount to the thesis that private investment is bound to fall short of full employment. Last, stagnationism was a constant theme in the Keynesian literature and, in the influential writings of Alvin Hansen, was converted into the very essence of the Keynesian message.[18] To show how widely stagnationism was held it is only necessary to mention that it was primarily responsible for the almost universal belief among economists in 1945 that the postwar era would commence with a sharp slump. The doctrine that industrialized countries in the twentieth century faced a chronic deficiency of effective demand because private investment was bound to fall behind full-employment savings was one of Keynes's novel predictions, which led him to recommend the 'comprehensive socialisation of investment' as a possibly permanent feature of the economic landscape; it was a false prediction and it was not essential to Keynesian economics but it was nevertheless a novel prediction as novelty is defined by Lakatos.

Another one of Keynes's erroneous predictions of a novel fact was the proposition that the average propensity to save is a declining function of income, a prediction which was unambiguously confirmed by cross-section budget studies of family expenditure patterns, which literally exploded in the late 1930s and early 1940s (see Mack, 1952, p. 65n). Then in 1946, Kuznets's *National Product Since 1869* brought home the distinction between cross-section data that confirmed and time-series data that refuted the prediction of a negative association between the saving–income ratio and the level of national income. The attempt to reconcile this contradiction resulted in the Duesenberry relative income hypothesis, the Modigliani–Bromberg life-cycle hypothesis and the Friedman permanent-income hypothesis, spanning more than a decade of theoretical and empirical work on the savings function inspired by Keynes's *General Theory* (Ackley, 1961, pp. 238–46).

Keynes had deliberately assumed a closed economy in *The General Theory* but the spending multiplier works just as well on the spending of foreigners on exports as on domestic spending. That the foreign trade multiplier is typically greater than unity and that income effects are quantitatively more important than price effects in bringing the balance of payments into equilibrium are other novel predictions of the Keynesian system, which followers of Keynes soon explored (for example, Metzler, 1942; Machlup, 1943) even if Keynes himself ignored them. The invention of the Phillips Curve in 1958, and the manner in which it was grafted on to Keynesian economics, is yet another example of the amazing fertility of the Keynesian system.[19] Of course, we have now moved well beyond the year 1948 which, we earlier argued, marked the completion of the Keynesian revolution as a process of gaining the endorsement of the economics profession. But it is worth remembering that there is a sense in which the Keynesian revolution is still going on. After degenerating in the 1960s and being virtually supplanted by monetarism, Keynesian economics has made a comeback in recent years.[20] The proliferation of implicit contract and principal agency theories of labour markets, not to mention quantity-constrained Walrasian and non-Walrasian disequilibrium theories, are all designed to explain the failure of labour markets to clear in the face of unemployment, – in short to give a new answer to the old Keynesian question. The spectre of Keynes continues to haunt macroeconomics as shown by the endless books and articles on 'what Keynes really meant', 'should have meant', and 'must have meant'.[21]

Conclusion

Keynes's consumption function, the downward sloping liquidity preference function and the downward sloping investment demand function were not themselves 'novel facts' because they were also used explicitly in the construction of the Keynesian system. Nevertheless, when interpreted in a particular way, they can be employed to predict novel facts, such as that a cut in money wages will have little effect on aggregate demand, that an increase in government expenditure will have a large, or at least a more than proportionate, effect on aggregate demand, and that a given increase in government expenditure financed by an equal increase in tax receipts will raise national income by the same amount as that given increase – the balanced budget multiplier is unity.[22] It was the prediction of these and other novel facts that allows us to describe the Keynesian research programme as 'progressive' and that accounts for the rapid approval of Keynesian economics by the majority of the economics profession.

Naturally, economists were shell-shocked by the Great Depression. They wanted action to induce a recovery and they were more or less agreed that loan-financed public works would accomplish that result. But the legacy of inherited theory was not focused on problems of output and employment. Thus, one might be tempted to say that Keynesian economics succeeded because it rationalized the policy conclusions that most economists wanted to advocate anyway. But that can at best explain a predisposition to give Keynesian economics a favourable hearing, not its wholehearted endorsement. That requires that other methodological criteria, such as simplicity, tractability, elegance, generality and fertility, are satisfied and that, in addition, the Keynesian schema promises to predict observable events with greater accuracy than its orthodox rivals. That particular expectation was fulfilled, rightly or wrongly, by the experiences of the Second World War, but long before that Keynesian economics had made its novel predictions appear extremely likely. This was an irresistible recipe for professional success, particularly as Keynesian economics sought not so much to supplant orthodox economics as to complement it; as Keynes said repeatedly in *The General Theory*, once full employment is achieved, 'classical economics' comes back into its own.

What makes economists adopt a new research programme? Economics is not physics; it is not just a body of substantive findings about the economy but also a policy science and is therefore influenced by the value judgements and political preconceptions of economists. Nevertheless, new economic doctrines do not find a ready audience among economists unless they can promise to produce new findings about the economy that are eventually confirmed by experience or by historical and statistical analysis. Thus, it was not just ideology, an animus against capitalism, a desire to cock a snook at the older generation, or simply a preference for something new that drove economists into the Keynesian camp. Keynes had caught a measure of substantive truth about the workings of an economic system that had not been vouchsafed to his predecessors. It was, therefore, perfectly 'rational', in the strict sense of Lakatos, for economists in the 1930s to have adopted Keynesian economics.

Notes

1. In my earlier paper (1976, p. 162) I made the mistake of citing 'the chronic tendency of competitive market economies to generate unemployment' as Keynes's principal novel prediction. This may have been a Kuhnian 'anomaly' but it is not a 'novel fact' in the sense of Lakatos.

2. Hands (1985, pp. 10–12) also cites the development of general equilibrium theory since 1930 as another strike against Lakatos and indeed as *'the fundamental enigma* to any rationalizing methodology'. Since then Weintraub (1985) has tried to meet Hands' argument by contending that general equilibrium analysis forms the empirically immune 'hard core' of a progressive research programme called neoclassical economics and that the mathematical analyses of the existence and stability of equilibrium over the last 50 years represent a 'hardening' of that hard core. In this way, Weintraub accommodates Walrasian general equilibrium theory to the Lakatosian framework. I am not altogether convinced by Weintraub's argument but that is a question for another day and another essay.

3. As Schumpeter (1946, p. 71) said:

   I have sometimes wondered why Keynes attached so much importance to providing that there may – and under his assumptions generally will – be less than full employment in *perfect equilibrium of perfect competition.* For there is such an ample supply of verifiable explanatory factors to account for the actual unemployment we observe at any time that only the theorist's ambition can induce us to wish for more.

4. Some such answer to Hands may be read into Samuelson (1985, pp. 289–90).

5. I know of no study of the diffusion of Keynesian economics in different countries but in Italy, for example, it was not until the 1960s that Keynesian economics was fully accepted by most Italian economists. Keynes was rejected by all the leading prewar Italian economists, such as Luigi Einaudi, Constantino Bresciani Turroni, Giovanni Demaria and Giuseppe Papi, and this resistance continued even after the Second World War. The first Italian textbook to incorporate Keynesian theory was F. Di Fenizio, *Economia politica* (1949) but this stood out for that very reason among the older texts then in use (see Fusco, 1964, 1984).

6. See Lekachman (1967) and Stewart (1967) for examples of such mythmaking; it is interesting to compare the first edition of Stewart (1967) with the third edition (1986, particularly chs. 3, 4, 5), which takes account of some of the recent scholarship on the 1930s. Robinson and Eatwell (1973, p. 47) manage to cram at least five of these myths into one page.

7. 'It is from their writings [Hayek and Robbins]', says Winch (1969, p. 190) 'that we get the clearest notion of the contrasts which lie beneath the analytical debates initiated by Keynes.' Perhaps, but that only leaves us even more puzzled as to why Keynes chose to ignore their works.

8. But for the United States there was Douglas (1934) or Clark (1935), books which Keynes also ignored. Keynes's failure to cite any of the influential works of Clark, the co-discoverer of the multiplier and the discoverer of the accelerator (see Stoneman, 1979), is particularly striking.

9. Schumpeter (1946, pp. 66–7) was particularly aware of these ideological elements in Keynes's appeal and went so far as to assert that *'This is* what the Keynesian Revolution amounts to' (see also Winch, 1969, pp. 339–50).

10. The classic reference to this literature is Haberler (1946); for a brief but striking summary, see Hutchison (1953, pp. 404–8).

11. A perfect illustration of the simplification that Keynes wrought is an article by Nicholas Kaldor, written a year before the publication of *The General Theory*, advocating wage subsidies as a cure for unemployment. This pre-Keynesian idea has come back into circulation in recent years (Layard and Nickell, 1980) but what is interesting in Kaldor (1936) is the tortured manner in which the macroeconomic issue of subsidizing the employment of labour is argued in the microeconomic terms of the elasticity of the demand for labour in industry as a whole. Amusingly enough, Keynes wrote to Kaldor categorically denying that a general subsidy of labour is capable of increasing aggregate employment (Kaldor, 1936, pp. viii–ix), which calls to mind the old quip that Keynes did not always understand his own theory.

12. This is only worth saying because it has been so frequently denied by members of the Keynesian 'circus', who insist that the IS–LM interpretation of Keynes is 'bastard Keynesianism' and a sort of plot of neoclassical reactionaries to empty Keynesian economics of its essential content (see Coddington, 1983, ch. 6).

13. Keynes never succeeded in demonstrating this proposition beyond a shadow of doubt but simply piled Ossa on Pelion to make it seem highly likely, employing arguments that were in fact all borrowed from the writings of Pigou (Patinkin, 1982, pp. 137–42; Addison and Burton, 1982; Casson, 1983, pp. 48–52, 161–2).

14. It is often said (after Keynes) that if the marginal propensity to consume were greater than unity, the instantaneous multiplier would be negative and hence income would actually decline for any small increase in aggregate demand. It is not always realized, however, that this conclusion depends entirely on the one-period definition of saving and investment.

15. Another recent historical controversy about unemployment in the interwar period relates to the payment of unemployment benefits as a causative factor. See Deacon (1987) and Garside (1987, p. 74). There is the further American revisionist thesis, made familiar by the writings of Milton Friedman, that monetary mismanagement caused the Great Depression and hence that it is only monetary policy that could have brought about a recovery (see Gandolfi and Lothian, 1977; and Brunner, 1981).

16. Klein (1966) was written in the late 1940s and is to some extent spoiled by the attempt to 'sell' Keynes to the reader; but its biggest fault is simply that it is insufficiently detailed, and that it is infected by Keynes's own straw man picture of 'classical economics'. Winch (1969, chs. 8–11) is the best account we have but it is overtly concerned with the policy implications of the Keynesian message. Howson and Winch (1977) is useful but is concentrated exclusively on Keynesian policy advice. Patinkin (1976) and Clarke (1988) are concerned with the making of *The General Theory*, not the Keynesian revolution, and Patinkin (1982), while directly relevant to the story of the Keynesian revolution, is focused on rivals to Keynes.

17. The first five are articles and are all reproduced in Wood (1983). The sixth is a short book by Robinson (1937).

18. Hansen had started out as a critic of Keynes but by 1938 had become the first of the many old guard converts to Keynesianism (that was eventually to include Pigou himself). Through his bi-weekly seminar at Harvard University, Hansen soon became the central figure in the Americanization of Keynes, publishing a string of widely read expositions of Keynesian economics, culminating in his still valuable *Guide to Keynes* (1953).

19. That fertility is also demonstrated by the manner in which Roy Harrod (and later Evsey Domar, Joan Robinson, and Kaldor) quickly converted Keynes' short-period analysis into a long-period theory of economic growth. Similarly, the interaction of the multiplier and accelerator gave birth to a wholly new brand of economic dynamics, first broached in Harrod's *Trade Cycle* (1936), a book that appeared within six months of *The General Theory*, showing that the Keynesian apparatus could be employed to generate a simple but powerful theory of business cycles as well as a theory of steady-state growth. But neither of these two developments involved the prediction of novel facts but merely the exploration of potentially promising territory.

20. Lipsey (1981) has gone so far as to contend that Keynesian macreconomics is still a 'progressive' research programme within Lakatos' definition of the term: it continues to make

strong predictions which conflict with those of its principal rivals and these predictions have a good track record.

21.   Ever since Leijonhufvud (1968) taught the profession to use Keynes as a launching pad to announce a new polemical position on macroeconomic questions, the game of speculating 'what Keynes would have said if ...' has become a major growth industry. *The General Theory* has virtually become a holy scripture, so much so that a recent guide to Keynes, a chapter-by-chapter commentary on *The General Theory*, is named *Macroeconomics After Keynes* (Chick, 1983). Similarly, Fletcher (1987) treats every pronouncement of Keynes as sacrosanct and decisive against all criticism. One can only endorse Patinkin's plea that future work in macroeconomics might 'have the courage to cut the umbilical cord to Keynes' (Patinkin, 1982, p. 158).

22.   Although this proposition did not enter the public literature until 1945, it was simultaneously discovered in 1942 by Walter Salant and Paul Samuelson and a year earlier by Jorgen Gelting, a Danish economist (Samuelson, 1975).

References

Ackley, G. (1961), *Macroeconomic Theory*, New York: Macmillan.

Addison, J.T. and Burton, J. (1982), 'Keynes's Analysis of Wages and Unemployment Revisited', *Manchester School*, **50** (1), March.

Ambrosi, G.M. (1981), 'Keynes and the 45-Degree Cross', *Journal of Post-Keynesian Economics*, **3** (4), Summer.

Andvig, J.C. (1983), *Ragnar Frisch and the Great Depression*, Oslo: Norsk Utenrikspolitisk Institutt.

Blaug, M. (1976), 'Khun versus Lakatos *or* Paradigms Versus Research Programmes in the History of Economics', in Latsis (1976).

Blaug, M. (1980), *The Methodology of Economics*, Cambridge: Cambridge University Press.

Blaug, M. (1985), *Economic Theory in Retrospect*, (4th ed.) Cambridge: Cambridge University Press.

Bleaney, M. (1985), *The Rise and Fall of Keynesian Economics*, London: Macmillan.

Booth, A. (1987), 'Britain and the 1930s: A Managed Economy', *Economic History Review*, 2nd Series, **60** (4), November.

Brunner, K. (ed.) (1981), *The Great Depression Revisited*, Boston: Martin Nijhoff.

Capie, F. (1987), 'Unemployment and Real Wages' in Glynn and Booth (1987).

Casson, M. (1983), *Economics of Unemployment: An Historical Perspective*, Oxford: Martin Robertson.

Chick, V. (1983), *Macroeconomics after Keynes: A Reconsideration of the General Theory*, London: Phillip Allan.

Clark, J.M. (1935), *Strategic Factors in Business Cycles*, New York: National Bureau of Economic Research.

Clarke, P. (1988), *The Keynesian Revolution in the Making*, Oxford: Clarendon Press.

Coddington, A. (1983), *Keynesian Economics: The Search for First Principles*, London: Allen and Unwin.

Cohen, I.B. (1980), *The Newtonian Revolution*, Cambridge: Cambridge University Press.

Cohen, I.B. (1985), *Revolution in Science*, Cambridge, MA: Harvard University Press.

Collard, D. (1981), 'A.C. Pigou, 1877–1959' in D.P. O'Brien and J.R. Presley (eds), *Pioneers of Modern Economics in Britain*, London: Macmillan.

Collins, R.M. (1981), *The Business Response to Keynes 1929–1964*, New York: Columbia University Press.

Corry, B.A. (1978), 'Keynes in the History of Economic Thought: Some Reflections' in A.P. Thirlwall (ed.), *Keynes and Laissez Faire*, London: Macmillan.

Davis, E.G. (1981), 'R.G. Hawtrey, 1879–1975', in O'Brien and Presley (1981).

Davis, R.J. (1971), *The New Economics and the Old Economists*, Ames, Iowa: Iowa State University Press.

Deacon, A. (1987), 'Systems of Interwar Unemployment Relief' in Glynn and Booth (1987).

Douglas, P.H. (1934), *Controlling Depressions*, New York: W.W. Norton.

Fletcher, G.A. (1987), *The Keynesian Revolution and its Critics*, London: Macmillan.

Fusco, A.M. (1964), 'Gli Economisti Italiani di Fronte Alla "Rivoluzione Keynesiana" ', *Cahiers Vilfredo Pareto*, **3**.

Fusco, A.M. (1984), 'Keynes in Italia' in *Tra Presente e Passato. Scritti Vari di Economia*, Napoli: Giannini Editore.

Gandolfi, A.E. and Lothian, J.R. (1977), 'Did Monetary Forces Cause the Great Depression? A Review Essay', *Journal of Money, Credit and Banking*, **9**, November.

Garside, W.R. (1987), 'The Real Wage Debate and British Interwar Unemployment', in Glynn and Booth (1987).

Garvey, G. (1975), 'Keynes and the Economic Activities of Pre-Hitler Germany', *Journal of Political Economy*, 1975, reprinted in Wood (1983).

Gilbert, R.V. *et al.* (1938), *An Economic Program for American Democracy*, New York: Vanguard Press.

Glynn, S., (1987), 'Real Policy Options', in Glynn and Booth (1987).

Glynn, S. and Booth, A. (eds) (1987), *The Road to Full Employment*, London: Allen and Unwin.

Haberler, G. (1946), *Prosperity and Depression*, New York: United Nations.

Hands, D.W. (1985), 'Second Thoughts on Lakatos', *History of Political Economy*, **17** (1), Spring.

Hatton, T.S. (1987), 'The Outline of a Keynesian Solution' in Glynn and Booth (1987).

Hazlitt, H. (1960), *The Critics of Keynesian Economics*, Princeton, NJ: Van Nostrand.

Howson, S. and Winch, D.N. (1977), *The Economic Advisory Council, 1930–1939*. Cambridge: Cambridge University Press.

Hudson, M. (1985), 'German Economists and the Depression of 1929–1933', *History of Political Economy*, **17** (1), Spring.

Hutchison, T.W. (1953), *A Review of Economic Doctrines 1870–1929*, Oxford: Oxford University Press.

Hutchison, T.W. (1978), *On Revolutions and Progress in Economic Knowledge*, Cambridge: Cambridge University Press.

Hutt, W.H. (1963), *Keynesianism: Retrospect and Prospect*, Chicago: Regnery.

Johnson, H.G. (1971), 'The Keynesian Revolution and the Monetarist Counter-Revolution', *American Economic Review*, 1971, reprinted in E.S. and H.G. Johnson, *The Shadow of Keynes*, Chicago: University of Chicago Press, 1978.

Jones, B.L. (1972), 'The Role of Keynesians in Wartime Policy and Postward Planning, 1940–1946', *American Economic Review*, **62** (2), May.

Kaldor, N. (1936), 'Wage Subsidies as a Remedy for Unemployment', *Journal of Political Economy*, reprinted in *Essays on Economic Policy, I*. London: Duckworth, 1964.

Keynes, J.M. (1936), *The General Theory of Employment Interest and Money*, reprinted in *The Collected Writings of John Maynard Keynes*, vol. VII, London: Macmillan, 1973.

Klein, L.R. (1966), *The Keynesian Revolution*, (2nd edn.), New York: Macmillan.

Kohn, M. (1986), 'Monetary Analysis, the Equilibrium Method, and Keynes's 'General Theory' ', *Journal of Political Economy*, **94** (6), December 1986.

Kuhn, T.S. (1957), *The Copernican Revolution*, Cambridge, MA: Harvard University Press.

Latsis, S. (1976), ed., *Method and Appraisal in Economics*, Cambridge: Cambridge University Press.

Layard, P.R.G. and Nickell, S.J. (1980), 'The Case for Subsidising Extra Jobs', *Economic Journal*, **90**, March.

Leijonhufvud, A. (1968), *On Keynesian Economics and the Economics of Keynes*. New York: Oxford University Press.

Leijonhufvud, A. (1976), 'School, "Revolutions" and Research Programmes in Economic Theory', in Latsis (1976).

Lekachman, R. (1967), *Age of Keynes*, Harmondsworth: Penguin Books.

Lipsey, R.G. (1981), 'The Understanding and Control of Inflation', *Canadian Journal of Economics*, **14** (4), November.

Machlup, F. (1943), *International Trade and the National Income Multiplier*, Philadelphia: Blakiston.

Mack, R.P. (1952), 'Economics of Consumption', *Survey of Contemporary Economics*, vol. 2, ed. B.F. Haley, Homewood, IL: Richard D. Irwin.

Mehta, G. (1974), *The Structure of the Keynesian Revolution*, London: Martin Robertson.

Mehta, G. (1979), 'The Keynesian Revolution', *International Journal of Social Economics*, **6** (3).

Metzler, L.A. (1942), 'Underemployment Equilibrium in International Trade', *Econometrica*, **10**, April.

Middleton, R. (1985), *Towards the Managed Economy: Keynes, the Treasury and the Fiscal Policy Decline of the 1930s*, London: Methuen.

Middleton, R. (1987), 'Treasury Policy on Unemployment' in Glynn and Booth (1987).

O'Brien, D.P. and Presley, J.R. (1981), *Pioneers of Modern Economics in Britain*. London: Macmillan.

O'Brien, P.K. (1987), 'Britain's Economy Between the Wars: A Survey of a Counter-Revolution in Economic History', *Past and Present*, **115**, May.

Patinkin, D. (1976), 'Keynes' Monetary Thought. A Study of its Development', *History of Political Economy*, **8** (1), Spring.

Patinkin, D. (1982), *Anticipations of the General Theory?* Oxford: Basil Blackwell.

Peden, G.C. (1983), 'Keynes, the Treasury and Unemployment in the Later Nineteen-Thirties', *Oxford Economic Papers*, 1980, reprinted in Wood (1983).

Peden, G.C. (1984), 'The "Treasury View" on PUblic Works and Employment in the Interwar Period', *Economic History Review*, Second Series, **37** (2).

Peden G.C. (1988), *Keynes, The Treasury and British Economic Policy*, London: Macmillan Education.

Robinson, J. (1937), *Introduction to the Theory of Employment*, London: Macmillan.

Robinson, J. and Eatwell, J. (1973), *An Introduction to Modern Economics*, London: McGraw-Hill.

Samuelson, P.A. (1975), 'The Balanced-Budget Multiplier: A Case Study in the Sociology and Psychology of Scientific Discovery', *History of Political Economy*, **7** (1), Spring.

Samuelson, P.A. (1985), 'Succumbing to Keynesianism', *Challenge*, January-February, reprinted in K. Crowley (ed.), *The Collected Scientific Papers of Paul A. Samuelson*, vol. V, Cambridge, MA: The MIT Press, 1986.

Schlesinger, J.R. (1956), 'After Twenty Years: The General Theory', *Quarterly Journal of Economics*, reprinted in Wood (1983).

Schumpeter, J.A. (1936), 'Review of *The General Theory Journal of the American Statistical Association*', reprinted in Wood (1983).

Schumpeter, J.A. (1946), 'John Maynard Keynes 1883–1946', *American Economic Review*, reprinted in Wood (1983).

Skidelsky, R. (1975), 'The Reception of the Keynesian Revolution' in M. Keynes (ed.), *Essays on John Maynard Keynes*, Cambridge: Cambridge University Press.

Skidelsky, R. (1977), 'The Political Meaning of Keynesian Revolutions' in R. Skidelsky (ed.), *The End of the Keynesian Era*, London: Macmillan.

Stanfield, R. (1974), 'Kuhnian Scientific Revolutions and the Keynesian Revolution', *Journal of Economic Issues*, **8** (1), March.

Stein, H. (1969), *The Fiscal Revolution in America*, Chicago: Chicago University Press.

Stewart, M. (1986), *Keynes and After*, (3rd edn.), Harmondsworth: Penguin Books.

Stoneman, W.E. (1979), *A HIstory of the Economic Analysis of the Great Depression in America*, New York: Garland Publishing.

Weintraub, E.R. (1985), *General Equilibrium Analysis: Studies in Appraisal*, Cambridge: Cambridge University Press.

Winch, D. (1969), *Economics and Policy*, London: Hodder and Stoughton.

Wood, J.C. (1983), *John Maynard Keynes: Critical Assessments*, (4 vols.), London: Croom Helm.

5 John Hicks and the methodology of economics

Sir John Hicks's career in economics spans more than 50 years, in the course of which he has published 14 books, including six collections of almost 100 essays. In some of these, particularly *Value and Capital* (1939) and *A Revision of Demand Theory* (1956), there are hints of Hicks's general attitude to the nature of economics, but it is only recently that he has become more explicit about his views on the methodology of economics. A 1976 essay on ' "Revolutions" in Economics' voiced doubts about the applicability of Lakatos's philosophy of science to economics; the opening and closing chapters of *Causality in Economics* 1979 threw up similar doubts about the wider question of empirical testing in economics; and, finally, an essay written in 1983 with the pointed title of 'A Discipline Not a Science' decisively parted company with all varieties of empiricism, Popperianism, falsifiability, or call it what you will, in economics.

Economics as a discipline not a science
After observing that economic theories can offer no more than 'weak explanations' for economic events because they are always subject to a *ceteris paribus* clause – a feature that he appears to believe is unique to economics – Hicks concludes:

> ... it becomes clear that they cannot be verified (or falsified) by confrontation with fact. We have been told that 'when theory and fact come into conflict, it is theory, not fact, that must give way' [a quote from R.G. Lipsey]. It is very doubtful how far that *dictum* applies to economics. Our theories, as has been shown, are not that sort of a theory; but it is also true that our facts are not that sort of fact. (Hicks, 1983, pp. 371–2).

Economic facts, he goes on to say, are not the data produced by replicable, controlled experiments but the testimony of observers in historical time. For that reason alone, economic facts are frequently defective.

> A lack of consilience between theory and fact, in economics (when that cannot be ascribed, or readily ascribed, to the weakness of the theory ...) is most commonly due to a lack of correspondence between the terms in which the theory runs, and the terms in which the fact is described. ... When that clash occurs, it may be that theory should be improved, so as to run more closely in the terms in which the relevant facts are commonly described but it may also be that the description of the facts should be improved, so that we may think about them more clearly. I believe it is this last ...

which is the special function of economic theory. Though the concepts of economics (most of the basic concepts) are taken from business practice, it is only when they have been clarified, and criticized, by theory, that they can be made into reliable means of communication. Now once one recognizes that this is what economic theory very largely is doing, one sees that the use of models, which are themselves quite unrealistic, may be extremely defensible. . . . I might indeed go on to maintain that the *Value and Capital* model, of General Equilibrium under Perfect Competition, can be defended in much the same way . . . it is a laboratory, in which ideas can be tested.

I have quoted this statement at length because it is simply astonishing, both in its general drift and in its careful choice of words. First, we are told that when there is 'a lack of consilience between theory and fact', that is, when an economic theory appears to be refuted by the evidence, this can sometimes be ascribed to the 'weakness' of that theory. Now I would have thought instead that it can sometimes, and even frequently, be ascribed to the falseness of that theory. Second, we are told that a much more common reason for the failure of theory to agree with the facts is the lack of an adequate specification of what philosophers of science call 'correspondence rules' for translating the analytical variables of the theory into the terms in which observational data are expressed; improving this translation, refining the specification of 'correspondence rules', is, according to Hicks, 'what economic theory very largely is doing'. Now, again, I was under the impression that what economic theory very largely is doing is providing causal explanations of the workings of the economic system, so as to enable us accurately to predict the effect of a change in an exogenous variable on one or more of the endogenous variables of the theory.

When economic theory comes into conflict with the facts, such as they are, let us by all means re-examine the quality of the data and the correspondence rules that must be employed to compare the implications of the theory with the data. These are points well worth making provided that we are reminded that there may come a point when the clash between theory and data cannot be explained away in these terms. Unless we are prepared to admit that all economic theories may be false and may have to be abandoned eventually, we are furnished with an unqualified licence to theorize as we like. But Hicks is silent throughout this essay on economics as 'A Discipline Not a Science' on the crucial question of whether we are ever permitted to place any bars on the proliferation of possible economic theories, or indeed how we are to choose between them. If the improved 'description' of the facts is, as he says, 'the special function of economic theory', it is not clear to me how one would decide whether one theory contributes more to this end than another, since apparently all economic theories are equally true.

But of course truth, substantive truth, has nothing whatever to do with it. Economics, Hicks is telling us, is a game, a discipline game played according to certain formal rules – logical consistency, simplicity, elegance, and generality –

but still a game, and truth does not come into it.[1] Such a methodological standpoint immediately reminds us of Keynes's famous declaration in the introduction to the *Cambridge Economic Handbooks*, which Hicks indeed quotes with approval:

> . . . the Theory of Economics does not furnish a body of conclusions immediately applicable to policy. It is a method rather than a doctrine, an apparatus of the mind, a technique of thinking, which helps its possessor to draw correct conclusions. (Hicks, 1983, p. 375)

Keynes never did tell us how one would know that a conclusion drawn by an economist was correct – and neither does Hicks.

Realism as a desideratum of economic models
Although economic theories cannot be verified or falsified, they must nevertheless satisfy standards of 'realism'. This is a theme to which Hicks frequently returns. Thus, in his prefatory remarks to the reprint of his essays on *Money, Interest and Wages*, he observes:

> All models are simplifications of reality; they leave out things which are judged to be unimportant, for the purpose in hand, in order to make it possible to think more clearly about the things that are retained. What is left out, and what is to be retained, is chosen with reference to the problem in hand. It is perfectly proper to use some sort of model for one purpose, and another for another. (Hicks, 1982, p. 128)

We are not told how to judge whether a particular model is appropriate to 'the problem in hand', but we are warned not to confuse the question of the inner logic of an economic model with 'the question of applicability of the model to particular empirical data – whether in relation to those data, it is a good model or not' (Hicks, 1982, p. 219). But if economic models cannot be verified or falsified, how are we supposed to relate them to empirical data? The only criterion that Hicks ever offers is that of choosing among models in accordance with the 'realism' or descriptive accuracy of their assumptions.

For example, growth models incorporating neutral technical progress are rejected because 'The real world is not in a steady state, never has been, and (probably) never can be' (Hicks, 1965, pp. 183, 201; 1977, pp. xv–xvi; 1983, p. 109); Chamberlin's tangency solution in the theory of monopolistic competition 'does correspond with a certain region of reality' (Hicks, 1983, p. 141); scale economies are of sufficient importance in the modern world to make perfect competition a useless standard for judging optimum organizations of production (Hicks, 1983, p. 153); income effects for finely defined commodities are likely to be small, so that 'in strictness the law of demand is a hybrid; it has one leg resting on theory, and one on observation' (Hicks, 1956, p. 59); the factor-price-equalization theorem is largely irrelevant to the determination of international prices because 'a general tendency to increasing returns to scale would seem to be nearer the facts' (Hicks, 1983, p. 231); the fact that market structures in modern economies are increasingly characterized by price-making rather than price-taking behaviour is 'verified by the most common observation', thus justifying the use of 'fixprice' rather than 'flexprice' models (Hicks, 1977, p. xi; 1982, pp. 225, 229, 234–5); the phenomenon of reswitching – a fall in the rate of interest leading to a substitution of labour for capital instead of the other way around – is dismissed as 'being on the edge of things that could happen' because it would involve the improbable situation in which the lower construction costs of a new technique are offset by its longer construction period and higher operating costs (Hicks, 1973, pp. 44–6; 1977, p. 9); finally, the view that the labour market is a special kind of market in which a sense of 'fairness' about wages directly affects efficiency, in consequence of which money wages exert an independent influence on the volume of employment, is correct 'both as a matter of theory and as a matter of history' (Hicks, 1963, p. 318).[2]

Such casual empiricism likewise colours Hicks's retrospective judgement of some of the great economists of the past. Thus, the classical conceptions of flexible wages and fixed coefficients of production are defended as realistic in the circumstances of the day (Hicks, 1967, p. 147; 1979, p. 47), and the decline of Ricardian economics in the second half of the nineteenth century is attributed to the waning importance of the scarcity of land (Hicks, 1983, p.38). In the same way, Keynes's assumption of an exogenous money wage is deemed to be justified by the facts of the 1930s (Hicks, 1977, p. 81), but changes in methods of collective bargaining and in monetary institutions have rendered Keynes's analysis increasingly obsolete (Hicks, 1983, p. 38). Because the 'facts' of economics are subject to continual, non-repeatable change, economic theories are forever doomed to be valid only for the historical circumstances in which they are born. Therefore, if there are 'revolutions' in economics, they are merely changes of attention because what Kuhn called 'loss of content' in successive 'paradigms' is considerable. It would seem, therefore, that every 'well chosen' economic theory is true for its time (Hicks, 1981, p. 233), and the job of the historian of economic thought is to make sense of these well chosen ideas in the light of their historical context. Such 'relativism' is, of course, perfectly defensible if only we were given some help in distinguishing the well chosen from the ill-chosen theories of the past. If Ricardo was correct for his time, was Malthus also correct for the same time even when he argued in diametrical opposition to Ricardo?

Positive versus normative economics

Hicks has always upheld the distinction between positive and normative economics, and of course, a great deal of his output has been concerned with normative economics of the cost–benefit variety in which problems of true or false take second place to problems of good and bad. Nevertheless, his writings on questions of positive economics seem to me to suffer from a continuous unwillingness to face up to the question of how it is that we ever discover whether a piece of positive economics is true or false. On the one hand, we are asked not to regard economics as a science but only as a discipline, a form of applied logic without any empirical content. Without worrying too much about the honorific label of 'science', Hicks' object in calling economics a discipline rather than a science is, as we have seen, to discourage attempts to knock out economic theories by empirical testing. At the same time, we seem to come equipped, according to Hicks, with considerable background knowledge about the workings of economic systems that enable us to know when assumptions about economic behaviour or the operation of economic institutions are realistic or not. But arguments employed to throw cold water on empirical judgements about the implications of economic theories surely apply with equal force to empirical judgements about the assumptions of economic theories.

On the one hand, 'There is much economic theory which is pursued for no better reason than its intellectual tradition; it is a good game . . . [like] pure mathematics' (Hicks, 1979, p. viii) but, on the other hand, 'What we want, in economics, are theories which will be useful, practically useful' and 'I have always held (as I said in the preface to *Value and Capital*) that theory should be "the servant of applied economics"' (Hicks, 1983, pp. 15, 361). So, presumably, there are well chosen economic theories embodying realistic assumptions that somehow illuminate the workings of real-world economic systems even though they can never be validated with reference to empirical evidence. If we should ever find ourselves in the situation in which we are confronted with two such competing economic theories, each purporting to address the same 'problem situation', such as Keynesian fiscalism and Friedmanian monetarism, we may apparently choose between them in terms of the respective degrees of realism of their assumptions (Hicks, 1975, p. 4). Unfortunately, it is easy to show that theories with patently unrealistic assumptions *may* be true and that, contrariwise, theories with extremely realistic assumptions *may* be false. To hold that economic theory should be practically useful and yet to deny that there is any place for empirical testing in economics is simply inconsistent.

Moreover, the Robinson-Keynes-Hicks description of economics as *merely* a 'box of tools' is incompatible with the Hicksian claim that the ultimate purpose of economic theorizing is to devise optimum or, at any rate, superior economic policies. If economics cannot aspire to any substantive knowledge of economic relationships, it cannot speak with authority about questions of economic policy. It may be true to say, after Marshall, that economics is 'not a body of concrete truth, but an engine for the discovery of concrete truth', but if economics is to be practically useful, we do well to underline some of the concrete truths we have discovered. In other words, either economics is simply an intellectual game or else it is something more than just a 'discipline'.

Take, for example, the simple policy question of whether a specific tax on a commodity will raise its price, but by less than the amount of the tax. The relevant 'discipline' is the Marshallian cross of demand and supply, but, by itself, this cannot give us any answer to the question we have posed. To answer it, we must assume that the demand curve for the commodity is negatively inclined and the supply curve positively inclined. But those assumptions imply knowledge of 'concrete' truths and therefore go beyond the 'engine' on its own. Thus, even on so simple a question, it is not enough to take our stand on economics as merely a technique of thinking.

Causality in economics

One problem is that Hicks constantly evades fundamental questions of economic methodology even in works that appear on the surface to be directly concerned with them. *A Theory of Economic History* (1969) raised high hopes that light would be thrown on the famous question of the nature of historical explanation and, in particular, on how historical explanations differ from the explanations afforded by economic models. But it soon turned out that the term 'theory' in this book denoted a general, non-deterministic scheme of social evolution within which different forms of economic life may be distinguished; it is something like a stage theory, but not in the strict sense that endogenous developments are relied on to account for the passage from one stage to another. Hicks gives great prominence to the growth of markets and market exchange via the emergence of middlemen and merchants, and employs various 'models' to explain some of the specific changes within particular stages of development, such as the 'lag of wages behind industrialization' during the Industrial Revolution due to the dramatic switch from circulating to fixed capital. At no point, however, does he raise the question of whether any of these models are true, or rather, how one would find out if they are true. His 'theory of economic history' is simply another 'story'; it is a plausible and possibly significant story but, like so many of the other stories of historians, we are given no aid in choosing between it and a large number of other equally plausible accounts of the same set of historical events. Similarly, *Causality in Economics* (1979) appeared in its opening pages to deliver the goods we had long been waiting for:

> All experimental sciences are, in the economic sense, 'static'. They have to be static, since they have to assume that it does not matter *at what date* an experiment is performed. There do exist some economic problems which can be discussed in these terms; but there are not many of them. . . . The more characteristic economic problems are problems of change, of growth and retrogression, and of fluctuation. The extent to which these can be reduced into scientific terms is rather limited. . . . As economics pushes on beyond 'statics', it becomes less like science, and more like history. (Hicks, 1979, p. xi)

Having emphasized the temporal nature of all economic phenomena in contrast to 'science', in which the passage of time is rarely critical – but what of biology, geology, and astronomy? – Hicks moves on to observe that economics is also unique in being concerned with the consequences of purposive individual decisions. One might have imagined that this would lead on naturally to a consideration of intentional modes of causal explanation – the reasons of economic agents are the causes of their action – methodological individualism, *Verstehen* doctrine, and the like. For instance, there is the question that cannot fail to worry a macroeconomist: if aggregate economic outcomes are frequently and perhaps invariably the unintended consequences of individual actions, can such outcomes be reduced to individual action and, if not, what becomes of methodological individualism? But Hicks does not stop to raise such questions, and instead moves on to observe that most effects in economics are produced by a multiplicity of causes and hence that causality always involves the implicit or explicit use of counterfactuals (the *modus tollens* form of logical reasoning according to which if A is the cause of B, then non–A implies non–B). Thus, theorizing is necessarily involved in every causal assertion in economics. This is perfectly true and might have been employed to question Friedman's as-if, empty-box interpretation of economic theories but, again, this is not the route chosen by Hicks.

The point about counterfactuals leads straight on to the final point, which is indeed the main thesis of the book, that causation in economics is not necessarily Humean in character, cause always preceding effect in time; it may be 'static' if cause and effect exist more or less permanently or 'contemporaneous' if the relevant time period connecting cause and effect is stretched out. Much is made of the concept of 'contemporaneous causality' – 'the characteristic form of the causal relation in modern economics' – in the middle chapters of the book dealing with Keynesian economics, but the concept seems at best a new word for 'simultaneous determination'. The purpose of Hicks's distinction between three types of causality seems to fit general equilibrium theory into the language of causality, whereas past practice has been to refuse to give general equilibrium theory a causal interpretation. It is true that there is something very peculiar about general equilibrium theory – namely, that it is compatible with any and all economic events – but I doubt that we learn very much by calling simultaneous determination 'causal determination' in a special sense of the word 'cause'.

The last chapter of *Causality in Economics* questions the applicability of Neyman-Pearson techniques of statistical inference to economics because the time-series observation that econometricians commonly employ are not random drawings from a known population. This is, of course, the now almost standard justification for the replacement of Neyman-Pearson techniques by Bayesian methods of inference. But this is not how Hicks's argument proceeds. Both

Neyman-Pearson and Bayes depend on cardinally measurable probabilities. Many economic events occur with a frequency, argues Hicks, that cannot be expressed in cardinal numbers and sometimes not in any numbers at all; there is both Knightian uncertainty and true ignorance about the occurrence of many economic events. If so, that certainly kills off any notion of econometric testing as a court of last resort for choosing between competing economic theories. Unfortunately, it also kills off the idea that well chosen models with realistic assumptions will somehow throw light on the real world and prove useful to policy-makers, which, as we have seen, is one of Hicks's abiding beliefs.

I have probably been very unfair to what I regard as the rather thin philosophical content of *Causality in Economics*. However, I have summarized it fairly[3] and others must judge its significance for themselves. What is clear, however, is that it was written in apparent ignorance of the simply enormous literature on the difficult philosophical concept of causality, not to mention an even larger literature on the problem of causal explanation in the social sciences.

For example, it is a mistake to suppose that causal statements are decisively tested by counterfactual statements. When events have multiple causes, as they usually do in the social sciences, the truth of a counterfactual statement is neither necessary nor sufficient for the truth of a causal statement: if A is not *the* but simply *a* cause of B (but so is C, D, and so on), the statement that A is a cause of B may be true even though the statement that the non-occurrence of A implies the non-occurrence of B is false (Elster, 1983, pp. 34–40). Mackie's (1975, p. 62) INUS condition for causality – A is a cause of B if A is an Insufficient but Necessary part of a condition that is itself Unnecessary but Sufficient for B – comes much closer to the sorts of causal propositions we often encounter in economics. Addison *et al.* (1984) illustrate the INUS condition by examining the well known proposition that investment is a cause of economic growth: this proportion may well be true, and yet we can get economic growth even without extra investment; investment by itself is insufficient, but it is a necessary part of a larger set of conditions (such as entrepreneurship, an efficient financial system, a stable government, and so on) that is sufficient and yet not strictly necessary to produce growth. How we test the truth of an INUS causal statement is, of course, another story, but suffice it to say that we cannot refute it simply by considering counterfactuals.

The younger Hicks and the older Hicks

In a perceptive review of Hicks's *Economic Perspectives*, Leijonhufvud (1979) noted the peculiar relationship between Hicks the Younger – the Hicks who reformulated the orthodox theory of consumer behaviour in terms of indifference curves, interpreted Keynes in terms of the IS-LM apparatus, and revived and refined general equilibrium theory – and Hicks the Older, who has come to be increasingly sceptical of general equilibrium theory and indeed of all static analysis that is not 'securely in time', who insists that all labour and most commodity markets are fixprice markets, and who contends that useful economic theory must incorporate stylized institutional facts. The Younger Hicks is widely read and constantly cited, while the Older Hicks is generally neglected and rarely cited, all of which is to say that the Older Hicks undermines the achievements of the Younger Hicks in opposition to the prevailing mainstream of professional opinion that the Younger Hicks had done so much to establish.[4]

But a deeper reason for the relative neglect of the Older Hicks is the deeply private tone of much of Hicks's recent writings, a dialogue in fact with his former self, which we are invited to sample but perhaps not fully to share. Thus, there are frequent references to Keynes, Hawtrey, Robertson, Hayek, and Wicksell, all major figures in pre-First World War economics, but current writers like Friedman, Lucas, and Tobin are rarely mentioned even when he is discussing macroeconomic issues of inflation and the formation of expectations. Moreover the illusiveness of Hicks's laconic literary style – 'I am no longer convinced', 'it is not as persuasive as it once appeared to me', 'one may now have grave doubts', and so on – makes it difficult to pin down the criteria he employs to arrive at his judgements. I am not at all sure, therefore, that I have succeeded in capturing the standards he implicitly invokes in appraising economic theories. For example, there is his frequently expressed admiration for Keynes with 'his keen nose for the actual, the current actual' (Hicks, 1977, p. 141n), and this despite the fact that Hicks finds Keynes's arguments in some respects inconsistent and even incoherent (Coddington, 1979, pp. 979–80). But what is not clear is the grounds on which Keynesian economics is given such high marks by Hicks. Is it because Keynesian economics 'illuminated' the depression in the 1930s? Is it because it implied 'correct' policy conclusions? Is it because it was well corroborated by empirical evidence? Or is it instead, as I suspect, because Keynesian economics provided a simple, elegant, and robust economic model with dramatic policy implications, which moreover proved fruitful in the quantification of economic data? After all, Hicks wrote a textbook in economics, *The Social Framework* (1942), which was clearly inspired by the balance-sheet approach of the Keynesian schema. Nevertheless, and despite the numerous occasions on which Hicks has returned to probe the foundations of the Keynesian system, I have been unable to discover the precise basis for Hicks's high opinion of Keynes. And what is true of his judgement of Keynes is also true of many of his other theoretical appraisals.

By way of conclusion

What is clear is that Hicks generally attaches greater importance to certain formal criteria for appraising economic theories – consistency, simplicity, elegance, and generality – than to empirical criteria, particularly in relationship to the implications rather than the assumptions of economic models. I am not the first to have noticed this (see, for example, Maes, 1984, p. 180). It is also clear that, whatever his misgivings about empirical testing in economics before the Second World War, such misgivings have become much stronger in recent years, culminating in the explicit condemnation of all attempts at economic testing in his 1983 *Collected Essays on Economic Theory.*

I once made the bold assertion that most modern economists are 'innocuous falsificationists', that is, they pay lip service to the Popperian view that the validity of economic theories must be judged *in the final analysis* by the accuracy of their predictions, and occasionally they even practise what they preach (Blaug, 1980, p. 127). Evidently, Hicks is an exception to this characterization and, considering his enormous influence on the shape of modern economics, his is no minor exception.[5] Yes, indeed, some would say, and this only goes to demonstrate the sterility of *pre*scriptive Methodology with a capital M and the importance of *de*scriptive methodology with a lower-case m: we need to study what economists actually do and not what they should do (McCloskey, 1983). It is, however, impossible rigidly to divorce the two, and even those who profess to be totally open-minded about the best practice in economics find themselves driven to criticize actual practice (Caldwell and Coats, 1984).[6] Besides, I have been preoccupied in this chapter less with what Hicks does than with what he says he does. What Hicks says is that economic theories cannot be tested for their truth value, and yet he does not deny, or at least he does not appear to deny, that economic theories have truth value: they are not merely conventional instruments for organizing our background knowledge but genuine causal explanations of what does happen and why it so happens. Moreover, some economic theories are said to be better than others even though we are somehow precluded from ever comparing them in terms of their power to account for empirical evidence. There is nothing wrong with such a position, but it does lead inevitably to the conclusion that economic theory is a subject precisely like pure mathematics, an intellectual game to be justified in its own terms. And that position is incompatible with the notion of economics as the handmaiden of economic policy, which Hicks has consistently upheld. I conclude, therefore, that it is impossible to extract any coherent methodology of economics from the writings of Hicks.

Notes
1. Since we are gathered here to celebrate Johannes Klant's retirement as Professor of the Methodology and History of Economics at the University of Amsterdam, it may be worth adding that his book, *The Rules of the Game*, does not endorse Hicks's view of economics as 'a discipline not a science'. Klant is perfectly aware of the inherent difficulties of achieving falsifiable general theories in a subject like economics, and he makes no bones of the fact that economics contains a generous mixture of metaphysics and purely formal models. But he is also convinced that economics has achieved some 'reasonably confirmed falsifiable hypotheses' and that economists should not abandon the aim of continually striving to achieve falsifiable theories (Klant, 1984, pp. 184–5).

2. I have found only one example in all of Hicks's writings in which he faults an economic theory because its implications, rather than its assumptions, are refuted by the evidence. Thus, he notes, the expectations theory of the term "structure of interest rates" has been "tested against the facts; and it has usually been found that it does not fit the facts very well" (Hicks, 1974, pp. 45–6).

3. Helm (1984) gives a sympathetic account of Hicks's views on methodology and compares them favourably with those of Friedman. He sums up (p. 124):

> Hicksian causality is the central building block of his non-positivistic methodology. . . . There are three components to his account of causality. The first relates to weak predictions and the *ceteris paribus* clauses mentioned above, and is his distinction between strong and weak causality. The second is his counterfactual account. The third is his relation between temporal ordering and his three possibilities: static, reciprocal, and contemporaneous.

See also Addison *et al.* (1984), who are less sympathetic but focus entirely on Hicks's account of 'static' causality.

4. As Hicks said himself in later years: 'They gave me a Nobel prize [1972] for my work on general equilibrium and welfare economics . . . work which has become part of the standard literature. But it was done a long time ago, and it is with mixed feelings that I found myself honoured for that work, which I myself felt myself to have outgrown' (1977, p. v).

5. As Lindbeck (1985, p. 42) notes: 'it is indeed remarkable how strong the intellectual influences of these four theorists [Hicks, Samuelson, Arrow, and Debreu] has been on our profession by influencing not only the choice of issues and methods but also the "style" of analysis and exposition.'

6. Both in his 1983 paper and in his 1985 book, McCloskey is much concerned with the bad rhetoric of significance tests in econometrics, arguing for Bayesian in preference to Neyman-Pearson methods. Actually, if the methodology of falsificationism, or what he calls "modernism," is as silly as he makes out, it is difficult to see why he is so concerned about econometric practice.

References

Addison, J.T., Burton, J. and Torrance, T.S. (1984), 'Causation, Social Science and Sir John Hicks', *Oxford Economic Papers,* **36** (1), pp. 1–11.

Blaug, M. (1980), *The Methodology of Economics*, London: Cambridge University Press.

Caldwell, B.J. and Coats, A.W. (1984), 'The Rhetoric of Economics: A Comment on McCloskey', *Journal of Economic Literature*, **22** (2), 575–8.

Coddington, A. (1979), 'Hicks's Contribution to Keynesian Economics', *Journal of Economic Literature*, **18** (3), pp. 970–88.

Elster, J. (1983), *Explaining Technical Change. Studies in Rationality and Social Change*, Cambridge: Cambridge University Press.

Helm, D. (1984), 'Predictions and Causes: A Comparison of Friedman and Hicks on Method,' *Oxford Economic Papers*, **36** (suppl.), pp. 118–34; reprinted in D.A. Collard *et al.* (eds), *Economic Theory and Hicksian Themes*, Oxford: Oxford University Press, 1984.

Hicks, J. (1956), *A Revision of Demand Theory*, Oxford: Oxford University Press.

Hicks, J. (1965), *Capital and Growth,*, Oxford: Oxford University Press.

Hicks, J. (1967), *Critical Essays in Monetary Theory*, Oxford: Oxford University Press.

Hicks, J. (1969), *A Theory of Economic History*, Oxford: Oxford University Press.

Hicks, J. 1973), *Capital and Time*, Oxford: Oxford University Press.

Hicks, J. (1974), *A Crisis in Keynesian Economics*, Oxford: Oxford University Press.

Hicks, J. (1975), 'What is Wrong with Monetarism?', *Lloyds Bank Review*, **118**, 1–13.

Hicks, J. (1977), *Economic Perspectives*, Oxford: Oxford University Press.

Hicks, J. (1979), *Causality in Economics*, Oxford: Blackwell.

Hicks, J. (1981), *Wealth and Welfare, Collected Essays on Economic Theory*, vol. I, Oxford: Blackwell.

Hicks, J. (1982), *Money, Interest and Wages, Collected Essays on Economic Theory*, vol. II, Oxford: Blackwell.

Hicks, J. (1983), *Classics and Moderns, Collected Essays on Economic Theory*, vol. III, Oxford: Blackwell.

Klant, J.J. (1984), *The Rules of the Game. The Logical Structure of Economic Theories*, London: Cambridge University Press.

Leijonhufvud, A. (1979), 'Review of J. Hicks *Economic Perspectives*', *Journal of Economic Literature*, **17**, pp. 525–8.

Lindbeck, A. (1985), 'The Prize in Economic Science in Memory of Alfred Noble', *Journal of Economic Literature*, **23** (1), pp. 37–56.

Mackie, J.L. (1975), *The Cement of the Universe. A Study of Causation*, Oxford: Clarendon Press.

Maes, I. (1984), 'The Contribution of J.R. Hicks to Macroeconomics and Monetary Theory', Ph.D. thesis, Katholieke Universiteit te Leuven.

McCloskey, D.N. (1983), 'The Rhetoric of Economics', *Journal of Economic Literature*, **21**(2), pp. 481–517.

McCloskey, D.N. (1985), *The Rhetoric of Economics*, Madison: University of Wisconsin Press.

PART II

HISTORY
OF ECONOMIC
THOUGHT

6   The economics of Johann von Thünen

Introduction

Johann Heinrich von Thünen (1783–1850) was a pioneer in the development of agricultural economics, an important early figure in the history of mathematical economics, one of the two or three independent discoverers of the so-called 'marginal productivity theory of distribution', and, above all, the 'father' of the economics of space.

Spatial economics is fundamentally concerned with the role of distance and area in economic life: it is not simply that distance, and hence transport cost, affect the location of production facilities and that specific markets have definite geographic limits, but that the twin forces of distance and area can be shown to have definite consequences for market prices. Throughout the nineteenth century, English Classical Political Economy virtually ignored spatial questions, despite the fact that Cantillon's *Essai sur la nature du commerce en général* (1775), James Steuart's *Principles of Political Economy* (1767), and Adam Smith's *Wealth of Nations* (1776) were full of insights into the economic effects of space. Indeed, it has been argued that spatial considerations played a major role in both the pamphlet literature and the great economic treatises of the eighteenth century; the separation of spatial economics from mainstream economics is a nineteenth-century development (Dockès, 1969; Hébert, 1981).

It cannot be argued, therefore, that Thunen[1] was the founder of spatial economics but, nevertheless, he was the first to put the subject on the map as a specialized branch of economics. Unlike Cantillon, Steuart, and Smith, Thünen had the vision to postulate an abstract geographical model that highlighted the roles of distance and area by its very construction. On the opening page of his *Isolated State*, Thünen tells us to consider an 'ideal' or 'isolated' state – a homogeneous, featureless plain without roads or navigable rivers and restricted to the use of horse-drawn wagons as the only mode of transportation, having a single town at its centre producing all manufactured articles and supplied by the farmers in the plain with all its agricultural products, and closed off to the outside world by an impenetrable wilderness on all sides – and asks us to discover the principles which would, in such circumstances, determine the prices that farmers receive for their products, the rents that are earned by various units of land, and the associated pattern of land use that accompany such prices and rents. This notion of a closed economy in idealized space was a radically new idea, which fully justifies Thünen's claim to the title of 'father' of the economics of space.

121

But perhaps more remarkable than the invention of this concept of abstract space is Thünen's grasp of both the strengths and the weaknesses of all such abstract devices. Thünen combined unusual powers of rigorous abstract reasoning and equally unusual patience in the gathering of empirical data and, indeed, it is doubtful whether it is possible to find any other figure in the history of economic thought who so strikingly excelled in both the deductive *and* the inductive skills of an economist. As Schumpeter (1954, p. 465) said of Thünen and Ricardo: 'If we judge both men exclusively *by the amount of ability of the purely theoretical kind* that went into their work, then, I think, Thünen should be placed above Ricardo or indeed above any economist of the period, with the possible exception of Cournot.' In addition, however, Schumpeter added that Thünen's detailed farm records, patiently collected over a number of years and constantly revised in the light of his theoretical discoveries, make him 'one of the patron saints of econometrics. Nobody, before or after, ever understood so profoundly the true relation between "theory" and "facts" ' (Schumpeter, 1954, p. 466). Last, there is Thünen's brilliant originality:

> Ricardo or Marx (or whoever it is among the theorists of that period who holds the place of honour in the reader's scale) worked on problems that presented themselves from outside by means of analytical tools that had been forged before. Thünen alone worked from the unformed clay of facts and visions. He did not rebuild. He built – and the *economic* literature of his and earlier times might just as well not have existed as far as his work is concerned'. (Schumpeter, 1954, pp. 466–7)

And yet *The Isolated State* was not widely read either in Thünen's day or in our own. He was, in the words of Dickinson (1969), 'a prophet with little honour in any country, but with even less in his own'.[2] Dickinson explains this neglect by three circumstances: Thünen was a liberal and free trader in an era when liberalism was anathema in Germany; Thünen was a 'pure' theorist who extolled Newtonian methods in the analysis of social problems in a country dominated by the antitheoretical bias of the Historical School; and Thünen lacked academic status and even a university degree. To these three factors, we may add three more: his book appeared in four instalments over a 37-year period, so that its final impact was necessarily long delayed; he made constant use of algebra and differential calculus long before mathematical economics had become an acceptable mode of expression in the social sciences; and, last, he wrote cryptically and obscurely, constantly moving back and forth among various central questions, usually without announcement or explanation. Even in a science as renowned for its badly written Great Books as economics (for example, Ricardo's *Principles*, Marx's *Capital*, Walras' *Elements*, and Keynes's *General Theory*), *The Isolated State* stands out as a formless monster: it represents, as we shall see, a collection of notes, comments, arithmetical examples, and mathematical formulae, which constantly interrupts the flow of its central analysis of an economy governed by transport costs by various digressions on crop-rotation schemes, the effects of diet on population size, the merits of different types of sheep rearing, and so on.

Nevertheless, Thünen always received respectful acknowledgements from the great economists. John Bates Clark (1908, p. viii) paid tribute to Thünen's discovery of the marginal productivity principle. Knut Wicksell (1934, I, pp. 116, 117, 121, 147, 177, 216–17, 268) likewise credited Thünen with literally inventing the marginal productivity theory of distribution, and added that, among all earlier writers, 'von Thünen was certainly the most advanced in his conception of the nature and origin of interest'.[3] But none gave greater praise than Alfred Marshall, the more remarkable in his case as he was not generally inclined to acknowledge inspiration from others: Thünen and Cournot are the only economists to whom Marshall expresses direct indebtedness and Thünen is perhaps the only economist of whom Marshall speaks repeatedly in unreserved compliments. In a footnote to the preface of his *Principles*, he correctly attributed the term 'marginal' to Thünen; in the text, he characterized Thünen's discussion of rent as 'noteworthy', observed that his analysis of location factors was based on 'brilliant researches', remarked that the problems involved in the unequal riskiness of different lines of business are 'well shown by von Thünen', and drew attention to the fact that Thünen deduced the concept of marginal productivity 'with characteristic breadth of view' (Marshall, 1961, I, pp. x, 144n, 400n, 442n, 522–3n; II, 582n, 690). In private, he said even more: in an undated fragment found among his papers after his death, he expressed the wish that 'someone would care for von Thünen':

> Cournot's work is now easily accessible, mainly through the good efforts of Professor Fisher. . . . I have long ago forgotten Cournot; and I may be wrong. But my impression is that I did not derive so much of the substance of my opinions from him as from von Thünen. Cournot was a gymnastic master who directed the form of my thought. Von Thünen was a bona fide mathematician, but of less power; his blunder as to the natural wage is not of the same order as Cournot's little slips. But to make up, he was a careful experimenter and student of facts with a mind at least as fully developed on the inductive as on the deductive side. Above all he was an ardent philanthropist. . . I loved von Thünen above all my masters. Professor Fisher has cared for Cournot. I would that someone would care for von Thünen. He should not, I think, be translated but an abstract of his work should be given, with translations of a good deal of his second volume. (Marshall, 1961, II, pp. 36–7)

The praise which such figures as Clark, Wicksell, and Marshall heaped on Thünen's contribution nevertheless did little to bring *The Isolated State* the recognition it deserved. It remains to this day among the least read of the great economic tomes of the nineteenth century[4] and the name of Thünen conjures up for most modern economists nothing else but the archaic and mysterious formula: 'the natural wage = $\sqrt{ap}$'. It is economic geographers and regional scientists that have adopted Thünen as their hero but, as any economist will confidently tell you, economic geographers and regional scientists are not really 'economists'. Be that as it may, this paper is mainly about the Thünen that geographers, location theorists, and regional scientists admire; it is only tangentially concerned with Thünen's marginal productivity theory, which is just about all that still gives 'economists' an interest in Thünen.

Life

Thünen was born on 24 June 1783 at his father's estate in the Jeverland District of the Grand Duchy of Oldenburg, near the North Sea Coast in East Friesland, which lies today just inside the Democratic Republic of Germany.[5] His father died when he was three years old and his mother remarried a timber merchant in Hooksiel, a small port on the Bay of Jade. He attended the local school in Hooksiel, and moved to Jever when he was thirteen to attend a secondary school, living with his maternal grandfather. He left school at the age of sixteen to gain practical experience in agriculture by working as an apprentice on a farm. At nineteen, he returned to his academic studies by entering the agricultural College at Gross-Flottbeck in Holstein, north-west of Hamburg and today a suburb of the city. Here he deepened his interests in agriculture and here in 1803, at the age of twenty, he wrote a paper, *Description of Agriculture in the Village of Gross-Flottbeck*, in which he sketched the idea of an 'isolated state', or as he originally called it, an 'ideal state', with the town at its centre and a definite pattern of land use throughout the region surrounding the town, which later became the keystone of his book.

It was just at this time that he read Albrecht Thaer's *Introduction to a Knowledge of English Agriculture* (1798), a seminal book in the formation of the progressive farming movement in Germany, advocating the principles of extensive farming and the introduction of the English crop-alternation system. Thünen enrolled himself in Thaer's seminar at Celle, a little further south near Hanover, and here he first studied the new science of agricultural statics, which figures prominently in several chapters in *The Isolated State*. From Celle, Thünen went to the University of Göttingen, still further south, where he studied philosophy, biology, economics and languages for two semesters. Then, in the summer of 1804, armed with a letter of introduction from Thaer, he embarked on an agricultural tour of Saxony and Mecklenburg, in the course of which he met the woman who became his wife in 1806.

After his marriage, he leased a farm from his brother-in-law in Western Pomerania, searching all the while for a suitable estate of his own. In 1810, a few days after his twenty-seventh birthday, he bought the 1,146-acre (464.3 hectares) Tellow estate, large even by modern day standards, lying 37 km south-east of Rostock in the former *Länd* of Mecklenburg. Mecklenburg was a remote area then and now: it contained no major navigable rivers and almost no major improved roads and the railway did not penetrate the area until the 1880s. The prevailing mode of agriculture in the region was the medieval three-field system of spring grain, winter grain and a fallow period. But the Mecklenburg improved system was coming in from the West, whose central feature was the seven-period alternation of cereal crops, root crops and a short grass ley. The reader of *The Isolated State* will find constant reference to this improved system of cultivation, which Thünen advocated enthusiastically.

The years 1810 to 1815 were largely taken up with working out a basic system of accounts for the Tellow estate. This initial period was followed by four more years of detailed calculations, after which the first draft of *Der isolierte Staat in Beziehung auf Landwirtschaft und Nationalökonomie* (The Isolated State in Relation to Agriculture and National Economy) was rapidly produced in 1818–19 (just when Ricardo was working on the second edition of his *Principles*). Thünen revised his draft in 1824 and published it in 1826.

This is the so-called first volume of *The Isolated State* (I), which completed Thünen's major contributions to rent and location theory. The book received complimentary reviews but, as letters to his brother reveal, Thünen was nevertheless disappointed with the reception of his book and slowly continued to work on a second volume that would extend the argument. The first volume was revised and reprinted in 1842, by which time he had already developed the famous formula for the 'natural wage'. The wage theory, however, was not published until 1850 as the first part of the second volume (II.1) of *The Isolated State,* appearing shortly after his death at the age of sixty-seven. This edition II.1 starts with a long introduction, summarizing the inquiry of I and elaborating his methodological views on the proper way of approaching the analysis of social problems. Other material on taxation, protective duties, population growth, human capital, and the construction of railways appeared as posthumous fragments in a second part of the second volume (II.2) of *The Isolated State* in 1863, selected by Hermann Schumacher, a friend of Thünen and his official biographer; a third volume (III), consisting of a dissertation on forestry, also appeared in 1863; even today there are further unpublished papers in the Thünen Archiv at the University of Rostock.

All through the years from 1810, Thünen was engaged in ceaseless agricultural improvements on his estate, on the basis of which he produced a steady flow of papers, which first appeared in the local Mecklenburg agricultural journal and subsequently found their way into *The Isolated State*. The University of Rostock granted him an honorary doctorate in 1830 in recognition of his work on practical agricultural questions.

In the last years of his life, and particularly from 1848 onwards, he took a new interest in social questions. He introduced a profit-sharing scheme for his tenants on the Tellow estate and was invited to stand for election to the liberal National Assembly at Frankfurt-am-Main, the so-called 'Professors' Parliament'; he declined on grounds of ill health but his two sons were elected instead. It is apparent from II.2 of *The Isolated State* that his policy views on problems of poverty show a remarkable parallel with those of John Stuart Mill: producers' cooperatives, profit-sharing, and an emphasis on thrift, education and the limitation of numbers (without, however, so much as a hint of birth control.

Thünen died on 22 September 1850 and was buried in the village churchyard of Belitz, next to Tellow. Under his name on the gravestone is engraved, in accordance with his own instructions, the formula for the natural wage: $A = \sqrt{ap}$

The first collected and only complete edition of *Der isoliert Staat* was edited by Schumacher in 1876. Further German editions of I, the volume beloved by geographers, and II.1, the volume favoured by economists, appeared in 1910, 1921, and 1931, and a selection of passages from these was published in West Germany as recently as 1951. The first French translation of I appeared in 1851, followed by II.1 in 1857. A Russian translation of I and II.1 appeared in 1857 and the first Italian translation of the same material was published in 1860 and then republished in 1857. A Czech translation appeared in 1926. The first English translation by Clara Wartenberg of almost the whole of I and selections from II.1 and II.2 did not see the light of day until 1966 (see Thünen, 1966), by which time Bernard Dempsey (1960) had already translated the whole of II.1.

Reader's guide to the first volume of *The Isolated State*
Chapter 1, boldly entitled 'Hypotheses', and consisting of only three short paragraphs, sets out the model of a closed economy in idealized space. Chapter 2, equally boldly entitled 'The Problem', and only slightly longer than Chapter 1, announces the celebrated land-use pattern of concentric rings. These passages have been endlessly quoted and rightly so: their almost Euclidean severity immediately rivets the attention of the reader.

Their purpose is deliberately to isolate transport costs as a linear function of distance from all the other factors (for example, climate, soil quality, topography, the pattern of demand of town dwellers, quality of farm management, technology of food preparation, quality of transport network) which influence the pattern of land use and the location of agricultural production facilities. Chapter 2 starts by asking: what will be the pattern of agricultural production around the central town in the Isolated State? but ends by noting that as the product changes in the concentric rings around the town, so will 'the entire farming system' (I, p. 2).[6] Thünen confusingly states two problems in one: what crop will be grown in different places as a function of distance from the market and at what intensity will that same crop be grown in different places as a function of the same distance? He thus has a 'crop theory' and an 'intensity theory' (Hall in Thünen, 1966, p. xxiv; Petersen, 1944, ch. 8). In fact, after laying down the notion of concentric rings in Chapter 2, Chapter 3 deals with both crop patterns and intensity methods of cultivation in the first ring, after which the next 16 chapters are exclusively concerned with the general application of the intensity theory to a single-grain crop.

Chapter 4 treats the pricing of grain the various rings on the assumption that all transport is by horse and wagon. Here we first learn of the Tellow estate and the calculation of transport costs in terms of 'natural units' of rye, the staple grain in North Germany at the time, which are afterwards converted into silver-money or *thalers* (I, pp. 8-10). Since horses have to be fed en route and since even some of the men's wages are customarily paid in kind, Thünen simplified his calculations by measuring all transport costs in bushels of grain, namely:

1. the number of bushels fed to horses on the journey together with
2. the grain paid in kind and
3. the grain-equivalent of cash wages, all expressed in terms of bushel-kilometres of transport performed.

Measured in this way, it was easy to show how many kilometres a bushel of grain could be transported before losing a specified proportion of its value.[7] Here, too, we get a first example of Thünen's tendency to provide a mathematical formula for all his basic propositions. What is grain worth x kilometres from the market? His answer (I, pp. 10–11) is:

$$1 \text{ bushel of rye } = \frac{2.73 - 5.5x}{182rx} \text{ thalers}$$

where r = the market price of grain at the starting point of a wagon journey.

He starts in Chapter 4 by finding an empirical formula for the farm price of grain, which depends directly on transport-per-km costs. His formula for the net farm price is based on a given market price of 1.5 thalers per bushel, which is governed jointly by the size of demand in the town and the costs of the marginal farmer who just finds it profitable to bring his grain to the market. From this fixed market price, transport costs are subtracted, net farm prices therefore falling progressively more slowly with increasing distance from the market. It is worth noting at this stage in the argument that Thünen's model is an example of partial, and not of general, equilibrium analysis. He says that the will solve the model for the crops grown in each location, the degree of intensity at which each crop is grown, the width of the successive rings of production, the rent of land at each location, and the market prices of all crops, but in fact he takes the prices paid by town dwellers from various agricultural products as given and only derives the prices received by farmers by deducting transport costs and rents from the given market price. In short, the demand-side in price determination is almost totally neglected and so are all changes in the technology of both food preparation and storing as well as changes in techniques of transportation. Or, to express the same point somewhat differently, when Thünen in the next chapter shows that ground rent in the isolated state will fall to zero at 371 km from the central town, he loses sight of the fact (as did Ricardo) that it is the level and pattern of demand for products that determines the location of the no-rent margin.

Assuming a given market price of grain, Chapter 5B studies output and costs under the *Mecklenburgische siebenschlägige Koppelwirtschaft* or *Koppelsystem* in which arable land rotates through seven courses with intensively used ley grass. We will henceforth call it the 'Improved System' because it is identical to the improved system of rotations introduced in England in the eighteenth century and increasingly adopted by Mecklenburg landowners in the first half of the nineteenth century. The figures employed by Thünen are derived from Tellow accounts but they are applied throughout the book to a standard area slightly smaller than Tellow: 100,000 square rods or 217 hectares. Thünen divides all costs into farm-based costs (agricultural wages, seeds, manure, fodder for horses) expressed in grain and town-based costs (agricultural implements) expressed in silver thalers, and assumes that at all times and under all systems of cultivation, three-quarters of costs are farm-based and one-quarter are town-based (I, pp. 28–9). As a result, farm-based costs will vary directly with grain prices, decreasing as grain prices decrease with increasing distance from the town, but town-based money costs are assumed to remain fixed (ignoring the fact that even these will incur rising transport costs). Since only a part of costs falls with falling grain prices, it follows that total costs fall more slowly than grain prices as we move away from the central market, which is one of his principal conclusions. There must come a point where the surplus of grain, expressed in money, no longer covers fixed money costs. Thünen calculates that this will happen at 371 km from the market under the Improved System, this being the actual distance at which the marginal farm unable to pay any rent will be situated. Under the standard Thünen assumption of uniform fertility, this type of rent is pure 'locational rent'.

In Chapters 12 and 13, Thünen calculates, in a similar way, the rent formula for the less intensive and older three-field system, which always yields a lower gross product but also a lower cost, and hence not necessarily a lower rent, than the Improved System. As a matter of fact, Chapter 14A shows that the ground rent of the Improved System falls faster than that of the three-field system and at a distance of 39.5 km from the central town, the formula gives equal rents for the two systems (I, pp. 115–16). Short of 39.5 km from the town, the more intensive Improved System produces an extra surplus over the three-field system, which may properly be called 'scarcity rent' (rent from the intensive margin in Ricardo). This scarcity rent is an addition to the locational rent which the more favourably situated farm cultivating the three-field system would also enjoy.

To round out Thünen's treatment of rent, we turn back to Chapter 5A, which first introduces the concept of ground rent, taking care to distinguish pure ground rent from interest on capital invested in buildings, fences and other improvements, and criticizing Adam Smith for failing to make that distinction (I, pp. 14–16). As he tells us in the second 1842 edition of *Der isolierte Staat* (I, p. 19), this chapter and indeed the whole of the first 1826 edition was written without knowledge of the works of Ricardo, who similarly distinguished rent from interest.

Chapter 5B introduces us to Thünen's peculiar use of the term *Reichtum*, or the fertility the soil has currently attained under cultivation, as distinguished from the *physische Beschaffenheit des Bodens*, the inherent physical quality of the soil (I, pp. 23–4). At this point, Thünen equates *Reichtum* with yield but later he assumes a simple functional relationship rather than an equivalence between degrees of fertility and yield in bushel-crops.

Chapters 6, 7 and 7B take up the science of agricultural statics (*Statik des Landbanes*) and expounds some of its fundamental propositions. Thünen explains in Chapter 7B that 'fertility' is the product of the humus content of the soil and its crop-producing capacity, given a certain application of fertilizer. The size of the harvest is in turn the product of the fertility of the soil and its rate of loss of plant nutrients as a result of one harvest. In the general theory of agricultural statics, fertility or the crop-producing capacity of the soil is proportional to its humus content and since only one type of soil is assumed for the isolated state, the term 'fertility' can be used for either concept. All earlier systems of statics, Thünen observes, were based on a simple and direct relationship between yield and fertility. But subsequent research has shown that the yields of two fields vary with the square roots of the respective humus contents of the fields. Even on one soil, increments of humus in the form of extra manure yield diminishing returns. Thus, although all the tables in *The Isolated State* showing the fertility of soil under various crop systems are strictly speaking inaccurate, Thünen decides to leave them untouched because all the important propositions of the book are based on a single soil of uniform fertility.

Chapter 8 deals with the ratio of tillage to pasturage in a three-field system. Chapter 9 compares the three-field system with the Improved System in respect of rye yields per acre.[8] The chapter also contains a brief reference to the Alternating Crop System (*Fruchtwechselwirtschaft*), the most intensive cultivation system know to Thünen (later in Chapter 17, he refers to the Belgian crop-alternation system, which is a somewhat less intensive five-course rotation). Another variation, to which Thünen also refers, is the intermediate six-course crop alternation system (*sechsschlägigen Fruchtwechselwirtschaft*). The comparison between alternative cultivation systems continues in Chapter 10.

In Chapter 11 Thünen addresses himself to the role of distance between field and farmstead and, hence, the question of the optimal location of farm buildings on an estate. If we take a field of regular shape – say, an equilateral triangle – and add the distances covered by the horses in manuring the field, dividing the resulting sum by the number of cartloads taken, we get the 'mean distance' covered between field and farmstead. Geometrically, this corresponds to a point on a diagonal line bisecting the plot. In the 1826 edition, Thünen declared himself unable to solve the problem mathematically. A solution was found by someone else in 1829, which Thünen criticizes quite correctly on technical grounds, thereby demonstrating his firm grasp of differential and integral calculus (I, pp. 99–102). The last few pages of the chapter criticize the location of farm buildings on most Mecklenburg and West Pomeranian estates.

Chapter 12, as mentioned earlier, takes up the determination of rent in the three-field system and Chapter 13 returns to the role of distance between field and farmstead in the three-field system. Chapter 14A then turns to the rent-comparison between the three-field and the Improved Systems, demonstrating, as we have said, that the latter enjoys no absolute advantage over the former under all possible grain prices: low grain prices and low yields both favour a less intensive use of land, and therefore, the three-field system. On the other hand, at higher net farm prices nearer the market, it will pay to choose a more intensive system of cultivation, in which a higher level of costs is associated with a later point of the onset of diminishing returns. Moreover, intensification brings a higher rent, but it stops being profitable at a smaller distance from the market. This fundamental theorem of the 'intensity theory' is really only hinted at in the first volume of *The Isolated State* but it is brought out fully in II.1, particularly Chapter 19 (see below), where Thünen develops the concept of the marginal product of units of capital and labour applied to land.

Chapter 14B restates his assumptions and asks: under what conditions and to what extent is it profitable to improve the soil? Chapters 15 and 16 explore the relationship between manure production and land under grain in the three-field system compared with the Improved System. The closing pages of Chapter 16 discuss the advantage of replacing the ley grass by cultivated feed crops which can be fed to the cattle indoors.

Chapter 17 compares the Belgian crop-alternation system and the Improved System, using some evidence on Belgium agriculture that had come Thünen's way. This chapter also contains a number of throw-away remarks on countries at different stages of economic development.

So far, the choice of farming systems has dealt solely with two factors: the net farm price and soil fertility yields. Chapter 18, however, discusses a number of other factors, after which Thünen once again summarizes the leading features of the three-field system, the Improved System, and the Alternating Crop System (I, pp. 163–4).

At this point we may sum up Thünen's contribution to the theory of rent. His theory of ground rent is based upon the same fundamental principles as that of Ricardo, except that he treats locational differences as the pure source of ground rent, adding differences in land fertility as a complicating circumstance, whereas

Ricardo of course operates with a model which reverses the order of priority of these two factors. Like Ricardo, but more explicitly than Ricardo, Thünen distinguished rent from interest and, unlike Ricardo, he deals explicitly with the competition between crops for a given acre of land; moreover, he takes realistic account of the time period required to withdraw capital from land that pays negative rent by failing to yield the going rate of interest.

The price of grain in the central town is determined by the production-plus-transportation costs of obtaining grain from the most distant estates whose produce is required to satisfy the town's demand for grain. Since grain sells at the same price regardless of where it is produced, and since grain produced on estates near the town enjoys low transport costs, ground rent will equal the saving in transport costs on the more favourably situated estates. Ground rent is therefore at a maximum in the first concentric ring, declining with increasing distance from the central town, reaching zero in the outermost ring at the frontiers of the isolated state. In the real world, differences in the fertility of different estates, which are not themselves related to location, will give rise to ground rent in the same manner as do differences in proximity to the central town. Thus, as a general rule, ground rent acts to equalize the total costs of obtaining grain from estates wherever they are located and whatever their soil quality.

All this refers to what Ricardo might have called (but did not) the *extensive margin of cultivation*. Thünen recognized, however, that ground rent may arise even if all land were equally situated and of equal fertility, owing to the fact that successive applications of capital and labour to the land of a given estate yield a diminishing increment of produce: 'scarcity rent' as distinct from 'locational rent' and 'differential rent'. Since all workers are paid the same amount and since every unit of capital earns a uniform rate of interest, there remains a surplus over wages paid for all intramarginal workers. Once again, this surplus accrues to the landowner as rent, thus equalizing the production costs of obtaining grain regardless of whether it is produced by the first or the last worker applied to a given acre of land. Thus, Thünen might have added (and almost did add in II.1), the phenomenon of rent serves the social function of limiting the use of scarce factors to the point where its marginal value product is equal in all uses. In the case of land, the exploitation of land is restricted by the landlord's rent to the point at which its marginal cost equals the cost on no-rent units of land. In consequence, equal additions of investment on more favourably situated, more fertile and more intensively cultivated acres of land will make equal additions to output and equal units of output will incur identical costs. In short, the creation of 'locational', 'differential', and 'scarcity' rents is one of the optimizing characteristics of a competitive market.[9]

Coming back to *The Isolated State*, we note that Chapters 19–32 turn away from the 'intensity theory' to the 'crop theory', from the question of how intensely to cultivate a given crop to the question of what crops to grow where.

Unfortunately, these two questions seem to be hopelessly intertwined because certain crops, such as wood, are by their nature land-using (a relatively high land to product ratio), whereas others, such as grain, are by their nature land-saving (a relatively low land to product ratio). The pattern of crop production in the successive rings of the isolated state has perhaps produced more confusion than any other subject taken up by Thünen – it is virtually *the* Thünen problem.

The standard view is that Thünen taught that so-called 'intensive crops' are always grown near the market, the high price of land near the central town justifying only intensive cultivation, so that his famous concentric rings are really rings of rising crop intensity as we approach the central town.[10] But in that case it is difficult to understand why Chapter 19 should assign the production of wood, an 'extensive crop', to the second ring around the central town, and why Chapter 26 should depict the sixth ring as given over to a whole series of intensive cash crops, such as oilseed, hop, tobacco, and flax. Something else is involved in the 'crop theory' that is missed in the standard view.

If we trace to its source this common misapprehension that crop intensity for Thünen necessarily rises towards the central market, there is little doubt that it stems from the belief that high crop intensity implies high yields per acre and that high yields imply high costs per acre (Hall in Thünen, 1966, pp. xxx–xxxi). On balance, it is of course true that yields and costs are frequently positively correlated, in consequence of which crop intensity does normally rise as we approach the central market. On the other hand, there are a few crops which have high yields and low costs, as for example, trees, and there are plenty of commercial and industrial crops, many of which are found in Thünen's sixth ring, that combine low yields and high costs.

When we say that a crop is intensive or extensive in the use of land, what we really mean is that the number of cost inputs that are applied up to the no-rent margin are small or large and this factor has no necessary connection with physical yield, or weight of product per unit of acre. One of two crops may have a higher yield per acre of a lower land requirement per unit of produce and yet be extensively produced because it is subject to rapidly diminishing returns that set in after only a few increments of capital and labour are applied to a given acre; it is, therefore, produced near the market (for example, forestry). On the other hand, a crop like grain for distilleries may have a low yield per acre or a high land requirement but because diminishing returns set in slowly, it is intensively cultivated; if, in addition, it has a relatively low production cost per unit of transport load, it is easily portable and will then certainly be cultivated far away from the market. For a large number of alternative crops, farm prices, output per acre, costs per acre, weight per unit of output, and the rate of spoilage over time all vary and of course all of these factors influence the distance from the market at which it is profitable to produce a crop. The general rule is that the sites nearest the market will be pre-empted by crops which experience the greatest reductions in total costs per unit of output, save the greatest sum of total costs, and produce the highest ground rent by virtue of their particular location.

Thünen always represents the pattern of total cost savings in terms of the costs per wagon load transported to the market, converting all other costs in terms of the per unit load. The comparison between alternative crops in Chapters 19 and 20 give rise to a number of generalizations about the precise location of different crops: with equal yields or bulk per acre, the crop with the lower production costs per wagon load will be cultivated nearer the market; with equal production costs per loads, the crop with the highest yield will be cultivated nearer the market; obviously, the more perishable crops will be cultivated, all else being equal, nearer the market; and, finally, production will generally, but not invariably, be ordered around the market according to a pattern of falling yields. All this applies to cases where yields and costs show contrary tendencies but if one crop shows both higher yields *and* higher production costs than another, we cannot resolve the location question without working out the production costs, transport costs, and ground rents of the alternative crops. It is precisely when yields and costs are positively correlated that the standard interpretation of Thünen's 'crop theory' breaks down.

For many if not most crops, Thünen's simpler generalizations about yields-versus-costs do work: forestry is carried on near the market because, compared with grain, it has both a high yield per acre and low production costs per wagon load, or, if you like, requires high transport costs relative to its value; butter is produced far from the market because it has a low yield per acre and high production costs that fall away rapidly as the distance from the market increases; likewise, wool has even lower yields and higher production costs and, therefore, should occupy the outermost ring of the isolated state (much of Chapter 30 on sheep-rearing is devoted to explaining why this did not apply at the time Thünen was writing); and, lastly, crops grown especially for industrial production (for example, grain grown for distilleries) are intensively cultivated far away from the market in locations where grain for flour does not pay because they have a low effective yield per acre (the crops are reduced in weight in the course of manufacturing) and high production costs (that is, farm costs plus manufacturing costs).

Having now cleared the ground, we can move more rapidly through the remainder of the book. Chapter 3 told us that garden vegetables, milk, hay and straw, and certain root crops will be produced in the first ring by a system of free cash-cropping (*Freie Wirtschaft*), whose central feature is the absence of fixed rotations. In one sense, Thünen's results for the first ring are simply due to the circumstances of the day and have little to tell us that is still relevant. The absence of refrigeration of products in transit and the slow speed of transportation in nineteenth-century Mecklenburg simply made it impossible to ship fresh milk and vegetables over great distances. Similarly, in Thünen's time a large proportion of total agricultural land had to be put aside to produce grain and fodder for horses. Every town in those days produced vast quantities of horse manure that had to be disposed of without excessive transport costs, which necessarily produced a small belt of market gardening of exceptionally high fertility and exceptionally high rents in the immediate neighbourhood of towns. Thünen also argues in Chapter 19, where we pick up our story again, that wood, both for fuel and for building purposes, cannot bear high transport costs and that it is, therefore, essential that some areas should be preserved for forests in fairly close proximity to each town (the second ring of the isolated state). In Chapter 20 he returns to the first ring to ask which use of the soil near the town will yield the highest rent. Chapter 21 takes us to the third ring and, once again, Thünen sets forth the assumptions that govern his argument (I, pp. 219–21). There follows a one-paragraph Chapter 22 on the production of grain in the fourth ring, and an equally short Chapter 23 on crop farming in the fifth ring.

Chapter 24 asks: how is the price of grain determined? By the marginal farmer is the answer, whose costs are so high that the going price leaves nothing over for rent. The source of ground rent is the subject of Chapter 25 and here Thünen distinguishes neatly between locational rent, differential rent and scarcity rent (without using these terms). Chapter 26A-C deals with livestock farming in the sixth ring; he calculates the net product associated with stock farming at varying distances from the town as production costs fall and transport costs rise; he likewise calculates the annual production costs per cow, using figures for Mecklenburg dairy farms in the period 1810–15, breaks down the labour costs of stock farming into a fixed money element and a decreasing rye element, and expresses the variation in price and costs at increasing distances from the town. In Chapter 26C, he discusses the relative nutritive value of meat, butter, potatoes, and grain, noting the different price and income elasticities of demand for these products (again without using these terms); this is perhaps the only place in the book where he pays some attention to the demand-side in price determination.

This concludes Section I of Volume I of *The Isolated State*. Section II is called 'Comparison of the Isolated State with Reality' and Chapters 27 and 28 consider some of the differences between the isolated state and the realities of an estate like Tellow. Thünen now begins to relax some of his assumptions, such as a given soil of uniform fertility, the absence of navigable rivers, and the lack of other than a single, central town in the plain (see, in particular, some further remarks on the role of abstractions in economic analysis, I, pp. 275–6). Chapter 29 deals with distilling and Chapter 30 with sheep farming, pointing out that fine merino sheep have been introduced into Germany too recently to permit firm generalizations about ground rent in sheep farming. The closing paragraphs of this chapter draw attention to the fact that there are differences among farmers in respect of managerial talent, which interfere with all neat generalizations about rent in relation to distance from the market.

Chapter 31 turns to the production of industrial crops and lays down several typical Thünen propositions about commercial crops (I, p. 295). There follows a detailed discussion of individual crops, such as rape, tobacco, chicory, clover seeds, and flax. Chapter 32 asks: at what prices can the various areas of the isolated state supply the town with flax and linen? It is here (see also II.2, pp. 119–33) that Thünen broaches questions of industrial location, having to do with the comparative transport costs of bringing raw materials to the place of manufacture and the manufactured product to the place of final sale, which Alfred Weber developed further in his *Theory of the Location of Industries* (1909).

Chapter 33 continues the argument about industrial products by considering the long-term effects on the wealth-producing capacity of the isolated state of restrictions on the production of flax and linen. The chapter ends with a Smithian passage on the 'invisible hand' which converts private selfishness into public altruism (I, p. 327).

Section 3, Chapters 34–38 is entitled 'The Effect of Taxation on Agriculture'. Earlier in Chapter 5B (I, p. 27), Thünen had announced the assumption that no taxes are paid to the state and it is only at this point that he drops this assumption. His analysis of the effects of taxation on agriculture in these next four chapters is in fact more sophisticated than anything found in Ricardo if only because Thünen carefully distinguishes the comparative statics effects of a tax from their actual effects over historic time. Chapter 38 on rent taxation is particularly interesting, first stating the well known Ricardian dictum that a tax on ground rent, being an intramarginal surplus, has no effect on output, and then qualifying the Ricardian dictum in the light of variations in the managerial abilities of different farmers.

The book closes with a set of famous diagrams of the isolated state 'drawn by a friend of mine' (I, p. 384). Unfortunately these graphical illustrations are somewhat misleading and have probably created the common misunderstanding that we spoke of earlier, according to which the concentric rings in the isolated state show a steadily declining intensity of cultivation with increasing distance from the market (Petersen, 1944, pp. 42–5). For one thing, these diagrams omit Thünen's distinction between firewood and constructional timber in the second ring, as well as all mention of industrial crops in the sixth ring. For another, they include the Alternating Crop System, which has no actual place in the analysis of *The Isolated State,* although it is of course briefly mentioned in Chapter 9.

Reader's guide to the second volume of *The Isolated State*
This brings us to the first part of the second volume of *The Isolated State*, published in 1850. The introduction to II.1, 'Summary and Critique of the Method Employed in Part One of this Work, and a Plan of Part Two', contains some of Thünen's most important remarks on the methodology of economics. It

opens with the magisterial sentences: 'Adam Smith taught me political economy, Thaer scientific farming. They are the founders of two sciences and many of their teachings will forever rank among the basic principles of science.' There follow nine questions 'which, in the teachings of these two great men, appeared to me incomplete', of which number 6 is: 'What is the natural wage, or what, in Nature's scheme of things, is the worker's rightful share of the product?'. It is the answer to this question that in fact dominates the content of II.1.

The next few pages (II.1, pp. 5–13) contain some powerful and highly quotable paragraphs on the advantages, and indeed indispensability, of the abstract-deductive method in economics, namely, the method of isolating the influence of a particular factor, while holding everything else constant, which, Thünen declares, is nothing but the method of constrained maximization in differential calculus. We can only marvel at Thünen's originality when we consider the fact that these pages were written some 20 years before the so-called 'marginal revolution' in economics.

With II.1, Chapters 15 and 19, we come at last to Thünen's theory of distribution and his formula for the 'natural wage'.

Thünen's treatment of distribution anticipates the whole of what later came to be known as the marginal productivity theory of distribution, and in some respects improves even on the presentation of John Bates Clark, which came almost 50 years later. Thünen varies the inputs of labour, while holding capital and land constant, and of course the inputs of land while holding capital and labour constant, and he even emphasizes the impact of variations in factor and product prices on the optimum input mix. His analysis culminates in the perfectly modern statement that net revenue is maximized when each factor is employed to the point at which its marginal value product (*Wert des Mehrertrags*) is equalized to its marginal factor cost (*Mehranfwand*). Although the discussion proceeds in verbal terms, illustrated by numerical examples, Thünen correctly points out that the marginal product of a factor is a partial differential coefficient of a multi-variable production function. Moreover, apart from clearly recognizing the distinction between fixed and variable factors, and between the average and the marginal returns of a factor, he took great care to define the inputs of capital, labour, and land in strictly homogeneous units, observing that this condition was rarely obtained in practice – this too was literally more than 60 years ahead of his time.

Thünen's illustrative examples in II.1 of the marginal product of labour in terms of the quantities of potatoes harvested from a field as the number of days used in picking potatoes is increased, and analogous examples of the marginal product of capital, take the form of a decreasing geometric series. This geometric series is precisely the 'law of the soil', which was independently rediscovered in the early twentieth century by two agronomists, the German E. A. Mitscherlich and the American W. J. Spillman, who were unaware of Thünen's earlier statement of the same law (Lloyd, 1969, pp. 28–9).[11] The production function corresponding to this series is non-linear, non-homogeneous, and yields mono-tonically decreasing average and marginal product curves that are concave from below (Lloyd, 1967, p. 30).

However, the particular production function which, according to Thünen, is said to characterize the actual output of the Tellow estate is in fact linearly homo-geneous with average and marginal product curves that are convex from below: it is indeed a particular case of the Cobb-Douglas production function, that old favourite of economists, reinvented in 1926 (Lloyd, 1969, pp. 32–3).

The function that Thünen gives (II.2 Chapter 3) is:

$$p = h (g + k)n$$

where p = product per unit of labour
        h = a given shift parameter, depending on the fertility of the soil and the diligence of human effort
        g = a positive constant
        k = the quantity of capital per unit of labour
and n = a positive parameter less than unity

Multiplying both sides by L, the number of labour units, we get:

$$P = pL = hL (g + k)^n = hL^{1-n} (gL + kL)^n$$

which is similar in form to the Cobb–Douglas production function:

$$P = hL^{1-n} K^n$$

where P = total output
        h = a given shift parameter denoting 'technical progress' in the widest sense of the term
        K = the total stock of capital
        L = the number of workers
and n = a positive parameter less than unity

Apart from his firm grasp of the practical objections to marginal productivity theory, grounded on the difficulty of holding both the quantity and the quality of the fixed factors constant, Thünen was also keenly aware of the limitations of marginal productivity theory in providing an ethical principle of distribution. He was convinced that the low wages and poverty of large sections of the working class under the circumstances then prevailing in much of Europe was due to overpopulation, lack of education and, above all, the absence of free land, which prevented workers from taking up and cultivating new land of their own. The United States was less troubled by poverty, he thought, because of free land available on the frontier. It was thoughts such as these that gave rise to the notion of a 'natural wage' that emerges, not spontaneously from a competitive process under a regime of private ownership of capital, but by the self-determination of voluntary agents creating their own capital on the frontier of the isolated state where land is free. Thünen claimed that his formula for the natural wage was approximated under frontier conditions in the United States but he nevertheless put it forward as an abstract theorem that held strictly true only under the assumptions of his model of the isolated state.

Thünen's formula has been endlessly ridiculed and only Wicksell, Schumpeter (1954, pp. 467–8) and Dempsey (1960, pp. 78–87) have given it anything like a fair hearing. Perhaps the most persistent misinterpretation is to suppose that Thünen's formula was meant to depict the long-run equilibrium wage rate that would prevail under normal conditions in a capitalist economy, whereas it was designed deliberately to reform the real world by means of profit-sharing in what would nowadays be called a 'labour-managed market economy'.[12] Moreover, this is not a question on which we have to read between the lines. Thünen says quite clearly: '*This wage, not originating in the relation of supply and demand, not measured by the needs of the worker, but proceeding from the free self-determination of the worker, this, √ap, I call the natural wage*' (II.1, p. 171). If he had called it the 'just wage', he might have been better understood.

Thünen derives his formula is several different ways. As a sample of his reasoning, suffice it to say that if we go to the frontier of the 'isolated state' where ground rent is zero, if labour is homogeneous and perfectly mobile, if the average product of labour exceeds subsistence levels, and if capital is also homogeneous and perfectly mobile, then:

$$(a + y) + q(a + y)z = p$$

where a = the known amount of grain necessary for the subsistence of a family
y = the unknown surplus of grain available for accumulation
$(a + y)$ = the unknown grain-wages of a working family
q = the known quantity of capital required per working family to develop new land, measured in $(a + y)$ units of grain
z = the unknown rate of interest
and p = the known average annual product of a working family when assisted by q units of capital

With perfect competition, it follows that:

$$z = \frac{[p-(a+y)]}{q(a+y)}$$

Thünen assumed that each working family converts its annual surplus, y, into capital, q, and that each wishes to maximize the annual returns to that capital, expressed as:

$$zy = \frac{[p-(a+y)]y}{q(a+y)}$$

This is maximized when:

$$\frac{d}{dy}\left\{\frac{[p-(a+y)]y}{q(a+y)}\right\} = 0$$

Thünen solves this equation for $(a+y)$, which yields $\sqrt{ap}$, the geometric mean between the necessary subsistence, a, and the average product of a working family, p (II.1, p. 171).[13] He now turns the problem around to find the amount of capital per family, q, which maximizes zy and solves for the wage as the remainder of the product after interest has been paid, showing that the wage that would emerge as the marginal product of labour in a labour-managed enterprise is, once again, $\sqrt{ap}$.

Most of the critics of Thünen's formula seize on the fact that his reasoning really takes the rate of interest, z, as given instead of treating it as an unknown to be determined. In addition, Thünen reduced capital to units of grain and ultimately to quantities of labour, which suggests that he was really thinking of capital as circulating capital, more or less ignoring fixed capital. In this he was simply the child of his time. Wicksell tried to simplify the presentation of Thünen's formula by measuring capital in terms of a 'year's effort', the excess of a year's wage over a year's subsistence, y, but this hardly improves the argument as y varies with a. Dickinson (1969, p.899) has shown that if Thünen had measured capital in terms of a, he would have found the arithmetic and not the geometric mean as the natural wage and, provided a and p are both positive and not equal to each other, the arithmetic mean, $(a+p)/2$, is actually greater than the geometric mean, $\sqrt{ap}$.

Finally, Thünen treated the concept of subsistence wages, a, as if it were subject to precise quantitative measurement; here, for once, he was behind the times because even Ricardo had warned his readers that the subsistence wage is a cultural and not a biological minimum, being influenced by workers' expectations and aspirations.

But perhaps none of these criticisms goes as deep as the objection to Thünen's implicit assumption that working families should aim at maximizing yz, the surplus of *one* year's wages, rather than the whole income from this year's labour and from all the invested capital they own; or, to put it another way, that they should aim at maximizing their short-run income from capital alone rather than their joint lifetime income of wages and profits. On deeper reflection, it appears that Thünen supposes that workers would divide themselves into the mutually exclusive categories: a first group that would produce capital goods (that is, seeds and foodstuffs); and a second group that would work with the physical capital produced by the first. In consequence, far from the analysis of a labour-managed market economy, what we get is a two-sector model in which one sector maximizes income from capital and the other maximizes income from work. It is this, and not the tendency to treat interest as a datum rather than a variable, to reduce capital illegitimately to labour, and to treat the subsistence wage as a definite, unproblematic entity, that is the fatal flaw in Thünen's theory of the natural wage.[14]

Even all this does not quite exhaust Thünen's contributions to economics. Although there is nothing about money and credit in the published versions of *Der isolierte Staat*, a recent study has shown that his unpublished papers on monetary theory are full of flashes of insight (Gordon, 1983). His contributions to human capital theory in II.2 (Chapters 12, 13) are better known and have been reviewed elsewhere (Kiker, 1968, pp. 39–44). Let us simply note that he was convinced of the positive influence of education on the productivity of labour, and, instead of simply assuming that schooling augments labour's product, he gave six cogent reasons why it might be expected to do so. He went on to consider the relationship between the costs of formal education and the wages of better educated workers, and, assuming the education industry to be operating in private hands under conditions of increasing costs, he deduced that this relationship was subject to two 'laws: under competitive conditions, the amount of capital that is profitably invested in the educational system is always (i) a decreasing function of the prevailing rate of interest; and (ii) an increasing function of the prevailing wage rate for raw labour.

Thünen's lasting influence on spatial economics

Despite Marshall's flattering references to Thünen's analysis of 'situation value', and despite Alfred Weber's path-breaking work on location of industrial plants, deliberately starting where Thünen had left off, mainstream economics throughout the nineteenth and first half of the twentieth century continued to neglect locational problems and, with it, the writings of Thünen. In his own country, he and the subject he created never entirely died out (Blaug, 1979). Elsewhere, however, the name of Thünen joined the ranks of 'forgotten economists of the past'. The revival in recent years of spatial economics and its close relative, regional economics, however have brought Thünen back to the fore.

It is true that modern changes in methods of transportation, in the preparation and storing of foodstuffs, and in the tastes and demands of town dwellers have condemned many of the details of Thünen's analysis of land use patterns to obsolescence. Urban-fringe farmers still benefit to some extent from lower transport costs to the market for many perishable products but the importance of their locational advantage has declined to the point where they can no longer compete with distant producers favoured by better land, cheaper labour, and lower taxes. Nevertheless, the spirit and even the letter of Thünen's analysis is still visible in such modern treatments of the location of agricultural facilities as Dunn's *The Location of Agricultural Production* (1954), Chisholm's *Rural Settlement and Land Use* (1962) and Alonso's *Location and Land Use* (1964). The opening paragraph of *The Isolated State* states, as we now realize, a typical linear programming problem with fixed technical coefficients and land availability as the single binding constraint on production activities, the rigorous treatment of which is nowadays found in Beckmann's *Location Theory* (1968). It is true that Thünen allows some variability between the inputs of capital and labour applied to land and that his model is better described as one of lumpy investments, as farmers switch between entire crop-rotation schemes, rather than rigidly fixed coefficients. It is this assumption of lumpiness which accounts for the sharp division of land in the isolated state into rings of specialized use; completely continuous land-capital-labour substitution possibilities will generate a more gradual transition between types of land use (see Isard, 1956, chs. 8, 10; Böventer, 1962; Bühr, 1970; Beckmann, 1972).

Although Thünen confined his attention largely to the location of agricultural producers in cases where they serve consumers at a central point, he said enough to suggest how the model can be generalized to the locational decisions of manufacturing establishments, and it is these questions of industrial location which naturally dominate the modern treatment of spatial problems. Nevertheless, although the problems of space are no longer those that preoccupied Thünen, his approach and working methods still colour the writings of spatial economists to this very day. It may be truly said that there are few other branches of economics that have been so thoroughly dominated for so long by the ideas of a single thinker: it is this which is the ultimate tribute to Thünen's genius.

Notes

1. We shall follow modern German usage by omitting *von* from his name.
2. For an account of the specifically German reactions to his work, see Petersen (1944, chs. 15–17), a book which, incidentally, is an indispensable handbook to Thünen's *Isolated State*.
3. Böhm-Bawerk (1959, pp. 111–16, 455–6), however, was more grudging in his respect for Thünen's interest theory as a 'motivated productivity theory'.
4. Karl Marx, who read everything, also read *The Isolated State* and quoted it in *Capital*: 'How has the worker been able to pass from the master of capital – as its creator – to being its slave?' 'It is to Thünen's credit that he asked this question,' Marx (1976, p. 772n) observes, adding: 'His answer is simply childish.' And that is all that Marx found worth quoting in Thünen!

5.   The biographical sources for Thünen's life are listed in Thünen (1966, pp. xii–xiii).

6.   The page references that follow refer to the definitive 1842 Rostock edition of *Der Isolierte Staat* in the case of I; to the 1850 Rostock edition in the case of II.1; and to the 1863 Schumacher edition in the case of II.2.

7.   Converting Thünen's figures for bushels per km into modern terms of tons per km, Colin Clark (1967, pp. 373–4) has calculated that Thünen's estimates of the average costs of a representative journey by horse wagon of 37 kms works out at 2.73 kms of rye-equivalent per ton-km of delivered weight. He compares this figure of 2.73 kms for wagon transport with some figures, past and present, of transport costs in low-income countries, ranging from the cheapest, boat transport at 1.0, to wagon-transport at 3.4, to pack-animal transport at 4.1, to the most expensive, human porterage at 9.0. In other words, Thünen's figures for transport by horse-wagon, while somewhat on the low side, appear to have been accurately calculated.

8.   Clark (1967, p. 375) demonstrates that the crop yields that Thünen recorded for Mecklenburg estates, including Tellow, were exceptionally (and perhaps even suspiciously) high by the standards of the time.

9.   Although Marx had read Thünen, he failed to understand him. In Marx, there is always a category of rent, called 'absolute rent', which arises from the monopoly of ownership of land by a separate class of landlords, inhibiting the free flow of capital from industry to agriculture. What Thünen's rent theory implies, however, is that even a socialist government that had nationalized all land would still have to charge a 'shadow price' for the use of land, corresponding to 'locational', 'differential' and 'scarcity' rents, to ensure the efficient allocation of natural resources.

10. Thus, Heimann (1964, p. 113) says that 'He [Thünen] assumed a land of homogeneous fertility with one city in the center, so that different locations would be distinguished only by differences in the cost of transporting the crop to the market. On this assumption, it is clear that the different branches of agriculture will situate themselves in concentric rings around the city in the order of decreasing intensiveness of cultivation, interrupted only in cases where the crop is bulky or perishable.' Rima (1972, p. 193) makes a similar remark. Grotewold (1959, p. 352) observes that 'some writers have stated as a general law that, according to von Thünen, the intensity of cultivation must decrease with increasing distance from the market', and adds, 'Such statements are very irritating if quoted outside their proper context.'

11. It must be added that this so-called 'law of the soil' is no longer regarded as valid.

12. Even Leigh (1960, p. 572), in a classic re-examination of Thünen's distribution theory, says that Thünen's 'natural wage' was meant to be 'a basic for analyzing the 'normal' rates of interest and wages supposed to prevail in the real world'.

13.
$$\frac{d}{dy}\left\{\frac{[p-(a+y)]y}{q(a+y)}\right\}=\frac{d}{dy}\left\{\frac{py-ay-y}{q(a+y)}\right\}=0^2$$

$$=\frac{q(a+y)(p-a-2y)-q(py-ay-y^2)}{q(a+y)^2}=0$$

therefore

$$(a+y)(p-a-2y)=py-ay-y^2$$
$$ap-a^2-2ay-2y^2=y^2$$
$$a^2+y^2+2ay=ap$$
$$(a+y)^2+2ay=ap$$
$$(a+y)=\sqrt{ap}$$

14. Leigh (1968, p. 19) sums up all the criticisms in a succinct paragraph: Thünen's expression for the 'natural wage', is

... no more than an intellectual curiosity. Neither *a* nor *p* can be analytically defined. There is no reason to suppose that a rational worker would want to maximize the annual interest on one year's savings. Measurement of a unit of capital by its wage cost alone is inconsistent with the assumption that each worker must use *q* units of capital, interest on which is part of the cost of the unit of capital. The importance of the work lies in its method of analysis and in the kinds of problems to which that method is applied.

References

Beckmann, Martin J. (1972), 'Von Thünen Revisited: A Neoclassical Land Use Model', *Swedish Journal of Economics*, 74 (1), March pp. 1–7.

Blaug, Mark, (1979), 'The German Hegemony of Location Theory: A Puzzle in the History of Economic Thought', *History of Political Economy*, Spring.

Böhm-Bawerk, Eugene von, (1959), *Capital and Interest*, I, in G.D. Huncke and H.F. Semholz, (eds), *History and Critique of Interest Theories*, South Holland, Illinois: Libertarian Press.

Böventer, Eduard von (1962), *Theorie des räumlichen Gleichgewichts*, Tübingen: Mohr (Siebeck).

Bühr, W. (1970), 'An Operational Generalized Version of Von Thünen's Model', *Zeitschift für die Gesamte Staatswissenschaft*, 126 Band/3 Heft pp. 117–28.

Clark, Colin (1967), 'Von Thünen's Isolated State', *Oxford Economic Papers*, 19 November, pp. 370–7.

Clark, John Bates (1908), *The Distribution of Wealth*, New York: Macmillan.

Dempsey, Bernard (1960), *The Frontier Wage*, Chicago: Loyola Press.

Dickinson, H.D. (1969), 'Von Thünen's Economics', *Economic Journal*, 79 (316), December, pp. 894–902.

Dockès, P. (1969), *L'espace dans la pensée économique du XVIᵉ au XVIIIᵉ siècle*, Paris: Flammarion.

Gordon, Donald F. (1983), 'Von Thünen's Unpublished Interest and Monetary Theory', mimeo.

Grotewold, A. (1959), 'Von Thünen in Retrospect', *Economic Geography*, 31 (1), January, pp. 346–55.

Hébert, Robert F. (1981), 'Richard Cantillon's Early Contributions to Spatial Economics', *Economica*, 48, February, pp. 71–9.

Heimann, Edward, (1964), *History of Economic Doctrines*, New York: Oxford University Press.

Isard, Walter (1956), *Location and Space-Economy*, Cambridge, Mass.: The MIT Press.

Kiker, Bernard F. (1968), *Human Capital: In Retrospect*, Columbia, South Carolina: University of South Carolina.

Leigh, A. H. (1946), 'Von Thünen's Theory of Distribution and the Advent of Marginal Analysis', *Journal of Political Economy*, reprinted in J.J. Spengler and W.R. Allen (eds) *Essays in Economic Theory*, Chicago: Rand McNally.

Leigh, A.H. (1968), 'Thünen, Johann Heinrich von', D.L. Sills (ed.) *International Encyclopedia of the Social Sciences*, vol. 16, New York: Macmillan and The Free Press.

Lloyd, Peter J. (1969), 'Elementary Geometric/Arithmetic Series and Early Production Theory', *Journal of Political Economy*, 77 (1), January–February, pp. 21–34.

Marshall, Alfred (1961), *Principles of Economics*, (9th (Variorum) edn), ed. C.W. Guillebaud, London: Macmillan.

Marx, Karl (1976), *Capital*, vol. 1 ed. E. Mandel, London: Penguin Books, 1976.

Petersen, A. (1944), *Thünen's Isolierte Staat. Die Landwirtschaft als Glied der Volkswirtschaft*, Berlin: Verlag von Paul Parey.

Rima, I.H. (1972), *Development of Economic Analysis*, Homewood, Ill.: Richard D. Irwin.

Schumpeter, Joseph A. (1954), *History of Economic Analysis*, New York: Oxford University Press.

Thünen, Johann Heinrich von (1966), *Von Thünen's Isolated State*, ed. P. Hall, Oxford: Pergamon Press.

Wicksell, Knut, (1934), *Lectures on Political Economy*, (2 vols), ed. L. Robbins, New York: Macmillan.

7   Classical economics

The label 'classical economics' is sometimes employed to refer quite simply to an era in the history of economic thought from, say, 1750 to 1870, in which a group of predominantly British economists used Adam Smith's *Wealth of Nations* as a springboard for analysing the production, distribution and exchange of goods and services in a capitalist economy. So broad a definition of classical economics must include such contemporary continental writers as Cournot, Dupuit, Thünen and Gossen, not to mention such British writers as Bailey, Lloyd and Longfield, who at first glance seem to stand outside the tradition founded by Adam Smith. It is difficult to resist the implication, therefore, that classical economics is more than a period in the history of economic thought: it seems to involve a definite approach to economic problems. The difficulty, however, is how to characterize this approach.

Shrugging aside such tendentious definitions of classical economics as those of Marx and Keynes – for Marx (1867, pp. 174–5n) classical political economy begins with Petty in the seventeenth century and ends with Ricardo, and for Keynes (1936, p. 3n) the classical school begins with Ricardo and ends with Pigou – the first question is whether it was Adam Smith or David Ricardo who established the 'essence' or 'core' or classical economics. Of course, Adam Smith laid down the main issues that economists debated for a century after him, but there is also little doubt that the Smithian tradition was in some sense transformed with the appearance of Ricardo's *Principles of Political Economy and Taxation* in 1817. Some writers have nevertheless insisted that Smith and not Ricardo was the lasting influence on the character of classical economics, contending that the leading features of Ricardo's theoretical system were soon rejected even by his avowed followers in the decade after his death in 1823. Others, however, have insisted that, despite all the criticisms of Ricardo that no doubt appeared in the late 1820s and early 1830s, later writers like John Stuart Mill and John Elliott Cairnes continued to operate right up to the 1870s with the central Ricardian theorem that the rate of profit, and hence the accumulation of capital, depends critically on the marginal cost of production in agriculture; in that sense, they remained trapped in the Ricardian system. But even this assertion presupposes the notion that the Ricardian system is essentially characterized as a theory about the determination of the rate of profit, a proposition which is by no means accepted by all historians of economic thought.

It is only after clearing up this problem of the relative significance of Smith's and Ricardo's ideas in shaping the central current of classical economics that we can take up the question of where to place the utility theories of value put forward by such writers as Lloyd, Longfield, Senior, Dupuit and Gossen, the abstinence theories of interest of Bailey, Senior, Rae and John Stuart Mill, the use of both supply and demand forces in the determination of international prices by Mill, the theory of general gluts and the denial of Say's Law of Markets by Malthus, and the exploitation theory of profits by Marx – in short, all the elements of economic theorizing in the period 1770 to 1870 that so clearly do not belong to the corpus of doctrines bequeathed by Adam Smith and David Ricardo. Likewise, it is only then that we can start talking about the end of classical economics in the 1870s and the nature of the 'marginal revolution' that may or may not have marked a decisive break in the continuity of orthodox economics.

The endless debate on what was classical economics is neatly illustrated by the simultaneous appearance of three books on classical economics: *Classical Economics Reconsidered* by Thomas Sowell (1974), *The Structure of Classical Economic Theory* by Robert Eagly (1974) and *The Classical Economists* by Denis O'Brien (1975). Of the three, Eagly takes the widest view of the length of time over which something called 'classical economic theory' ruled the roost, beginning with the physiocrats in the 1750s and ending with the Walrasian theory of general equilibrium in the 1870s. His view is not only that the whole of classical economics can be defined in terms of a single conceptual framework but that this framework revolves essentially around a particular concept of capital as a stock of intermediate goods invested in staggered production periods, the question of the pricing of final goods always relegated to the next period after output has already been determined by the size of the labour force and the technology of the previous period; in short, the key to classical economics is to be found in the so-called 'wages fund doctrine'. Whether this thesis is convincing or not, Eagly's book represents an extreme example of the tendency to define classical economics as one coherent body of ideas organized around a central unifying principle. The secondary literature is, of course, replete with other attempts to pin down once and for all the classical theory of economic growth (for example, Lowe, 1954; Samuelson, 1980), but few allege, as Eagly does, that their modelling of classical economics captures all the essentials of the writings of Quesnay, Smith, Ricardo, Mill and Marx, as well as McCulloch, Torrens, Bailey, Jones, Senior, Longfield, Babbage, Tooke, Wakefield, and so on.

Sowell, on the other hand, adopts the traditional definition of classical economics as, in effect, the School of Adam Smith, and he therefore excludes Marx and, more surprisingly, Malthus, Torrens and Senior at least in some respects from the mainstream of the tradition stemming from *The Wealth of Nations*. That tradition consisted, according to Sowell, of a common set of philosophical presuppositions, common methods of analysis and common conclusions regarding matters of substantive economic analysis: it comprised such major propositions as the labour theory of value, the Malthusian theory of population, Say's Law and the quantity theory of money and was predominantly oriented towards the issue of economic growth (although not in the modern sense of the term as a theory of the steady-state equilibrium growth path of an economy). However, Sowell admits that this picture has to be qualified after 1817 by such phrases as 'classical economics in its Ricardian form' because Ricardo worked a major change in Smith's eclectic mode of economic reasoning by adopting static equilibrium analysis as the only valid method of conducting an economic argument. At any rate, Sowell's treatment of classical economics leaves little doubt of the extensive and varied character of economics in the classical period, posing problems for anyone who seeks to define classical economics in one or two sentences.

Both Eagly's and Sowell's books are dwarfed by O'Brien's wide-ranging and comprehensive review of classical economics, which alone among the three begins with an incisive discussion of the extent to which the classical writers formed a 'scientific community'. (O'Brien's book also contains excellent annotated bibliographical notes on classical economics; indeed, O'Brien, Blaug (1985) and Spiegel (1983) between them review the whole of the secondary literature.) O'Brien follows Schumpeter in arguing that the Ricardian system represented an analytical detour from the main line of advance running from Adam Smith to John Stuart Mill; it was not a fatal detour, however, because the full Ricardian apparatus attracted hardly any followers and in any case was more or less abandoned by the 1830s. As we noted earlier, this Schumpeter–O'Brien thesis has been questioned by some (for example, Blaug, 1958; Hollander, 1977). The point is, however, that O'Brien's book perfectly illustrates our contention that any stand taken on the nature of classical economics as a whole depends critically on the attitude adopted towards the Ricardian metamorphosis of Smithian economics.

The Sraffa interpretation of Ricardo

Still more recently a new note has been struck in the old argument about the essential meaning of classical economics. Inspired by the publication of Sraffa's *Production of Commodities by Means of Commodities* (1960), a number of commentators have argued that classical economics is in effect a Sraffa-system, that is, an analysis of the manner in which a capitalist economy invests its surplus of net output over consumption, which is to say an output in excess of that required to reproduce that level of output, subject to the condition that goods and services are so priced as to maintain a uniform rate of wages and a uniform rate of profit on capital in all lines of investment. This approach, they contend, was buried in the 1870s when the central object of economic analysis became that of investigating the optimum allocation of resources whose quantities are given at the outset of the analysis; in reviving classical surplus analysis, Sraffa not only provides a promising new way of studying economic problems but also illuminates precisely what it was that united Smith, Ricardo and Marx, thus licensing the use of a single label such as 'classical economics' to cover them all (see Meek, 1973, 1977, the originator of the argument; and Dobb, 1973; Roncaglia, 1978; Walsh and Gram, 1980; Bradley and Howard, 1982; Eatwell, 1982; Garegnani, 1984; Howard and King, 1985).

As is well known, a Sraffa-system consists of a set of linear production equations, one for each commodity in the economy, and is intended to demonstrate that these equations are sufficient to determine all relative prices in long-run equilibrium irrespective of the pattern of demand, provided that

1. the output of each commodity is given;
2. the rate of profit on capital is uniform throughout the economy and
3. the real wage or (alternatively the rate of profit on capital) is somehow determined exogeneously.

On the face of it, such a theory does indeed appear to be very much like 'classical economics'. For example, after distinguishing between 'natural' and 'market' prices of commodities – or, as we would nowadays say, the long-run and short-run prices of commodities – Adam Smith focused much of his analysis on the determination of 'natural' prices, a tendency which became even stronger in the writings of Ricardo. Moreover, Smith and certainly Ricardo, not to mention Marx, always wrote as if demand played no role whatever in the determination of 'natural' price. We have all known ever since the work of Marshall that this neglect of demand can be justified if one assumes that commodities are produced under conditions of constant unit costs or constant returns to scale, the long-run supply curves of all industries being perfectly horizontal over the relevant range of output. Sraffa's production equations imply fixed coefficients of production and, again, we have known ever since the work of Leontief that fixed coefficients of production are sufficient (but not necessary) to produce constant costs. In short, Sraffa's demonstration that prices in his model are determined independently of demand is eminently 'classical'.

Likewise, there is no doubt that the concept of a uniform rate of return on capital, or rather defining 'natural' prices to be those generated by a stationary equilibrium in which the rate of profit has become equalized by interindustry mobility of capital, is typical of all economic writing in the century between 1770 and 1870. Finally, the real wage rate in classical economics is determined by so-called 'subsistence' requirements and these were defined by Ricardo, Mill and Marx in historical rather than physiological terms; in other words, it was assumed that the current 'natural' price of labour reflected the past history of the 'market' price of labour. The 'natural' price of labour was in effect determined by workers' attitudes to the size of their families but since the classical economists did little to analyse these attitudes, it is not too much to say that the so-called 'subsistence *theory* of wages' actually amounts to taking 'subsistence' as a datum (Schumpeter, 1954, p. 665). Once again, it can be argued that the Sraffian assumption of an exogeneous real wage is 'classical' in spirit.

There is no doubt that Sraffa's system captures many of the elements of 'classical economics'. It provides a further bonus, however, in illuminating classical economics. Generations of critics have tried to make sense of Ricardo's lifelong quest for an 'invariable measure of value' and have given it up as a hopeless task. Ricardo was troubled by the fact that any change in money wages will alter the structure of relative prices owing to the fact that capital and labour are combined in different proportions in different industries. Thus, a rise in wages or a fall in the rate of profit raises the prices of labour-intensive goods relative to the price of capital-intensive goods. This violates the labour theory of value according to which relative prices are determined by the physical quantities of labour expended on production independently of the rate at which labour is rewarded. To remedy this difficulty, Ricardo struck upon the notion of expressing all prices in terms of a commodity produced by a ratio of capital to labour that is a weighted average of the entire spectrum of capital–labour ratios in the economy; such a commodity, he believed, constitutes an 'invariable measure of value' in the sense of providing a standard of measurement that is invariant to changes in the ratio of wages to profits. In the same way, Sraffa measures all prices in terms of a 'standard composite commodity' that consists only of outputs combined in the same proportions as the non-labour inputs that enter into all the successive layers of its manufacture. Moreover, in one of the many elegant demonstrations in his book, Sraffa succeeds in showing that such a 'standard commodity' is in fact embedded in any actual economic system and that the proportion of net output going to wages in that reduced-scale system determines the rate of profit in the economy as a whole.

The explanation of this result depends on Sraffa's distinction between 'basic' commodities which enter directly or indirectly into the production of every commodity in the economy, including themselves, and 'non-basic' commodities which enter only into final consumption. If we treat labour itself as a produced 'means of production' then wage goods constitute examples of 'basic' commodities, that is, they are technically required to cause households to produce the flow of labour services. Ricardo clearly believed that wheaten bread was 'basic' in this sense but Sraffa parts company with Ricardo in rejecting any and all versions of the subsistence theory of wages; workers in Sraffa are primary, non-reproducible inputs. Nevertheless. there are plenty of other basics besides wage goods in an actual economy and the upshot of Sraffa's distinction between basics and non-basics is that the 'standard composite commodity' consists only of basics and indeed of all the basics in the economy; this collection of basics enters into the production of the invariant yardstick in a 'standard ratio', that is, in the same proportion as they enter into their own production. It turns out that relative prices and either the rate of profit or the rate of wages (depending on which one is given exogeneously) depend only on the technical condition of producing the 'standard commodity' and are in no way affected by what happens to nonbasic commodities. In a way this is obvious: a change in the cost of producing a non-basic no doubts alters its own price but, by the definition of a non-basic commodity, the effect stops there since the product in question never becomes an input into any other technical process. It is also obvious, at least intuitively, that an exogenous change in wages unconnected with a change in productive techniques alters the rate of profit but has no effect on relative prices measured in terms of the standard commodity for the simple reason that the change alters the measuring rod in the same way as it alters the pattern of prices being measured. The 'standard commodity' therefore provides an 'invariable measure of value', and Ricardo's old problem is at long last solved.

In developing his own ideas, Sraffa also advanced an entirely new interpretation of how Ricardo came to connect his theory of the determination of the rate of profit with the question of finding an invariable yardstick for measuring relative prices. In his early pamphlet *Essays on the Influence of a Low Price of Corn on the Profits of Stock* (1815), Ricardo wanted to show that the extension of cultivation to inferior soils depresses the rate of profit on capital throughout the economy by raising the marginal cost of producing 'corn', that is, wheat, the principal wage good consumed by workers. This is easy to demonstrate in a one-sector economy where the only output is wheat. However, from the beginning Ricardo operated with a two-sector economy in which an agricultural industry produces 'corn' and a manufacturing industry produces 'cloth'. Of course, if wage goods consist entirely of corn and if cloth is always purchased out of profits and rents, it is still easy to show that the rate of profit on capital depends decisively on the action of diminishing returns in agriculture. In agriculture, wheat is the only output and it is also the input both in the form of wages 'advanced' to workers to tide them over the annual production cycle and seeds to plough back into the next agricultural cycle; hence, the 'money' rate of profit in agriculture cannot possibly diverge from the 'wheat' rate of profit because any change in the price of wheat affects inputs and output in the same degree. Manufacturing, however, only uses wheat as one of its inputs (namely, in the form of wage goods), and since the rate of profit earned on capital must be equal in between the two industries in equilibrium, the price of wheat determines a definite price for cloth. If, for example. the rate of profit in agriculture falls due to the operation of diminishing returns, the price of cloth in terms of wheat must likewise fall to prevent cloth from being more profitable to produce than wheat. To reiterate: measuring all prices in terms of wheat, the 'money' rate of profit in industry is governed by the 'wheat' rate of profit in agriculture, which, in turn, depends entirely on the technology of producing wheat, the unique wage good; in one of

Ricardo's famous catchphrases: 'it is the profits of the farmer which regulate the profits of all other trades'.

This ingenious argument, which appears to explain the determination of the rate of profit in purely physical terms without the use of a theory of value, is known in the literature as the 'corn model'. In the preface to his edition of *The Works of David Ricardo* (1951), Sraffa argued that the corn model is implicit in Ricardo's 1815 *Essay*. To be sure, Ricardo never wrote it down in so many words because even in the *Essay* he could not swallow the assumption that wages are entirely spent on wheat, that all agricultural products are wage goods and that all manufactured products are luxuries which are never consumed by workers. Nevertheless, he did use wheat in the *Essay* as a measure for aggregating the heterogeneous inputs of agriculture on the assumption that all prices rise and fall with wheat prices, and he also employed arithmetical examples in which all inputs and outputs of both agriculture and manufacturing are expressed in terms of wheat. In the *Principles* he analysed an economy with many sectors in which a change in the terms of trade between wheat and cloth will alter real wages and hence the rate of profit on capital. Nevertheless, his preoccupation in this mature work with the 'invariable measure of value' may be read as an attempt to secure the same results obtained earlier with the aid of the corn model, that is, to tie the determination of the rate of profit directly to the production function of agriculture. Of course, if Ricardo could have ignored the varying proportions of labour and capital in different industries, he could have reached all his conclusions without the aid of an invariable yardstick of value. He had placed so much emphasis, however, on what Marx was to call the unequal 'organic composition of capital' that this route was closed to him. Hence, the quest for an 'invariable measure' with which to recapture the simple truth of the corn model. Here then is a rational reconstruction of Ricardo's arguments that accounts neatly for both the form and the drift of his reasoning.

A general equilibrium interpretation of Ricardo

Sraffa's interpretation of Ricardo has won wide assent even among those who otherwise remain sceptical about Sraffa's system in its own right. However, Samuel Hollander's recent re-examination of the whole of Ricardo's writings has taken sharp exception to Sraffa's reading (Hollander, 1979, pp. 123–90, 684–9). Ricardo, according to Hollander, never entertained the corn model even implicitly, never assumed that corn alone enters the wage basket, never argued that the rate of profit in agriculture determines the general profit rate and, above all, never assumed that real wages remain constant either because they are determined by the subsistence requirements of workers or because they are determined exogenously. What Hollander really objects to is the notion that 'distribution', that is, the rate of wages and the rate of profit, are determined in Ricardo as in Sraffa's own model independently of and indeed prior to the value of commodities, so that the former causally determines the latter. This is to be contrasted with the approach of Walrasian general equilibrium theory in which the pricing of factor services is determined simultaneously with the pricing of final consumption goods. It is simply not true, argues Hollander, that the history of economic thought can be neatly divided into two great branches, a general equilibrium branch leading down from Walras and Marshall to Samuelson, Arrow and Debreu today, in which all relevant economic variables are mutually and simultaneously determined, and a completely different branch leading down from Ricardo and Marx to Sraffa in which distribution takes priority over pricing because economic variables are causally determined in a sequential chain starting from a predetermined real wage (Pasinetti, 1974, pp. 42–4, even enlists Keynes into the ranks of the Ricardo–Marx–Sraffa school). Ricardo, Hollander insists, was essentially a general equilibrium theorist – and so were Adam Smith, John Stuart Mill and even Karl Marx (Hollander, 1973, 1981, 1982).

Before passing judgement on this dispute, it is worth noting that what has been called the 'neo-Ricardian' or 'Cambridge' interpretation of the history of economic thought claims superior merit for Ricardo because Ricardo divorced the question of distribution from the question of pricing. But this is precisely the grounds on which many prewar historians of economic thought attacked Ricardo! Thus, Frank Knight in a famous essay on 'The Ricardian Theory of Production and Distribution' (1956) poured scorn on classical writers like Ricardo because they utterly failed to approach the problem of distribution as a problem of valuation and this despite the fact that the effective demand for any factor of production depends on the distribution of income, which in turn depends at least to some extent on the pricing of factor services; in short, 'distribution theory has little meaning apart from a theory of general equilibrium' (Knight, 1956, pp. 41, 63). Similarly, Schumpeter (1954, pp 473, 568–9, 1171) spoke scathingly of the 'Ricardian Vice' whereby an already oversimplified economic model is further reduced by freezing one endogenous variable after another by special *ad hoc* assumptions. First, rent in Ricardo is determined as an intramarginal return to land treated as a factor in fixed supply; the location of the margin depends of course on the demand for agricultural produce, but this is in turn explained by the size of the population via the assumption of a perfectly inelastic demand for corn. Second, having 'gotten rid of rent' on the margins of cultivation, Ricardo then employed a subsistence theory of wages to determine the share of total-output-minus-rent that accrues to labour. Third, total profits in Ricardo are treated as a pure residual after the deduction of wages and rents, the rate of profit being determined as the quotient of total profits and the inherited stock of capital. In other words, the problem of distribution is explained by three totally different types of theories, which in turn are quite different from the principles employed to explain the pricing of goods and services, namely, the labour theory of value. How amazed Knight and Schumpeter would have been to see their critique stood on its head, so that what they regarded as vices are now viewed in certain quarters as virtues.

Ricardo versus Smith

Having expounded various interpretations of classical economics, it is time to attempt some sort of general assessment. To collect our thoughts, consider the number of problematic issues we have outlined above. Is the economics of Adam Smith something different from the economics of David Ricardo? Obviously there is no total break in the continuity of thinking, but nevertheless, is there a sufficient break to warrant the use of such dramatic language as the 'Ricardian Revolution'? Was this 'Ricardian Revolution' the implicit resort to something like the 'corn model' to produce a clear-cut explanation of the determination of the rate of profit, or was it simply a change in the style of economic reasoning? Was Ricardo soon repudiated, so that the Smithian tradition survived right down to John Stuart Mill and beyond, or are the later phases of classical economics dominated by the ideas of Ricardo rather than those of Adam Smith? Is there sufficient coherence around a definite core of ideas to permit us to talk at all of 'classical economics'? Is this core the notion of the origin and disposition of the 'economic' surplus and the proposition that distribution is independent of valuation? And, finally, is all of classical economics a primitive but prescient version of general equilibrium analysis?

We can deal quickly with the first question, the so-called 'Ricardian revolution'. With the exception of Hollander (1979, ch. 1), all modern commentators on classical economics agree that Ricardo altered both the scope, method and focus of economics. Even if we take only *The Wealth of Nations* among Smith's books and essays, the scope of economics for Adam Smith is enormous and perhaps wider than that for any economist before or after him. The first two books of *The Wealth of Nations* consist largely of what later came to be regarded as the very hallmark of orthodox economics: the theory of value and the theory of production and distribution, employing in the main the method of comparative statics. But even the 'Digression' on the value of silver in Chapter 11 of Book 1 takes up an unorthodox topic – namely, changes in the structure of prices over centuries with the aid of a method of analysis that might be called 'inductive' or 'historical'. Moreover, here as elsewhere in *The Wealth of Nations* there is a remarkable emphasis on the notion of 'increasing returns' so widely defined as to include the effects of both increases in the scale of production and changes in the method of production or technical progress. Despite the flowering of a considerable literature in recent years purporting to model Smith's 'theory of economic growth', few have succeeded in capturing this vital element in Smith's thinking, which Kaldor (1972) has consistently emphasized (but see Eltis, 1984, ch. 3). Moreover, this notion of increasing returns soon dropped out of classical economics, coming back only 90 years later with the writings of Karl Marx.

Similarly, there is the famous distinction in Book III of *The Wealth of Nations* between productive and unproductive labour with Ricardo and Mill accepted, which McCulloch and Senior denied, which Marx reinterpreted in a different way, but which nevertheless was never followed up and developed in any fruitful way. A simple explanation for this failure to elaborate Smith's distinction was that Smith made a mess of it, defining productive labour alternatively as labour which produces something tangible, produces a profit for its employer, and generates productive capacity that then creates a demand for additional employment. But another explanation is that the distinction between the employment of 'manufacturers' and 'menial servants', between wealth-creating and wealth-consuming activities, is only relevant in the context of long-run economic development, being partly a 'positive' account of different patterns of economic change in different nations and partly a 'normative' proposal for legislators seeking to maximize the rate of net investment in an economy. Although Mill was profoundly concerned with questions of economic development (see O'Brien, 1975, ch. 8), Ricardo had no real interest in the forces that govern the historical patterns of economic change, and for that reason alone the Smithian distinction between productive and unproductive labour, and the associated discussion of an optimum investment pattern between industries in Chapter 5 of Book II of *The Wealth of Nations*, was effectively laid to rest all through the heyday of classical economics.

Smith's interest in 'the different progress of opulence in different ages of nations' totally dominates Book III of *The Wealth of Nations* and is at work even in Book IV on mercantilist theory and policy and Book V on public finance. In this latter half of *The Wealth of Nations* there is little appeal to the comparisons of steady-state equilibria, which was to figure so heavily in practically everything that Ricardo wrote. But there are two other elements in these pages that are totally missing in Ricardo and even in Mill, namely, a concern with the incentive effects of different institutional devices for rewarding self-employed professionals and individuals employed in the public sector (Rosenberg, 1960) and a keen sense of the role of pressure groups in the formulation of economic policies (Peacock, 1975; West, 1976; Winch, 1983). Thus, the modern theory of property rights as well as the economic theory of politics may properly claim Smith as a forerunner. At any rate, neither of these two aspects of *The Wealth of Nations* has any echoes in the writings of those that came immediately after Smith.

Consider next the theory of international trade. There is a static equilibrium theory of the gains of foreign trade in Smith based on the principle of absolute rather than comparative advantage, and here no doubt Ricardo saw further than Smith. But there is also a dynamic theory of the gains of trade in Smith, the so-called 'vent-for-surplus' doctrine, according to which foreign trade widens the extent of the market and generates new wants; this view of foreign trade disappears in Ricardo and only comes back to classical economics with Mill (Bloomfield, 1975, 1978, 1981).

Smith's theory of money is also profoundly different from that of Ricardo, typically invoking the quantity theory of money in its dynamic eighteenth-century version in which the emphasis falls on the disequilibrium 'transition period' between an increase in the quantity of money and the rise in prices and not on the final equilibrium adjustment between money and prices (Laidler, 1981). In addition, Smith was an advocate of private, unregulated banking (qualified only by the prohibition of the issue of banknotes for small sums), reflecting the operation of Scottish banking, which was unregulated for over a century between 1716 and 1844. It was Henry Thornton who first rejected the Smithian tradition in his *Paper Credit of Great Britain* (1802), explicitly denying that the note issue in a free banking system would be self-regulating as Smith had argued. By the time of Ricardo it was orthodox to argue that the issue of banknotes was an obvious exception to the doctrine of laissez faire (White, 1984, ch. 3). Here too, the gulf between Smith and Ricardo is almost total.

There is no need to underline Ricardo's differences with Adam Smith over the labour theory of value, since Ricardo set out explicitly to criticize Smith's failure to apply the labour theory of value to a modern economy rather than a purely conjectural 'early and rude state of society'. But what is not so obvious is the fact that even in respect of labour as a measure of the 'real price' of commodities – Smith's tortured language in Book I, Chapter 5, for the problem of specifying an index number of economic welfare – Smith's view of labour is profoundly subjective, whereas Ricardo in his comparable Chapter 20 of the *Principles of Political Economy and Taxation* on 'value and riches' consistently treats labour as an objective, physical expenditure of energy. In the masterly tenth chapter of Book I of *The Wealth of Nations* on 'relative wages', Smith demonstrated that competition in labour markets equalize the net advantages of different occupations, that is, the monetary returns to units of disutility of labour. In other words, to the extent that labour is a 'measure of value' in Smith, it is labour conceived as 'toil and trouble' and reflects the preferences of workers as much as those of their employers. Although Ricardo, and for that matter Marx, never disputed this analysis of Smith, they ignored its implications and blithely treated labour as fundamentally homogeneous in quality, its role in the production of commodities being conceived as a brute reflection of purely technological data; in short, they took as given something like Sraffa's production equations. It is this, and not the famous debate over whether the value of commodities in Smith is determined by the labour 'commanded' by goods or the labour 'embodied' in their production, that represents the real watershed in the history of the labour theory of value (Robertson and Taylor, 1957; Gordon, 1959: Blaug, 1985, pp. 49–53).

But the most profound departure in Ricardo from the Smithian tradition is the notion that rent is in a class by itself as a source of income: it is 'unearned income', being an intramarginal return to purely natural differences in the quality of land which have nothing whatever to do with the activity of landlords. Despite Smith's references to landlords who 'love to reap where they have never sowed' and the 'conspiracy' of merchants, the Smithian world is one in which all economic interests are essentially harmonious or, at any rate, capable of being made harmonious by wise legislators. The Ricardian world, however, is one in which conflicting class interests are unavoidable. It is this unique element in the Ricardian system, which gave classical economics its sharp political edge, an edge that clearly worries so many of the minor classical economists, such as Jones, Senior and Longfield.

Finally, the central, and indeed sole, focus of the Ricardian system is the question: what determines the rate of profit on capital, or rather, what governs its changes over time? This is a question which never really troubled Adam Smith. He made it clear that profit is equalized among industries in the long run, but he had no explanation of how the level of the rate of profit is determined. To be sure, Smith believed that the rate of profit was eventually doomed to fall because of the exhaustion of profitable investment outlets. But he never emphasized this proposition and on balance he took an extremely optimistic view of the future prospects for economic growth. Ricardo too was essentially an optimist about the long-run growth potential of the British economy but only if the Corn Laws were repealed; he was thus motivated to argue the strongest possible connection between the rate of profit on capital and the real cost of producing wheat exclusively with domestic resources. In consequence, Ricardo viewed absolutely every aspect of economic activity, including monetary forces, currency arrangements, taxation, the financing of the public debt, and of course foreign trade, through the lenses of his theory of profits. Many readers of Ricardo have been deceived by the preface to his *Principles* – 'To determine the laws which regulate this distribution (of rent, profit, and wages), is the principal problem in Political Economy' - into believing that the Ricardian system is largely devoted to an analysis of the determination of the relative shares of land, capital and labour. But while Ricardo certainly had much to say about the issue of relative shares, and indeed was responsible for introducing this theme into economics, his analysis is in fact concentrated on rents per acre, the rate of the profit per unit of capital and the rate of wages per man. It is, in a word, a book about the pricing of factor services and that is (surely?) much less than the subject matter of *The Wealth of Nations*.

There is little doubt, therefore, that the scope of the science of political economy as conceived in *The Wealth of Nations* was sharply contracted in Ricardo's *Principles of Political Economy*. But, in addition, Adam Smith wrote much besides *The Wealth of Nations*. Quite apart from *The Theory of Moral Sentiments* and the remarkable essay on the *History of Astronomy*, the publication of the new University of Glasgow edition of the complete *Works and*

Correspondence of Adam Smith (1976–83) strongly suggests that he intended to round off his contributions by a major work on the theory of jurisprudence which he never lived to write; nevertheless, even in *The Wealth of Nations* he never lost sight of the fact that political economy may be considered as 'a branch of the science of a statesman or legislator', the latter being therefore something more comprehensive than the former. A number of recent commentators (Cropsey, 1957; Lindgren, 1973; Winch,1978; Skinner, 1979) have indeed insisted that all of Adam Smith's writings are held together by a unified vision of an all-embracing social science, which he unfortunately never succeeded in realizing to the full. Whether this thesis is persuasive or not, it certainly strengthens the contention that the economics of Adam Smith is conceived on grander lines than the economics of David Ricardo.

The corn model again

So there was what might be described in highly coloured language as a 'Ricardian revolution': what began as a criticism of some of 'Professor Smith's opinions' ended up as a wholesale revision of the legacy of Adam Smith.

What was the cornerstone of this 'revolution'? Was it the 'corn model'? It certainly was a denial of the Smithian cost-of-production theory according to which a rise in money wages would raise all prices, thus leaving the rate of profits unaffected. But that is not to say that Ricardo's fundamental theorem that 'profits vary inversely as wages' was based on an implicitly held corn model. It is true that the corn-model interpretation neatly rationalizes Ricardo's arguments in the early *Essay on Profits* in which the economy is conceived as consisting of two sectors but the rate of profit is determined exactly as it would be in a one-sector economy. In other words, Ricardo should have held the corn model for without it the *Essay* is simply logically inconsistent. Nevertheless, the corn-model version simply attributes far more rigour and consistency to Ricardo's analysis than is warranted (Peach, 1984). What Ricardo later put in place of the missing corn model was the 'invariable measure of value' which was designed to surmount two of his unresolved difficulties at one and the same time.

1. that workers consume both manufactured and agricultural goods, so that one can never be sure that the rising cost of producing wheat is directly transmitted to the rate of profit; and
2. that capital and labour combine in different proportions in different industries, so that a change in real wages for any reason whatsoever alters the structure of prices and, thus, affects the rate of profit even if nothing has happened to the technology of agriculture.

We noted earlier that Sraffa's *Production of Commodities by Means of Commodities* may be said to have vindicated Ricardo's belief in the existence of an 'invariable measure of value', capable of separating and measuring the effects of changes in technology from those due to changes in the rate of wage and profits. But doubts remain about the validity of this claim. In Ricardo, the divining rod of the invariable measure is supposed to be invariant (as Ricardo kept saying) not just to changes in wages in profits but also to changes in its own methods of production. Sraffa's 'standard commodity' fills the bill on the first score but fails on the second score: it is not invariant to changes in its own techniques of production and therefore falls short of solving Ricardo's problem of linking the determination of the rate of profit directly and unambiguously to the action of diminishing returns in agriculture. The truth is that there is no such thing as an 'invariable' yardstick that will satisfy all the requirements that Ricardo placed upon it (Ong, 1983). All of which is to say that, despite the fact that Ricardo was the first truly rigorous analytical economist, it is impossible to exonerate him from all analytical errors: he was at times inclined to square a circle using only a ruler and a compass!

Classical economics as surplus theory
We turn next to the thesis that classical economics is the economics of the creation and disposition of surplus output over consumption – a theory of the reproducibility of economic systems in the making – in sharp contrast to the later neoclassical theme of the allocation of *given* resources between competing ends, subject to the constraints of technology and existing property rights. Now, there can be little doubt that this is precisely the nature of the economics of physiocracy (Eltis, 1984, ch. 2), and it is little wonder that those who argue the surplus interpretation include the physiocrats in classical economics (Walsh and Gram, 1980, ch. 2). There is also little doubt that it captures much of the drift of *The Wealth of Nations* and turns up again in Mill's *Principles* and in Marx's *Capital*. On the other hand, it does not begin to do justice to dominant features of the Ricardian system and leaves out almost as much as it manages to include in the writings of the classical economists.

What does it tell us, for example, about the jewel in the crown of classical economics: Ricardo's law of comparative advantage as the foundation of the belief in free trade, which served throughout the whole of the nineteenth century as the litmus-paper test of an economic liberal? Ricardo treated foreign trade as a matter of moving along a static world production–transformation curve, constructed on the basis of *given* resources and the *given* techniques of production of the trading countries; the gains of foreign trade in his celebrated cloth–wine example show up in a global increase in physical output from given labour resources in Portugal and England. There is no hint here of 'surplus theory' and perhaps that is why the surplus interpretation of classical economics studiously avoids discussion of the theory of international trade.

It might be argued, however, that the subject of foreign trade lies outside the mainstream of classical economics because it violates the assumption of a uniform rate of profit on capital – if capital were mobile between countries, international trade would be based like intranational trade on absolute cost advantages. As a matter of fact, Thweatt (1976) has argued that Ricardo's view of foreign trade never went beyond the conception of absolute advantage and this despite the three-paragraph illustration of comparative advantage in his *Principles,* which may well have been written by James Mill rather than Ricardo. After all, free trade for Ricardo meant a policy appropriate to an advanced manufacturing nation in its relation with agrarian nations supplying it with food; the point of the chapter on foreign trade in the *Principles* is not to explain the gains of trade but to demonstrate that foreign trade only affects the rate of profit insofar as it leads to the importation of cheaper wage goods.

Be that as it may, less than a decade after the death of Ricardo, the young Mill (1844, but written in 1829) completed Ricardo's argument by showing that the division of the overall gains from foreign trade in the two countries depends on 'reciprocal demand', thus putting another nail in the coffin of the labour theory of value: even when goods are produced by labour alone within countries, the barter terms of trade between countries depend on both demand and supply. Cairnes subsequently extended the reciprocal demand approach even to domestic trade at least in respect of exchange between 'non-competing groups'. None of this has anything to do with the creation, accumulation and allocation of an economic surplus, and so the surplus interpretation must leave to one side the classical theory of international prices, the classical theory of balance of payment adjustments and with it the classical theory of monetary management.

But the shortcomings of the surplus interpretation extend even to classical theorizing about the operations of a closed economy. It can throw no light on the care with which Adam Smith spelt out the effects of a public mourning on the price of black cloth in Book I, Chapter 7, of *The Wealth of Nations,* so as to demonstrate that 'market' prices cannot permanently diverge from 'natural' prices because they imply profit opportunities for producers that will sooner or later be exploited; all this is to say that the surplus interpretation has little time for those short-run adjustments that formed the staple of much of the practical wisdom of classical economists grappling with day-to-day economic problems. Similarly, the surplus interpretation must pass over the doctrine of opportunity costs that was part and parcel of the legacy of Adam Smith, namely, that effective costs to producers are not expenditures incurred in the past but present opportunities foregone. As Buchanan (1929) showed many years ago, Ricardo's characteristic doctrine of 'getting rid of rent' by concentrating attention on the rentless margin of production implies that land has no uses alternative to the growing of wheat; while this may at a pinch be justified at a macroeconomic level, Smith's theory of rent, which recognizes the fact that land employed in cultivation must compete with land for grazing or urban use, is thus more truly in the tradition of analysing allocation with given resources than is Ricardo's. This Smithian emphasis on the competing uses for land, so that ground rent does enter into the price of agricultural goods, was never lost sight of by classical writers between Ricardo and Mill and comes back into its own in Mill's *Principles,* notably in Book II, Chapter 16, on rent theory.

The surplus interpretation is thus a limited view of classical economics, but it is not a misrepresentation. In one sense it is only fancy language for the old view that classical economics is essentially the economics of development, which starts from a fundamental contrast between augmentable labour and non-augmentable land given in quantity and asks how, under these circumstances, growth in the sense of per capita income can be maximized (Myint, 1948). Indeed, the notion that growth of population and the accumulation of capital are the great themes of classical economics in contrast to the question of efficient allocation of given supplies of the factors of production in neoclassical economics after 1870 is endorsed in many, if not in all, textbooks on the history of economic thought (for example, Blaug, 1985, pp. 295–6). So why all the fuss? Why all this insistence on the surplus interpretation in recent years?

A close reading of those who have advocated a reading of classical economics in terms of surplus analysis suggests two rather different motivations for the 'new' interpretation: one is to provide Marx with a respectable pedigree, or at least to display Marx as the true heir of bourgeois economics in its days of glory, solving the riddles that baffled Quesnay, Smith and Ricardo; the other is to reveal Sraffa as the true heir of the classical tradition, demonstrating that there is an old and venerable tradition of explaining the determination of prices without resorting to the preferences and satisfactions of consumers and without relying on a market mechanism to price both capital and labour. Each of these two strands of the surplus interpretation produces its own special distortions of classical economics.

It is certainly true that Marx was in many ways a direct descendant of Smith and Ricardo, and particularly of Ricardo. He took over from Smith the distinction between use value and exchange value (as well as the denial that the former had anything to do with the determination of the latter), the distinction between market and natural prices, together with the notion that the business of the economist is to explain natural prices as terminal states of long-run equilibrium outcomes, the distinction between productive and unproductive labour, the conception of historically increasing returns as a major force in the process of development, the tripartite division of national revenue into wages, profits and rents as the incomes of three distinct social classes – and much else. But he learned even more from Ricardo and particularly Ricardo's discovery that all the problems of the labour theory of value are reducible to the undeniable fact that capital and labour combine in different proportions in different industries, difficulties which may be resolved however by measuring all prices in terms of the price of a commodity produced by the 'average' industry. This was the key to Marx's 'transformation problem', which demonstrated that 'prices of production' must systematically diverge from labour 'values' if the rate of profit is to be uniform between industries, an insight which, Marx thought, had always eluded Ricardo. Marx hardly noticed that in correcting Ricardo's answer, he also corrected his question. Ricardo's problem had been: what determines the rate of profit? Marx's problem, however, was: what determines the rate of profit if profit is in the nature of unpaid labour, a mark-up on the outlays of wages disguised as a mark-up on all cost-outlays? But the nature of profit as 'earned' or 'unearned' income did not interest Ricardo: he devoted one sentence to this subject in the *Principles* and even this sentence was a throw-away remark.

Marx also learned from Ricardo how to reduce skilled labour to common labour by simply taking the structure of relative wages as given, thus missing the thrust of Smith's theory of relative wages, namely, that wages are not determined solely by the demand-side in labour markets. Marx discarded the Malthusian theory of population but retained the subsistence theory of wages relying on the 'reserve army' of the unemployed to keep wages fluctuating around subsistence levels. He failed to notice, however, that this made wages a function of the play of demand and supply in labour markets and not the labour costs of producing wage goods; in short, the pricing of wage goods in Marx does not conform to the labour theory of value. Like Ricardo, Marx conceded that the level of 'subsistence' is itself historically conditioned: it is a standard of living that workers have become accustomed to expect by past experience. Thus, even the 'natural' price of labour in Marx is not entirely cost-determined but depends on the preferences of workers. Once again, the 'value of labour power' in Marx does not conform to the labour theory of value.

Marx never paid much attention to Ricardo's doctrine of comparative advantage and apparently failed to notice that it too violates the labour theory of value. It is also doubtful whether he ever truly grasped the import of Ricardo's theory of differential rent and particularly its central implication that prices everywhere, and not just in agriculture, are determined by marginal rather than average costs of production.

Nevertheless, despite all the obvious differences between Smith and Ricardo on the one hand and Ricardo and Marx on the other in both analytical constructs and social vision, there are so many striking similarities between them that Marxian economics is simply unimaginable without Smith, Ricardo and (although Marx did not like to admit it) John Stuart Mill. Marx went further than any of them in his grasp of business cycles, his treatment of technical change and the so-called 'reproduction schema' – the true starting point of the modern theory of steady-state growth – but he never emancipated himself from his starting point in classical economics with all its strengths and all its weaknesses.

There can be little quarrel, therefore, with a surplus interpretation of classical economics that treats Marx squarely as one of the last classical economists. However, it is when this Marxian strand in the surplus interpretation is combined with the Sraffian strand that we begin to encounter a mythical classical economics that never existed. We are told that the data for the analysis of prices in classical economics are the same as those for Sraffa, namely:

1. the size and composition of output;
2. the techniques of production in use; and
3. the real wage rate.

These are contrasted with the data of neoclassical economics, namely, the preferences of individuals, the initial endowment of the factors of production among individuals and the existing techniques of production (for example, Eatwell, 1977, p. 62). We are even told that long-run prices in classical theory are *not* the outcome of the opposing forces of demand and supply and that classical 'natural' prices are *not* what (ever since Marshall) are called long-run 'normal' prices (Harcourt, 1982, p. 265) or that, although classical 'natural' prices are indeed the same as neoclassical long-run 'normal' 'prices, the theories advanced by classical and neoclassical economists for the determination of these long-run equilibrium prices are quite different (Garegnani, 1976, pp. 28–9). But there is actually no warrant for any of these assertions.

The size and composition of output is certainly not treated as given in Smith and to say so is to make nonsense of Smith's emphasis on secular economic development and the optimum balance of manufacturing and agriculture in the course of secular growth. Ricardo, on the other hand, frequently but not invariably treats the output of agricultural produce to be determined by the size of population via a perfectly inelastic demand for wheat (Barkai, 1965; Stigler, 1965). Thus, he does not assume the output of wheat (or any other product) to be a datum but to be an endogeneously determined variable, a function of population growth, which in turn is treated as an endogenous variable. He never squarely faced up to all the difficulties created for his argument by commodity-substitution as the price of 'corn' rises relative to 'cloth', but he certainly recognized the problem. There is no support, therefore, for the contention that he took the composition of output to be a datum, except provisionally at certain points in his argument for the sake of producing what he called 'strong results'. What we have said about Smith and Ricardo follows with double force for both Mill and Marx. So much, then, for this part of the attempt to bring the classical economists fully into the Sraffian fold.

We can agree that the classical economists took for granted an existing state of techniques – has there ever been an economist, apart possibly from Marx, who has not? – but the real question is whether they conceived of this state of techniques *à la* Sraffa as ruling out factor substitution. On balance, as we noted earlier, the answer to this question must be 'yes'. Ricardo of course recognized the problem the moment he introduced the chapter on machinery in the third edition of the *Principles* (1821), but by then he was thoroughly committed to his invariable standard of value, which necessarily rules out factor substitution. On the other hand, a special kind of factor substitution was built into his theory of differential rent in which variable doses of capital and labour combined in fixed proportions are applied in increasing amounts to a fixed quantity of heterogeneous land; it is this idea which of course led John Bates Clark and Philip Wicksteed in later years to hail Ricardo as the 'father' of marginal productivity theory. When we consider that the theory of differential rent was the very cornerstone of the Ricardian system, we can only gasp at Sraffa's bold declaration in the preface to his *Production of Commodities by Means of Commodities* (1960) that his own system, concerned as it is 'exclusively with such properties of an economic system as do not depend on changes in the scale of production or in the proportions of "factors"' is identical to the 'standpoint ... of the old classical economists from Adam Smith to Ricardo'.

Next, can it be argued that the classical economists took the real wage rate as a datum for their analysis of value and distribution? It is perfectly true that the much maligned theory of subsistence wages in factor amounts to saying that the subsistence wage is whatever has been the real wage for a long time. How long is long? About a generation, Malthus said, and Ricardo agreed. But such assertions did not help much in specifying the subsistence wage, since annual population growth had been positive for as long as anyone could remember, and a positive rate of population growth implied that market wages exceed the natural subsistence wage rate. So, in effect, the classical economists regarded real wages as data but that is not what they thought they were doing; after all, the only reason that the Malthusian theory of population was so quickly incorporated into the mainstream of classical economics was that it appeared to provide a truly endogeneous explanation of the determination of real wages. The long-run equilibrium wage rate, Malthus had taught, was that wage rate, which, given the historically conditioned habits and customs of the working class, encouraged them to reproduce a family of given size. Some classical economists, like Senior and McCulloch, came to doubt the validity of the Malthusian theory but never managed to put any other theory of the determination of long-run wages in its place. John Stuart Mill, on the other hand, found the Malthusian theory so suitable for his purpose of alleviating poverty through the self-help of the poor – birth control, education and the formation of consumer and producer cooperatives – that he espoused it more vehemently than even Malthus himself. All in all, there is simply no warrant for arguing that any classical economist (including Marx) *intended* to explain real wages by forces outside the purview of economic analysis.

Lastly, we come to the most grotesque distortion of all: the idea that any appeal to the forces of demand *and* supply in determining prices is necessarily alien to classical economics and that classical 'natural' prices have nothing whatsoever in common with Marshall's long-run 'normal' prices. Now, it is true that Ricardo (and Marx after him) propagated the misleading idea that demand and supply explanations only pertain to 'market' prices, whereas 'natural' prices are to be explained solely in terms of costs of production, as if costs can influence prices without acting through supply. Ricardo lacked the analytical apparatus to appreciate the fact that supply-side explanations of prices hold only if goods are produced under conditions of constant costs; this might well justify the neglect of demand in the case of the pricing of 'cloth' but certainly not on his own grounds in the case of the pricing of 'corn'. This marvellous confusion of language, encouraged by Ricardo's tendency to think of demand and supply as quantities actually bought and sold and not as schedules of demand and supply prices, was almost entirely cleared up by Mill in his masterful treatment of value in Book III of his *Principles* in which he noted that an equilibrium price is one which equates demand and supply in the sense of a mathematical equation and concluded that 'the law of demand and supply ... is controlled but not set aside by the law of cost of production, since cost of production would have no effect on value if it could have none on supply'. In fact, this is not very different from what Ricardo (1952, vol. IX, p. 172) once said in private to Jean Baptiste Say: 'You say demand and supply regulates the price of bread; that is true, but what regulates supply? the cost of production.'

Marshall's schema of market-period, short-period and long-period prices, of constant-cost, increasing-cost and decreasing-cost industries, and their accompanying diagrams of demand and supply, are indispensable aids to clear thinking about the determination of prices and imply nothing whatsoever about the truth or falsity of any particular theory of prices. To treat demand and supply as dirty words that classical economists would never have employed in the explanation of natural prices is to take their outmoded language at its face value and, indeed, to deny any analytical progress in the history of economics.

To reject Sraffian interpretations of classical economics is not to reject Sraffa's system on its own grounds. Whether or not it is faithful to both the spirit and the letter of classical economics, it is undeniably true that, like all advances in economic theory, it casts a new light on the ideas of the past. It has certainly made us think again about Ricardo's invariable measure of value and its intimate connection with Marx's transformation problem; it has illuminated the problem of joint production and the difficulties which this creates for the labour theory of value, however formulated; and it has highlighted the fact that any theory of prices necessarily involves some proposition about how total output is divided between wages and profits. Its impact on the ongoing debate about the great ideas of the past is perhaps best illustrated by the furore which it has created among

Marxian economists, suggesting for example, that the labour theory of value in Marx is both unnecessary and incapable of producing Marx's results (Steedman, 1977, 1981). But to endorse Sraffa's system as a tool for historical exegesis is not to say that it successfully models the essence of classical economics. Smith, Ricardo, Mill and Marx are simply richer than anything captured in *Production of Commodities by Means of Commodities*.

Classical economics as general equilibrium theory

Every extreme reaction produces a counter-reaction. The surplus interpretation of classical economics is a reaction against Marshallian interpretation of classical economics in which Ricardo and Mill are viewed as neoclassical theorists in embryo; for Marshall there was one and only one thread of continuous thought from Adam Smith to his own times (for example, Marshall, 1890, App. I). In reaction to the surplus interpretation, Hollander has argued that, from Ricardo onwards, classical economics was, for all practical purposes, general equilibrium theory; there never was any 'marginal revolution'. Since this assertion is, to say the least, surprising, let us quote his own words:

> Ricardian economics – the economics of Ricardo and J.S. Mill – in fact comprises in its essentials an exchange system fully consistent with the marginalist elaborations. In particular, their cost-price analysis is pre-eminently an analysis of the allocation of scarce resources, proceeding in terms of general equilibrium, with allowance for final demand, and the interdependence of factor and commodity markets. (Hollander, 1982, p. 590)

It is evident that by 'general equilibrium theory', Hollander means a number of interconnected propositions, such as efficient allocation of given resources among alternative uses subject to the principle of diminishing marginal returns, the simultaneous determination of both quantities and relative prices with the aid of the principle of equality between demand and supply, and the consequent interdependence between equilibrium in product and factor markets. Perhaps we have already said enough to suggest that if this is what is meant by general equilibrium theory, there is no sense in which we can subscribe to Hollander's interpretation of classical economics.

Hollander has spelled out his meaning in great detail in a major work on *The Economics of David Ricardo* (1979). In interpreting Ricardo as a general equilibrium theorist, Hollander found himself revising more or less the entire body of Ricardian scholarship, implying that absolutely everybody else before him had radically misinterpreted Ricardo. To convey the flavour of his iconoclasm, consider the following small sample of the extraordinary conclusions of this book (for a complete list, see O'Brien, 1981, pp. 354–5):

1.   Ricardo's method of analysis was identical to that of Adam Smith.

2. Ricardo's theory of money was not very different from that of Smith.
3. Ricardo treated the pricing or products and the pricing of factors as fully interdependent.
4. Ricardo's profit theory did not originate in a concern over the Corn Laws, and Ricardo never believed, even in his early writings, that profits in agriculture determine the general rate of profit in the economy.
5. Ricardo's value theory was essentially the same as that of Marshall in that it paid as much attention to demand as to supply, and Ricardo never regarded the invariable measure of value as an important element in his theory.
6. Ricardo could have established his fundamental theorem of the inverse wage-profit relationship without his invariable yardstick and he frequently took the short-cut of assuming identical capital-labour ratios in all industries to give the answers he looked for.
7. Wages in Ricardo are never conceived at any time as constant or fixed at subsistence levels.
8. Ricardo never assumed a zero price-elasticity of demand for corn, making the demand for agricultural produce a simple function of the size of population.
9. Ricardo did not predict a falling rate of profit or a rising rental share and never committed himself to any clear-cut predictions about any economic variable.
10. Ricardo was never seriously concerned about the possibility of class conflict between landowners and everybody else or between workers and capitalists.

There must be something wrong with an interpretation of Ricardo that produces so many conclusions diametrically opposed to what every commentator has found in Ricardo, not only since his death but even while he was still alive. The distortions produced by the surplus interpretation of classical economics are therefore as nothing compared with those generated by Hollander's general equilibrium interpretation.

Walsh and Gram (1980) provide a more reasonable version of the general equilibrium characterization of classical economics: they take the view that general equilibrium analysis encompasses more or less the whole of the history of economic thought, but they distinguish between pre-Walrasian general equilibrium analysis of the allocation of the economic surplus over successive time periods and post-Walrasian general equilibrium analysis of the allocation of given resources within the same time period. One difficulty with their argument is that they never inform the reader what precisely is meant by 'general equilibrium analysis'. If we mean a discussion of the determination of both product and factor prices which proceeds in terms of an explicit or implicit set of simultaneous equations in order to ensure that the number of unknowns to be determined are equal to the number of equations written down, then obviously classical economics is not general equilibrium analysis: factor pricing in classical economics is invariably explained on different principles from those governing the pricing of products. If we go further and demand that such a discussion must include not just a demonstration of the existence of a unique equilibrium solution for the vector of factor and product prices but also an analysis of the stability and determinacy of the set of equilibrium prices, such as Walras himself struggled to provide, then even more obviously classical economics is not general equilibrium analysis. But what Walsh and Gram seem to mean by general equilibrium analysis is simply any analysis that involves the simultaneous determination of prices and one distributional variable on the assumption that other factor prices are given; in short, they define general equilibrium analysis to be nothing more nor less than Sraffian economics. Their book therefore collapses the general equilibrium interpretation of classical economics into the surplus interpretation, sharing the deficiencies of both in equal proportions.

Finally, Arrow and Hahn (1971, pp. 1–3) join the fray in the introduction to their textbook on general equilibrium theory. In contrast to Walsh and Gram, they are perfectly explicit about what is meant by general equilibrium theory: if it means anything it implies some notion of both determinateness and stability, that is, the relations describing the economic system are sufficient to determine the equilibrium values of its variables, and a violation of any one of these relations sets in motion forces to restore it. They go on to introduce a new note into the argument: general equilibrium theory is typically associated with the doctrine of unintended consequences - equilibrium outcomes may be and usually are different from those intended by individual actors - and the doctrine that competition is a social mechanism that is capable of achieving a determinate and stable set of equilibrium prices. In all these senses of the term, they count Adam Smith as a 'creator' of general equilibrium theory and Ricardo, Mill and Marx as early expositors. They add, however, that there is another sense in which none of the classical economists had a 'true general equilibrium theory': no classical economist gave explicit attention to demand as a coordinate element with supply in determining prices, and hence classical economics determined the prices but not the quantities of commodities, the only exception to this statement being their treatment of agricultural output; on the other hand, Mill's theory of foreign trade was 'a genuine general equilibrium theory'.

To this brief, but incisive, discussion of the sense in which classical economics is or is not general equilibrium theory, one must add one word of caution: it is the subtle but nevertheless unmistakable difference in the conception of 'competition' before and after the 'marginal revolution'. The modern concept of perfect competition, conceived as a market structure in which all producers are price-takers and face perfectly elastic sales curves for their outputs, was born with Cournot in 1838 and is foreign to the classical conception of competition as a process of rivalry in the search for unrealized profit opportunities, whose outcome is uniformity in both the rate of return on capital invested and the prices of identical goods and services but not because producers are incapable of making prices. In other words, despite a steady tendency throughout the history of economic thought to place the accent on the end-state of competitive equilibrium rather than the process of disequilibrium adjustments leading up to it, this emphasis became remorseless after 1870 or thereabouts, whereas the much looser conception of 'free competition' with free but not instantaneous entry to industries is in evidence in the work of Smith, Ricardo, Mill, Marx and of course Marshall and modern Austrians (Stigler, 1957; McNulty, 1967; Littlechild, 1982). For that reason, if for no other, it can be misleading to label classical economics as a species of general equilibrium theory except in the innocuous sense of an awareness that 'everything depends on everything else'.

Summary

We have reviewed the recent upswell of new and startling interpretations of classical economics in the light of developments in modern economics, such as the economics of development, growth theory, general equilibrium theory, and Sraffian analysis. In itself there is nothing surprising about this, nor is it a new phenomenon: every turn and twist in the history of economic thought has always been attended by a fresh look at the past. Marx in propounding his own treatment of the 'laws of motion' of capitalism felt impelled to re-examine the ideas of his predecessors over more than a thousand pages. Jevons, Menger and Walras, the triumvirate that is said to have launched the 'marginal revolution', accompanied the exposition of their 'new' economics by scathing denunciations of the fallacies of classical political economy. Marshall, in seeking unsuccessfully to reconcile a static with a dynamic treatment of economic problems, naturally looked with sympathy at the work of his classical forebears and struggled to depict them as slightly exaggerating one side of the truth in contrast to Jevons, who exaggerated the other. Perhaps therefore the recent proliferation of definitely new but conflicting interpretations of the essential meaning of classical economics is simply an expression of the fact that modern economists are divided in their views and hence quite naturally seek comfort by finding (or pretending that they can find) these same views embodied in the writings of the past.

References

Arrow, K.J. and Hahn, F.H. (1971), *General Competitive Analysis*, San Francisco: Holden-Day.
Barkai, H. (1965), 'Ricardo's Static Equilibrium', *Economica*, **32**, February, pp. 15–31.
Blaug, M. (1958), *Ricardian Economics: An Historical Study*, New Haven, Conn: Yale University Press.
Blaug, M. (1985), *Economic Theory in Retrospect* (4th edn.), Cambridge: Cambridge University Press.

Bloomfield, A.I. (1975), 'Adam Smith and the Theory of International Trade' in Skinner and Wilson (1975).

Bloomfield, A.I. (1978), 'The Impact of Growth and Technology of Trade in Nineteenth-century Economic Thought', *History of Political Economy*, 10(4), Winter, pp. 608–35.

Bloomfield, A.I. (1981), 'British Thought on the Influence of Foreign Trade and Investment of Growth, 1800–1880', *History of Political Economy*, 13(1), Spring, pp. 95–120.

Bradley, I. and Howard, M.C. (1982), *Classical and Marxian Political Economy*, London: Macmillan.

Buchanan, D. (1929), The Historical Approach to Rent and Price Theory, *Economica* 9(26), June, 123–55.

Cropsey, J. (1957), *Polity and Economy: An Interpretation of the Principles of Adam Smith*, The Hague: Nijhoff.

Dobb, M. (1973), *Theories of Value and Distribution since Adam Smith*, London: Cambridge University Press.

Eagly, R.V. (1974), *The Structure of Classical Economic Theory*, New York: Oxford University Press.

Eatwell, J. (1977), 'The Irrelevance of Returns to Scale in Sraffa's Analysis', *Journal of Economic Literature*, 15(1), March, pp. 61–8.

Eatwell, J. (1982), 'Competition' in Bradley and Howard (1982).

Eltis, W. (1984), *The Classical Theory of Economic Growth*, London: Macmillan.

Garegnani, P. (1976), 'On a Change in the Notion of Equilibrium in Recent Work on Value and Distribution' in M. Brown, K. Sato and P. Zarembka (eds), *Essays in Modern Capital Theory*, Amsterdam: North-Holland.

Garegnani, P. (1984), 'Value and Distribution in the Classical Economists and Marx', *Oxford Economic Papers*, 36(2), June, pp. 291–325.

Gordon, D.F. (1959), 'What Was the Labour Theory of Value?', *American Economic Review*, 49(2), May, pp. 462–72.

Harcourt, G.C. (1982), 'The Sraffian Contribution: An Evaluation' in Bradley and Howard (1982).

Hollander, S. (1973), *The Economics of Adam Smith*, Toronto: University of Toronto Press; London: Heinemann Educational Books.

Hollander, S. (1977), 'The Reception of Ricardian Economics', *Oxford Economic Papers*, 29(2), July, pp. 221–57.

Hollander, S. (1979), *The Economics of David Ricardo*, Toronto: University of Toronto Press; London: Heinemann Educational Books.

Hollander, S. (1981), 'Marxian Economics as "General Equilibrium" Theory', *History of Political Economy*, 13(1), Spring, pp. 121–55.

Hollander, S. (1982), 'On the Substantive Identity of the Ricardian and Neoclassical Conception of Economic Organization: The French Connection in British Classicism', *Canadian Journal of Economics*, 15(4), November, pp. 586–612.

Howard, M.C. and King, J.E. (1985), *The Political Economy of Marx*, (2nd edn), London: Longman.

Kaldor, N. (1972), 'The Irrelevance of Equilibrium Economics', *Economic Journal*, 82, December, pp. 1237–55.

Keynes, J.M. (1936), *The General Theory of Employment, Interest and Money*, in *The Collected Writings of John Maynard Keynes*, vol. VII, London: Macmillan, 1973.

Knight, F.H. (1956), *On the History and Method of Economics*, Chicago: University of Chicago Press.

Laidler, D.E.W. (1981), 'Adam Smith as a Monetary Economist', *Canadian Journal of Economics*, 14(2), May, pp. 187–200.

Lindgren, J.R. (1973), *The Social Philosophy of Adam Smith*, The Hague: Martinus Nijhoff.

Littlechild, S.C. (1982), 'Equilibrium and the Market Process' in I.M. Kirzner (ed.), *Method, Process and Austrian Economics*, Lexington, Mass.: D.C. Heath.

Lowe, A. (1954), 'The Classical Theory of Economic Growth', *Social Research*, 21, Summer, pp. 127–58.

Marshall, A. (1890), *Principles of Economics*, London: Macmillan.

Marx, K. (1867), *Capital: A Critique of Political Economy*, trans. B. Fowkes, Harmondsworth: Penguin Books, 1976.

McNulty, P.J. (1967), 'A Note on the History of Perfect Competition', *Journal of Political Economy*, **75**(4), August, pp. 395–9.

Meek, R.L. (1967), *Economics and Ideology and Other Essays*. London: Chapman & Hall.

Meek, R.L. (1973), *Studies in the Labour Theory of Value*, (2nd edn), London: Lawrence & Wishart.

Meek, R.L. (1977), *Smith, Marx and After*, London: Chapman & Hall.

Mill, J.S. (1844), *Essays on Some Unsettled Questions on Political Economy*, London: London School of Economics, 1948.

Myint, H. (1948), *Theories of Welfare Economics*. Cambridge, Mass.: Harvard University Press.

Myint, H. (1958), 'The "Classical Theory" of International Trade and Underdeveloped Countries', *Economic Journal*, **68**, June, pp. 317–37.

O'Brien, D.P. (1975), *The Classical Economists*. London: Oxford University Press.

O'Brien, D.P. (1981), 'Ricardian Economics and the Economics of David Ricardo', *Oxford Economic Papers*, **33**(3), November, pp. 352–86.

Ong, N-P. (1983), 'Ricardo's Invariable Measure of Value and Sraffa's "Standard Commodity"', *History of Political Economy*, **15**(2), Summer, pp. 207–27.

Pasinetti, L.L. (1974), *Growth and Income Distribution: Essays in Economic Theory*, Cambridge: Cambridge University Press.

Peach, T. (1984), 'David Ricardo's Early Treatment of Profitability: A New Interpretation', *Economic Journal*, **94**, December, pp. 733–51.

Peacock, A. (1975), 'The Treatment of the Principles of Public Finance in *The Wealth of Nations*' in Skinner and Wilson (1975).

Ricardo, D. (1951–73), *The Works and Correspondence of David Ricardo*, ed. P. Sraffa, Cambridge: Cambridge University Press.

Robertson, H.M. and Taylor, W.L. (1957), 'Adam Smith's Approach to the Theory of Value', *Economic Journal*, **67**, June, pp. 181–98.

Roncaglia, A. (1978), *Sraffa and the Theory of Prices*, New York: Wiley.

Rosenberg, N. (1960), 'Some Institutional Aspects of the *Wealth of Nations*', *Journal of Political Economy*, **68**(6), December, pp. 557–70.

Samuelson, P. (1978), 'The Canonical Classical Model of Political Economy', *Journal of Economic Literature*, **16**(4), pp. 1415–34.

Schumpeter, J.A. (1954), *History of Economic Analysis*, New York: Oxford University Press.

Skinner, A.S. (1979), *A System of Social Science: Papers Relating to Adam Smith*, Oxford: Clarendon Press.

Skinner, A.S. and Wilson, T. (1975). *Essays on Adam Smith*, Oxford: Clarendon Press.

Sowell, T. (1974), *Classical Economics Reconsidered*, Princeton: Princeton University Press.

Spiegel, H.W. (1983), *The Growth of Economic Thought*, Durham, North Carolina: Duke University Press.

Sraffa, P. (1960), *Production of Commodities by Means of Commodities*, Cambridge: Cambridge University Press.

Steedman, I. (1977), *Marx after Sraffa*, London: New Left Books.

Steedman, I. (ed.) (1981), *The Value Controversy*, London: Verso Editions and New Left Books.

Stigler, G.J. (1957), 'Perfect Competition, Historically Contemplated', *Journal of Political Economy*, **65**(1), February, pp. 1–17.

Stigler, G.J. (1965), 'Textual Exegesis as a Scientific Problem', *Economica*, **33**, November, pp. 447–50.

Thweatt, W.O. (1976), 'James Mill and the Early Development of Comparative Advantage', *History of Political Economy*, **8**(2), Summer, pp. 207–34.

Walsh, V. and Gram, H. (1980), *Classical and Neoclassical Theories of General Equilibrium*, New York: Oxford University Press.

White, L. H. (1984), *Free Banking in Britain: Theory, Experience and Debate, 1800–1845*, Cambridge: Cambridge University Press.

8 Marginal cost pricing: no empty box

Introduction

The belief that 'efficiency' and 'equity' can somehow be separated represents one of the oldest dreams of economics. A half-century before Pareto, J.S. Mill distinguished between the immutable 'laws of production' and the pliant 'law of distribution' in an attempt to persuade his readers that questions about the size of the cake can be divorced from questions about its slices. Virtually every economist before Pareto analysed particular economic policies as if it were possible, first, to discuss the effects on allocative efficiency given the distribution of income and, second, to round off the analysis by adding a value judgement about the associated changes in income distribution. The two stages of the argument were never clearly distinguished, however, so it was often difficult to see just where interpersonal comparisons of utility entered in.

The value of Pareto's definition of social welfare was to make the distinction between efficiency and equity crystal clear. But Pareto continued to believe that significant pronouncements about economic policy could be laid down solely on the basis of efficiency considerations, and the same ideal inspired the advocates of the 'new' welfare economics that flourished in the 1930s. In particular, the 'new' welfare economics featured the doctrine that the Pareto optimality conditions for maximum economic welfare required all prices to equal marginal costs, even in cases where marginal costs were less than average costs for the entire range of operations of an enterprise, so that total costs are never recovered by receipts from sales. This, in a nutshell, is the concept of marginal cost pricing (MCP).

What I want to do in this paper is to take you through the tortured history of MCP, moving quickly through the prewar phases of the debate, which have been so brilliantly reviewed by Nancy Ruggles (1947, 1949), and somewhat more slowly through the postwar phases and particularly the recent years. This will not be history of economic thought for its own sake: the story has a point. In the course of telling it, it will quickly become apparent that MCP is one of those orthodox doctrines that has been continually criticized and rejected by experts in the field of public utility pricing but nevertheless remains part and parcel of the corpus of received economic ideas. Even now, the precise status of the concept is a matter of frequent misunderstanding.

The prewar period

The doctrine that the whole of the overhead costs of decreasing-cost industries or 'natural monopolies' must be financed out of general tax revenues, and that the price of their output must depend only on marginal operating costs, makes its first explicit appearance in the railway literature of the late nineteenth century, in particular in the writings of such railway economists as Wilhelm Launhardt and Arthur Hadley, although hints of it are found in the much earlier work of Jules Dupuit and his disciples at the Ecole des Ponts et Chaussées in Paris.[1] When Harold Hotelling resurrected the concept of MCP for public enterprises in a famous paper (Hotelling, 1938), he advanced the general principle that the resulting deficits of decreasing-cost industries must be financed out of 'lump-sum taxes', that is out of taxes that do not affect the behaviour of economic agents at the margin because they leave the *pattern* of post-tax income the same as that of pre-tax income. His claim for the superiority of MCP and the exclusive reliance on neutral, lump-sum taxes was based on the 'new' welfare economics in the sense of Pareto. Hotelling's advocacy of MCP ran almost immediately into a barrage of furious criticism.

Ruggles's classic review of the debate surrounding the Hotelling thesis included many of the great names of modern economics, such as Frisch, Lerner, Samuelson, Lewis, Meade, Coase and many others. It was a confusing discussion, which, we can now see, involved almost as many fallacies as valid objections. Some argued, incorrectly, that prices need only be proportional, not equal, to marginal costs, in which case it might be possible to meet all the marginal conditions of Pareto optimality and at the same time cover total costs out of sales receipts. Some thought that MCP required identical tariffs for public utilities during peak and off-peak periods, whereas the exact opposite is true. Some said that perfect price discrimination would satisfy the marginal conditions, which is true, and that perfect price discrimination is preferable to MCP, which is not true, since discriminatory charges are only one of many ways of pricing intramarginal units. In particular, a special form of price discrimination, namely multipart pricing, with a fixed, uniform 'admission' fee to all users or consumers to finance overhead costs plus a variable charge equal to marginal costs to recover operating costs, was held to be superior to MCP because it satisfied the benefit principle of taxation at the same time that it solved the deficit problem of decreasing-cost industries. Finally, it was argued that MCP failed to provide a profit–loss test of misconceived investment, and that any change from average cost pricing to MCP without compensation payments by gainers (consumers of the public service) to losers (all taxpayers) necessarily leads to a change in income distribution, which is to say that the results of MCP are simply not comparable with those of average cost pricing.

After sorting out the sense from the nonsense in these criticisms, Ruggles nevertheless rejected the Hotelling thesis. At best, Hotelling had shown that a shift to MCP would entail a *potential* Pareto improvement (PPI), not an actual one. He believed that, if deficits were financed by lump-sum taxes, the case for MCP rested on *actual* Pareto improvements because lump-sum taxes fall only on the intramarginal consumers' and producers' surpluses. Ruggles argued that Hotelling was simply wrong, because even lump-sum taxes are borne in part by those who make little or no use of a public service and hence involve a redistribution of income between users and non-users. Either we must decide to ignore this effect by assuming that the utility of income is the same for all individuals, which takes us right back to the 'old' welfare economics of Marshall and Pigou, or we must deny that the associated redistribution is uniquely related to the incomes of users and non-users, which may or may not be true, depending on the public service in question.

Ruggles's criticism of Hotelling has withstood the test of time, and it is now a commonplace of writers on welfare economics to declare that the 'new' welfare economics can only approve a potential Pareto improvement: an actual Pareto improvement requires the addition of a specific distributional judgement. This admission is sometimes regarded as marking the effective failure of the 'new' welfare economics, which had, after all, promised to provide important and significant statements on policy issues without invoking interpersonal comparisons of utility, thus separating questions of allocative efficiency from those of distributive equity. If the conclusions of welfare economics have to be confined to potential Pareto improvements rather than actual ones, the sceptics argue, the promised separation of efficiency and equity is achieved only at the cost of practical irrelevance. Hotelling himself believed that taxes on land rents, inherited income and current income all qualified as neutral, lump-sum taxes, from which it followed that a PPI could always be realized in practice. The notion that taxes on land rents and inherited incomes are lump-sum taxes that do not affect the marginal conditions for maximizing welfare must be put down as a piece of old-fashioned, nineteenth-century economics. Stranger still was Hotelling's notion that an income tax is a lump-sum tax when an income tax obviously alters the marginal rates of substitution between work and leisure.[2] That leaves us with a poll tax or head tax as the only candidate for a lump-sum tax. Unfortunately, such taxes appear to be politically impracticable. If so, there would seem to be no way in which we could ever realize a PPI in practice without committing ourselves to some interpersonal comparison of utility.

The postwar period: phase I
The late 1950s saw a number of major contributions to the debate, all of which endorsed Ruggles' central conclusion that the impracticability of lump-sum redistributions of income or wealth represented the Achilles heel of the theory of MCP.

A careful reading of Ian Little's knock-down assault on the doctrine of marginal cost pricing in his *Critique of Welfare Economics* (1957) shows that it rests essentially on second-best reasoning, that is, the impossibility in a mixed economy of achieving first-best conditions, coupled with a denial of the view that the redistributive effects of a switch from average cost pricing to MCP in public services is random. On the other hand, here and there he made a number of concessions to MCP. In general, Little concluded that cases of zero or near-zero short-run marginal costs (for example, museums, parks, bridges, passenger trains, buses, broadcasting, water supply and uncongested roads) justified zero or near-zero prices so as to equate demand to supply. Nevertheless, in the final analysis he insisted that 'nationalized industries should *at least* aim to cover total costs' (Little, 1957, p. 201); and it is precisely this conclusion that typifies the standpoint of all those who oppose MCP.

Similarly, Jan de Graaff's devastating survey of the 'new' welfare economics in 1957 returns again and again to the impossibility of separating efficiency from equity because of the impracticability of lump-sum redistributions of income or wealth (de Graaff, 1957, pp.77–80). The assertion that lump-sum transfers are not practicable, or even that they are not feasible – a much stronger assertion – is so common in the literature (see for example Samuelson, 1948, pp.147–9) that we ought to spend a moment examining it.

Lump-sum transfers are frequently, but incorrectly, defined as taxes and subsidies that do not influence any economic decision, which of course guarantees the conclusion that the set of lump-sum transfers is empty. Instead, they should be defined as transfers that do not directly change the terms of any economic choice, or, more precisely, as transfers that do not produce substitution effects. In principle, we can think of at least four types of taxes that will meet this requirement:

1. a poll tax or an undifferentiated, uniform levy on everyone;
2. a differential head tax, which is a function of the personal characteristics of individuals, provided these characteristics are not subject to choice, such as age, measured IQ in the preschool years or the number of letters in one's last name;
3. an excise tax on goods, the demand for which is completely price-inelastic; and
4. an equiproportionate tax on all economic alternatives, including not only leisure but all of the non-pecuniary advantages of different occupations.

It is sometimes said that differential lump-sum taxes and subsidies are not feasible because the information on which we would like to base such transfers is not observable and, moreover, economic agents have incentives not to reveal it (Atkinson and Stiglitz, 1980). It is evident that this objection applies with full force to the last two of the four types, but it is not easy to see why it should apply to the first two. A poll tax or a differential head tax is perfectly feasible from an economic point of view. Of course, such taxes are politically impossible because no elected government would swallow the notion of arbitrary levies unrelated to the economic circumstances of taxpayers. At any rate, let us stop saying that lump-sum transfers are not feasible when what we really mean is that they are politically inconceivable.[3]

To return to de Graaff. Like Little, he too rejects MCP on second-best grounds:

> It seems fairly clear that the conditions which have to be met before it is correct (from a welfare viewpoint) to set prices equal to marginal costs in a particular industry are so restrictive that they are unlikely to be satisfied in practice. The survival of the marginal cost pricing principle is probably no more than an indication of the extent to which the majority of professional economists are ignorant of the assumptions required for its validity. How else can we account for the glib advocacy of the principle in a society where the marginal rate of income-tax is certainly not zero, where optimum taxes are certainly not imposed on both imports and exports, where external effects in consumption are of the first importance, where uncertainty and expectation play a major role in making life worth living, where ...? (de Graaff, 1957, p. 154)

In the following year, Coenraad Oort published a book-length study of *Decreasing Costs as a Problem of Welfare Economics* (Oort, 1958), which once again rejected MCP, particularly as a guide to pricing the products of decreasing-cost industries. To stop at the demonstration that MCP creates the conditions for a PPI, while handing over to politicians the job of converting a potential into an actual Pareto improvement, he concluded, is to abandon policy-making at the point where all the interesting economic issues first arise (Oort, 1958, pp.149-50).

Since all these writers agree, there would seem to be little left to say about MCP. Nevertheless, we have not yet taken account of Jack Wiseman's 'empty box' paper (Wiseman, 1957), the most frequently cited and most uncompromising of all the attacks published on MCP in the 1950s. Wiseman did not mince words:

> No general pricing rule or rules can be held unambiguously to bring about an 'optimum' use of resources by public utilities even in theory. Indeed, failing some universally acceptable theory of public economy, the economist can offer no *general* guidance at all to a government how to decide a price policy for such utilities.

Wiseman's argument is based essentially on the fact that there exists no method of implementing the MCP rule for decreasing-cost industries – which for him comprise the typical case – that does not entail a system of financing the resulting deficit, thus altering the distribution of income, which alteration however cannot be evaluated according to the 'new' welfare economics. In short, decreasing-cost industries provide the outstanding example of how pricing rules based on principles of allocative efficiency necessarily imply a simultaneous decision about income distribution.

Wiseman made two further points, both of which have proved to be productive of further developments. He rejected multipart pricing as a solution to the problem of deficits in decreasing-cost industries because it failed to avoid interpersonal comparisons of utility. Multipart pricing, we recall, consists of a lump-sum licence fee to cover deficits and a variable charge per unit of utilization equal to the marginal cost of provision (such two-part tariffs are now common in many countries, for example telephone charges in the United Kingdom). The uniform licence fee, Wiseman noted, may be interpreted as an admission charge to a voluntary 'club' of users, whose members decide unanimously on quantity and price. It is true that multipart pricing changes the distribution of income among users of the service, but this does not matter because it is the product of a voluntary and unanimous choice. If the fixed admission charge did not discourage potential customers, the two-part tariff would be Pareto-efficient. However, since the admission charge is essentially a regressive head tax, the two-part tariff is not distributionally neutral, and its adoption therefore implies an interpersonal comparison of utility. A later paper by James Buchanan took up this idea of economic 'clubs', applying it to the study of efficiency rules for allocating impure 'public goods' characterized by excludable benefits, resulting in what is now a vast if inconclusive literature on the economic theory of clubs (see Sadler and Tschirhart, 1980).

Wiseman also made much of the fact that the MCP principle gives no guidance in selecting the appropriate time period for deciding on public utility prices, and hence no guidance in selecting the length of the relevant planning period. He argued that the only practical planning period is one as long as the lowest common multiple of the life periods of the assets involved, implying that MCP would always have to be supplemented by or associated with an exercise in investment planning.

Martin Farrell (1958) wrote what is generally considered to be the definitive reply to Wiseman. It is noteworthy that he concedes all the standard, second-best arguments against MCP, avoids discussion of the special difficulties created by decreasing-cost industries, and ultimately rests his case for MCP on the still greater deficiencies of average cost pricing.[4] But William Vickrey (1955), writing two years before the Wiseman attack, had used exactly the same sort of argument as Farrell:

> One may for various and sufficient reasons hesitate to embrace marginal cost pricing in all its ramifications as an absolute standard. But no approach to utility pricing can be considered truly rational which does not give an important and even a major weight to marginal cost considerations.

He conceded that popular notions of equity, the need to provide internal efficiency checks on the operation of public enterprises and the high cost of raising the revenues required to implement MCP in the case of 'natural monopolies', such as railroad freight services, made it desirable to depart from the strict MCP rule in a number of cases. Nevertheless, in most cases – and he singled out railroad passenger services as a good example – pricing based on incremental costs yields better results than the type of pricing based on 'fully distributed costs' which is commonly practised by public enterprises in most countries. He concluded:

> In general marginal cost pricing must be regarded not as a mere proposal to lower rates generally below the average cost level but rather as an approach which implies a drastic rearrangement of the patterns and structure of rates. Indeed, it is this restructuring of rates that is likely to be the greatest contribution of marginal cost pricing to the improvement of the overall efficiency of our economy. (Vickrey, 1955, p. 114)

Similar sentiments with particular reference to railroad pricing were voiced by a team of economists led by William Baumol a few years later (Baumol *et al.*, 1962).

In all of these defences of MCP that were penned in the late 1950s, we have clearly travelled a long way from the dogmatic pronouncements of the early advocates of MCP in the golden halo created by the 1938 Hotelling paper. The new argument for MCP is not that it is a perfect policy rule for public enterprises, but that it is a policy rule superior to average cost pricing.

The postwar period: phase II

The early 1960s witnessed a new twist to the MCP debate, which seemed at last to answer Wiseman's earlier criticism that MCP requires a decision on the length of the run over which marginal costs are defined, and yet provides no basis for such a decision. The answer takes its cue from the well known theorem that short-run and long-run marginal costs coincide when capacity is optimally adjusted to demand – from which it follows that any difference between the short-run and the long-run implications of MCP is a sure sign that capacity is not adjusted to its optimal level. If there is excess demand at a price determined by short-run marginal costs, MCP tells us that prices must be raised until demand equals capacity. At the same time, however, capacity should be raised to meet the demand that would be forthcoming at the price that is optimal on the basis of long-run marginal costs. In other words, if there is an optimal investment policy, there is no contradiction between short-run and long-run MCP, and if there is such a contradiction, it constitutes a criticism not of the MCP principle, but of the investment policy that is being pursued.

This argument is the gist of the contributions of a number of French economists, particularly Marcel Boiteux and Pierre Massé, who were connected with Electricité de France in the late 1940s and 1950s.[5] They noted that, in electricity pricing at any rate, there was little alternative to pricing based on long-run marginal costs. 'Short-run marginal costs' could mean the cost either of increasing output quickly or of increasing it temporarily; but, whatever the operational meaning of the term, administrative constraints on frequent tariff charges forced managers of electricity generating boards to focus on permanent output changes and hence on long-run marginal costs (Turvey, 1969a).

The theory of optimal capacity of the French engineers-cum-economists has been vigorously taken up by Ralph Turvey in his writings on the pricing problems of the British electricity industry. In his major study, *Optimal Pricing and Investment in Electricity Supply* (1968), Turvey defines long-run marginal costs in present-value terms as 'the greatest worth of all system costs as they will be with the increment in load which is to be costed, less what they would be without that increment', and shows that information about the structure of marginal costs is provided as a byproduct of the calculations required for rational investment planning. Elsewhere, too, Turvey has come down firmly on the side of MCP as a second-best pricing rule, arguing that the prices of public enterprise products sold within the public sector should equal their long-run marginal costs, while those sold outside the public sector should be proportional to long-run marginal costs, the markup over marginal costs being determined by the prices of their private sector substitutes (Turvey, 1969b).[6]

The striking feature of the French contributions to the MCP literature is their total failure to deal with the problem of deficits in decreasing-cost industries – which, indeed, is hardly ever mentioned.[7] If there really are 'natural monopolies' – that is, public enterprises in which costs continue to decline monotonically for all foreseeable levels of output – it is of little help to be told that short-run marginal costs will be equal to long-run marginal costs when capacity is optimally adjusted, because the optimum level of capacity of 'natural monopolies' is infinitely large. It is true, of course, that the evidence that there are increasing returns to scale in most public services is actually very thin, and it has been argued that even decreasing costs in railways are really due to excess capacity and do not represent a true long-run equilibrium phenomenon.[8] But even if we reject the notion of genuine decreasing-cost industries, the problem of deficits forms an integral part of the MCP principle.

Most UK and US writers on MCP illustrate the problem of deficits with examples of nationalized industries, such as railway transport, the demand for which has been shrinking for such long periods that financial deficits are really due to excess capacity. In that case, even prices equal to short-run marginal costs will not cover long-run marginal costs and will generate financial losses. We can, of course, raise prices to cover average costs in order to remove the deficit, but that only redistributes the social costs of carrying excess capacity, from all taxpayers to users of the service. The French writers on MCP avoid discussing such issues of equity connected with pricing rules of public enterprise because they appear to be thinking of the electricity industry, for which demand is growing and for which costs are almost certainly non-decreasing in the long run.

The postwar period: phase III

We are now very close to the heart of the matter, which, in popular parlance, is the question, 'Should public enterprises be expected to pay their own way?' Those who advocate MCP, even with many 'ifs' and 'buts', deny any presumption that public enterprises ought always to make a profit or even to break even; they focus on current costs, and treat historic costs as bygones that are forever bygones. Furthermore, they insist on keeping questions of allocation and pricing analytically separate from questions of finance and equity. On the other hand, those who reject marginal cost pricing in any and all of its varieties, maintaining that only average cost pricing provides an accounting check on management and denying that efficiency and equity can ever be separated, end up insisting that every public enterprise must be expected to pay its own way, which paradoxically undermines the very case for public ownership that gave rise to the debate on public utility pricing in the first place. In other words, the opponents of MCP would appear to solve the pricing problem of public enterprises by dissolving it.[9]

We come now to the last and most recent phase of the long controversy over the Hotelling thesis. The views of the early advocates of MCP, such as Hotelling and Lerner, that Pareto optimality requires MCP in the public sector on the assumption that prices are equated to marginal costs in the private sector is nowadays dismissed as extraordinarily naive. Given imperfect competition, uncorrected externalities and non-lump-sum taxes, MCP in public enterprises can be only a second-best solution. But apart from all these considerations, there is the old problem of financing the deficit of decreasing-cost industries. Since the deficit must be financed by taxation, and since any tax other than a poll tax or an arbitrary head tax induces price distortion, MCP must involve the problem of maximizing output in the presence of an added constraint: the revenues of government must equal the algebraic sum of the deficits (or surpluses) of the individual firms in the economy – which is precisely the definition of a second-best problem. Even if there is no such thing as a 'natural monopoly', public enterprises or privately regulated enterprises may be required by law to meet historic as well as current costs, in consequence of which MCP would once again involve the problem of maximizing output subject to an added revenue constraint. In either case, MCP is inherently a second-best problem, at least so long as lump-sum taxes are ruled out as being impossible in practice. It can be shown, however, that the second-best case for MCP requires not that prices equal marginal costs, but that prices deviate systematically from marginal costs. It is this theorem that Baumol and Bradford have labelled the 'Mislaid Maxim', in the sense that it goes back to the public finance literature of the 1920s, for example to Pigou (1928), and even further back to the public utility pricing literature of the nineteenth century.[10]

Far from setting prices equal to, or even proportionate to, marginal costs, second-best, quasi-optimal prices should deviate unequally from marginal costs throughout the economy, the deviation in any particular case being greater, the more price-inelastic is the demand for the product in question. In the simple case where all cross-elasticities of demand are zero, the rule is that the deviation from marginal costs for any one product should be inversely proportional to its price elasticity of demand (Baumol and Bradford, 1970). This idea of an optimal set of deviations from MCP in a second-best world is now a recognized feature of modern discussions of applied welfare economics, being the other side of the coin of the currently fashionable topic of 'optimal taxation' (see Atkinson and Stiglitz, 1980, pp. 461–74).

These developments are clearly a far cry from the original Hotelling article. Neverthless, they remain in the Hotelling tradition, not simply because long-run marginal costs remain the reference point to pronouncements on optimal resource allocation, but because the century-old separation of efficiency from equity characterizes second-best as it did first-best welfare economics. Even in this literature, the First Commandment of the 'new welfare economics' - 'Thou Shalt Not Make Interpersonal Comparisons of Utility' - is scrupulously obeyed. But for this First Commandment, we could meet the revenue constraint that inhibits us from achieving a first-best solution by average cost pricing rather than marginal cost pricing. The case for MCP, or, as we should now say, the case for making MCP a point of departure for a set of optimal prices, stems basically from the fundamental conditions for Pareto-optimal efficiency; and, of course, Pareto optimality is defined only with reference to a particular distribution of income or, rather, resource endowments. If we are unwilling to divorce efficiency from equity, at least for the sake of argument, neither the concept of MCP nor that of optimal deviations from MCP makes any sense.

Cost–benefit analysis

In the final analysis, therefore, it is the willingness to analyse efficiency arguments apart from problems of income distribution that divides the advocates from the critics of MCP. The fundamental distinction between efficiency and equity is rarely defended in so many words by modern writers on MCP, but it is frequently and explicitly discussed in the literature on cost–benefit analysis.

Cost–benefit analysis appraises economic projects in terms of their net total benefits over total costs on the assumption that it is desirable to maximize the sum of producers' and consumers' surpluses. But producers' surplus is simply the absolute value of the money amount by which the total costs of production of a particular output exceed the revenue which that output yields under strict MCP, while the consumers' surplus is the money amount by which the consumers' total valuation of that output exceeds the revenue they have paid out, again under strict MCP. Hence, cost–benefit analysis subsumes the MCP principle and is unthinkable without it.[11]

Virtually all modern exponents of cost–benefit analysis are careful to point out that it can only show that a particular project is capable of generating a PPI in which gainers could compensate losers and still themselves remain better off. It offers no opinion on whether such compensation payment *should* be made; that is, it stops at the point at which it has enumerated the gains and losses to various individuals and ventures no judgement on how these gains and losses should be distributed. Since the actual adoption or rejection of a project by a public authority implies both a cost–benefit calculation and a distributional judgement, a number of writers have in recent years suggested that such distributional judgements should be integrated into cost–benefit analysis by means of weights attached to the benefits that accrue to various income groups.

This proposal to use distributional weights has been vigorously opposed by Arnold Harberger (1971, 1978) on a number of different grounds. He argues, first, that economists are unlikely to agree on any particular set of weights. The view that distributional weights ought to decline with income, because of some notion of diminishing marginal utility of income, would no doubt command universal assent among economists. Nevertheless, the distributional weighting functions reflecting this viewpoint can be shown to involve vastly different weights. Even the suggestion of a single premium magnifying the net benefits of beneficiaries below the poverty line is problematic. In general, the use of distributional weights would in most cases make project evaluation depend critically on how the project is actually financed. Hence, if we are concerned to reach a professional consensus in the area of applied welfare economics, we are well advised to ignore distributional effects in cost–benefit analysis.

Besides, even conventional valuations of social income, in which an increase in the size of the national income is regarded as 'good' and a decrease as 'bad', in effect assume that the size of the cake can be treated independently of the sharing out of its slices. In evaluating a change in national income, we typically accept base-year or final-year prices as if the choice involved no value judgement, and we ignore concomitant changes in the distribution of income, thereby attaching equal weights to the gainers and losers of the change. To do anything else would mean that we could not welcome an increase in measured national income without prior agreement on the social welfare function.

Harberger is not denying that the evaluation of the distributional effects of an economic project forms part of the decision to accept or reject the project. The argument is simply that, instead of incorporating distributional weights into cost–benefit analysis, we should sum the monetary value of costs and benefits algebraically across relevant individuals or groups of individuals, leaving the addition of alternative distributional weights to a later stage. In this way we can show that society may have to pay a price in terms of efficiency for each incremental distributional 'benefit' obtained. In one of the most perceptive appraisals of cost–benefit analysis that I know of, Alan Williams (1972) comes to identical conclusions: he rejects the concept of amalgamating efficiency and equity effects but recommends attaching incidence calculations to each cost–benefit appraisal, so that the principles underlying distributional weights can be gradually improved.

Equity versus efficiency again

We end this long and complex story, therefore, by reasserting the old distinction between efficiency and equity which runs right through the entire literature on welfare economics, as far back as Pareto, Pigou, Marshall and even Ricardo, and without which its elaborately constructed apparatus collapses like a house of cards. This is not to say that efficiency questions are 'positive', 'objective' economics, involving no value judgements. Even first-best Pareto optimality rests on definite value judgements, as Alan Peacock has recently reminded us (Rowley and Peacock, 1975). Efficiency is necessarily a value-laden concept, and cannot be freed from the notion that it is somehow more desirable than inefficiency.[12] Nevertheless, there is little advantage, and much disadvantage, in cluttering up the conclusions of welfare economics by indiscriminately combining the value judgements underlying the concept of Pareto optimality with those relating to the economic justice of different distributions of income.

Consider, for example, what is implied by the opposite attitude. If we refuse, even in principle, to distinguish allocative efficiency from distributive equity, we must perforce reject the whole of welfare economics and with it any conventional presumption in favour of competitive markets - and, indeed, in favour of the price mechanism as a method of allocating scarce resources. Arguments for coordinating economic activity by markets would then have to be expressed in terms of political philosophy – for example, that markets diffuse economic power – and economics would in consequence have to become a totally different subject.[13] Moreover, it is perfectly clear that economists do judge such practical questions as, Should parking meters be used to control road congestion? Should public transport be free? Should governments subsidize petrol, medical care and public housing? and so on by means of sequential reasoning, in which the efficiency of various alternatives is judged before considering any possible adverse distributional effects that may or may not be capable of being offset by taxes and transfers (for evidence see Brittan, 1973). It is true that most decisions of public policy proceed exactly the other way round: they are expressly designed to aid a favoured group at the expense of every other, the more so as the benefits of economic policies are often extremely visible, whereas the costs are so widely diffused that most people are hardly aware of paying any part of it. Jacob Viner once defended the economist as 'the special custodian for society of the long view in economic matters' (Viner, 1958, pp.112–13). Similarly, we must insist on the role of the economist as a special custodian for society of the efficiency view of economic problems, because all the evidence suggests that, if economists do not draw attention to the trade-off between efficiency and equity, no one else will.

The subjectivity of costs

Even so, we are not yet home and dry. Recent years have seen an entirely new objection to MCP, new in the sense that it makes explicit an objection that one can now see has been at the back of much of the criticism of MCP. It is an argument that has been vigorously advocated by James Buchanan, who goes so far as to claim that it represents the outlook of an entire 'school', of LSE economists (Buchanan, 1970; Buchanan and Thirlby, 1973).

Buchanan argues that opportunity costs in the real world are personal, subjective valuations of the utility of foregone alternatives, and not the objective market prices of resources that figure in the diagrams of textbooks in price theory. In a world of fully competitive equilibrium, he readily admits, objective *ex post* cost data would indeed coincide with subjective *ex ante* estimates of foregone alternatives; but in actual situations of disequilibrium, imperfect knowledge and pervasive uncertainty, there is no reason to think that the two are systematically related. Buchanan mentions some practical implications of his argument and is particularly scathing about cost–benefit analysis; he is silent, however, on the question of the pricing of public utilities.

However, in a critical assessment of Buchanan's argument, Karen Vaughn (1980) specifically considers the problem of pricing rules for regulated monopolies. It is, of course, precisely when governmental decisions pre-empt market decisions that models of markets in full equilibrium are likely to be particularly misleading. In other words, the Buchanan critique cuts most deeply at the very point under consideration: if in practice the regulatory agency has no method for ascertaining the costs perceived by the regulated enterprise, MCP falls to the ground.

But this is merely to say that MCP suffers all the shortcomings of applied welfare economics cast in the traditional Paretian mould: it is a proposition about the nature of end-point equilibrium states and has nothing whatever to say about the process by which an actual economy converges on equilibrium. Economists have usually been confident that, provided one is certain about one's destination, the journey to that destination is of little consequence; in other words, they have shrugged off the political and administrative problems of imposing MCP on an enterprise pursuing a pricing rule based on average costs. Much doubt has recently been cast on that approach by Demsetz (1968), Stigler (1975a) and Alan Peacock (1979) himself. Faced with a genuine natural monopoly situation, it is no longer as obvious to the present generation of economists as it was to previous generations that only outright nationalization or regulation of some kind can achieve the MCP solution required by Paretian principles. Nevertheless, this is no objection to MCP in cases where the industry has long been in public ownership or subject to public regulation. And, besides, the natural monopoly case is only half the story of MCP.

Conclusions

So, Ruggles, Little, Graaff, Oort and Wiseman notwithstanding, the theory of MCP is no empty box. Of course, MCP is a method, not a dogma. It is grounded in Pareto optimality and the maximization of consumers' and producers' surpluses, but, then, so are all the policy views of economists. In addition, MCP requires empirical judgements on a product-by-product basis about market structure, indivisibilities, externalities and elasticities of demand and supply; in short, it is a systematic check-list of what to look for in pricing a public service. It does not, therefore, furnish any simple pronouncements about public pricing, except perhaps that public enterprises should not necessarily be expected to break even and that almost any pricing rule is better than average cost pricing. Moreover, standing by itself, it furnishes no case for nationalizing or regulating all industries with natural monopoly characteristics.

These may be simple truths, but nevertheless they directly contradict popular doctrine about public sector pricing. Here as elsewhere, economists find themselves solidly ranked against some of the great myths of our times.

Notes

1. See Ekelund and Hébert (1983) and the literature cited there, not least their own researches.
2. Most of the early participants in the controversy over the Hotelling thesis agreed with Hotelling that an income tax is superior to an excise tax as a method of raising revenue to finance the MCP system. This thesis, soon to be known as the 'excess burden of indirect taxation', attracted almost as much debate in the 1940s and 1950s as the concept of MCP. It took almost two decades to arrive at the correct view, namely that there is no simple way of ranking taxes according to their 'excess burden' (see Walker, 1955, and Musgrave, 1959, ch. 7).
3. This conclusion is essentially due to Oort (1958, pp. 40-4, 122-5).
4. Farrell (1958) is reprinted with considerable amendment, taking account of Wiseman (1959), in Turvey (1968a).
5. See Drèze (1964), Turvey (1964) and Nelson (1968).
6. See also Turvey and Anderson's popular exposition of MCP in the electricity industry (Turvey and Anderson, 1975). This concludes:

   If we ignore complications relating to income distribution, externalities and pricing distortions elsewhere, and if we ignore stochastic variations in demand and in the availability of productive capacity, the rules for optimal resource allocation are simple. There is the pricing rule that price should equal whichever is the higher of marginal operating costs, or the price necessary to restrict demand capacity. There is also the investment rule that the present worth of the dual (shadow) value of capacity should be equated with its marginal capacity costs (p. 355).

7. I owe this insight to Millward (1971, pp. 244–5).
8. The typical long-run average cost curve of a firm appears to be L-shaped, falling at first then becoming horizontal, which is to say that there is no evidence for continually falling costs even in the case of railways. In other words, while there is clear evidence of unexploited economies

184 Economic theories, true or false?

of scale in many industries, there are few unambiguous cases of 'natural monopolies'; see Johnston (1960); Walters (1963, 1968); Smith (1955); Silbertson (1972).

9. For an admittedly confusing example of this style of anti-MCP reasoning see Melody (1974) and the reply by Kahn (1974). The tension between these two points of view is at the back of the complex argument of Nove (1973). He rejects the belief of 'many economists [who] insist on identical criteria in the nationalized and private sectors' and yet recommends Wiseman's 'proper scepticism about marginal cost pricing' in the apparent belief that MCP suggests that every part of an integrated public enterprise should be run at a profit and that there should never be cross-subsidization between them. But the MCP philosophy suggests the very opposite, so Nove's criticisms are properly directed not at MCP, but at average cost pricing.

10. Pigou (1928) contains an extensive summary of optimal pricing solutions for an industry in which MCP fails to recover total costs, including a statement of the 'Mislaid Maxim'. Thus, a decade before Hotelling's paper Pigou had already conceived MCP as a second-best problem.

11. As Millward (1971) has said, 'It is amazing how the topic of marginal cost pricing has been bombarded with criticisms, many of which are equally applicable to cost–benefit analysis which often escapes scot-free' (p. 282). Actually, this is less amazing when it is realized that the intimate connection between MCP and cost–benefit analysis is little appreciated even by those who malign MCP.

12. Only a minority of economists would disagree with this view, principally Archibald and Hennipman. For details see Blaug (1980, pp. 142–8).

13. As Mishan (1971) has said,

If economists reject welfare economics, they may well have to reject also the economists' conventional presumption in favour of a competitive market. The economist could of course approve of the market for other than allocative reasons: for instance, on the grounds that it is a cheap and relatively non-political administrative institution for coordinating economic activity (p. 308).

References

Atkinson, A.B. and Stiglitz, J.E. (1980), *Lectures on Public Economics*, Maidenhead, Berkshire: McGraw-Hill.

Baumol, W.J. and Bradford, D.F. (1970), 'Optimal Departures from Marginal Cost Pricing', *American Economic Review*, **60**.

Baumol, W.J. *et al.* (1962), 'The Role of Cost in the Minimum Pricing of Railroad Services', *Journal of Business*, **35**; reprinted in Munby (1968).

Blaug, M. (1980), *Methodology of Economics*, London: Cambridge University Press.

Brittan, S. (1973), *Is There an Economic Consensus? An Attitude Survey*, London: Macmillan Press.

Buchanan, J. (1970), *Costs and Choice*, Chicago: Markham.

Buchanan, J. and Thirlby, G.F. (eds) (1973), *LSE Essays on Cost*, London: Weidenfeld and Nicolson.

Demsetz, H. (1968), 'Why Regulate Utilities? *Journal of Law and Economics*, **11**.

Drèze, J.H. (1964), 'Some Post-war Contributions of French Economists to Theory and Policy', *American Economic Review*, **56**.

Ekelund, R.B. and Hébert, R.F. (1983), *A History of Economic Theory and Method* (2nd edn), Maidenhead, Berkshire: McGraw-Hill.

Farrell, M.J. (1958), 'In Defence of Public Utility Price Theory', *Oxford Economic Papers*, **10**.

De Graaf, J. (1957), *Theoretical Welfare Economics*, London: Cambridge University Press.

Harberger, A. (1971), 'Three Basic Postulates for Applied Welfare Economics', *Journal of Economic Literature*, **9**.

Harberger, A. (1978), 'On the Use of Distributional Weights in Social Cost Benefit Analysis', *Journal of Political Economy*, **86**.

Hotelling, H. (1938), 'The General Welfare in Relation to the Problems of Taxation and of Railway and Utility Rates', *Econometrica*, **6**; reprinted in K.J. Arrow and T. Scitovsky (eds) (1969), *Readings in Welfare Economics*, Homewood, Illinois: Irwin Press.

Johnston, J. (1960), *Statistical Cost Analysis*, New York: McGraw-Hill.

Kahn, A.E. (1974), 'Economic Theory as a Guideline for Government Intervention and Control: A Comment' *Journal of Economic Issues*, **8**.

Little, I.M.D. (1957), *Critique of Welfare Economics*, Oxford: Oxford University Press.

Melody, W.H. (1974), 'The Marginal Utility of Marginal Analysis in Public Policy', *Journal of Economic Issues*, **8**.

Millward, R. (1971), *Public Expenditure Economics: An Introductory Application of Welfare Economics*, Maidenhead, Berkshire: McGraw-Hill.

Mishan, E. (1971), *Cost-Benefit Analysis*, London: Allen and Unwin.

Munby, D. (ed.) (1968), *Penguin Modern Economics Readings: Transport*, Harmondsworth, Middlesex: Penguin Books.

Musgrave, R.A. (1959), *The Theory of Public Finance*, New York: McGraw-Hill.

Nelson, J.R. (ed) (1968), *Marginal Cost Pricing in Practice*, Englewood Cliffs, New Jersey: Prentice-Hall.

Nove, A. (1973), *Efficiency Criteria for Nationalised Industries*, London: Allen and Unwin.

Oort, C. (1958), *Decreasing Costs as a Problem in Welfare Economics*, Amsterdam: Drukkerij Holland.

Peacock, A.T. (1979), *The Economic Analysis of Government*, Oxford: Martin Robertson.

Pigou, A.C. (1928), *Study of Public Finance*, London: Macmillan Press.

Rowley, C.K. and Peacock, A.T. (1975) *Welfare Economics: A Liberal Restatement*, Oxford: Martin Robertson.

Ruggles, N. (1947), 'The Welfare Basis of the Marginal Cost Pricing Principle', *Review of Economic Studies*, **17**.

Ruggles, N. (1949), 'Recent Developments in the Theory of Marginal Cost Pricing', *Review of Economic Studies*, **19**: reprinted in Turvey (1968a).

Samuelson, P.A. (1948), *Foundations of Economic Analysis*, Cambridge, Massachusetts: Harvard University Press.

Sadler, T. and Tschirhart, J.T. (1980), 'The Economic Theory of Clubs: An Evaluative Survey', *Journal of Economic Literature*, **18**.

Silbertson, A. (1972), 'Economies of Scale in Theory and Practice', *Economic Journal*, **83**.

Smith, C.A. (1955) 'Survey of Empirical Evidence on Economies of Scale in NBER', in *Business Concentration and Price Policy*, Princeton, New Jersey: Princeton University Press.

Stigler, G.I. (1975), *The Citizen and the State: Essays on Regulation*, Chicago: University of Chicago Press.

Turvey, R. (1964), 'Marginal Cost Pricing in Practice', *Economica*, **31**.

Turvey, R. (ed.) (1968a) *Penguin Readings in Modern Economics: Public Enterprise*, Harmondsworth, Middlesex: Penguin Books.

Turvey, R. (1968b), *Optimal Pricing and Investment in Electricity Investment*, London: Allen and Unwin.

Turvey, R. (1969a), 'Marginal Cost', *Economic Journal*, **79**.

Turvey, R. (1969b), 'The Second Best Case for Marginal Cost Pricing', in J. Margolis and H. Guitton (eds), *Public Economics*, London: Macmillan Press.

Turvey, R. and Anderson, D. (1975), *Electricity Economics*, Baltimore: Johns Hopkins University Press.

Vaughn, K.I. (1980), 'Does it Matter that Costs are Subjective?' *Southern Economic Journal*, **46**.

Vickrey, W. (1955), 'Some Implications of Marginal Cost Pricing for Public Utilities', *American Economic Review*, **45**.

Viner, J. (1958) *The Long View and the Short View*, Glencoe, Illinois: The Free Press.

Walker, D. (1955), 'The Direct-Indirect Tax Problem; Fifteen Years of Controversy', *Public Finance*, **10**.

Walters, A.A. (1963), 'Production and Cost Functions: An Econometric Study', *Econometrica*, **31**.

Walters, A.A. (1968), *The Economics of Road User Charges*, Baltimore: Johns Hopkins University Press.

Williams, A. (1972), 'Cost–Benefit Analysis: Bastard Science and/or Isidious Poison in the Body Politic', *Journal of Public Economics*, **1**.

Wiseman, J. (1957), 'The Theory of Public Utility Price: An Empty Box'. *Oxford Economic Papers*, **9**; reprinted in Buchanan and Thirlby (1973).

Wiseman, J. (1959), 'The Theory of Public Utility Prices: A Further Note', *Oxford Economic Papers*, **11**.

9 Nicholas Kaldor, 1908–86

Introduction – biographia

Modern economics, like modern physics, is a subject in which reputations are made and unmade by essays rather than books. Nicholas Kaldor is a case in point. Unlike the great economists of the nineteenth century, he has never put his ideas together in a single comprehensive treatise and has instead scattered his ideas over some 90 articles, half a dozen of which have become classics of their kind. He has candidly admitted changing his mind more than once on some vital questions and has explained his own failure to write the 'Great Book' by the belief that he might yet change it again (Kaldor, 1978b, p. xxix). The willingness to rework his pet theories when they are upset by the discovery of some hitherto unsuspected fact is one of the features that give almost all his writings a fresh and lively quality – that and his constant insistence that fruitful economic analysis must be grounded in empirically derived 'laws' or statistical regularities. His own description of his work in the last twenty years perfectly captures this pragmatic element in his approach – to economic questions:

> I tried to find what kind of regularities can be detected in empirically observed phenomena and then tried to discover what particular testable hypotheses would be capable of explaining the association . . . It is an approach which is more modest in scope (in not searching for explanations that derive from a comprehensive model of the system) and also more ambitious in that it directly aims at discovering solutions (or remedies) for real problems. (Kaldor, 1978b, p. xviii; also Kaldor, 1985, p. 8)

Kaldor's intellectual career breaks rather neatly into three well-defined phases, as he would be the first to agree (Kaldor, 1986). In the first phase, spanning the 1930s, his efforts were largely critical and polemical. His very first published article (Kaldor, 1934) contained a systematic account of the 'cobweb' theorem and invented its name. In addition, he effectively attacked Chamberlain's excess capacity theorem (Kaldor, 1938) and Hayek's theory of the trade cycle (Kaldor, 1939a, 1942) and traded blows with Frank Knight over the Austrian theory of capital (Kaldor, 1937). In the closing years of that decade, he announced the discovery of the compensation principle in welfare economics (Kaldor, 1939b) and the notion of optimum tariffs in the theory of international trade (Kaldor, 1940b) besides constructing an original model of the trade cycle (Kaldor, 1940a). During the war years and early postwar period, he emerged as one of the most vigorous of Keynes's many disciples and yet by, say, 1950 he had still failed to place a unique stamp of his own on the development of economic theory.

The second phase began in the mid-1950s with a series of papers on the theory of economic growth, embodying the concepts of 'two' saving rates, a mark-up theory of pricing and the 'technical progress function', which formed essential ingredients of what soon came to be known as post-Keynesian economics. Simultaneously, he published a book on *The Expenditure Tax* (Kaldor, 1955), which launched him on a new career as a tax reformer.

His inaugural lecture as Professor of Economics at Cambridge University in 1966, *Causes of the Slow Rate of Economic Growth of the United Kingdom,* marked the onset of the third and final phase of his intellectual development. Convinced that manufacturing industry is characterized by conditions of increasing returns to scale, he broke decisively with the notion of single-sector growth models, including his own, and adopted instead a multi-sector account of the growth process according to which the growth of demand for manufacturing products determines the rate of growth of total output in the economy. The new scheme was designed not merely to explain the differential rates of growth of industrialized countries in recent years, but indeed the entire evolution of the capitalist system. In short, he had at long last arrived at a unique vision of his own of what Adam Smith had called 'the nature and causes of the wealth of nations'.

Kaldor's contributions have ranged so far and wide as to preclude even a summary of them in anything less than a book. We will therefore focus here on the last two phases of his career, labelled for convenience Kaldor II and III, saying little, however, about his views on taxation (Kaldor, 1979a, 1979b) or his writings on international finance (Kaldor, 1963).

Nicholas Kaldor was born in Budapest, Hungary in 1908, the son of a Jewish barrister. As a boy he attended the 'Model Gymnasium' in Budapest, a private school which has produced an almost endless series of famous Hungarians. After a year at the University of Berlin, he moved to Britain in 1927 to study at the LSE, graduating in 1930. Two years later he was appointed an assistant lecturer at the LSE, becoming a lecturer in 1934 and a reader in 1942. He left the LSE in 1947 to become Director of the Research and Planning Division of the Economic Commission for Europe, serving eventually as one of a small group of experts to author the influential UN report *National and International Measures for Full Employment* (1949). He returned to academic life as a fellow at King's College, Cambridge in 1949, becoming a reader in 1952, and a Professor of Economics in 1966. He retired from academic life in 1975.

Throughout this latter period at Cambridge he also served as a tax adviser to the government of India, Sri Lanka, Mexico, British Guyana, Turkey, Iran, Venezuela and Ghana, capped by his appointment as Special Adviser to the Chancellor of the Exchequer of two British Labour governments during the years 1964–68 and 1974–76. Among his many contributions to the economic policies of the Labour government were the Selective Employment Tax (1966–72), a payroll tax designed to discriminate against employment in service industries and the Regional Employment Premium (1966–76), designed to subsidize manufacturing employment in depressed areas. But his pleas for an expenditure tax to replace the taxation of income and his opposition to Britain's entry into the Common Market (Kaldor, 1971b, 1971c) fell on deaf ears. He was raised to the peerage in 1974. His speeches to the House of Lords, published under the title of *The Economic Consequences of Mrs Thatcher* (1983) – echoing the title of Keynes's *Economic Consequences of the Peace* (1919) – reveal his brilliance as a political debater with an audience of non-economists. Two lectures to an academic audience, published as *The Scourge of Monetarism* (1982), leave no doubt of his scathing rejection of the policies of the current Conservative government in Britain (see also Kaldor, 1970a).

Kaldor's conviction that manufacturing holds the key to Britain's economic growth rate has been widely disseminated in recent years (John Eatwell's BBC TV series *Whatever Happened to Britain?*, shown in 1984, was pure Kaldor) and indeed were more or less officially adopted by the Labour Party in the run-up to the election. Thus whatever are our ultimate judgements on his views, they clearly merit a considered hearing.

A theory of economic growth

Kaldor's theory of economic growth was propounded in a series of six papers published between the years 1956 and 1962, marking a gradual evolution of the details of the theory without affecting its substantial outlines. It began as a simple Keynesian theory of macrodistribution (Kaldor, 1956), to which was then added a so-called 'technical progress function', a mark-up theory of pricing and a particular investment function (Kaldor, 1957). The investment function was then reformulated (Kaldor, 1958), which produced further changes in the final version of the model (Kaldor, 1962). The original macrodistribution theory is plain sailing; complications only arise when considering the full-blown theory of growth, particularly in its final mature version. We shall not attempt to expound Kaldor's growth theory in all its details[1] but merely to sketch its main outlines, touching upon its peculiar strengths and weaknesses.

A necessary prelude to Kaldor's macrodistribution theory is the growth equation of Roy Harrod. This created the modern conception of the theory of economic growth in the form of a statement of the requirements for steady-state, indefinite expansion:

$$G = s/C$$

where $G = dY/Y$, the actual proportionate rate of growth of national income,

$C = dK/dY$, the marginal capital-output ratio

and $s = S/Y$, the average saving-income ratio (which is assumed to equal the marginal savings-income ratio)

Since planned saving, S, must equal planned investment, I, in equilibrium, we have what Harrod calls the 'warranted' rate of growth, G_w:

$$G_w = \frac{dy}{Y} = \frac{dY}{I}\frac{S}{Y} = \frac{dY}{dK}\frac{S}{Y} = \frac{s}{C}$$

Harrod went on to define G_n as the 'natural' or full employment growth rate resulting from the rate of growth of the labour force and the rate of technical progress as reflected in the average productivity of labour, both of which are taken to be exogenously determined. If we define C_r, as the incremental capital–output ratio required to equip the increasing number of workers at full employment, the Harrod equation for G_n becomes:

$$G_n = s/C_r$$

Kaldor's 'alternative theory of distribution' can now be rendered into the terminology of Harrod. Starting with the identity:

$$Y = W + P \tag{1}$$

where Y = national income, W = total wages and P = total property income, we postulate constant but different average equals marginal propensities to save out of wages and profits, s_w and s_p, so that total savings, S, is given by:

$$S = s_w W + s_p P \tag{2}$$

or, substituting for W from (1)

$$S = s_w(Y—P) + s_p P$$

and rearranging

$$S = (s_p - s_w)P + s_w Y \tag{3}$$

Dynamic equilibrium requires that $I = S$, which implies that:

$$I = (s_p—S_w)P + s_w Y \tag{4}$$

Equation (4) can be divided by Y and rearranged to obtain the share of profits in national income, P/Y.

$$I/Y = (s_p - s_p)P/Y + s_w \tag{5}$$

$$\frac{P}{Y} = \frac{1}{s_p - s_w} \frac{I}{Y} - \frac{S s_w}{s_p - s_w} = \frac{I/Y - s_w}{s_p - s_w}$$

Thus, a condition for both positive profits and a positive profit share is that:

$$S_w < I/Y < S_p$$

In the special 'classic' case in which the propensity to save out of wage income is assumed to be zero, equation (5) reduces to:

$$\frac{P}{Y} = \frac{I/Y}{s_p} \tag{6}$$

By the Harrod growth equation, $I/Y = S/Y = s = GC$, and so we have in general:

$$\frac{P}{Y} = \frac{G_w C - s_w}{s_p - s_w}$$

or in the special 'classic' case,

$$\frac{P}{Y} = \frac{G_w C}{s_p} \tag{7}$$

At full employment, with growth at its 'natural' rate, $G_n C_r = {}_s$, this 'classic' case becomes:

$$\frac{P}{Y} = \frac{G_n C_r}{s_p} \tag{8}$$

What Kaldor has shown, therefore, is that the share of profits (and also the rate of profit on capital) varies directly with the growth rate of income, the capital–output ratio and workers' saving rate, but it varies inversely with the capitalists' saving rate. At full employment, with growth at the 'natural' rate, the saving propensities determine the profit share, such that the more capitalists consume (the smaller is s_p), the larger is their relative share. Or, to put it differently, with income given at the full employment level and investment given exogenously so as to be consistent with full employment, steady-state growth as defined by Harrod is only possible through changes in the aggregate saving–income ratio; once we follow Kaldor by distinguishing two given saving propensities out of wages and profits and assume $s_w = s_p$, so that total savings is a weighted average of s_p and s_w, the weights being the relative shares of capital and labour, it follows immediately that the shifting of income between workers and capitalists is the only thing that makes steady-state growth possible. This is hardly an earth-shattering conclusion, since everything else but the relative shares of capital and labour is in effect given by the assumption of steady-state growth.[2]

Needless to say, this simple macrodistribution theory was widely criticized, and even ridiculed, on the grounds that it was rested upon two distinctly Harrodian notions: a technically predetermined capital–output ratio unaffected by relative input prices and a 'natural' full employment growth path defined independently of variations in the saving propensities out of wages and profits. It was in reaction to the first of these criticisms that Kaldor (1957) amplified the original version of his model by the addition of a 'technical progress function', which served to determine the capital–output ratio in the steady state.

Rejecting the neoclassical concept of an aggregate production function defined for a given state of technical knowledge and the associated notion of 'disembodied' technical progress taking place independently of capital accumulation, Kaldor begins by making technical progress a function of gross investment. He argues that entrepreneurs always choose that technique which gives the greatest increase in output per worker at the lowest investment per worker, irrespective of the factor-saving nature of the technique. In other words, every economy can be characterized by a 'technical progress function', relating the rate of growth of output per worker to the rate of growth of capital per worker.

In Figure 9.1, the vertical axis shows the percentage rate of growth of labour productivity, y/n, lower case letters denoting (here as elsewhere in this paper), proportionate rates of growth. The horizontal axis shows the percentage rate of growth of investment per worker, i/n. The technical progress function cuts the vertical axis at some positive rate of growth of labour productivity to show that

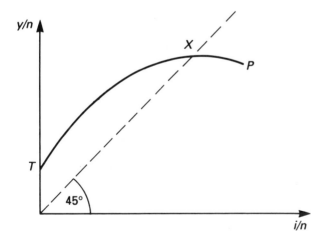

Figure 9.1   The technical progress function

there will always be some 'disembodied' technical progress, and is concave from below, indicating 'diminishing returns' to ever higher rates of growth of investment per worker. The broken 45°-1ine shows all the points where output per worker and investment per worker grow at the same rate. Hence, an economy in steady-state growth must be somewhere on the 45°-1ine. It must at the same time be somewhere on its technical progress function, from which it follows that the intersection X is the only point where steady-state equilibrium is possible. To the left of X, output per worker is growing faster than the flow of investment per worker, so that the (stock) capital to output ratio is falling; to the right of X, investment per worker is growing faster than output per worker, so that the capital-output ratio is rising; but at X, the capital–output ratio is constant, technical progress is 'neutral' (as measured by the capital–output ratio) and all the critical rates of growth, output, labour, the flow of investment, the stock of capital – as well as the share of wages and profits in output – are likewise constant over time.

The entire argument depends, partly on the position of the technical progress function which expresses what Kaldor calls the 'technical dynamism' of an economy (that is, the willingness of entrepreneurs to invest in new ways of making goods) and partly, and perhaps more critically, on the forces that actually drive an economy towards point X. Kaldor leaves the former unexplained. With regard to the latter he discusses various ways in which an economic system will converge on X, all of which depend on variations in the gap between the actual and expected profit margins of the typical firm in positions of less than, or more than, full employment. It is evident, therefore, that the stability of the position X depends in turn on a theory of pricing that determines profit margins and on a theory of investment.

Kaldor's pricing theory is identical in all three versions of the model (Kaldor, 1957, 1958 and 1962), being a Kalecki-type mark-up theory whereby prices are marked up on labour costs, which are taken to be constant up to the level of full capacity. The investment function, however, is different in each of the three versions of the model. In the first version of 1957, investment is explained as a function of each firms' desired capital–output ratio, which is taken to be an increasing function of the expected rate of profits, thus combining the familiar acceleration principle of investment with Kalecki's 'principle of increasing risk'. This model turned out to have special implications for the stability of steady growth, deriving from the fact that it made investment relatively insensitive to changes in the current rate of profit. Thus, in the second version, Kaldor altered the assumptions about producers' expectations with regard to profit margins; even so, this made steady growth only slightly more stable.

Finally, in the third version, the investment function was radically revised and the old view of a homogeneous capital stock was replaced by the notion of vintage capital, thus implying further changes in the definition of the technical progress function. The new investment function is that firms aim to maximize the growth rate of their sales, subject to the constraint that profitability over a pay-off period of four to five years is sufficient to avoid the risk of bankruptcy or takeover bids. The new technical progress function postulates a relationship between the growth rate of labour productivity and the growth rate of investment per head but now only on newly installed equipment. In consequence, the argument that automatic forces will drive the economy to the position of neutrality on the technical progress function, thus sustaining steady-state growth, is made more plausible but still not perhaps entirely convincing.

Even sympathetic commentators have remained sceptical about Kaldor's arguments with respect to the stability of steady-state growth (Kregel, 1971, pp. 139–40, 203–7; Kregel, 1973, p. 192) if only because it implies that apparently anti-Keynesian conclusion that full employment is the 'natural' condition of capitalism in long-run equilibrium. Kaldor is a post-Keynesian economist in that he rejects many if not all the standard assumptions of the neoclassical approach to economic growth: optimizing behaviour, smoothly adjusting competitive markets, continuous factor substitution, aggregate production functions, malleable capital, a single saving function, the dependence of investment on the available flow of savings, and the like. In one respect, however, he stands alone among post-Keynesians in rejecting the Keynesian concept of 'unemployment equilibrium', at least for purposes of studying growth problems. Joan Robinson, for example, has been primarily concerned (as was Harrod) to emphasize the obstacles which are liable to prevent the attainment of a 'Golden Age' of steady-state growth in an unplanned capitalist economy, whereas Kaldor has always insisted that 'a theory of growth should be based on the hypothesis of full employment' (Kaldor, 1960b, p. 12).

Kaldor supported his assumption of full employment partly by reference to historical experience and partly by references to a theorem which was intended to show that there cannot be unemployment on a balanced growth path in which planned saving equals planned investment (Kaldor, 1958, pp. 24–9). This theorem seems, after due consideration, to depend on the assumption that the marginal propensity to invest exceeds the marginal propensity to save over the range of output below levels of full employment and thus on a static investment function related to the *level* of output and not, as in the acceleration principle underlying his treatment of the investment function, to *changes* in the level of output (Hacche, 1979, pp. 194–6, 206–14). Be that as it may, it raises the perplexing question as to what one may legitimately assume for purposes of growth theory. Growth theory is an intellectual game played according to certain rules, but it is far from clear what governs the rules one may adopt. That is true about the assumption of full employment, but it is also true about rules-of-thumb governing the investment process.

We may sum up Kaldor's growth theory by saying that it is perhaps the only model of economic growth in which technical progress emerges as the main engine of economic growth, determining the share of investment in income, the share of profits, the average life of equipment, and the rate of growth of productivity of both labour and new capital but, of course, being itself essentially unexplained; it simply determines the level of the technical progress function (the slope being of no particular significance). But that is not the only unique feature of Kaldor's growth theory. Different growth theories have advanced various defences of steady-state growth theory and some have claimed that theories of steady growth have direct empirical relevance in the sense that the broad facts about growth in advanced industrial economies correspond more or less closely to the main results of growth theory (see Hacche, 1979, pp. 26–8). But only Kaldor has consistently adhered to the view that his principal objective is the explanation of 'the characteristic features of the economic process as recorded by experience' (Kaldor, 1958, pp. 177–8). The history of capitalist development over the last century, he contends, testifies to the validity of the following six 'stylized facts':

1.   a steady rising trend in the growth of output and output per unit of labour;
2.   a steady rise in the amount of capital per worker, however capital is measured;
3.   a trendless rate of profit on capital, well in excess of the pure long-term rate of interest as revealed by the yield of gilt-edged bonds;
4.   a constant capital–output ratio;
5.   a high correlation between the profit share and the investment income ratio and, moreover, the wage and profit shares of income as well as the investment–income ratio are constant in the long run; and
6.   wide variations in the growth rate among different economies at any one time. (Kaldor, 1958, pp. 2–3)

Neoclassical growth theory is perfectly capable of accounting for Kaldor's stylized facts with appropriate assumptions about production functions, technical progress, population growth and saving propensities. Indeed, so elastic is the apparatus provided by neoclassical growth theory that it is capable of accounting *ex post* for any facts whatsoever. But only Kaldor's theory seeks to explain these facts in a genuine, causal sense, so that its validity can be said to stand or fall on the occurrence of certain 'stylised facts'.

Unfortunately, many of Kaldor's 'stylised facts' are not facts at all.[3] Facts (1), (2) and (3) are not in dispute; arguments only begin when confronting facts (4) and (5). The capital–output ratio in Britain (that is, the ratio of the constant replacement costs of domestic reproducible fixed capital to the gross domestic product at constant factor costs) declined more or less steadily in the last half of the nineteenth century, from a value of 5 in 1855 to 3.7 in 1900; it then rose and fell back in the period leading up to the First World War and continued in a downward course up to the Second World War; in the 1960s and 1970s it stood at just below 4, only exceeding its mid-nineteenth-century value of 5 in the late 1970s. In the USA the capital–output ratio likewise declined throughout the first half of the twentieth century, recovering most of this fall, however, in the 1950s and 1960s. In a fit of generosity, we might therefore endorse Kaldor's carefully phrased assertion of fact (4): 'Steady capital–output ratios over long periods; at least there are no clear long-term trends either rising or falling, if differences in the degree of utilisation of capacity are allowed for' (Kaldor, 1958, p. 2). But if so, the clock-time implied by the term 'long periods' will have to be stretched to run to 50 years or more. There is actually little evidence in the data to suggest the notion that there is some 'steady trend' or 'normal' relationship between capital and output; which is what Kaldor's stylized fact (4) clearly suggests.

We can be even more categorical about the evidence on relative shares relating to fact (5): the share of wages in aggregate income in both Britain and the USA has increased ever since the nineteenth century and, correspondingly, the share of profits has steadily fallen; and this is true no matter how wages or profits are measured. There never was a law less lawlike than the so-called 'Bowley's Law' of the long-run constancy of the relative shares of wages and profits in total income. Given the lack of a systematic long-term trend in the capital–output ratio and a downwards trend in the profit share, the rate of profit on capital, which is simply the quotient of the profits–income and the capital–output ratios, has shown a downward trend at least in Britain (although less obviously so in the USA).

Fact (5) also suggests that there is a correlation between the profit share and the investment–income ratio. Broadly speaking, such a relationship is indeed found for the last half of the nineteenth century and the interwar period in the twentieth century, but it breaks down completely in the 40 years since the Second World War, which saw a substantial rise in the investment–income ratio without any corresponding rise in the share of profits.

Some commentators (Hacche, 1973, p. 252) add a seventh stylized fact to Kaldor's list, namely, little deviation over the long term from a state of full employment, and as we have seen this is certainly one of the stylized facts to which Kaldor repeatedly appeals. A complete assessment of this claim would take us into the treacherous territory of historical unemployment statistics, which before the 1930s were largely based on members of trade unions rather than all members of the labour force. But even a cursory knowledge of economic history suggests that we will have to explain away the increasing concern with the problem of unemployment in the closing decades of the nineteenth century, probably indicative of rising actual levels of unemployment, the well attested growth of unemployment in Britain all through the 1920s and of course mass unemployment throughout the industrialized world during the Great Depression of the 1930s. Against this, we can point to the postwar boom of the 1950s and 1960s as a long period of sustained full or nearly full employment – the very period in which Kaldor was developing his growth theory. But what reason do we have for regarding the postwar boom as typical of long-run growth under capitalism, while rejecting the interwar slump, not to mention the current slump, as atypical? Here, as elsewhere, neither Kaldor nor anyone else has provided us with standards for judging the appropriate length of time for identifying those long-run forces that comprise the staples of modern growth theory.

On balance we must conclude that if Kaldor's growth theory is interpreted as Kaldor would have us interpret it, namely as an explanation of the common experience of the growth process in industrialized countries, the theory has in fact been explaining the wrong things. On the best evidence, even the aggregate features of long-run growth do not correspond to anything that can be described by a steady-state process. It may well be that Kaldor now accepts as much.[4] At any rate, when in 1966 he turned to explaining Britain's poor postwar growth performance, he drew none of his arguments from his own growth model and instead based his reasonings on yet another 'stylized' fact about long-run economic growth associated with the writings of Colin Clark: the shift of labour in the process of 'industrialization' from primary to secondary and from secondary to tertiary activities (that is, from agriculture and mining to manufacturing and then to the service industries). This involved much more than the replacement of a one-sector model of growth by a multi-sectoral explanation. It represented the rejection of all growth modelling based on the conception of a long-run steady state, adopting instead a 'stage theory' of capitalist development in which the economy is forever in a condition of dynamic disequilibrium.

'Laws of growth'

In the course of his inaugural lecture at the University of Cambridge in 1966 on the causes of Britain's low growth rate, Kaldor (1966b) presented two 'laws' of growth to account for the differences in the growth rates of industrialized countries, to which he subsequently added a third 'law' (Kaldor, 1968), which largely displaces the first two. These three laws have been the subject of a considerable debate, which has left its mark on Kaldor's own interpretation of their significance. The three laws may be baldly stated as:

1. there is a strong positive correlation in all industrialized countries between the rate of growth of manufacturing output and rate of growth of GDP;
2. there is a strong positive correlation in all industrialized countries between the rate of growth of labour productivity in manufacturing and the growth of manufacturing output – this is the so-called Verdoorn Relation, named

after its discoverer, the Belgian economist Paulus Verdoorn (Thirlwall and Thirlwall, 1979); and

3. there is a strong positive correlation in all industrialized countries between employment growth in manufacturing and the rate of growth of GDP, just as there is a strong negative correlation between employment growth outside manufacturing and the rate of growth of GDP.

We need to consider Kaldor's arguments for each of these three laws and then to assess their implications for Kaldor's explanation of international growth differences.[5]

Kaldor's first law
Taking a cross-section of 12 OECD countries over the period 1952–64, Kaldor found a strong positive correlation between the growth rate of manufacturing output, g_M, and the growth rate of GDP, g_{GDP}

$$(9)$$

$$g_{GDP} = 1.153 + 0.614 \, g_M \qquad r^2 = 0.959$$
$$(0.040)$$
$$\text{(standard error in parenthesis)}$$

This high correlation between the two variables, he argued, is not the simple result of the fact that manufacturing output constitutes a large proportion of GDP because there is also a significant positive association between the overall rate of growth of GDP and the *excess* of the growth of manufacturing over non-manufacturing output. He found no correlation between the rate of growth of GDP and the growth rate of agriculture or mining, but he did find a significant correlation between GDP growth and the growth of services. He insisted, however, that the growth rate of services should be attributed to the growth of GDP rather than the other way round, on the unconvincing grounds that the demand for most services is in fact derived from the demand for manufacturing output. To this critical argument we will return below. Subsequent research by colleagues of Kaldor essentially confirmed the first law for a larger number of countries and a longer time period

Why should GDP grow faster whenever manufacturing output grows faster than the overall rate of output, that is, when the share of the manufacturing sector in the total economy is increasing? Kaldor offered essentially two answers to this question. The first is that the fast growth of manufacturing draws labour from other sectors which harbour 'disguised unemployment' in the sense that there is no relationship between growth of output and employment growth in these sectors; hence, the transfer of labour to manufacturing causes no decline in the output of these sectors to offset the growth of manufacturing itself. A second answer is that the expansion of manufacturing is peculiarly subject, for reasons somehow inherent in the nature of manufacturing itself, to dynamic economies of scale which steadily reduce unit costs as output grows over time. These dynamic economies of scale are brought about by 'induced' technical progress embodied in new capital, by external economies accruing to each firm as a result of the expansion of the whole industry, and by learning-by-doing as a function of cumulative output in the past. They are not to be confused with static increasing returns to scale according to which larger plants, all else being equal, yield lower unit costs, although this probably applies to manufacturing too.

Kaldor's second law

Taking the same cross-section for the same group of countries, Kaldor replicated Verdoorn's Relation, which states that the growth of labour productivity in manufacturing, p_M, is positively correlated with the growth of manufacturing output, g_M:

$$p_M = 1\ 035 + 0.484\ g_M \qquad \qquad r^2 = 0.826 \qquad (10)$$
$$(0.070)$$

(standard error in parenthesis)

Since the output of the manufacturing sector is equal to the productivity of labour (value added per worker) multiplied by the volume of employment, it follows that after taking logs of all three variables to express a relationship between growth rates that:

$$g_M = p_M + e_M \qquad \qquad (11)$$

where e_M = the rate of growth of employment in manufacturing. Thus, by way of an example, if manufacturing output is growing by 5 per cent per annum and the productivity of labour in manufacturing is rising by 2 per cent per annum, employment in manufacturing must be growing at 3 per cent per annum. Therefore, an alternative way of testing the Verdoorn Relation is to regress e_M on g_M, which results in a similar equation to the previous regression of p_M on g_M:

$$e_M = -1.028 + 0.516\ g_M \qquad r^2 = 0.844 \qquad (12)$$
$$(0.070)$$

(standard error in parenthesis)

In both equations, the Verdoorn coefficient is about 0.5, asserting that a one per cent increase in the growth rate of manufacturing output, g_M, leads to 0.5 per cent increase in the productivity of labour, p_M and equally a 0.5 per cent increase in manufacturing employment, e_M. The effect is not necessarily confined to manufacturing. Kaldor found a similar Verdoorn Relation in public utilities and the construction industry but he found none in agriculture, mining, transport and communication.

Productivity growth in manufacturing is faster, the faster the rate of growth of manufacturing output (Kaldor's second law) and the rate of growth of manufacturing output is faster, the faster the rate of growth of GDP (Kaldor's first law). What, however, determines the growth of manufacturing itself? That question is perhaps best answered in terms of the constraints inhibiting the growth of any sector, such as a low income elasticity of demand for the product of that sector and an inadequate supply of labour or capital or both. Kaldor originally doubted that British manufacturing was in any way constrained on the demand-side and took the view that the effective constraint was on the side of labour arising from the small proportion of the labour force employed in British agriculture. Britain had reached a stage of economic maturity in which there was no low-productive sector outside manufacturing capable of supplying labour to an expanding manufacturing sector. He later withdrew this conclusion of the 1966 lecture (Kaldor, 1968, 1978b, p. xx), replacing it with the view that British manufacturing is effectively constrained by a lack of export growth.

Whichever version of the Verdoorn Relation we adopt, that is,

$$p_M = a + bg_M$$

or (employing the identity $p_M = g_M - e_M$)

$$e_M = -a + (1 - b) g_M,$$

$$\tag{14}$$

the problem of which is cause and which is effect remains. Kaldor assumed that the growth of labour productivity is entirely 'induced' by the growth of output, in which case it is perfectly correct to regress p_M on g_M. The opposite view is to argue that productivity growth is entirely autonomous and causes output to grow faster, say, by stimulating demand through a reduction in prices rather than being caused by fast output growth. Similarly, Kaldor assumed that employment growth is determined by output growth, in which case it is difficult to see how he could have argued simultaneously that the growth of output in manufacturing is constrained by the shortage of labour. It was precisely this contradiction that led Rowthorn (1975) to attack Kaldor's demonstration of Verdoorn's Relation. The Verdoorn Relation can be specified, not just in two, but in four different ways:

$$p_M = a + bg_M \qquad 0 < b < 1 \tag{13}$$

$$e_M = -a + (1-b)g_M \tag{13a}$$

$$g_M = \frac{a}{1-b} + \frac{b}{1-b} e_m \tag{13b}$$

and, substituting (3) into (1),

$$p_M = \frac{a}{1-b} + \frac{b}{1-b} e_M \qquad (13c)$$

These four versions will only yield identical estimates if the equations are exact without error. Rowthorn criticized Kaldor for estimating the Verdoorn co-efficient 'indirectly' using the first two specifications rather than 'directly' using the fourth specification, according to which productivity growth is determined by employment growth as implied by the notion of a labour constraint. In addition, Rowthorn showed that his estimates of equation (13c) were sensitive to the inclusion or exclusion of Japan as an 'outlier' in the relationship between p_M and e_M; excluding Japan yielded an estimate of the Verdoorn coefficient, b, that was not significantly different from unity, thus refuting the notion of increasing returns to scale. In reply, Kaldor discarded the notion of a labour constraint and hence returned to his own formulation of the Verdoorn coefficient in the form of equation (13a), showing that the exclusion of Japan did little to alter its significance, and concluding: 'a sufficient condition for the presence of static or dynamic economies of scale is the existence of a statistically significant relation-ship between e and g, with a regression .. coefficient which is significantly less than 1' (Kaldor, 1975a, p. 893).

Nevertheless, the problem of possibly spurious correlation has continued to dog the discussion on the Verdoorn Relation. In the first place, it is all too easy to see why changes in the productivity of *labour* in a sector should be positively associated with the growth of output of that sector, if only because labour is a quasi-fixed factor: when output declines, it is difficult to lay off labour rapidly and when output expands, it takes time to recruit new labour. In consequence, output per unit of labour will appear to rise when output growth accelerates. Thus, the Verdoorn Relation has now been confirmed on British time-series data over the period 1900–1977 and US time-series data for the period 1953–78. But the problem with time-series data is that short-run cyclical factors will generate a regression coefficient of about one-half when e_M is regressed on g_M; this is the result of 'Okun's Law', namely that employment fluctuates less than output over the business cycle for reasons that appear to be related to labour market institutions, and which proves nothing one way or the other about static or dynamic returns to scale (McCombie, 1983, p. 421).

In the second place, it is difficult to provide a microeconomic foundation for the Verdoorn Relation, and certainly neither Kaldor nor Verdoorn (1980) himself have ever provided a microeconomic explanation. Employers are motivated to minimize costs per unit of output and that implies maximizing total factor productivity rather than labour productivity – that is, output divided by the weighted sum of labour and fixed capital, the weights being the shares of value added paid to labour and capital respectively. The productivity of labour is frequently taken to be an easily observable proxy for total factor productivity and, in particular, the rate of change of labour productivity is frequently taken to be a very good proxy for the rate of change of total factor productivity. Actually, there is absolutely no reason to believe that the two will vary neatly in tandem over a run of years or even over the duration of a single business cycle. Indeed, the average annual growth of labour productivity in a sector is not even a good proxy for the average annual charge of labour costs per unit of output in that sector, not to mention the average annual change of average costs per unit of output (the inverse of total factor productivity).

Thus, by way of an example, the average annual growth of labour productivity in British manufacturing shows extreme year-to-year variations over the decade of the 1970s and early 1980s, whereas labour costs per unit of output in British manufacturing rose sharply but continuously in the 1970s and less sharply but again more or less continuously in the early 1980s (NEDC, 1985, p. 25). The distinction between the two measures arises partly from variations in hours worked but more fundamentally from variations in the annual rate of growth of nominal earnings. The distinction between labour productivity and total factor productivity on the other hand, arises entirely from variations in the rates of investment per worker

The notion that the Verdoorn Relation must have something to do with the growth of capital in a sector, an element omitted in the equations estimated by Kaldor, has persuaded a number of investigators to estimate the determinants of productivity growth by including, among other things, capital accumulation on the right-hand side the equation, which generally improves the goodness of fit of the Verdoorn equation (Chatterji and Wickens, 1983; Michl, 1985). Even when we revert to the simple one-variable regression of productivity growth on output growth, there have been signs of a break in the Verdoorn Relation as a result of the universal decline in productivity growth in manufacturing in all industrialized countries since 1973: the statistical fit of the Verdoorn Relation has deteriorated over the 1970s and early 1980s compared with earlier periods (Michl, 1985). One reason for this phenomenon may be that reductions in the growth of output do not affect labour productivity symmetrically with increases in the growth of output: slow or negative growth seems to result in reductions of capacity and a closing down of plants embodying worst-practice technique, thus reducing the association between labour productivity and output.

For this and other reasons, the recent era of productivity slowdown has witnessed the proliferation of 'radical' interpretations of the determinants of labour productivity, resting on a breakdown of the tacit willingness of workers to cooperate with management, a willingness which never is, and never can be, fully specified in a labour contract (see, for example, Kilpatrick and Lawson, 1980; Weisskopf et al., 1984). This view is the precise opposite of Kaldor's because it denies that labour productivity is 'induced' by output growth, insisting instead that it is a prime cause of output growth. The truth probably lies somewhere in between these two polar extremes and that suggests immediately that the Verdoorn Relation must be estimated by means of simultaneous equations expressing both the effect of productivity growth on output growth and the effect of output growth on productivity growth.

In principle, either causal sequence is plausible. A rapid growth of output due to rising demand may lead to rapidly rising output per man by allowing firms to reap the advantage of static economies of scale and by permitting the use of the latest, best-practice technique. On the other hand, rapid productivity growth, whether due to endogenous technical progress or a change in industrial relations, reduces costs and prices and thus permits a higher rate of growth of output. But whatever is the initial stimulus, there is every likelihood that the forces set in motion will be mutually self-reinforcing, so that over time output growth stimulates greater productivity, which in turn stimulates greater output growth,[6] all of which is to say that single-equation estimates are unlikely to identify the Verdoorn Relation.

The only attempt to estimate the Verdoorn Relation within a simultaneous equations framework is the study by Parikh (1978). Parikh was fundamentally concerned with establishing the labour-constraint hypothesis, which, as we mentioned before, Kaldor subsequently abandoned. Moreover, the Parikh study suffered from a number of technical deficiencies (McCombie, 1981, pp. 214–15, 1983, pp. 424–6). Thus, the precise significance of the Verdoorn Relation remains an open question to this day.

However, even Kaldor himself no longer attaches any significance to the acceptance or rejection, of the Verdoorn Relation. In his view, the choice is between a neoclassical supply-oriented view of the growth process, according to which the growth of output is essentially cited by the growth of factor inputs, or a Keynesian demand-oriented approach, according to which growth in an economy is essentially limited by the volume of demand and, in an open economy, by the balance of payments: there is enough disguised unemployment in the non-industrial sectors to provide the manufacturing sector with an elastic supply of labour; likewise, capital is automatically provided by the profits generated by the growth process itself and is in no sense a binding constraint. In Kaldor's own words:

> The existence of increasing returns to scale in industry (the Verdoorn Law) is not a necessary or indispensable element in the interpretation of these equations [relating p_{GDP}, q_M, e_M] Even if industrial output obeyed the law of constant returns, it could still be true that the growth of industrial output was the governing factor in the overall rate of economic growth... so long as the growth of industrial output represented a net addition to the effective use of resources and not just a transfer of resources from one use to another. That would be the case if (a) the capital required for industrial production was (largely or wholly) self-generated – the accumulation of capital was an aspect, or a by-product, of the growth of output; and (b) the labour engaged in

industry had no true opportunity-cost outside industry, on account of the prevalence of disguised unemployment both in agriculture and services. There is plenty of direct evidence to substantiate both of these assumptions
>   The important implications of these assumptions is that economic growth is demand-induced, and not resource-constrained. (Kaldor, 1975a, pp. 894–5)

Nevertheless, despite this repudiation of the assumption of dynamically increasing returns to scale, Kaldor has continued to rely in all his subsequent writings on the notion that growth is inherently cumulative, which necessarily implies some notion as dynamically increasing returns to scale. Be that as it may, Kaldor's second law needs to be replaced by a third law.

Kaldor's third law
Regressing g_{GDP} on e_M and e_{NM} (employment is non-manufacturing), Kaldor found that the faster the growth of manufacturing output in an economy, the faster is the rate of labour transference from non-manufacturing to manufacturing

$$g_{GDP} = 2.899 + 0.821\ e_M\ 1.183\ e_{NM}$$
$$(0.169)\quad (0.367)\qquad R^2 = 0.842$$
$$\text{(standard errors in parenthesis)} \tag{15}$$

This, the third law, states that the growth of GDP in an economy is positively related to the growth of output and employment in manufacturing and negatively associated with the growth of employment outside manufacturing. In short, manufacture is the engine of growth in GDP and the growth of manufacturing is not constrained by a shortage of labour, being fundamentally export-led.

The evidence for Kaldor's third law is even more difficult to assess than the evidence for the first two laws. The statistical evidence is entirely confined to the proposition that productivity growth in the economy as a whole depends critically on the growth of manufacturing and does not bear on the associated proposition that the growth of manufacturing is export-led. Kaldor's theory of export-led growth is one of a family of such theories (Thirlwall, 1982, 11). His argument is essentially that of Hicks', namely, that the long-run growth rate of an economy depends on the growth of autonomous demand and that export demand is the main component of autonomous demand in an open economy. Thus, differences in the growth performance of Western European countries are due primarily to differences in the rate of growth of exports, which set up a virtuous circle in which higher exports promote investment, which in turn leads to a higher rate of productivity, lower export prices and still higher exports. Whatever the validity of such models of export-led growth, the fact is that they do not require Kaldor's third law, namely, the notion that manufacturing is the engine of GDP growth because the faster the rate of growth of manufacturing output, the faster is the rate of growth of labour productivity in manufacturing.

This proposition clearly depends on the hypothesis of dynamic economies of scale in manufacturing. The idea of dynamic economies of scale – costs decreasing over real time in a manner not captured in traditional static theories of returns to scale – is not unique to Kaldor (see Hirschleifer, 1962; Spence, 1981) but what is uniquely Kaldorian is to attach such dynamic economies of scale exclusively to manufacturing. It is difficult to see why the private service industries, such as banking, insurance, communications and wholesale and retail distribution, should not be similarly subject to dynamic economies of scale. The third law of growth, according to which GDP growth is negatively associated with the growth of non-manufacturing employment, is a thin reed on which to hang the denial of dynamic economies of scale outside manufacturing.

Kaldor has little to say about the policy implications of his 'laws' of growth. Presumably what is implied is that demand management must form an integral part of any national policies designed to stimulate growth in stagnating economies like those of Britain. But that conclusion is derivable from any version of neo-Keynesian macroeconomics. A more pointed implication of the Kaldorian growth 'laws' is that what is important is not just a stimulus to overall aggregate demand but a quite specific stimulus to demand for the output of manufacturing, and in particular overseas demand for manufacturers. For example, anything that will improve the competitiveness of manufactured goods, including not just lower prices but also non-price improvements in delivery time, reliability, design, after-sales service, and so on should, according to Kaldor, serve to lift the balance-of-payments constraint on British economic growth. Now, this central element in the Kaldorian position rests on little more than a series of single-equation regressions, which are made to carry far more weight than they are capable of supporting. Apart from these single-equation regressions, no argument is provided to justify the view that manufacturing is absolutely critical to the growth process.

In the case of Britain, for example, it is of course perfectly true that much of the alarming growth of unemployment in the last six to seven years has been the result of an unprecedented contraction in the size of the manufacturing sector. Manufacturing output has been contracting by more than 1 per cent a year on average over the last decade but, on the other hand, the output of the service industries has been expanding by almost 2 per cent a year over the same period. But this fall in the share of employment and output in manufacturing, and the concomitant rise in the share of services, shows up in the figures for all OECD countries and appears to be a common feature of all mature economies. It has been far more pronounced in Britain than elsewhere (with the possible exception of the USA) but it is certainly not unique to Britain and thus provides only slender support for the Kaldorian emphasis on manufacturing as the key to the growth process.

Similarly, approximately two-thirds of Britain's visible exports have traditionally consisted of manufactures. The sharp contraction of British manufacturing could certainly have caused serious balance-of-payments deficits were it not for North Sea oil and, of course, when North Sea oil runs out in the 1990s, there is no guarantee that invisible exports in the form of services will automatically fill the gap created by the decline of manufacturing. On the other hand, they may very well succeed in filling the entire gap – recall that Kaldor's first 'law' found a high correlation between the growth rate of GDP and the growth of output of both manufacturing and services. Once again, the recent change in the composition of British exports cannot itself justify Kaldor's view that manufacturing holds the key to economic growth in Britain as elsewhere.

Similarly, without denying the important role of demand in explaining the disparate growth rates of advanced countries, it is difficult to swallow the Kaldorian notion that, say, rapid growth in Japan and low growth in Britain can be adequately explained without considering supply-side differences in the two countries in attitudes to work, enterprise and innovation, not to mention differences in industrial relations, government policies towards industry, social security provisions, and so on. And yet that is what is implied by Kaldor's studious insistence that demand and demand alone can account for international differences in growth rate.

Conclusion

Kaldor has not been loath to draw the logical conclusions of his recent thinking about international differences in growth rate. The mould of that thinking is essentially different from that of mainstream neoclassical thinking with its reliance on such concepts as general equilibrium, perfect competition, constant returns to scale, marginal productivity payments and allocative efficiency as the central economic problem. In two powerful essays written in the early 1970s (1972, 1975b), he attacked not just static equilibrium analysis but the very concept of equilibrium itself as the nub of what is wrong with standard economic theory. [7] Both of these essays called for more dynamic thinking in economics unrelated to equilibrium relationships between variables, but failed to emphasize that the repudiation of equilibrium economics involves not just abandoning orthodox microeconomics but also Keynesian macroeconomics and all varieties of growth theory, including that of Kaldor II, leaving little else but Kaldor III growth laws as the sum of the content of economics. Needless to say, this is a prospect which will not be welcomed by everyone. Nothing is more difficult than to turn an entire discipline around, asking it in effect to jettison its own history over the last 200 years. It is doubtful whether even so formidable a figure as Kaldor can expect to succeed in so daunting a task.

Kaldor certainly asks Big Questions and attempts to answer them in a Big Way. In this sense, he is a true heir of Adam Smith. The emphasis on difference in growth rates as the key problem of economics, the constant appeal to the principle of increasing returns to scale, and even the reliance on stylized facts as furnishing the basis of both the premises of economic theory and the checks on its conclusions, all remind us of Adam Smith. In other respects, however, his analysis lacks the historical and sociological breadth of Adam Smith, being narrowly geared to the growth problems of Britain in recent decades. Moreover, his is essentially a one-man research programme. His ideas link up with the rest of post-Keynesian economics but do not marry very well with the writings of other members of the school, such as Sraffa, Robinson and Kalecki, all of which depend in one degree or another on the concept of equilibrium. Moreover, Kaldor's ideas have developed little since the mid-1970s and have attracted few disciples. There are now any number of schools that have repudiated neoclassical economics and have attempted to move towards a new style of dynamic economics, such as the neo-Austrians, 'evolutionary economics' and the 'new institutional economics' (see Langlois, 1986), none of which have found inspiration in the writings of Kaldor. In short, judged by academic, rather than political, standards, his ideas must be judged as having failed to take off.

Notes

1. For an outstanding exposition of Kaldor's entire growth theory, paying due attention to the successive versions of the model, see Hacche (1979, Chapters 11–13; see also Wan (1971, pp. 82–9).
2. See for example, Bronfenbrenner (1971, pp. 416–21); Pen (1971, pp. 187–90); Johnson (1973, pp. 199–204); and Jones 1975, pp. 146–9). C.E. Ferguson (1969, p. 322) sums up the criticisms:

   the Kaldor model simply determines the profit share that is consistent with full employment, given an exogenous level of investment and the unequal propensities to save. This is far from a theory of distribution .A basic condition of the model is that I must equal S, *ex-ante* and *ex-post*. There is no behavioral equation to explain investment; it simply must equal desired saving. Since P/Y depends on the investment–income ratio, there is also nothing in the model to explain distributive shares. P/Y is what it is because in equilibrium it is related to I/Y, and I/Y is what it is because it can be nothing else. Just as relative shares are technologically determined in neoclassical theory, so they are psychologically determined in Kaldor's theory, being ultimately determined by the propensities to save.

   Note the phrase 'There is no behavioral equation to explain investment', which Kaldor clearly took to heart.
3. Hacche (1979, Chapters 14, 15) provides a superb account of the British–US evidence relating to Kaldor's six stylized facts, on which the subsequent comments in the text are largely based.
4. In 1972, he noted that 'The capital–output ratio in the United States has been falling over the past 50 years whilst the capital/labour ratio has been steadily rising' (Kaldor, 1978b, p. 148) and elsewhere he has conceded that output under capitalism is always constrained by the level of effective demand, so that full employment is far from the typical situation in modern industrialized economy.
5. For an earlier and highly sympathetic account of Kaldor's three laws, to which we are heavily indebted, see McCombie (1981) and Thirlwall (1983)
6. For an attempt to discuss these forces systematically, see Kennedy (1971, chs. 6, 7).
7. 'The powerful attraction of the habits of thought engendered by "equilibrium economics" has become a major obstacle to the development of economics as a *science* – meaning by the term

"science" a body of theorems based on assumptions that are *empirically* derived (from observations) and which embody hypotheses that are capable of verification both in regard to the assumptions and the predictions' (Kaldor, 1975b, p. 176).

References

Bronfenbrenner, M. (1971), *Income Distribution Theory*, London: Macmillan.

Chatterji M. and Wickens M.R. (1983), 'Verdoorn's Law and Kaldor's Law: A Revisionist Interpretation', *Journal of Post-Keynesian Economics*, Spring.

Hacche, G. (1979), *The Theory of Economic Growth: An Introduction*, London: Macmillan.

Hirschleifer, J. (1962), 'The Firm's Cost Function: A Successful Reconstruction, *Journal of Business*, July.

Jones, H. (1975), *An Introduction to Modern Theories of Economic Growth*, London: Thomas Nelson.

Johnson, H.G. (1973), *The Theory of Income Distribution*, London: Gray-Mills.

Kaldor, N. (1934), 'The Determinateness of Static Equilibrium', *Review of Economic Studies*, February, repr in Kaldor (1960a).

Kaldor, N. (1937), 'The Controversy on the Theory of Capital', *Econometrica*, July, repr in Kaldor (1960a).

Kaldor, N. (1938), 'Professor Chamberlin on Monopolistic and Imperfect Competition', *Quarterly Journal of Economics*, May, repr in Kaldor (1960a).

Kaldor, N. (1939a), 'Capital Intensity and the Trade Cycle', *Economica*, February, repr in Kaldor (1960b).

Kaldor, N. (1939b), 'Welfare Propositions in Economics', *Economic Journal*, September, repr in Kaldor (1960a).

Kaldor, N. (1940a), 'A Model of the Trade Cycle', *Economic Journal*, March, repr in Kaldor (1960b).

Kaldor, N. (1940b), 'A Note on Tarrifs and the Terms of Trade', *Economica*, November, repr in Kaldor (1960b).

Kaldor, N. (1942), 'Professor Hayek and the Concertina-effect', *Economica*, November, repr in Kaldor (1960b).

Kaldor, N. (1956), 'Alternative Theories of Distribution', *Review of Economic Studies*, 23 (2), repr in Kaldor (1960a).

Kaldor, N. (1957), 'A Model of Economic Growth', *Economic Journal*, December, repr in Kaldor (1960b).

Kaldor, N. (1958), 'Capital Accumulation and Economic Growth' in F. Lutz (ed.), *The Theory of Capital*, London: Macmillan, repr in Kaldor (1978a).

Kaldor, N. (1960a), *Essays on Value and Distribution*, London: Duckworth.

Kaldor, N. (1960b), *Essays on Economic Stability and Growth*, London: Duckworth.

Kaldor, N. (1962), 'A New Model of Economic Growth' (with J.A. Mirrlees), *Review of Economic Studies*, 24 (3), repr in Kaldor (1978a).

Kaldor, N. (1963), 'The Case for an International Commodity Reserve Currency' (with A.G. Hart and J. Tinbersen) *Essays on Economic Policy*, vol II (London: Duckworth).

Kaldor, N. (1966), *Causes of the Slow Rate of Economic Growth in the United Kingdom*, Cambridge: Cambridge University Press, repr in Kaldor (1978a).

Kaldor, N. (1968), 'Productivity and Growth in Manufacturing Industry: A Reply', *Economica*, November.

Kaldor, N. (1970a), 'The New Monetarism', *Lloyds Bank Review*, July, repr in Kaldor.

Kaldor, N. (1971b), 'The Dynamic Effects of the Common Market', *New Statesman*, 12 March, repr in Kaldor (1978b).

Kaldor, N. (1971c), 'The Common Market - A Final Assessment', *New Statesman*, 22 October, repr in Kaldor (1978b).

Kaldor, N. (1972), 'The Irrelevance of Equilibrium Economics', *Economic Journal*, December, repr in Kaldor (1978b).

Kaldor, N. (1975a), 'Economic Growth and the Verdoorn Law - A Comment of Mr Rowthorn's Article', *Economic Journal*, December.

Kaldor, N. (1975b), 'What is Wrong with Economic Theory?', *Quarterly Journal of Economics*, August, repr in Kaldor (1978b).

Kaldor, N. (1978a), *Further Essays on Economic Theory*, London: Duckworth.

Kaldor, N. (1978b), *Further Essays on Applied Economics*, London: Duckworth.

Kaldor, N. (1979a), *Reports on Taxation*, vol. I London: Duckworth.

Kaldor, N. (1979b), *Reports on Taxation*, vol. II, London: Duckworth.

Kaldor, N. (1986), 'Recollections of an Economist', *Banco Nazionale del Lavoro Quarterly Review*, March.

Kennedy, K.A. (1971), *Productivity and Industrial Growth, The Irish Experience*, Oxford: Clarendon Press.

Kilpatrick, A. and Lawson, T. (1980), 'On the Nature of Industrial Decline in the UK', *Cambridge Journal of Economics*, March.

Kregel, J.A. (1971), *Rate of Profit, Distribution and Growth: Two Views*, London: Macmillan.

Kregel, J.A. (1973), *The Reconstruction of Political Economy: An Introduction to Post-Keynesian Economics*, London: Macmillan.

Langlois, R.N. (1986), *Economics as a Process: Essays in the New Institutional Economics*, London: Cambridge University Press.

McCombie, J.S.L. (1981), 'What Still Remains of Kaldor's Laws?', *Economic Journal*, March.

McCombie, J.S.L. (1983), 'Kaldor's Laws in Retrospect', *Journal of Post-Keynesian Economics*, Spring.

Michl, T.R. (1985), 'International Comparisons of Productivity Growth: Verdoorn's Law Revisited', *Journal of Political Economy*, Summer.

NEDC (1985), *British Industrial Performance*, London: National Economic Development Council.

Parikh, A. (1978), 'Differences in Growth and Kaldor's Laws', *Economica*, February.

Pen, J. (1971), *Income Distribution*, London: Allen Lane/The Penguin Press.

Rowthorn, R. (1975), 'What Remains of Kaldor's Law', *Economic Journal*, March.

Spence, M. (1981), 'The Learning Curve and Competition', *Bell Journal of Economics*, Spring.

Thirlwall, A.P. and Thirlwall, G. (1979), 'Factors Governing the Growth of Labour Productivity' (translation of P.J. Verdoorn's original article in *L'industria*, 1949), *Research in Population and Economics*, Autumn.

Thirlwall, A.P. (1982), *Balance-of-Payments Theory and the United Kingdom Experience*, London: Macmillan.

Thirlwall, A.P. (1983), 'A Plain Man's Guide to Kaldor's Growth Laws', *Journal of Post-Keynesian Economics*, Spring.

Verdoorn, P.J. (1980), 'Verdoorn's Law in Retrospect: A Comment', *Economic Journal*, June.

Wan, H.Y. (1971), *Economic Growth*, New York: Harcourt Brace Jovanovitch.

Weisskopf, T.E., Bowles, S. and Gordon, D.M. (1984), 'Hearts and Minds: A Social Model of US Productivity Growth', *Brookings Paper on Economic Activity*, 1.

10 Economics through the looking glass

Introduction

There is in economics, or at least among the overwhelming majority of its disciples, broad agreement as to what represents the corpus of their subject. This corpus revolves around the concept of maximizing behaviour, whether it be by the individual, firm or institution. There are, of course, 'Schools' of economic thought which take a heterodox view of economics and some are openly and vociferously critical of neoclassical economics. Indeed internal controversy and challenges to a discipline are a sign of its vitality and are to be welcomed. However, these schools represent a minority fringe of intellectual activity. But when a group of academics, purporting to collect together a magisterial survey of economic knowledge, mistakes the fringe for the solid core of the discipline, whether overtly or by more subtle devices, then this is cause for concern. *The New Palgrave Dictionary* has been heralded as a major publishing event and like its predecessor has the potential to become an important part of the economist's library. Yet it fails to supply the teacher, student and layman with a balanced overview of economics today. It is, to be perfectly frank, an idiosyncratic work. In this paper I take the opportunity to expose the nature of the biases and deficiencies of *The New Palgrave* based on a full reading of its four volumes and over 4 million words.

The first *Palgrave Dictionary of Economics* was published in three volumes almost a century ago by R. H. Inglis Palgrave, then editor of *The Economist*. It was called a dictionary but it was really an encyclopedia of economics, the first compendium of its kind in English. It was a highly uneven work but it did contain numerous entries by some of England's leading contemporary economists and its major biographical articles instantly became classical references. It was re-edited in the 1920s by Henry Higgs but the rise of monopolistic competition theory and the Keynesian revolution soon rendered even that edition obsolete. By the 1950s economic theory had moved so rapidly in a mathematical and econometric direction that both the original and the re-edited Palgrave were hardly of interest to economists without a training in the history of economic thought. The masterly and comprehensive *International Encyclopedia of the Social Sciences,* edited by David L. Sills and published in 17 volumes in 1968 (with a biographical supplement in 1979), devoted something like a quarter of its 10,000 pages to economics. It took stock of new developments in the subject and continues to this day to serve as a major reference work in economics.

Nevertheless, there was much talk all through the 1970s of an Encyclopedia of Economics that would update and extend the treatment of economics in the Sills encyclopedia. Macmillan, the publisher of both Palgrave and Sills, considered at least two American proposals for such an encyclopedia and finally decided in 1983 to launch a *New Palgrave*. For its editors, they chose John Eatwell, Murray Milgate and Peter Newman.

New Palgrave editors are anti-neoclassical
This was a strange choice in at least two senses: none of the three editors is American and yet the subject of economics is nowadays overwhelmingly dominated by Americans; moreover, none of the three editors believes in mainstream or so-called 'neoclassical' economics and two of them are in print as rejecting it root and branch. John Eatwell is a Fellow and Lecturer in Economics at Trinity College, Cambridge, co-author with Joan Robinson of an off-beat textbook, *An Introduction to Modern Economics* (1973), and the presenter of the BBC-TV series *Whatever Happened to Britain?* (1982). He is a post-Keynesian and neo-Ricardian economist, a follower of Nicholas Kaldor when it comes to the ills of the British economy and a disciple of Piero Sraffa in the higher reaches of economic theory. Murray Milgate, one-time student of Eatwell and now Associate Professor at Harvard University, is the author of *Capital and Employment* (1982), a book which aspires to combine Keynes' theory of income determination with Sraffa's theory of value and distribution.[1] Peter Newman of Johns Hopkins University (but British-born and British educated) is a mathematical economist who has also worked on the demographic problems of developing countries. He would seem, at first glance, to belong to a wholly different school of thought from Eatwell and Milgate. But in fact Newman's early article-review (1962) of Sraffa's *Production of Commodities by Means of Commodities* (1960) proved to be extremely influential for the burgeoning Sraffa Industry.[2] In short, even Newman is a Sraffian of sorts.

Whatever we may think of the validity and significance of the economics of Sraffa, it is a fact that Sraffians are a tiny minority among modern economists. Apart from the Universities of Cambridge and Manchester and two or three polytechnics, it is difficult to round up more that a dozen Sraffians in Britain. There are hardly any in America's 3,000 institutions of higher learning. The real centre of the Sraffa School is in Italy – for no better reason than that Sraffa was Italian (even though he spent almost his entire adult life at Cambridge). The leadership of the Sraffa 'Church' in Italy is shared between Sraffa's literary executor, Piero Garegnani of the University of Rome, and Luigi Pasinetti of the Universita Cattolica del Sacro Cuore in Milan; but there are dozens of enthusiastic followers in many Italian universities – of whom 16 appear in this dictionary – and the 'house' journal of the Sraffians, *Political Economy, Studies in the Surplus Approach,* is published twice a year in Turin. In the rest of Europe and elsewhere in Asian, Africa and Latin America, it may be possible to collect another five or six self-declared Sraffians but not many more than that.

A Sraffian trio – a tendentious dictionary

To have invited three Sraffians to edit a new Palgrave dictionary of economics is roughly equivalent to asking three atheists to edit an encyclopedia of Christianity: it is conceivable that such a trio would carry out its task with studious impartiality, but it is not very likely. And, indeed, it has not come to pass in this case. *The New Palgrave* is a tendentious work that fails to reflect the mainstream of orthodox doctrine in economics and that does not even do justice to the entire range of dissenting and heterodox opinion.

The editors clearly saw *The New Palgrave* as a signal opportunity to put their particular views on the map. At the same time, they were aware that a dictionary of economics along entirely Sraffian lines would not be commercially viable. They solved this problem with characteristic *chutzpah*. Instead of attempting to present a balanced account of controversial issues in economics, including a frank admission of certain fundamental methodological and ideological disagreements among members of the profession, they simply let a thousand flowers bloom, leaving it to the reader to separate the perennials from the weeds. As they say in their preface:

> On many non biographical subjects, we have tried to capture diversity and vivacity of views by having multiple entries, under similar but different titles. In this way we hoped to obtain essays that present the results and methods of research with fairness and accuracy, but not necessarily from a 'balanced' point of view. Such a view in these cases should be sought externally, as it were, using the system of cross-references to consult other relevant entries. This means more work for the reader but should yield correspondingly greater reward (*New Palgrave*, I, p. ix)

Do the four volumes of *The New Palgrave* represent 'the results and methods of research with fairness and accuracy', if not necessarily from 'a "balanced" point of view'? Not when the results and methods touch on what Sraffians regard as sensitive issues, such as, for example, the ideas of Ricardo, Marx, Keynes and Sraffa himself. In the entire 4,100 pages and over 4 million words of the dictionary there is a large number of extremely sympathetic and even adulatory expositions of Marxian economics but not one single critical account of any of Marx's ideas (with the possible exception of Ernst Gellner on the Economic Interpretation of History, II, pp.47–51).Similarly, there are some 50 expositions of Sraffian economics under various headings but only two entries – namely, my own on Classical Economics (I, pp. 434–44) and Paul Samuelson's on Sraffian Economics (IV, pp. 452–60) – which even begin to entertain the possibility that Sraffa's words may not represent the alpha and omega of economics. A sample count of pages in *The New Palgrave* shows that Marx and Sraffa are quoted more frequently – indeed, much more frequently – than Adam Smith, Alfred Marshall, Leon Walras, Maynard Keynes, Kenneth Arrow, Milton Friedman, Paul Samuelson or whoever you care to name. This indicates a lack of balance in the dictionary which appears elsewhere in the length of entries devoted to certain topics, to the very choice of titles for some entries, and even to the selection of the more than 900 economists who agreed to contribute.

'Curious results'

The Eatwell-Milgate-Newman policy of publishing multiple entries with slightly different titles for identical subjects constantly produces curious results, in which the outcome of the study of any topic depends principally on the reader's tenacity in following up all the cross-references (placed oddly at the end of the articles). To give two examples, Charles Goodhart in an essay on the 'Monetary Base' denies categorically that the supply of money is an exogenous variable, that is to say that the monetary authorities are able to increase or decrease the money supply at will (III, p. 50). But Karl Brunner in an entry on 'money supply', the third reference cited at the end of Goodhart's article, equally categorically insists the very opposite: 'the monetary authorities can effectively control the money stock' (III, p. 528). This is a famous bone of contention about 'monetarism', because if Goodhart is right, monetarism is a nonsense. Now, on the face of it, there is nothing wrong with either argument (there is a pertinent entry here by Meghnad Desai on 'endogenous and exogenous money, II, pp. 136–7), but a good editor would have invited both authors to refer to each other's diametrically opposed viewpoints, or else would have ensured such a cross-reference editorially. Similarly, Alan Peacock extols economic freedom (II, p. 33–5) as freedom for the individual; whereas C. B. Macpherson castigates individualism (II, pp. 75–7) as the ideology of the bourgeoisie, but the two essays are not cross-referenced to each other – almost as if the editors failed to realize that economic freedom *is* individualism. It would be easy to give many more instances of this sort of confusion arising from unannounced conflicts of opinion in multiple entries on identical subjects. On balance, a policy of presenting competing opinions under the *same* title would have been vastly preferable to the Eatwell-Milgate-Newman policy of several entries under *different* titles on what is in fact one and the same topic.

The New Palgrave is avowedly a dictionary of economic theories and doctrines (I, p. ix). There are indeed articles on institutions such as 'Auctions' (I, pp. 138–44) and 'Financial Intermediaries' (II, pp. 340–8), and Robert Heilbroner and Alec Nove write on 'Capitalism and Socialism' (I, pp. 347–53; IV, pp. 398–407), each with equal vigour and sceptical disdain of standard opinion on these explosive institutional topics. But *The New Palgrave* is clearly not the place to go for descriptions of how the World Bank operates or how different countries regulate the pricing policies of public utilities. Accepting this limitation, and hence the focus on questions of economic theory, the dictionary nevertheless demonstrates an almost shocking disregard for students, journalists, writers, politicians and lay readers. The original *Palgrave* was addressed to 'the student with such assistance as may enable him to understand the position of economic thought at the present time'. But this new edition is unhesitatingly addressed to the professional economist. The level of analytical competence required to read many of the entries on on even such standard topics as demand, supply and equilibrium is forbiddingly high, and all the mathematical essays sail upwards into the stratosphere of algebraic topology, optimal control theory and dynamic programming without so much as a consoling word for undergraduates whose mathematics does not extend much beyond differential calculus and linear algebra.

Now, obviously, modern economics is an increasingly mathematical subject and, equally obviously, any encyclopedia of modern economics must contain an account of recent developments in mathematical economics, as well as much economics mathematically treated. But to have allowed John Chipman to write 30,000 words – a thick pamphlet or a small book and the longest entry in the volume – on 'International Trade' (II, pp. 922–52) with no concessions to the 'average' literary economist, not to mention the mythical 'general reader', amounts to an abnegation of editorial responsibility.[3] This brand of formalism, a revelling in technique for technique's sake, is certainly a feature of much modern economics; yet an encyclopedia of economics would hardly seem an appropriate place to advertise it. Entries like those of Stephen Robinson on 'Convex Programming' (I, pp. 647–59), William Parry on 'Ergodic Theory' (II, pp. 184–7), Richard Savage on 'Random Variables' (IV, pp. 54–64), and many more like it, read like chapters in a textbook of advanced mathematical economics and statistics. One expects articles such as 'Duality' by Peter Newman (I, pp. 924–34), 'Lyapunov Function' by Charles Henry (II, pp. 256–9), 'Non-linear Programming' by Michael Intriligator (III, pp. 666–70), and 'Turnpike Theory' by Lionel McKenzie (IV, pp. 712–20) to be difficult – and they are – but it is not easy to see why essays on such standard topics as 'Aggregate Demand Theory' by Hugo Sonnenschein (I, pp. 47–50), 'Demand Theory' by Volker Böhm and Hans Haller (I, pp. 785–91), 'Financial Markets' by Nils Hakansson (II, pp. 351–4), and 'Perfect Competition' by Ali Khan (III, pp. 831–4) have to be presented in a style that makes them virtually unintelligible to those outside the coterie of mathematical economists.

The mind-boggling obscurity of many of the articles is part and parcel of the editors' master plan: its purpose is to dispel the worry that mainstream economists might otherwise have felt about a dictionary edited by three Sraffians. Mainstream economists are all too inclined to equate professional competence with a technically demanding style. Formalism has an iron grip on much of modern economics: to be intelligible is to be suspect.[4] In short, in some quarters the high proportion of unreadable entries in *The New Palgrave* will be regarded as proof positive that high professional standards have been maintained.

Gold amidst the dross

With that caveat, there is nevertheless much in these volumes to praise. Clearly, with 2,000 entries, including 700 biographies, there are bound to be hits as well as misses. Some of the biographies of the great economists of the past are little masterpieces – 'Edgeworth' by Peter Newman (II, pp. 84–98), 'Fisher' by James Tobin (II, pp. 369–76), 'Malthus' by John Pullen (III, pp. 280–5), 'Marshall' by John Whitaker (III, pp. 350–63), 'Smith' by Andrew Skinner (IV, pp. 357–74), and 'Walras' by Donald Walker (IV, pp. 852–62) – but there are also striking biographies of living or recently deceased economists, such as 'Friedman' by Alan Walters (II, pp. 420–7), 'Kaldor' by Adrian Wood (III, pp. 3–8), 'Kalecki' by Karl Laski (III, pp. 8–14), 'Meade' by David Vines (III, pp. 400–6), and 'Joan Robinson' by Luigi Pasinetti (IV, pp. 212–17). In addition, there are hundreds of biographies of minor twentieth-century economists, which are simply not available anywhere else.

Among the entries on various subjects, there are many that rehearse analyses and arguments well known from other sources. Ronald Jones is excellent on Heckscher-Ohlin trade theory (II, pp. 520–7) but he has written so often on this theme elsewhere that the sense of discovery is gone: that is true of many other entries, such as Gerard Debreu on 'Existence of General Equilibrium' (II, pp. 216–19), Becker on 'the family' (II, pp. 281–6), Wassily Leontief on 'Input-Output Analysis' (II, pp. 860–4), Don Patinkin on 'Keynes' (III, pp. 19–41), Gordon Tullock on 'Public Choice' (III, pp. 1040–4), William Baumol on 'Ramsey Pricing' (IV, pp. 49–51), and Armatya Sen on 'Social Choice' (IV, pp. 382–93). That being said, I can recommend the entries in Table 10.1 as saying something new, or at least expressing it in a new form.

But my favourite single entry is the one on the Coase Theorem by Robert Cooter (I, pp. 457–60), an explanation of one of the most profound and yet most misunderstood ideas in the whole of welfare economics. The Coase Theorem is the proposition that 'market failure' due to externalities in either production or consumption can sometimes, and perhaps even frequently, be cured by a mere change in legal entitlements; in that case what is required to cure the ills of the market is not government intervention but a change in property laws. Cooter unpacks this theorem and demonstrates elegantly that it is, at best, a quarter-truth. In other words, there is much gold amidst the dross but on balance, and particularly when read from cover to cover – which I can testify takes only four to five weeks if one gives up eating and sleeping – *The New Palgrave* conveys a slanted picture of modern economics. I say nothing about the omission of entries for many important topics (Table 10.2), and many recognized branches of economics – the economics of education (except as another term for human capital

Table 10.1 Genuinely fresh entries

Entry	Author	Vol./Pages
Bayesian inference	Arnold Zellner	I:208–18
Behavioural economics	Herbert Simon	I:221–5
Biological application of economics	Gordon Tullock	I:246–7
Co-determination and profit-sharing	Mario Nuti	I:465–9
Division of labour	Peter Groenewegen	901–6
Economic theory and the hypothesis of rationality	Kenneth Arrow	II:69–74
Experimental methods in economics	Vernon Smith	II:241–9
Game theory	Robert Aumann	II:460–82
Equilibrium, development of concept	Murray Milgate	I:178–82
Efficient market hypothesis	Burton Malkiel	II:120–3
Hunting and gathering economies	Vernon Smith	II:697–9
Neutrality of money	Don Patinkin	III:639–45
Paradoxes	Neil de Marchi	III:796–9
New classical macro-economics	Stanley Fisher	III:647–50
Pareto-efficiency	Brian Lockwood	III:811–13
Probability	Ian Hacking	III:977–83
Quantity theory of money	Milton Friedman	IV:3–19
Rent control	Kurt Klappholz	IV:143–5
Real-cost doctrine	John Maloney	IV:103–4
Second best	Peter Böhm	IV:280–3
Statistical inference	D.V. Lindley	IV:490–3
Welfare economics	Allan Feldman	IV:889–94

theory), comparative economic systems, cultural economics, and the history of economic thought – despite the existence of professional journals exclusively devoted to each of these specializations.[5] The index is of some help in locating a perfunctory reference to two or three of these omitted subjects, but in general the index is not to be trusted because it seems to have been prepared by computer using a list of key terms. Thus, if we are interested in the new household economics of Gary Becker, the index does nothing to relate separate references to the 'new household economics', 'household production', 'family', and 'fertility, determinants of', even though all these refer to one and the same complex of ideas. Similarly, the index cites 'Verdoorn's Law'[6] but does not refer to Kaldor's endorsement of it in all his later writings. Such examples of poor indexing could be multiplied almost indefinitely.

Table 10.2   Omitted topics

Automation	Mixed economy
Bank deposit multiplier	Occupational licensing
Debt management	On-the-job training
Director's Law (or its corollary,	Output budgeting
the median voter theorem)	Producer's surplus
Earnings differentials	Stages of growth
Empirical testing	State provision of education (there
Factors of production	is one on state provision of
Falsification	medical services)
Flexitime	Stock markets
Fringe benefits	Vacancies
Grants economics	Voucher schemes
Internal labour markets	Work sharing
Labour force participation rate	

I shall also say nothing (or almost nothing) about occasional instances of editorial sloppiness, such as bibliographies entirely omitted or cut short in biographical entries or the inconsistent use of one or another system of referring to the secondary literature (I, pp. 231, 266; II, pp. 519, 569, 640, 666; III, pp. 17, 60, 102, 131, 142, 218, 267, 301, 325, 362, 442, 814; IV, pp. 228, 233, 245, 249, 259, 287, 350, 768, 770, 832) – only a petty mind like my own would even notice it. And being petty I cannot forego a comment on the irritatingly small print-size adopted by Macmillan in belated imitation of the original *Palgrave* (8 on 9 point Monotype Times in double columns); compare that with the magnificent and generous typeface of the Sills *International Encyclopedia of the Social Sciences,* which is always a visual pleasure to read. On the plus side, however, is the superb proofreading of the Macmillan editor, Margot Levy. I found only 13 misprints in over 4,000 pages (I, pp. 286, 331, 545, 570; II, pp. 25, 642, 645, 657, 861; III, pp. 55, 266, 442, 527, 782; IV, pp. 494, 988), but only two of these (I, pp. 286, III, pp. 442) were serious.

What is Sraffian economics?

The New Palgrave is designed, as we have said, to promote Sraffian economics. But what is Sraffian economics? This is not the place for yet another exposition of the Sraffian system but it is worth spending some time describing the flavour and the upshot of Sraffa's slim volume with the strange title, *Production of Commodities by Means of Commodities* (1960).[7]

Sraffa's book contains no introduction or conclusion but it does carry the intriguing subtitle: 'prelude to a critique of economic theory'. From various hints in the book, the economic theory in question appears to be the whole of the post-

1870 marginalist or neoclassical tradition. According to this tradition, goods and services as well as the factors of production are determined in the first instance by demand and supply and ultimately by the pattern of consumer preferences, the prevailing techniques of production and the ownership of productive factors among individual economic agents – that is, tastes, technology and endowments. Sraffa proceeds to criticize this type of theorizing by claiming that it is perfectly possible to explain the determination of relative prices by technology alone without any reference to consumer demand. However, this technology must preclude substitution among the factors of production in response to changing wage and interest rates; it must be technically rigid or, in the language of input–output analysis, it must be of the fixed coefficients variety – that is, so many workers per ton of steel, so many spades per bushel of corn, and so on. Now, we all learned in school that to solve a system of simultaneous equations, you need at least as many equations as unknowns, and it is a simple mathematical fact that a set of *known* fixed coefficients do not give us enough equations to determine the value of all the *unknown* prices in the economy. Thus, to determine prices, we have to assume something besides the technical structure of production, and that something is either the real wage rate of labour (assuming there is only one kind of labour) or the uniform rate of profit on capital.

Suppose we take the real wage as given. In that case, Sraffian economics concludes with the demonstration that it is possible to determine all relative prices in the economy and the rate of profit on capital simply from a specification of technology and an assumed wage rate; consumer demand has nothing to do with it. Of course, demand determines *how much* of each product is produced but not at what *price* it will be sold; demand determines the *composition* of total output, and by implication the *volume* of total output, but not the relative *values* of one kind of output compared with another. We have returned to the labour theories of value of Adam Smith, David Ricardo and Karl Marx for whom prices were determined exclusively by the costs of production.

If we recall our elementary economics handed down since the days of Alfred Marshall a century ago, it appears that we are in a world where supply curves are horizontal lines, in consequence of which demand determines quantity but supply determines price. When supply curves are horizontal lines, it costs twice as much to produce a double amount of anything, three times as much to produce a triple amount, and so on; unit costs are constant because a large plant is simply a small plant scaled up. In the short run, this is an almost inconceivable case – you can always squeeze a bit more out of any plant even when it is operated at full capacity but only at rising costs per unit of output. But in the long run – that is, when all possible ways of producing more output have been exhausted – it is a perfectly conceivable case. It is the case which Marshall labelled 'constant returns to scale'.

Early in his career, when he was only 28 years old, Sraffa made his reputation with an article, 'The Laws of Returns under Competitive Conditions' (1926), in which he argued that, from a strictly logical point of view, the only long-run supply curve that properly represents the general run of cases in a perfectly competitive economy is, not a normal upward-sloping or a perverse downward-sloping supply curve, but a horizontal, constant-cost supply curve. Sraffa spent the rest of his life editing the works, speeches and letters of Ricardo. Then in 1960 he produced the mysterious little book which demonstrated that the only admissible case of perfectly competitive price determination, the case of constant costs, is precisely the one which rules out factor substitution in response to changing factor prices, which is the be-all and end-all of marginalist economics. It implies that fixed coefficients of production, or a 'linear technology' as we would say nowadays, form the appropriate general framework for thinking about price determination in the real world. (Sraffa, 1960). It follows from this that demand is not coordinate with supply in determining prices, that consumers are not sovereign and indeed have no direct influence on the pricing process, and in particular that factor prices are not determined in the same way as the prices of consumer goods.

This explains why John Eatwell, in a key entry in *The New Palgrave* on 'Returns to Scale (IV, pp. 165–6), is absolutely adamant in denying that there is any such thing as real-world decreasing or increasing returns to scale – unit costs falling or rising as plants get bigger. According to him, the famous long-run U-shaped cost curve of the standard textbooks (Figure 10.1) is a bogus concept and 'the only really satisfactory formal characterisation of returns of scale is that of constant returns' (IV, p. 166; also IV, p.448). So, if he is to be believed, it is simply

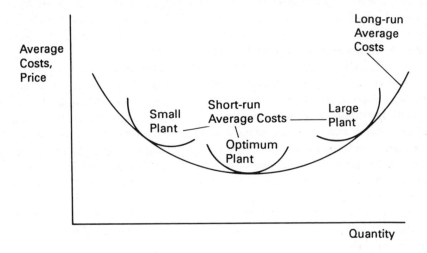

Figure 10.1   Standard cost curve

meaningless to talk about an *optimum* plant designed to minimize unit costs, which implies that plants can be too large or too small, and it is equally meaningless to define a 'natural monopoly' in the standard way as an industry whose technology dictates a scale of operations so large that average costs are minimized with only one monopoly producer. In any case, the motive for Eatwell's assault on the standard orthodox doctrine of varying returns to scale is to defend the neglect of demand in Sraffa's theory of value.[8]

Sraffa had to assume the wage rate to get any answers at all, and that wage rate is therefore determined outside the model by political rather than economic factors, by the class struggle rather than the process of competition – fill in whatever you like. In Sraffian language, the theory of value is divorced from the theory of distribution and, moreover, the latter takes priority over the former. First we take a distributional variable as determined by political forces, and then with the aid of a set of engineering blueprints for the production of every commodity in the system we can solve for all relative prices in our economic model, including the remaining distributional variables. So, goodbye to the theory of consumer behaviour and the so-called marginal productivity theory of distribution of neoclassical economics, according to which trade unions can influence wages but only within definite limits, and goodbye in particular to general equilibrium theory, that strange, orthodox doctrine that everything depends on everything else and that no economic variable has any priority over any other. And all this in 92 pages!

'Beautiful technical puzzles'
This is the gist of Sraffa's central message but along the way his book, despite its brevity, generates a number of beautiful technical puzzles, most of which it then proceeds to solve. For example, it had long been known that 'joint production' complicates the exposition of almost any theory of value and defeats any theory of value that is entirely supply-determined, such as the old labour theory of value or Sraffa's own linear production model. By 'joint production' we mean a situation in which two or more outputs are produced inseparably from the same set of inputs, the familiar examples being meat and wool from sheep and petrol and oil from petroleum. Such cases were traditionally regarded as somewhat exceptional but Sraffa, inspired by some older classical discussions of the issue, realized that they invariably arise in every use of fixed capital in the sense that production employing machinery typically produces some final product and, as a by-product, an older but still usable machine; in other words, every instance of production employing durable capital is an example of joint production.

Now, in the first part of his book, Sraffa gets rid of the complication of joint production by examining only cases of single-product industries employing 'circulating capital' – that is, raw materials and short-lived implements that are fully used up in one cycle of production. For this sort of make-believe world he generates a number of his elegant results, which, however, are not sustained for the real-world case of multi-product industries employing fixed capital examined in part two of his book. Since the book contains no conclusion, it is left to the reader to decide whether any of the elegant theorems of part one are of much practical significance. In any case, so many hints and allusions of how the apparatus might conceivably be amplified are strewn along the way that there is plenty of scope for the analytically inclined disciple to refine and extend the model.[9] A veritable academic industry has grown up extolling and elaborating Sraffian economics. As Paul Samuelson asks in his highly critical account of Sraffian economics in *The New Palgrave:* 'Did any scholar have so great an impact on economic science as Piero Sraffa did in so few writings?' (IV, p. 460).[10]

Re-interpreting history
With Sraffa as the fountainhead of a new brand of non-marginalist economics, Ricardo and Marx appear naturally as predecessors and Keynes and Kalecki as fellow travellers, similarly rejecting orthodox economics but from a macroeconomic rather than a microeconomic standpoint. The result is a far-reaching Sraffian reinterpretation of the entire history of economic thought. The economic thinking of the last 200 years, Sraffians tell us, reveals two great branches: a general equilibrium branch leading down from Jevons, Walras and Marshall to the neoclassical economics of the Arrows and Samuelsons of today, in which all the relevant economic variables are mutually and simultaneously determined, and a Ricardo-Marx-Sraffa branch in which distribution takes priority over pricing because economic variables are causally determined in a sequential chain starting from a predetermined real wage. This reinterpretation has been disseminated in a number of books and articles by Sraffian 'true-believers' over the last 20 years and is given full-star billing in *The New Palgrave.* It figures prominently in Garegnani's 12,000-word essay on the 'Surplus Approach to Value and Distribution' (IV, pp. 560–73), whose basic elements, he insists, are to be found in what others previously labelled English classical political economy.

The notion that Sraffa's 1960 book is at once the revival and culmination of a grand old tradition that was first buried and then forgotten by those wicked neoclassical economists involves a great deal of 'making-it-up-as-you-go-along' accounts of what such classical economists as Adam Smith, David Ricardo, John Stuart Mill and Karl Marx actually believed. They took as given, we are told, the available technology, the real wage rate and both the volume and composition of total output, and on the basis of these parameters explained the determination of relative prices and the rate of profit or interest (Garegnani, IV, pp. 560–2; Giorgio Gilibert, I, p. 424; C.A. Gregory, I:613; Eatwell, I, pp. 3, 538, 539, 698, III, p. 599; Heinz Kurz, I, p. 357; Massimo Pivetti, I, pp. 872–5; Carlo Panico, II, pp. 106, 877; Geoffrey Harcourt, III, p. 924). How extraordinary that this is precisely what

Sraffa did! In other words, Adam Smith's *Inquiry into the Nature and Causes of the Wealth of Nations* is not, as many of us have believed, a study of the factors conducive to growth and development in a dynamic capitalist society but rather an essay in the theory of price determination in a stationary state *à la* Sraffa, according to which all variations in output are ruled out by definition. Similarly, Ricardo's *Principles of Political Economy and Taxation* is not a study of the natural resource scarcities that erode the inducement to invest in a tariff-ridden economy like that of Britain in the years after the Napoleonic Wars but a technical exercise in the distributional implications of 'the corn model', a primitive version of Sraffa's 'standard commodity' (G. De Vivo, I, p. 671, IV, pp. 183–98; Donald Harris, I, p. 446).

First we read Sraffian economics backwards into the works of Smith, Ricardo and John Stuart Mill and then we proclaim with triumph: 'Sraffa (1960) deserves the credit for having elaborated a consistent formulation of the classical surplus approach to the problem of capital and distribution' (Heinz Kurz, I, p. 359).

But enough said. My essay on 'Classical Economics in *The New Palgrave*' (especially I, pp. 439–42) attempts to sort out the sense and nonsense in the surplus interpretation of English classical political economy and I shall not go over that ground again here. Interestingly enough, not a single one of the articles on the surplus approach to value and distribution in classical economics written by Sraffians and cited above contains any cross-reference to my own essay on classical economics.

All this is far from an antiquarian intellectual issue. Every new paradigm or school of thought in economics must sooner or later acquire its own pedigree because a new way of looking at the present always entails a new way of looking at the past. At the same time, a new way of looking at the past instils confidence in the belief that one has at long last found the one and only truth and can become a powerful method of enlisting new devotees. It is no wonder then that Sraffian economics has invaded the history of economic thought, seeking to supplant the standard neoclassical interpretations of what the economists of the past were all about.

Marxian economics

Marxian economics presents a special problem to Sraffians. In one sense, Marx was the last of the classical economists whose thinking was thoroughly steeped in the concepts and modes of thought of Ricardo. However, Marx was also highly critical of Ricardo for his failure to consider economic problems in an historical context, and the Marxian 'vision' soared above that of Ricardo and even the larger vision of Adam Smith and John Stuart Mill. Moreover, there is so much growth and development economics in Marx, so much economic dynamics focused on technical progress and business cycles, that Marxian economics cannot be easily fitted into a history of economics which has Sraffa standing at its very pinnacle. Indeed, Sraffian economics has already produced its first great heresy. Ian Steedman's brilliant book in *Marx after Sraffa* (1977) employs Sraffa's apparatus to argue that the labour theory of value in Marx is not only redundant but actually unworkable as soon as joint products and choice of techniques are admitted into the analysis. Orthodox Marxists reacted with fury to this neo-Ricardian apostasy (Steedman, 1981; Fine, 1986; also Murray Milgate on Neo-Ricardianism, II, p. 637).[11] And to this day Sraffian economics has a neo-Marxist and a post-Marxist wing, that is, those who rank Sraffa below and those who, like Steedman, rank him above Marx.

Table 10.3   Entries on Marxian economics

Author	Vol./Pages
Edualdo Da Silva	I:4–5, IV:749–51
Anwar Shaikh	I:9–10, 333–6, II:249–51, III:347–8, 755–7, IV:574–6
George Catephores	I:76–8
A. Hussain	I:495–6
Willi Semmler	I:540–2
N. Okishio	I:580–4
Andrew Glynn	I:638–40, III:390–4
Peter Kenway	I:724–6, IV:105–7
Alice Amsden	II:728–33
G. De Vivo	III:88–9
William Lazonick	III:89–92
Ernest Mandel	III:367–82
John Roemer	III:383–6
Richard Jessop	III:489–91
Paul Sweezy	III:541–4
Ross Thomson	III:963–6
Fabio Petri	IV:66–8
Meghnad Desai	IV:335–7, 789–91
E.K. Hunt	IV:688–90
Krishna Bharadwaj	IV:830–2

None of these internecine battles is allowed to appear in *The New Palgrave*. Literally every article on Marxian economics in the four volumes is written by an avowed Marxist (Table 10.3). And although Steedman is a contributor to *The New Palgrave* he was not invited to give an account of his Sraffa-inspired critique of Marx. To say that the treatment of Marx in *The New Palgrave* is one-sided is to state the obvious. To give just one example, there is a perfectly appalling entry on the Labour theory of value by Fernando Viannello (III, pp. 107–13), which concludes that the only thing that can be said against the labour theory of value is that it cannot be defended in the way that Marx defended it. This is rather like reading an entry on phlogiston in a dictionary of chemistry that calmly sets out the pros and cons of phlogiston theory and then chides Joseph Priestley for defending it poorly. How could the editors have passed an entry like this one?

Keynesian economics
An important part of the Sraffian history of economic thought is the Keynesian epoch and precisely why the Keynesian revolution failed in the 1950s to be replaced first by 'the neoclassical synthesis' and, then, by monetarism in the 1960s and rational expectations in the 1970s. The standard reason given for the collapse of Keynesian economics is the appearance of 'stagflation' in the late 1960s and early 1970s and the apparent failure of Keynesian economics to explain the phenomenon. But a contributory reason was the lack of a coherent micro-foundation for the macroeconomic hypotheses of Keynes. The Sraffian account of the demise of the Keynesian revolution, however, is quite different. It is that Keynes' message was vulgarized and distorted; that its profoundly anti-orthodox implications were quietly buried and that Keynes himself sowed the seeds of that demise by compromising with the neoclassical theory of value and distribution. It follows that a consistent Keynesian must complete the revolution that Keynes inaugurated by repudiating neoclassical economics in its entirety.

This Sraffian story is set forth in a large number of entries in *The New Palgrave* on the Keynesian revolution, and indeed in almost enough entries to neutralize Don Patinkin's long, brilliant biographical entry on Keynes, which runs for 22 pages along standard lines. The balanced tone of Patinkin's essay is thus offset by Murray Milgate's strident entry on Keynes' *General Theory* (III, pp. 46–7). This is immediately followed by three tendentious pages on the Keynesian revolution by Lorie Tarshis (III, pp. 47–50), and elsewhere essays by Geoffrey Harcourt on 'Bastard Keynesianism' (I, pp. 203–4) and 'Post-Keynesian Economics' (IV, pp. 924–7), Carlo Panico on 'Liquidity Preference' (III, pp. 213–16), and a programmatic statement by John Eatwell on 'Imperfectionist Models' (II, pp. 726–8) complete the Sraffian story of how the revolution in both vision and method which Keynes inaugurated was gradually but steadily betrayed by a veritable conspiracy on the part of those evil orthodox economists.

The switching debate
Apart from believing that Sraffa has now provided them with a solid core of value and distribution theory upon which to build a new economics, Sraffians are also convinced that neoclassical economics contains a fatal logical flaw: capital cannot be valued independently of the rate of profit or interest and therefore the latter cannot be determined by the marginal productivity of capital as orthodox

theory requires. Furthermore, a technique of production that is rendered unprofitable by a rise in the rate of interest may become once more profitable by a further rise in the rate of interest, a paradoxical result known as 'reswitching'. Finally, in consequence of reswitching, we cannot in general draw a negatively inclined demand curve for capital – we cannot in general argue that a fall in the rate of interest will induce more investment, and vice versa for a rise in the rate of interest. Having at one time denied all this, the leaders of neoclassical economics now concede the possibility of both reswitching and 'capital-reversing' (Tatsuo Hatta, I, pp. 354–6; and Samuelson, IV, p. 437; see also Heinz Kurz, I, pp. 347–62; Luigi Pasinetti and Roberto Scazzieri, I, pp. 363–7, IV, pp. 162–4, 172–3).[12] But, of course, they deny that it implies the demise of neoclassical economics; what it implies, they say, is the falseness of some simple parables of orthodox classroom teaching, as for example that economic growth requires more 'waiting' because roundabout production is time-consuming, which extra waiting will always depress the rate of interest, which will invariably stimulate additional investment, and so on and on.

Exceptions prove the rule!

The Sraffian conviction that neoclassical economics is fatally defective because it does not permit invariant generalizations about the relationship between the relevant economic variables must stem from the prior belief that there are universal ''laws' of economics. Only when there are universal laws can we say that exceptions disprove the rule. But there are no *universal* laws of economics. As every Cambridge student of elementary economics knows, even the famous 'law of demand' that price is inversely related to quantity has an exception in the case of Giffen goods, the demand for which *increases* if their price is raised. Nevertheless, we do not for that reason abandon the presumption that demand curves are highly likely to be negatively inclined if only because no statistician has ever produced a convincing example of a positively inclined demand curve (Donald Walker on 'Giffen Goods', II, pp. 523–4; also III, p. 798). Similarly, we can easily prove that supply curves may be negatively inclined, so that a rise in price induces a *reduction* in supply, and yet we continue to insist that they are positively inclined in the overwhelming preponderance of cases, a rise in price inducing an increase in supply. In short, we make use of the Marshallian cross of demand and supply in almost every piece of economic reasoning but we know perfectly well that our general rules have exceptions. We simply say with Marshall that 'the central doctrines of Economics are not simple and cannot be made so'. Why should we not adopt a similar attitude to reswitching and capital-reversing? It is true that they are *possible* but it is also true that they are highly *unlikely*, and that as yet no one has observed a single real-world example of either reswitching or capital-reversing – as Edmond Malinvaud points out (II, p. 960).

It is ironic that the intolerance of Sraffians to any exception whatsoever to the standard neoclassical theorems is matched by a great deal of tolerance towards complications introduced into Sraffa's model by the presence of joint production. Thus, in the second part of Sraffa's *Production of Commodities by Means of Commodities,* dealing with multi-product industries and the use of fixed capital as a leading species of the genus of joint products, Sraffa notes that his 'standard commodity' may now include negative amounts of some commodities, that the relative value of commodities can no longer be reduced to 'dated quantities of labour', and that one cannot even be certain that the real wage is always inversely related to the rate of profit: in short, that the famous Sraffian yardstick, the standard commodity, and the equally acclaimed linear wage-profit frontier of single-product industries probably has no economic significance in a real world of multi-product industries (John Woods on 'Invariable Standard of Value', II, p. 969, and Bertram Schefold on 'Joint Production', II, pp. 1031–2). This is not in itself a reason for discarding the whole of Sraffa, but it is certainly to say that there are no universal truths in Sraffa just as there are none in Walras and Marshall.

Mid-air economics
The house that Sraffa built is an elegant construction, full of wonderful and surprising nooks and crannies, but it has its foundations planted firmly in mid-air. The degree of abstraction adopted by Sraffa is so high that even questions of economies or diseconomies of scale cannot arise because changes in the absolute amount of any input or output are rigorously excluded. Thus, we may not ask whether supply curves are negatively or positively inclined because there are no supply *curves* in Sraffa: producers do not supply more or less at various prices for the simple reason that prices never vary; they simply are what they are in consequence of assumed technology and a certain rate of wages for labour. Taking certain data as lying outside the realm of an economic model developed for one purpose does not of course preclude a theoretical explanation of their determination at a later stage for another purpose. Sraffa's book was published in 1960, and one might have expected that some progress would have been made in the intervening 28 years in analysis of the size and composition of output, choice of techniques – if there is indeed a choice – and the real wage of a capitalist economy. But as a matter of fact, Sraffian economics has been almost wholly moribund. Even Sraffa's prolegomenon to a critique of orthodox economics has never been extended or refined.[13] Some of the brain-teasers that Sraffa introduced, such as reswitching and joint production, have indeed been further explored but not a single application of the Sraffian model to the 'way things are' has been forthcoming in 28 years. Yes, it takes a long time in economics to make any practical use of theoretical innovations but, surely, it is time to ask whether

it is perhaps something about the very nature of Sraffa's approach that has so far made it totally irrelevant to practical issues.

General equilibrium theory

There is a trade-off in economics between rigour and relevance. Theories that are truly rigorous are rarely practically relevant, and theories that are eminently relevant to practical questions are rarely rigorous analytically. We witness this trade-off in Sraffian economics and we witness it again in general equilibrium theory, that jewel in the crown of neoclassical economics.

Proof not practice

There is, moreover, an intimate connection between Sraffian economics and general equilibrium theory. Frank Hahn (1984, p. 353) has said quite rightly that 'there is no correct neo-Ricardian proposition which is not contained in the set of propositions which can be generated by orthodoxy'; and by 'orthodoxy' he means a disaggregated general equilibrium theory as found in the writings of, say, Arrow and Debreu. General equilibrium theory was invented more than a century ago by Leon Walras who was the first to seize on multi-market equilibria as the central economic problem and to pose its solution as analogous to the algebraic problem of solving a set of simultaneous equations. Walras' procedure was to write down a set of abstract demand and supply equations on the assumption of perfect competition, perfect price flexibility and perfect factor mobility and then to 'prove' the existence of a solution for this set of simultaneous equations by counting the number of equations and unknowns; if they were equal, he concluded that simultaneous equilibrium in all markets was at least possible.

This strictly static picture of the determination of equilibrium was then followed up by a quasi-realistic explanation of how the competitive mechanism might establish such an equilibrium in practice, namely by automatic price adjustments in response to the appearance of excess demand and supply. Walras labelled these adjustments '*tâtonnement*', that is, 'groping' by trial and error on the part of independently acting buyers and sellers, and their role in general equilibrium theory troubled him all his life.

The task which he had set himself was to show that the relative prices which emerge from the process of competition are the same as the roots of his system of demand and supply equations in which the unknowns are the equilibrium quantities and prices. The difficulty was to allow for disequilibrium trading at other than market-clearing prices because these alter the distribution of goods among buyers and sellers before equilibrium is reached, thus changing the final equilibrium solution itself to one that differs from that dictated by the original set of equations. Walras hankered initially after a realistic description of the temporal sequence of price adjustments by which actual markets reach a final equilibrium solution. Indeed, he was persuaded by studies of the Paris stock exchange that his own mechanism of *tâtonnement*, in which prices are altered by a fictional auctioneer in accordance with excess demand or supply but no quantities are allowed to be exchanged until the equilibrium price is reached, might be construed as an example drawn from real life. But in successive formulations of his theory, he gradually abandoned the aim of descriptive realism and settle for the view that the *tâtonnement* process was at best an abstract model of how real-world markets move to equilibrium.

Competition as outcome rather than process
Markets for most goods and services are not like auctions at Christie's or Sotheby's, and in this sense we can conclude only that Walras ultimately gave up the effort to provide a convincing account of how real-world competitive markets achieve multi-market equilibrium. In some sense such an account has never been provided even to this day. Of course, modern mathematical economists establish the existence, stability and determinacy of general equilibrium by more elegant reasoning than that employed by Walras – for example, they introduce the unrealistic but highly simplifying assumption that there are forward markets for absolutely all goods and services in the economy – but that is not to be confused with a realistic description of actual buying and selling, involving costly acquisition of information about alternative trading opportunities and the irreversible lapses of time between successive transactions.

Modern Austrian economists, such as Friedrich Hayek, Israel Kirzner and Don Lavoie, go so far as to suggest that the Walrasian approach to the problem of general equilibrium is a cul de sac: if we want to understand the *process* of competition rather than the nature of the end-state achieved by competition, we must begin by discarding such *static* reasoning as is implied by any and all versions of general equilibrium. And, indeed, it is a shocking truth that modern economics comes equipped with a rich analysis of the nature of equilibrium as the final outcome of the workings of the competitive mechanism and yet is virtually silent on the precise means by which buyers and sellers resolve their differences on the way to final equilibrium. It is as if a cartographer supplied us with a detailed map of Rome, assured us that all roads led to it, and yet could give us no indication of how one actually sets about going to Rome. This failure to give an account of the process of competition is shocking because most of the acclaimed virtues of competition derive from its dynamic characteristics in fostering technical dynamism and cost-cutting innovations. But these are the disequilibrium features of the process of competition that have disappeared by the time we come to consider the final equilibrium. In short, whatever the virtues of equilibrium analysis, it is of little help in explaining the true merits of competition.

Abstraction or description?
It is interesting to not that attitudes to Walrasian general equilibrium theory have gone through a 180-degree revolution since Walras' own times. Walras himself seems to have conceived of his model as an admittedly abstract but not misleading representation of the manner in which competition drives prices to their equilibrium values in a capitalist regime. Similarly, when general equilibrium theory was revived in the 1930s, having almost disappeared from view in the previous 50 years, it was common to regard it as a reasonable approximation to the description of an actual capitalist economy. Thus, in the great Socialist Calculation Debate of the 1930s, Oskar Lange argued that socialism could employ a procedure for equilibrating prices that was similar to that ostensibly employed under capitalism, namely a Walrasian *tâtonnement* (Tadeusz Kowalik on the Lange-Lerner Mechanism, III, pp. 129–31, and W. Brus on 'Market Socialism' III, p. 337).[14] However, the Walrasian system is nowadays defended as a purely formal statement of the concept of general equilibrium, telling us what we *mean* by a logically consistent equilibrium model; not even the most enthusiastic advocates of general equilibrium theory pretend for one moment that it provides any kind of description of or prescription for a capitalist economy.

Since general equilibrium theory is no longer regarded as having much, if any, empirical content, it might be advisable to discard the very term 'general equilibrium *theory*' and to speak instead of general equilibrium as a 'framework' or 'paradigm'. This indeed accords with the practice of its most prominent spokesmen (Hahn, 1984, pp. 45–6). Enormous intellectual resources have been invested in the last 40–50 years in continually refining and elaborating this general equilibrium framework. Yet it is questionable even now whether these efforts have thrown any light on the way economic systems function in practice. Worse than that is the thought that the general equilibrium construction, by its very nature of emphasizing the end-state rather than the process of competition, may be the wrong starting point from which to approach a substantive explanation of the workings of an economic system.

Back to Sraffa
But what has all this to do with Sraffian economics? Simply this: Sraffian economics, like Walrasian economics, is obsessed with the mathematical metaphor of simultaneous equations, with the counting of equations and unknowns, with the end-state equilibrium solution of a set of relative prices rather than the process of prices groping towards their equilibrium values. How do we know in Sraffa that the real wage is a datum that is not determined by the same economic forces that govern all other prices? Because there are not enough equations to determine all relative prices as well as the rate of profit and the rate of wages. The *form* of the argument is exactly the same as that of Walras; the *content* is different only because Sraffa makes different assumptions from those employed by

Walras.[15] Sraffians like to claim that distributional variables are determined prior to the prices of final goods and services, but their theory baldly asserts this by assumption – it does not establish this, or indeed any other, *causal* claim about the sequential determination of economic variables.

Sraffa, like Walras, believed that a satisfactory theory of value and distribution in a capitalist economy should explain the long-period position of the economy. Long-period analysis has been largely abandoned in mainstream economics since about the 1920s, to be replaced by short-period analysis of temporary equilibria. This is something which Sraffians regard as one of the most deplorable features of modern orthodox economics, and they hope to bring about a renaissance of the economics of the long run (Carlo Panico and Fabio Petri on 'Long-run and Short-run', III, pp. 238–40, and Eatwell on 'Natural and Normal Conditions', III, pp. 598–9). But this slavish commitment to long-period analysis merely exacerbates the practical irrelevance of most Sraffian economics. Keynes once contemptuously dismissed the long run as a situation in which we are all dead:

> Economists set themselves too easy, too useless a task if in tempestuous seasons they can only tell us that when the storm is long past the ocean is flat again. (Keynes, 1971, p. 65)

Yet this is precisely that which Sraffians seek to make the only world that economics must address.

Theory without relevance
The empirical content of both Sraffian and Walrasian economics is nil because no theoretical system couched in such completely general terms could possibly predict any economic event or, to use Popperian language, forbid any economic event that might conceivably occur. It is true that Walrasian systems can be simplified by aggregation, as for example the famous Hicks-Hansen IS-LM version of Keynesian economics reduced to four equations; it is also true that the qualitative or comparative static properties of such simplified general equilibrium systems can be checked against empirical observations (does investment increase when the interest rate declines?, and so forth). Likewise, Herbert Scarf's computational algorithm for solving general equilibrium systems (I, pp. 556–62) has encouraged a number of economists in recent years to employ large-scale general equilibrium models to provide numerical estimates of the impact of policy changes, such as amendments of the tax system. But few of these models have been tested to check whether they give more accurate answers than much simpler partial equilibrium models (T.J. Kehoe on 'Comparative Statics', I, pp. 517–21). And let us not forget that the superiority of such applied general equilibrium models is fundamentally an empirical question because their construction is costly. Taking account of all interdependencies is in some sense better

than ignoring them, but it is also much harder work and the pay-off in predictability may not warrant the extra effort. In any case, the construction of *applied* general equilibrium models is a far cry from abstract proofs of the existence, stability and determinacy of *theoretical* general equilibrium models, which have earned several economists the kudos of a Nobel Prize.

As for theoretical general equilibrium models, it is worth noting that all-round multi-market equilibrium is a feature of certain *models* of the economy and not necessarily a reflection of how that economy is constituted. Counting the number of linear equations and unknowns to make sure that they are equal is a necessary condition for the existence of a mathematical solution of a set of simultaneous equations, which is *analogous* to the simultaneous determination of a set of equilibrium prices in all the markets of an economy, but that is not to say that prices are actually determined simultaneously; a *sequential* process of price determination – first the price of coal, then the price of steel, and then the price of automobiles – is perhaps a more plausible representation of how prices come to be set in the course of competitive rivalry.

In any case, the question is not one of approving or condemning the Walrasian apparatus *in toto,* but of deciding whether it deserves quite as high a place in the pecking order of professional prestige in economics as it currently enjoys; in particular, whether it does not constitute something like a blind alley, an intellectual game, from the standpoint of generating substantive hypotheses about economic behaviour. As Franklin Fisher puts it in his brief but illuminating entry on 'Adjustment Processes and Stability':

> ...the very power and elegance of [general] equilibrium analysis often obscures the fact that it rests on a very uncertain foundation. We have no similarly elegant theory of what happens *out* of equilibrium, of how agents behave when their plans are frustrated. As a result, we have no rigorous basis for believing that equilibrium can be achieved or maintained if disturbed. (I, p. 26; also John Geanakoplos, I, p. 123)

This lacuna in general equilibrium theory produces the curious anomaly that perfect competition is possible only when a market is in equilibrium. It is impossible when a market is out of equilibrium for the simple reason that perfectly competitive producers are price-takers, not price-makers. But if no-one can make the price, how do prices ever change to produce convergence on equilibrium? (Jean-Paul Benassy on 'Disequilibrium Analysis', I, pp. 858–62; also A. P. Kirman on 'Measure Theory', III, pp. 434–5). But, despite such admissions of the severe limitations of the Walrasian apparatus (see also Paul McNulty on 'Competition, Austrian Conception', I, pp. 536–7, and Thomas Rothenberg on 'Simultaneous Equations Models', IV, pp. 344–7), most of those writing on general equilibrium theory in *The New Palgrave* have little doubt of its usefulness (Frank Hahn, I, pp. 136–8; Herbert Scarf, I, p. 556; Gerard Debreu, II, pp. 216–18, III, p. 402; Lionel McKenzie, II, pp. 509–10; and Takashi Negishi,

IV, p. 595). Unfortunately, they never specify the criteria by which they judge its positive utility.

Methodology
The editors of *The New Palgrave* were no doubt disinclined to question any claims of practical relevance on behalf of general equilibrium theory if only because 'what is sauce for the goose...'. After all, the peculiarity of the Sraffian critique of orthodox economics is that Sraffian economics is itself a species of the genus of general equilibrium models and has to be defended, in formal terms, in the same way that general equilibrium theory is defended. Those who lay siege to a citadel defended by gunpowder cannot afford to renounce the use of explosives!

Thus, Sraffians have a vested interest in the methodological faith that patently abstract economic theories may somehow contain startling implications for economic policy. How this trick is performed is never explained and, in general, *The New Palgrave* gives little guidance on the crucial issue of the connection between theory and policy. Mainstream economists are frequently too sanguine about the practical relevance of abstract economic theory, but at least they pay lip-service to the doctrine that economic theories, like all scientific theories, must ultimately be judged in terms of their testable implications for economic events. Sraffian economists, on the other hand, deny this methodological standard which indeed they are fond of ascribing to the noxious influence of the philosophy of 'positivism' on modern economics (Shaun Hargreaves-Heap and Martin Hollis on 'Determinism', I, p. 876–8). No wonder then that virtually all the entries on methodology in *The New Palgrave* are devoted to denouncing empirical evidence as the litmus paper test of substantive propositions in economics (for example, Hargreaves-Heap on 'Epistemological Issues in Economics', II, pp. 166–8).[16] In that light, the absence of entries for 'Testing', 'Falsification', 'Verification' and 'Validation' in *The New Palgrave* takes on a new meaning.

Limitations of econometric methods
Stefano Zamagni tells us quite rightly that

> ...since no scientific law, in the natural scientific sense, has been established in economics, on which economists can base predictions, what are used and have to be used to explain or to predict are tendencies or patterns expressed in empirical or historical generalisations of less than universal validity, restricted by local and temporal limits' (II: 54).

But N.F.R. Crafts, in a perceptive discussion of the contribution of economics to economic history, concedes that 'most work applying economics to history, does not involve tests of competing hypotheses', and that the 'new economic history', which does involve such tests, employs standards of proof that are too low to convince the sceptical historian (II, p. 39). That leaves us with econometrics as a method of testing 'tendencies or patterns' expressed in empirical generalizations. There was a time, just before and after the Second World War, when great hopes were pinned on econometrics as the means by which economic theories might be conclusively appraised. But in recent years a deep sense of malaise has come over the subject as the severe limitations of econometric methods have come home to its practitioners. Economic theories abound in unobservable latent variables, poorly specified *ceteris paribus* clauses, and unspecified functional forms and dynamic relationships. These theories are then tested on data that are the legal by-products of public and private economic transactions rather than the results of specially designed experiments. No wonder then that econometric results are almost always ambiguous.[17]

Rhetoric or verification?

Nevertheless I would agree with Hashem Pesaran's pessimistic survey of econometric accomplishments, which concludes that the only cure for the shortcomings of econometrics is more and better econometrics (II, p. 19). The central issue remains that of choosing among competing economic theories in the light of empirical evidence, that is, to provide some external check on our wish to believe what we would like to believe. That issue is barely touched upon in a rambling essay by Vivian Walsh on 'Philosophy and Economics' (III, pp. 861–8). Likewise, Bruce Caldwell tells us that positivism is dead; but he has nothing to say on what might replace it (IV, pp. 921–3). One answer to the death of positivism is rhetoric: the study and practice of persuasive expression. There are no methodological criteria for validating economic theories, Donald McCloskey tells us, but simply different reasons for believing them:

> Consider, for example, the sentence in economics, 'The demand curve slopes down'. The official rhetoric says that economists believe this because of statistical evidence – negative coefficients in demand curves for pig iron or negative diagonal items in matrices of complete systems of demand – accumulating steadily in journal articles. These are the tests 'consistent with the hypothesis'. Yet most beliefs in the hypothesis come from other sources: from introspection (what would I do?); from thought experiments (what would they do?); from uncontrolled cases in point (such as the oil crisis); from authority (Alfred Marshall believed it); from symmetry (a law of demand if there is a law of supply); from definition (a higher price leaves less for expenditure, including this one); and, above all, from analogy (if the demand curve slopes down for chewing gum, why not for housing and love too?). As may be seen in the classroom and seminar, the range of argument in economics is wider than the official rhetoric allows. (IV, p. 174)

But is the official rhetoric any better than the unofficial one? Are there good reasons for believing any economic proposition and who is to tell us how to distinguish these from bad reasons? It used to be thought that the standards for appraising scientific theories came from a subject called 'philosophy of science' or 'methodology', but McCloskey would have us go even further than those who pronounce and welcome the death of positivism by pronouncing the death of anything called methodology. McCloskey speaks idly of good and bad reasons for believing one or another economic theory but will not tell us how he knows whether a reason is good or bad.

But no matter.[18] The point is that McCloskey's 'rhetoric of economics' does at least aim to make economists acutely aware of their reasons for believing what they believe. One of my principal complaints of the endless reiteration of neo-Ricardian, Sraffian economics in *The New Palgrave* is that no reasons whatever are given for believing that Sraffian economics is better than any other economics. It is as if Sraffians believed that economic theories are embedded in self-contained and basically incommensurable 'paradigms', in consequence of which there can be no rational method of comparing the relative merits of different economic theories (Peter Urbach on Paradigms, III, p. 795–7). At any rate, I can see no other grounds for a simply astonishing failure to defend their firm belief in Sraffian economics by anything other than the bland declaration that it *is* significant.

More methodology

Economics is a peculiar subject. It looks just like a science both in its formal structure and in its basic concern with observable reality. And yet economics does not reveal the sort of cumulative progress in the practical manipulation of reality that is one of the abiding characteristics of physics, chemistry, geology and parts of biology. Modern economists cannot predict either individual or aggregate economic behaviour very much better than Léon Walras could, or Adam Smith for that matter, and yet they remain committed to 'piecemeal social engineering', that is, to the use of collective action to improve the performance of the economy. It is not this that constitutes the peculiarity of economics as a subject because it may well be that the economy is simply harder to understand than Mother Nature, being less amenable to replicable laboratory experiments. The peculiarity of economics is rather that the vast majority of economics, whether orthodox or heterodox, are indifferent to the failure of economics to generate an ever-growing body of practically useful predictions on a par with the so-called 'hard sciences.

Some economists even go so far as to say that economics is a kind of social mathematics that must be assessed in the same terms that we assess progress in pure mathematics. But even those who proclaim this view of economics – mathematical economists are naturally very fond of this sort of defence – admit that economics must take a stand on questions of economic policy and, of course, this implies that economists have knowledge of how the economic system functions: we *can* say whether privatization improves the quantity and quality of the goods privatized; we *do* know whether exchange rates can be controlled and we also know whether this serves to control inflation; a reduction in the public sector borrowing requirement *will* cut down both inflation and unemployment; and so on. In other words, economics must be an empirical science, at least in part, in which case why is there so little concern with the poor empirical track-record of modern economics?

Ah, but all this is 'methodology' and methodology, any economist will tell you, is a dirty word, a subject peddled by people who like to talk about economics instead of doing it. *The New Palgrave* perfectly reflects this methodophobia of modern economics by the scant attention given to methodological topics, not to mention the persistent sneering at questions of empirical testing.

Conclusion

Despite dozens, and perhaps as many as 100, articles in *The New Palgrave* that I would not hesitate to recommend to anyone, I shudder to think that the work as a whole will have no rival form many decades to come and will probably remain the standard reference work on economics well into the next century.

It gives a hopelessly distorted picture of where economics is now. For better or for worse, and despite all the arguments and counter-arguments, the vast majority of economists the world over subscribe to the received corpus of neoclassical economics centred around the concepts of utility-maximizing households and profit-maximizing enterprises. There are Marxian economists, radical economists, post-Keynesian economists, behavioural economists, experimental economists, old American institutional economists, new institutional economists, evolutionary economists, and Austrian economists, but even all these added together only amount to a 25 per cent dissenting penumbra around a 75 per cent core of orthodoxy. On Mondays, Wednesdays and Fridays, I think that this is a good thing: economics is a solidly established profession with a definite point of view. On Tuesdays, Thursdays and Saturdays I deplore it: the orthodox majority stifles discussion and refuses to answer criticisms of its methods. But the fact remains that there is a broad consensus on a kind of economics which is consistently denigrated in every third or fourth entry of *The New Palgrave*.

Macmillan, the publisher of *The New Palgrave*, collected tributes to the volume prior to publication. Frank Hahn, Professor of Economics at Cambridge and current President of the Royal Economic Society, contributed the following encomium on the basis of what I take to be a selected sample of entries:

> For the doubtful the first move is to look for omitted topics. This will end in failure. The second move is to think of eminent economists who have not contributed. This too will fail. The third move will be to sample those entries on matters well known to the doubter. Here he will look for obscurities, slovenliness and incompleteness. He will largely look in vain. After that he is ready to learn and to enjoy himself. The Dictionary

shows economics to be a discipline with exacting standards and considerable achievements . . . one can now with confidence say to the critic: 'go and consult Palgrave'.

I am one of the doubtful. I found it easy to tot up many omitted topics and even easier to think of eminent names that do not appear.[19] I also found many obscurities and instances of slovenliness and incompleteness. In addition, I repeatedly encountered examples of bias, special pleading and formalism.

I would rarely direct a *student* to any article in *The New Palgrave* but I might direct a *colleague* to consult it, drawing his attention, however, to the fact that it is at least in large part an encyclopedia of economics from a most peculiar and singular standpoint, namely, that of a small band of enthusiasts in Cambridge and various universities in Italy who seek to emulate the Keynesian revolution by promoting a new brand of subversive economics that is Sraffian in theory and Marxian in politics. Orthodox economics, they contend, is little more than intellectual window-dressing for the political belief in the market as a self-regulating mechanism. To criticize orthodoxy is not enough because intellectuals abhor a mental vacuum as nature abhors a physical one. But Sraffa, Marx and Keynes somehow combined together to provide an alternative theoretical platform from which to launch the Holy War against neoclassical economics. From the perspective *The New Palgrave* is simply another fusillade in a continuous battle. The editors are, of course, entitled to their point of view but, when one considers that a dictionary of this kind only appears every 20–30 years and stands as a testimony to an entire generation of professional economists, one can only tear one's hair out at the magnitude of the opportunity that has been missed.

Notes

1. Eatwell and Milgate also edited a collection of papers, *Keynes's Economics and the Theory of Value and Distribution* (1983), which exemplifies the same aim.
2. Newman showed that Sraffa's ideas could be neatly expounded with the aid of certain properties of non-negative square matrices traditionally associated with the names of Perron and Frobenius, two German mathematicians of the early years of this century, since when all Sraffian economics has come to be written in terms of Perron–Frobenius algebra.
3. Ian Steedman writes on 'Foreign Trade' (II, pp. 406–11) in words and diagrams but his entry is not an account of the phenomenon of foreign trade but a critique of neoclassical trade theory from the standpoint of Sraffa and Cambridge capital theory. More to the point, however, is Comparative Advantage by Ronald Findlay (I, pp. 514–17).
4. Colander and Klamer (1987) have shown that American postgraduate education in economics is thoroughly technique-ridden.
5. There is an entry for 'Human Capital' (II, pp. 681–90), but this is only part, although a central part, of the economics of education. There is an entry for 'Performing Arts' (III, pp. 841–3), but again this is only an aspect of cultural economics. A glance at the contents of 'Current Periodicals' in the *Journal of Economic Literature* would have informed the editors of the existence of the *Economics of Education Review* and the *Journal of Cultural Economics*. The editors profess a great interest in viewing current economic ideas in historical perspective (I,

p. x), yet they refuse to acknowledge the history of economic thought as a recognized field of specialization. I admit to a personal concern about all three of these omissions.

6. Verdoorn's Law is the finding that the productivity of labour depends on the rate of growth of an industry; in consequence, growth breeds more growth in the same way that success breeds success. Kaldor based his theory of manufacturing as the engine of an economy's growth on Verdoorn's Law.

7. I have tried to explain Sraffian economics once before in an IEA publication (Blaug, 1975, pp. 21–32).

8. The issue of varying returns to scale is not just an argument about the theory of the firm, because Nicholas Kaldor and Martin Weitzman have argued that some form of increasing returns to scale is a necessary condition for genuine involuntary unemployment à la Keynes. If there were strictly constant returns to scale in all aspects of technology, there could be no involuntary unemployment because any unemployed worker could always set himself up as a mini-firm (see S. Vassilakis on 'Increasing Return to Scale', II, p. 763.).

9. For references to such refinements, Neri Salvadori on Basics and Non-Basics (I: 201).

10. It is worth noting that this essay by Samuelson was unsolicited, as is made evident by the publisher's early Prospectus for *The New Palgrave* (August 1986) in which Samuelson is listed as writing on 'Wicksell and neo-classical economics' but not on 'Sraffian economics'.

11. I have discussed the Steedman critique of Marx in more detail elsewhere: in my *Methodological Appraisal of Marxian Economics* (Blaug, 1980).

12. Tatsuo Hatta argues that reswitching and capital-reversing is 'Fully explicable within neo-classical theory, being no more (and no less) than one of the many intractable problems caused by the presence of complementarity' (I, p. 356).

13. The one promising extension has been that of Steedman and Metcalfe to the Heckscher–Ohlin–Samuelson theory of international trade (Steedman, 1979).

14. Despite subject entries on socialism, socialist economics and market socialism, and biographical entries on Oskar Lange and Ludwig von Mises, the Socialist Calculation Debate, so crucial to the revival of general equilibrium theory and the rise of modern welfare economics in the 1930s, is nowhere discussed at length in *The New Palgrave* (Lavoie, 1985).

15. In an entry on 'Models and Theory', Vivian Walsh struggles unconvincingly to deny this assertion (III, p. 483).

16. J. Geanakoplos in a penetrating essay on the Arrow–Debreu model of general equilibrium (I, pp. 16–24) expresses a number of doubts about it but he too fails to reveal his standards.

17. Lawrence Boland, no Sraffian, writes an entry on 'Methodology' (III, pp. 455–8) but hardly mentions testing, falsification and verification. Similarly, he writes on 'Stylised Facts' (IV, pp. 535–6) in Kaldorian growth theory but ignores the *fact* that almost all of Kaldor's stylized facts were not facts at all (H. Uzawa on 'Models of Growth', III, p. 485).

18. Stanley Fisher reports that Samuelson's 'major disappointment in economics in the last forty years has been the failure of econometric evidence to settle disputes' (IV, p. 240).

19. I have examined McCloskey's *Rhetoric of Economics* (1986) elsewhere (Blaug, 1987).

20. The list of contributors reads like a 'who's who' in economics, but not quite. I ought to know: a comparison of the names of the 900 contributors to *The New Palgrave* and the 1,000 most frequently cited living economists in my *Who's Who in Economics* (1986) shows an overlap of only about 500 names. Of course, those who do not appear in *The New Palgrave* may have been among the 200 or so economists who were asked to contribute but declined to do so (see I, p. x).

References

Blaug, M. (1975), *The Cambridge Revolution: Success or Failure?* (2nd edn.), London: IEA Paperback no. 6.

Blaug, M. (1980), *Methodological Appraisal of Marxian Economics*, Amsterdam: North-Holland.

Blaug, M. (1986), *Who's Who in Economics* (2nd edn.) Brighton: Wheatsheaf Books.

Blaug, M. (1987), 'Methodology with a Small *m*', *Critical Review*, **1**(2), Spring.

Colander, D.C. and Klamer, A. (1987), 'The Making of an Economist', *Journal of Economic Perspectives*, **1**(2), Fall.

Eatwell, J. and Milgate, M. (eds) (1983), *Keynes's Economics and the Theory of Value and Distribution*, London: Macmillan.

Eatwell, J. and Robinson, J. (1973), *An Introduction to Modern Economics*, London: McGraw-Hill.

Fine, B. (ed.) (1986), *The Value Dimension. Marx versus Ricardo and Sraffa*, London: Routledge & Kegan Paul.

Hahn, F. (1984), *Equilibrium and Macroeconomics*, Oxford: Blackwell.

Keynes, J.M. (1971), 'A Tract on Monetary Reform' in *The Collected Writings of John Maynard Keynes*, vol. IV, London: Macmillan for the Royal Economic Society.

Lavoie, D. (1985), *Rivalry and Central Planning. The Socialist Calculation Debate Reconsidered*, Cambridge: Cambridge University Press.

McCloskey, D. (1986), *Rhetoric of Economics*, Madison: University of Wisconsin Press.

Milgate, M. (1982), *Capital and Employment*, London: Macmillan.

Newman, P. (1962), 'Production of Commodities by Means of Commodities', *Schweizerische Zeitschrift für Volkwirtsschaft und Statistik*, **98**, March

The New Palgrave: A Dictionary of Economics (4 vols), (1987) ed. J. Eatwell, P. Milgate and P. Newman, London: Macmillan.

Sraffa, P. (1926), 'The Laws of Returns under Competitive Conditions', *Economic Journal*, 36, December,

Sraffa, P. (1960), *Production of Commodities by Means of Commodities*, Cambridge: Cambridge University Press.

Steedman, I. (1977), *Marx After Sraffa*, London: New Left Books.

Steedman, I. (1979), *Fundamental Issues in Trade Theory*, London: Macmillan.

Steedman, I. *et al.* (1981), *The Value Controversy*, London: New Left Books.

Name Index

Ackley, Gardiner 98, 99, 100
Addison, John 103, 114, 117
Albert, Michael 64, 82
Alchian, Armen 64
Alonso, Walter 141
Althusser, Louis 34, 75
Ambrosi, G.M. 91
Amir, Samin 79
Amsden, Alice 222
Anderson, D. 183
Andvig, Jan 92
Angell, James 92
Applebaum, Eileen 61
Archibald, Christopher 184
Aristotle 36, 38
Arrow, Kenneth 72, 117, 151, 166, 212, 215, 226
Atkinson, Anthony 173, 179
Aumann, Robert 215
Azariadis, Costas 68

Babbage, Thomas 145
Bach, G.L. 81
Bailey, Samuel 144, 145
Bakhunin, Michael 51
Baran, Paul 58, 78
Barkai, Hyman 161
Barrett, Michele 65
Baumol, William 18, 34, 176, 178, 179, 214
Becker, Gary 72, 214, 215
Beckmann, Martin 141
Bell, Peter 34
Benassy, Jean-Paul 230
Bergmann, Barbara 72
Bernstein, Eduard 50, 52
Bharadwaj, Krishna 222
Blackburn, Robert 83
Blaug, Mark 24, 35, 41, 52, 59, 60, 62, 74, 77, 82, 88, 89, 92, 116, 140, 146, 154, 159, 184, 236, 237

Block, Fred 79
Bloomfield, Arthur 154
Blundell-Wignall, Anthony 28, 30, 34
Boddy, Raford 78
Bohm, Peter 215
Bohm, Volker 213
Böhm-Bawerk, Eugene von 18, 19, 41, 141
Boiteux, Marcel 176
Boland, Lawrence 237
Booth, Allen 98
Bortkiewicz, Ladislaus von 18, 25
Bose, Arun 27, 28, 35, 82
Boventer, Eduard von 141
Bowles, Sam 30, 34, 41, 67, 68, 75–8, 82, 83
Bradford, D.F. 178, 179
Bradley, Ian 147
Braverman, Harry 52, 83
Bresciani Turroni, Constantino 102
Brewer, Anthony 34, 79
Brittan, Samuel 181
Bronfenbrenner, Martin 32, 35, 45, 57, 58, 66, 75, 81, 206
Brunner, Karl 103, 212
Brus, W. 228
Buchanan, Allen 35
Buchanan, David 158
Buchanan, James 175, 182
Buhr, W. 141
Burton, John 103

Cain, Glen 70, 71
Cairnes, John Elliot 144, 158
Caldwell, Bruce 2–7, 116, 232
Calva, Guillermo 68
Cannan, Edwin 93
Cantillon, Richard 121
Carnoy, Martin 67, 71, 75
Capie, F. 92
Casson, Mark 93, 103
Catephores, George 27, 30, 35, 51, 222
Chamberlin, Edwin 28, 109, 186

239

Subject Index